In Praise of *Living Economics*

"*Living Economics* is a superb book. Peter Boettke's passion for excellence in teaching and for his subject, mainline economics (the sort of basic economic reasoning that draws on the ideas of a line of thinkers from Adam Smith through the Austrians to people like Jim Buchanan and Elinor Ostrom), shines through on every page. It is vintage Boettke: engaging, witty, and chock full of insight. This book should be put in the hands of every first-year student of economics, if only to show them what they are missing!"

> —**Bruce Caldwell**, Research Professor of Economics and Director, Center for the History of Political Economy, Duke University

"Economics as it should be, *Living Economics* is a solid book that counters the excessive simulation of modern academic economics while, at the same time, avoiding the temptation to extend application of the logic beyond reasonable limits. Boettke concentrates on the primary purpose of economics, which is to convey an understanding of how, within properly designed institutional constraints, operative markets generate and distribute value without overt conflict."

> · —**James M. Buchanan, Jr.**, Nobel Laureate in Economic Sciences; Advisory General Director of the Center for Study of Public Choice and Distinguished Professor Emeritus of Economics, George Mason University

"Peter Boettke's book *Living Economics* not only is splendidly characterized by broad erudition, solid analysis, shrewd observation, and expositional clarity, it appears at a propitious moment. We are in a presidential election year, with most political spokespersons relying on embarrassingly superficial and bastardized economic diagnosis and rabble-rousing prescription. And the bulk of professional economists persist in putting precious and arid formalism over substantive content. It is high time—but Professor Boettke thinks that it is not too late—to join the impressive and long-persisting caravan of scholars promoting a feel for, sense of, and interest in the contribution which genuine economics can make to a free and increasingly prosperous society."

> —**William R. Allen**, Professor Emeritus of Economics, University of California, Los Angeles

D1041271

"Boettke's passion for economics and the clarity of his vision make *Living Economics* a pleasure to read. No reader will fail to benefit from his broad and deep insights."
— **Steven E. Landsburg**, Professor of Economics, University of Rochester; author, *The Armchair Economist*

"I am very pleased with Peter Boettke's book *Living Economics*, which has fully captured the essence of my work and that of others on what good economics is all about and why understanding it is so important."
— **Gordon Tullock**, University Professor Emeritus of Law and Economics, George Mason University

"Peter Boettke's insightful and wide-ranging book *Living Economics* is not simply about teaching economics: it is a joyous exercise in teaching us through the great teachers of economics. This volume shows us how the mainline of economic teaching from Smith through Hayek to contemporary thinkers such as Buchanan and Ostrom has analyzed the core features of economic cooperation while recognizing the cognitive limits of economic and political actors, and indeed of economic analysis itself. All students of the moral sciences need to learn Boettke's master lesson: 'We have to understand man as a fallible yet capable chooser, who lives within an institutional framework that is historically contingent.'"
— **Gerald F. Gaus**, James E. Rogers Professor of Philosophy, University of Arizona

"With *Living Economics*, Peter Boettke cements his reputation not only as one of the leading Austrian economists of our time, but as one of the most compelling and engaging communicators of economic ideas. Teachers will derive inspiration from his essays and policy officials will likely gain a little humility regarding their ability to improve upon undesigned economic processes. All readers of this book will be hard pressed not to come away sharing Boettke's enthusiasm for economics as 'a deadly serious discipline that tackles vital questions of wealth and poverty, of life and death,' as well as 'an amazing framework for thinking about human behavior in the real world, including all human endeavors, . . . that is entertaining and downright fun.'"
— **Susan E. Dudley**, Research Professor of Public Policy and Director, Regulatory Studies Center, George Washington University; former Director, Office of Information and Regulatory Affairs, U.S. Office of Management and Budget

"Through his scholarly and entrepreneurial work, Peter Boettke has transformed a sometimes hostile, sometimes neutral, field of economics into a thoroughgoing revival of Austrian ideas in the worlds of thought and action that is in full flower today. *Living Economics* reveals how Boettke has been the energetic catalyst so pivotal to this transformation. This book provides wonderful insight into how this future has been brought about."

> —**Richard E. Wagner**, Hobart R. Harris Professor of Economics, George Mason University

"Reading the wonderful book *Living Economics* by Peter Boettke made me start loving economics, and I am sure it will inspire many more readers to do the same. It makes me optimistic for the return of real economics."

> —**Nassim Nicholas Taleb**, Distinguished Professor of Finance and Risk Engineering, New York University Polytechnic Institute; author, *The Black Swan: The Impact of the Highly Improbable*

"There exist noteworthy works that survey economic thought and others that provide insights into current economic challenges. This highly unusual book does both at once and very successfully. Interpreting and contrasting major contributions to economics in clear prose, it also identifies the policy implications of key economic insights. Insightful, instructive, and also entertaining throughout, Peter Boettke's *Living Economics* can be read profitably by academics, policy makers, students, and a wide range of other constituencies concerned about our economic institutions."

> —**Timur Kuran**, Professor of Economics and Political Science and the Gorter Family Professor of Islamic Studies, Duke University

"Peter Boettke has spent a career not just as a scholar of economics, but as an educator of both the general public and generations of students. In *Living Economics*, he reflects on the importance of teaching and of his own teachers in spreading the ideas of the mainline of economic thinking from Smith, Say and Wicksteed to Mises, Hayek, Buchanan, Coase, and Friedman, including his own contemporaries. This book is essential reading, especially in a time when the tradition of sound economics Boettke focuses on is under increasing threat by old fallacies and new politicians. The passion for ideas and economic theory that permeates these pages is exactly the inspiration one gets from a great teacher. Peter Boettke is indeed that."

> —**Steven G. Horwitz**, Charles A. Dana Professor of Economics, St. Lawrence University

"The truly wonderful book *Living Economics* shows students and scholars alike why Peter Boettke is one of the most original scholars and teachers of his generation. Boettke's goal is to form minds young and old in the way that his was formed, and thus the lessons of this book come from across the intellectual spectrum. Boettke's masterful ability to deftly meld a variety of approaches to economics into a lens through which to view the world shows the possibilities of economics analysis at a time when its status is much in question and breathes new life into the dismal science."

—**Steven G. Medema**, Professor of Economics, University of Colorado, Denver

"*Living Economics* by Peter Boettke is aptly titled. It's all about what he received from his teachers (broadly defined) and what he, in turn, has imparted to his students. Boettke's deep scholarship, serious reflections and passion for economics come through on every page. Accordingly, unlike most economics prose, *Living Economics* can be safely read before driving. Indeed, *Living Economics* is full of surprises—like an entire chapter on my former professor, Kenneth Boulding. Boettke's treatment of that great economist hits the nail on the head. The book is well suited for anyone with an interest in economics and finance and should be a required supplemental text for principles of economics courses, as well as courses on the history of economic thought."

—**Steve H. Hanke**, Professor of Applied Economics, Johns Hopkins University

"Loaded with content well worth reading and carefully arrayed gems from the history of thought, Peter Boettke's *Living Economics* is literally his personal statement about living with and living through economics. But be careful as you read. Boettke's love affair with economics is contagious. You will find yourself cheering for more."

—**Bruce Yandle**, Professor of Economics Emeritus, Clemson University

"*Living Economics* is a fascinating discussion of the increasingly-acknowledged-as-important field of Austrian economics and its main contributors. But more important is Peter Boettke's lessons not only on the importance of teaching about Austrian economics but on how economics should be taught generally. *Living Economics* makes a useful tool for both students and their teachers."

—**Walter E. Williams**, John M. Olin Distinguished Professor of Economics, George Mason University

"In *Living Economics*, Peter Boettke has written a compelling book that is part intellectual autobiography and part a discussion on what economics is, and how it should be taught. Professor Boettke's love of economics comes through on every page, and the book is filled with insights on the nature of economics and how it should be presented to students. His sympathy toward free-market ideas and the Austrian school of economics comes through clearly, and much of the book is devoted to discussing the ideas and work of major scholars who have influenced him. The book is delightful to read, and will appeal to both students and teachers of economics."

> —**Randall G. Holcombe**, DeVoe Moore Professor of Economics, Florida State University

"This set of essays is Peter Boettke at his best; they are instructive, learned, entertaining and brilliant. Not only is *Living Economics* a must read but it is a very enjoyable read for today's economists and social scientists."

> —**Richard Swedberg**, Professor of Sociology, Cornell University

"In *Living Economics*, Boettke expresses well the 'joy of economics,' the expansion of one's own understanding of the process of social coordination we all benefit from, and the pure pleasure in communicating that understanding to students and others. He draws upon a deep well of teaching and guiding both undergraduate and graduate students and his lively advocacy of 'mainline economics,' as opposed to 'mainstream economics,' makes for an important read for anyone seeking to understand what economics is really all about."

> —**P. J. Hill**, Professor Emeritus of Economics, Wheaton College

"We have here a fascinating reflection that stems from more than a quarter century of Peter Boettke's scholarship and masterful teaching. One cannot close this book without a renewed appreciation of the core insights of economics that run from Adam Smith to F.A. Hayek to James Buchanan and others. On page after page *Living Economics* bubbles over with enthusiasm, as Boettke shows that our tradition is intellectually rich, robust and exciting to learn. The economic way of thinking, properly understood, studies real people. And Boettke clearly shows that our everyday lives are at stake if the lessons of economics continue to be misunderstood by pundits, politicians and the bulk of a misguided economics profession."

> —**David L. Prychitko**, Professor of Economics, Northern Michigan University

Living
ECONOMICS

PETER J. BOETTKE

Living ECONOMICS

YESTERDAY, TODAY, AND TOMORROW

The INDEPENDENT INSTITUTE

Oakland, California

UFM
universidad
FRANCISCO MARROQUIN

The Independent Institute
100 Swan Way, Oakland, CA 94621-1428
Telephone: 510-632-1366
Fax: 510-568-6040
Email: info@independent.org
Website: www.independent.org

Cover Design: Keith Criss
Interior Design and Composition by Leigh McLellan Design

Library of Congress Cataloging-in-Publication Data
Boettke, Peter J.
    Living Economics : yesterday, today, and tomorrow / Peter J. Boettke.
      p. cm.
    Includes bibliographical references and index.
    ISBN 978-1-59813-075-1 (pbk. : alk. paper)—ISBN 978-1-59813-072-0
(hbk. : alk. paper)
    1. Economics—Study and teaching. 2. Economics. 3. Economics—History. I. Title.
    HB74.5.B64 2012
    330—DC23   2012008378

16 15 14 13 12   5 4 3 2

*To My Teachers
and to Those I Have Had the Privilege to Teach*

Contents

PART III On the Practice of Economics

PART IV Conclusion

Preface

> It is no crime to be ignorant of economics, which is, after all,
> a specialized discipline and one that most people consider to be a
> "dismal science." But it is totally irresponsible to have a loud and
> vociferous opinion on economic subjects while remaining in this
> state of ignorance. —Murray N. Rothbard[1]

MY LOVE AFFAIR with economics began in the fall of 1979. The
summer prior to that I had experienced the long lines for gasoline, and I was
confused and frustrated by the experience for a variety of reasons. Economics
erased my confusion and targeted my frustration on the cause of the shortages.
I was hooked.

In many ways, the logic of economic reasoning came naturally to me once I
started studying. My first readings in the field were Henry Hazlitt's *Economics
in One Lesson,* and Bettina Bien Greaves, ed., *Free Market Economics: A Basic
Reader* (which included Leonard Read's "I, Pencil"). These were followed by
various essays and excerpts from books by Ludwig von Mises related to the
problems of socialism and interventionism and the benefits of the free market
economy, and then Milton and Rose Friedman's *Free to Choose.* By the time I
finished *Free to Choose,* I would never think about the world around me the same
way. I saw everything through the economic lens—from the most mundane
human activities to the most profound. To me, economics is simultaneously

---

1. Murray Rothbard, *Egalitarianism as a Revolt Against Nature* (Auburn, AL: Ludwig von
Mises Institute, 1974, 2000), 202.

the most entertaining discipline in the human sciences and the most important discipline in the policy sciences as it ultimately answers fundamental questions about human life and death.

It is my hope that the following essays capture not only my thirty–plus year love affair with economics as a discipline, but also the sheer joy I get from economic inquiry and inviting my students to join me in that inquiry. I believe that much of modern economics has lost its way, and I am actively engaged in trying to get the teaching and doing of economics back on track. Following one of my teachers—Kenneth Boulding—I use the term "mainline economics" to describe a set of propositions that were first significantly advanced in economics by Thomas Aquinas in the thirteenth Century and then the Late Scholastics of the fifteenth and sixteenth centuries at the University of Salamanca in Spain (especially the Christian clerics, Francisco de Vitoria, Martin de Azpilcueta, Diego de Covarrubias, Luis de Molina, Domingo de Soto, Leonardo Lessio, Juan de Mariana, and Luis Saravía de la Calle).[2] These insights were further developed in economics from the Classical School of Economics (both in its Scottish Enlightenment version of Adam Smith and the French Liberal tradition of Jean-Baptiste Say and Frederic Bastiat), to the early Neoclassical School (especially the Austrian version of Carl Menger, Ludwig von Mises, and F.A. Hayek), and finally with the contemporary development of New Institutional Economics (as reflected in the property rights economics of Armen Alchian and Harold Demsetz; the new economic history of Douglass North; the law and economics of Ronald Coase; the public choice economics of James Buchanan and Gordon Tullock; the economics of governance

---

2. Rodney Stark, *The Victory of Reason: How Christianity Led to Freedom, Capitalism, and Western Success* (New York: Random House, 2005); Alejandro A. Chafuen, *Faith and Liberty: The Economic Thought of the Late Scholastics* (Lanham, Md.: Lexington Books, 2003); Murray N. Rothbard, *Economic Thought before Adam Smith: An Austrian Perspective on the History of Economic Thought*, vol. 1 (Brookfield, Vt.: Edward Elgar, 1995), 51–64, 97–133; Marjorie Grice-Hutchinson, *The School of Salamanca: Readings in Spanish Monetary Theory, 1544–1605* (Oxford University Press, 1952) and *Early Economic Thought in Spain 1177–1740* (London: Allen & Unwin, 1978); Laurence S. Moss, ed., *Economic Thought in Spain* (Aldershot, England: Edward Elgar, 1993); Raymond de Roover, *Business, Banking, and Economic Thought in Late Medieval and Early Modern Europe* (Chicago: University of Chicago Press, 1976); and Joseph Schumpeter, *History of Economic Analysis* (New York: Oxford University Press, 1954).

associated with Oliver Williamson and Elinor Ostrom; and the market process economics of Israel Kirzner). The core idea in this approach to economics is that there are two fundamental observations of commercial society: (1) individual pursuit of their self-interest, and (2) complex social order that aligns individual interests with the general interest.

In the mainline of economics, the "invisible hand postulate" reconciles self-interest with the general interest not by collapsing one to the other or by assuming super-human cognitive capabilities among the actors, but through the reconciliation process of exchange within specific institutional environments. It is the "higgling and bargaining" within the market economy, as Adam Smith argued, that produces social order. The "invisible hand" solution does not emerge because the mainline economist postulates a perfectly rational individual interacting with other perfectly rational individuals within a perfectly structured market, as many critics suppose. Such idealizations would be as alien to Adam Smith as they would be to F.A. Hayek. Instead, for those who "sit in the seat of Adam Smith" man is a very imperfect being operating within a very imperfect world. Sound economic reasoning, by focusing on exchange, and the institutions within which exchange takes place, explains how complex social order emerges through the aid of prices and the entrepreneurial market process.

The mainline of economics, in my narrative, is to be contrasted with the "mainstream" of economic thought. Mainline is defined by a set of positive propositions about social order that were held in common from Adam Smith onward, but mainstream economics is a sociological concept related to what is currently fashionable among the scientific elite of the profession. Often the mainline and the mainstream dovetail, but at other times they deviate from one another. It is at these moments of deviation that acts of intellectual entrepreneurship are acutely needed by those working within the mainline of economics to recapture the imagination of mainstream economics, getting the discipline back on track.

My research has primarily been in the area of comparative political and economic systems and the consequences with regard to material progress and political freedom. In addressing these questions, I have also had a particular interest in twentieth century economic thought and the methodology of the social sciences because of my judgment that much suffering throughout the socialist and less developed worlds in the twentieth century was caused by bad ideas in economic theory and public policy and that these bad ideas were promulgated because of misguided notions in the philosophy of science as applied to the social sciences. It has become an important part of my research and teaching efforts to explore and tell the tale of this mistaken intellectual path. The Austrian School of Economics, its ideas, its historical figures, and its fate in the economics profession and public policy discourse has been a source of continued intellectual inspiration for me since my undergraduate days, and is no doubt evident throughout all my writings.

A trip I made to Universidad Francisco Marroquin (UFM) with my close colleague and friend, Chris Coyne, in June of 2011 inspired this particular book. UFM is an amazing institution of higher learning in economics. We were both impressed by the commitment of the entire intellectual community at UFM to sound economic reasoning and to high quality teaching of economics. Throughout the campus of UFM, there are images of the great economists throughout the history of the discipline and the core ideas that they sought to communicate in their writings. The various essays in this collection are my attempts to communicate those core ideas of the mainline of economic science from Adam Smith to J.B. Say to Philip Wicksteed to Ludwig Mises to F.A. Hayek to James Buchanan to Vernon Smith to Elinor Ostrom, and many others in-between, and currently practicing economists.

Economics teaches us many things, but to me the most important is how social cooperation under the division of labor is realized. This is what determines whether nations are rich or poor; whether the individuals in these nations live in poverty, ignorance, and squalor or live healthy and wealthy lives full of possibilities. If the institutions promote social cooperation under the division of labor, then the gains from trade and innovation will be realized. But, if the institutions, in effect, hinder social cooperation under the division of labor, then life will devolve into a struggle for daily existence. Economics, in other words, gives us the key intellectual framework for understanding how we can live better together.

This theme of what Mises called "the law of association" is also what animated the founder of UFM, Manuel Ayau—who in his own books stressed this idea of social cooperation under the division of labor. In the essays in this book, I repeatedly stress the role of property, prices, and profit/loss for providing economic actors with the incentives, information, and the spur for innovation that is required to achieve the complex economic coordination and the social cooperation among anonymous actors that characterizes a peaceful and prosperous society.

It is with this shared vision of the nature and significance of economic science and the commitment to teaching that I am especially thrilled to be publishing this book with the Independent Institute and UFM Press. I want to thank David Theroux, President of the Independent Institute, and Giancarlo Ibarguen, the current President of UFM, for the opportunity to do so. It is an honor to work with these two men who have dedicated their lives to the promotion of sound economic reasoning both inside and outside of the academy. I do hope this book will make a minor contribution to the goal of spreading the economic way of thinking.

I want to thank the staff at my office at GMU and the Mercatus Center for helping in the preparation of this manuscript for publication: Peter Lipsey, Liya Palagashvili, David Currie, Carly Reddig, and Matthew Boettke. I also benefited greatly from editorial suggestions from David Theroux, Roy Carlisle, and Alex Tabarrok. Responsibility for remaining errors are exclusively my own.

I also want to thank the wonderful teachers of economics I have had over the years from Hans Sennholz at Grove City College to James Buchanan, Gordon Tullock, Kenneth Boulding, and Don Lavoie at George Mason. I also was fortunate to have some established figures in the discipline take me under their wing and mentor me at a formative stage of my career: Warren Samuels, Peter Berger, and especially Israel Kirzner, who I worked alongside of for eight years at NYU. It was a dream come true for me to work at NYU (the home of Ludwig von Mises) and to work in close collaboration with Israel Kirzner.

In graduate school, I bonded quickly with two fellow students and they have traveled this entire journey with me—Steve Horwitz and David Prychitko. I don't say thanks to them nearly enough for making me a better teacher and better economist by setting a professional standard early in our careers that we have all tried to maintain. It is my sincere hope that these essays have met that standard even in the areas that they disagree most strongly with me. In one of the essays in this collection, I give the advice to students that they have to choose their teachers wisely because you will teach as you are taught, and that they have to choose whom they read wisely because you will write like those you read. I should add that you must choose your friends wisely because it will be your friends who help set the standard of argument you strive to meet and who will honestly tell you when you are falling short of that standard. Steve and Dave have respectively been those close friends of mine since we entered this profession as teachers and scholars in the 1980s.

And finally, I would like to thank all the wonderful students I have had the privilege to teach throughout my career and especially those I have had the great honor of serving as their dissertation advisor. I don't know if they realize just how much I have learned from them and how much pride I take in their developing careers as first-rate teachers of economics, significant contributors to the development of mainline economics, and to their amazing abilities to communicate sound economic reasoning not only to their students but to the general public as well.

As I write this, we are living through particularly turbulent economic times. It is a time when we need sound economic reasoning more than ever, rather than the sort of "emergency room" economics that has dominated public policy since 2008. Armed with the truth of the mainline of economic teaching from Adam Smith to F.A. Hayek, and with the great communication skills that these former students of mine have, I am confident that high quality representatives of sound economic reasoning are growing in number and will ultimately beat back economic ignorance and special interest politics, shifting the tide of public opinion in the direction of sound economics. As Milton and Rose Friedman argued in *Free to Choose*[3] (1980, 272): "A tide of opinion once it flows strongly tends to sweep over all obstacles, all contrary views."

We all have a lot of work to do to get economics back on track. Let's go to work.

---

3. Milton Friedman and Rose Friedman, *Free To Choose* (New York: Harcourt, Brace & Jovanovich, 1980), 272.

1

Economics for Yesterday, Today, and Tomorrow

The latest "new economics," and in my opinion rather the worst for fallacious doctrine and pernicious consequences, is that launched by the late John Maynard (Lord) Keynes, who for a decade succeeded in carrying economic thinking well back to the dark age. . . . The serious fact is that the bulk of the really important things that economics has to teach are things that people would see for themselves if they were willing to see. . . . "The time has come to take the bull by the tail and look the situation square in the face." —Frank H. Knight[1]

Introduction

AN IMPORTANT UNSUBTLE point should be stressed in every economic conversation with peers, students, policymakers, and the general public concerning the great recession since 2008. John Maynard Keynes was wrong in both his analysis of capitalist instability and reasons for persistent unemployment in 1936, and he was wrong in 2008. The ideas Keynes developed in *The General Theory of Employment, Interest, and Money* (1936) were as wrongheaded in the nineteenth century as they were in the twentieth century, and as they are in the twenty-first century. Keynesian economics is simply bad economics. And it is vitally important to always remember that in the field of economics, bad

---

1. Frank H. Knight, "The Role of Principles in Economics and Politics," *American Economic Review* 41, no. 1 (1951): 1–29, in *Selected Essays of Frank H. Knight*, edited by Ross Emmett, vol. 2 (Repr., Chicago: University of Chicago Press, 1999), 362–63, 364, 365.

economic ideas lead to bad public policies, which in turn result in bad economic outcomes.[2] The realization of this string of logically connected "bads" might be long and varied, but it is inevitable. The Keynes of *The General Theory* was never right when it came to how an economy operates, let alone how to fix it when it teeters during crises. And the resurrection of Keynes among professional economists, public intellectuals, and especially politicians and policymakers in the wake of the global financial crisis of 2008 has been one of the most disappointing developments I have witnessed in my career as an economist.

Keynes was wrong because his analysis was based on a set of flawed premises. The earlier analysis of "effective demand" failure was first pioneered by Malthus but vehemently opposed by Ricardo and the other "classics," and was forced, according to Keynes, to exist "below the surface, in the underworlds of Karl Marx, Silvio Gesell or Major Douglas."[3] Keynes believes that the complete victory of the "classics" is a mystery and reflects an unwillingness of professional economists after Malthus to recognize that disconnect between their theory and the basic facts of observation. "It may well be that the classical theory," Keynes argued, "represents the way in which we should like our Economy to behave. But to assume it actually does so is to assume our difficulties away."[4]

But there are good reasons why economists forced these theories into the underworld of economic opinion. They reflected bad economic analysis. What I mean by that is that these theories implicitly assume away scarcity and believe the fundamental problem of modern society is poverty amidst plenty; they explicitly deny both actor rationality and the coordinating role of prices,

---

2. It is important to stress that simple and straightforward answers in economics need not be simple-minded answers—see http://austrianeconomists.typepad.com/weblog/2008/10/simple-answers.html, and as I will stress throughout, the only real economics is relative price economics, so the discussions of "macroeconomic policy" without reference to the role of prices get us nowhere. This is the underlying message of the argument, that although there may be macroeconomic problems of inflation, unemployment, and industrial fluctuations, there are only microeconomic explanations and solutions. Prices have to be allowed to do their job both of telling the truth and of redirecting the allocation of resources.

3. John Maynard Keynes, *The General Theory of Employment, Interest and Money* (1936; Repr., New York: Harcourt, Brace & Jovanovich, 1964), 32.

4. Keynes, *General Theory*, 34.

as well as the function prices serve in guiding decisions and the feedback and discipline provided by profit and loss.[5] If you postulate a world of post scarcity, then neither the coordinating role of the price system, nor the incentives of the property rights structure is critical, and if you don't allow the individuals that populate your economy to learn from market signals, and you don't allow those signals to actually work, then of course the economy will not work! This is not mysterious. Without prices and the market process continually guiding economic actors on a path of learning and discovery "amid the bewildering throng of economic possibilities,"[6] the economic future will indeed be ensnared by the "dark forces of time and ignorance."[7]

It is important to stress, as J.B. Say did in his *Letters to Mr. Malthus* (1821), that all discussions of overproduction or underconsumption make reference to the price system. The cure to a "glut," Say argued, was neither monetary expansion nor fiscal stimulus, but allowing the prices to adjust to clear the market. In response to Malthus's theory of the "general glut," Say painstakingly explains how the market process coordinates the production plans of some with the consumption demands of others through market price adjustments. Say simply points out that "the slightest excess supply beyond the demand is sufficient to produce a considerable alteration in price."[8] And this focus on market prices and the role price plays in the self-regulation of the market economy (and not his value theory, as Malthus had argued), Say argues, forms the true cornerstone of Adam Smith's lasting contribution to the science of political economy.[9]

---

5. F.A. Hayek, *The Pure Theory of Capital* (Chicago: University of Chicago Press, 1941), 374. Hayek argues that Keynes's economics "is based on the assumption that no real scarcity exists, and the only scarcity with which we need concern ourselves is the artificial scarcity created by the determination of people not to sell their services and products below certain arbitrarily fixed prices." In footnote 1 on that page, Hayek adds that Keynes's economics is essentially a return to a "naïve early stage of economic thinking" and can hardly be regarded as an improvement in economic thinking.
6. Ludwig von Mises, *Socialism: An Economic and Sociological Analysis* (1922; repr., Indianapolis, IN: Liberty Fund, 1981), 101.
7. Keynes, *General Theory*, 155.
8. Jean Baptiste Say, *Letters to Mr. Malthus* (1821; repr., New York: Augustus M. Kelley, 1967), 59.
9. Say, *Letters*, 20.

It is this last point raised by Say that I want to emphasize, namely that the cornerstone of Adam Smith's economics is his analysis of the price system and the self-regulating capacity of the market economy. This is where we find what is enduring in economics, whereas what is fleeting is found in that underworld of economic thinking that denies that analysis. Unfortunately, as has been pointed out by thinkers such as F.A. Hayek, James Buchanan,[10] and more recently Luigi Zingales, the Keynesian message appeals to technocrats and politicians.[11]

This is the economists' age-old plight, what is fleeting in economics is politically popular, whereas what is enduring in economics is politically unpopular. Hayek describes the economists' conundrum as consisting of being called upon to consult with politicians on matters of pubic policy more often than any other social scientists, only to have their advice based on the principles of the science dismissed as soon as it is uttered. Not only are the teachings of the discipline dismissed, but public opinion on the matters at hand seems to run in precisely the opposite direction of that of the economist. This position, Hayek argued, was not unique to his time, as it has been the plight of classical economists as well.[12] But what is most fascinating as an issue for a theory of social change is that economists' ideas in general are not dismissed because public opinion clearly reflects the ideas of economists of the previous generation. Unfortunately, the ideas that dominate are those that Keynes pointed to that had been relegated

---

10. James M. Buchanan and Richard Wagner, *Democracy in Deficit,* in *The Collected Works of James M. Buchanan*, vol. 7 (1977; repr., Indianapolis, IN: Liberty Fund, 2000), 4. Buchanan and Wagner argue that "Keynesian economics has turned the politicians loose; it has destroyed the effective constraint on politicians' ordinary appetites."

11. Luigi Zingales, "Keynesian Principles: The Opposition's Opening Remarks," *The Economist*, March 10, 2009, http://www.economist.com/debate/days/view/276. Zingales argued: "Keynesianism has conquered the hearts and minds of politicians and ordinary people alike because it provides a theoretical justification for irresponsible behavior. Medical science has established that one or two glasses of wine per day are good for your long-term health, but no doctor would recommend a recovering alcoholic to follow this prescription. Unfortunately, Keynesian economists do exactly this. They tell politicians, who are addicted to spending our money, that government expenditures are good. And they tell consumers, who are affected by severe spending problems, that consuming is good, while saving is bad. In medicine, such behaviour would get you expelled from the medical profession; in economics, it gives you a job in Washington."

12. See F.A. Hayek, "The Trend of Economic Thinking," in *The Collected Works of F. A. Hayek*, vol. 3 (1933; repr., Chicago: University of Chicago Press, 1991), 17.

to the underworld. This is precisely the situation we find ourselves in today. And as economic educators, we must, as the epigraph from Knight argues, stare the situation square in the face, acknowledge the ugly and unpleasant nature of things in our profession and the body politic, and take up the challenge of teaching the principles of economics to those who refuse to learn and in most instances even seriously listen.

What Adam Smith Did *Not* Say, and What He Did Say

Adam Smith was not the first economic thinker. But Adam Smith synthesized existing knowledge and did so in a way that has captured the imagination of intellectuals ever since. His is one of the towering achievements in the scientific and literary history of Western civilization. Even to this day, Smith's legacy is hotly debated.

A new generation of scholars such as Emma Rothchild and Sam Fleischacker are battling to save Smith's legacy from the Adam Smith tie-wearing conservative policy community.[13] Stressing the human and egalitarian sides of Smith's theory, they seek to counter the reading of Smith that focuses exclusively on self-interest and market efficiency. This caricature of Smith, as this egalitarian and progressive reading of Smith points out, is false. Smith never said "Greed works" and that is that. His argument is much different. But the Smith of Rothchild and Fleischacker is also a confused caricature. Smith was not an egalitarian social democrat. He was an analytical egalitarian, but he was also a classical liberal political economist. *The Wealth of Nations* develops the positive science of political economy, and Book V can be read as an attempt to provide a set of rules that an enlightened statesman who desired to produce the "good society" could follow on the basis of that positive science.[14] In Smith's work, the scale and scope of government is limited. While not nonexistent, it is limited to basically the "night watchman" state of classical liberal political philosophy: protections from foreign aggressors, protection of person and property and the

13. Emma Rothschild, *Economic Sentiments* (Cambridge, MA: Harvard University Press, 2001); Samuel Fleischacker, *On Adam Smith's* Wealth of Nations (Princeton, NJ: Princeton University Press, 2004).
14. Two of my favorite examples are Smith's four maxims of taxation and his warning about the "juggling trick" of debasement to pay off public debt.

administration of justice domestically, and the provision of essential public works. Only a distorted reading of Smith could produce either the institutionally antiseptic "self-interest"–only interpretation, or the Smith as precursor of the modern social democratic welfare state. The more modern social democratic reading of Smith is a consequence of the caricature prevalent in our culture of the "self-interest" reading as that of the laissez-faire economists in general. To distance Smith from the "economists," they offer an interpretation that is more compassionate to the poor and the dispossessed.

An older literature exists in intellectual history, which also tried to drive a wedge between Smith's *Theory of Moral Sentiments* (1758) and *The Wealth of Nations* (1776). Called the *Das Adam Smith Problem*, it argued that Smith built his theory of moral sentiments on human sympathy, whereas self-interest drove his theory of the economy. In one book we get other-regarding behavior, whereas in the other we get self-regarding behavior—how can we reconcile these works? Many attempts have been made to address this problem, including Vernon Smith's "The Two Faces of Adam Smith." The bottom line is that the "problem" is really not a problem.

The Wealth of Nations is about social order among strangers—a social order in which our span of moral sympathy moves far beyond the realm of the familiar. "In civilized society," Smith argued, man "stands at all times in need of the co-operation and assistance of great multitudes, while his whole life is scarce sufficient to gain the friendship of a few persons."[15] The market economy is about cooperation in anonymity, cooperation with strangers. In the chapter just before the cited passage, Smith presents the reader with the basic mystery of economic life. The number of exchange relations that must be coordinated to produce even the most common products we take for granted "exceeds all computation."[16]

The source of the wealth of nations arises from social cooperation under the division of labor, and to realize this social cooperation certain fundamental institutions in society must be in place—the delineation and enforcement of private property, the keeping of promises through contract, and the acceptance

---

15. Adam Smith, *An Inquiry into the Nature and Causes of the Wealth of Nations* (1776; repr., Chicago: University of Chicago Press, 1976), bk. I, 18.
16. Smith, *Wealth of Nations*, bk. I, 15.

of the legitimacy of the transfer of property by consent. Benevolence would not be able to achieve this social cooperation under the division of labor. The relationships exist at the outer bounds of our span of moral sympathy. But when the institutions of property, contract, and consent are in place, then the self-interest of individuals can be marshaled to realize the mutual gains from trade and the benefits of every refined division of labor in society. Our moral sentiments do not disappear as the span of moral sympathy moves from the intimate order to the extended order of the market. They are omnipresent, but we must be mature about them; otherwise, our moral intuitions will be in conflict with the moral demands of the market order. The moral sentiments within a commercial society manifest themselves in more general rules of just conduct (related to the institutions of property, contract, and consent), rather than specific outcomes of just division given a fixed resource endowment. The rules of the intimate order do not transfer to the extended order without sacrificing the gains from social cooperation under the division of labor, in which case we sacrifice the extended order itself.

Smith certainly did not teach that individuals should pursue their self-interest at all costs. But he also didn't even teach the more subtle presentation that the pursuit of self-interest will automatically translate into public benefits. *The Wealth of Nations* actually has plenty of examples in which the pursuit of self-interest can lead to socially undesirable outcomes. His discussion of the vocation of teaching in Oxford (bad) and in Glasgow (good) provides a classic example.[17] In Glasgow, the teacher had a strong incentive to provide valuable instruction because salary was a function of fees paid by the students, whereas in Oxford, because an endowment guaranteed a teacher's salary, the professors had long ago given up even the pretense of teaching. Smith's work is full of such comparative institutional analysis. The pursuit of self-interest in one case leads to a socially desirable outcome, whereas in the other it leads to an undesirable one. The key point: Smith's analysis does not turn on the behavioral postulate of self-interest but instead on the institutional specifications that are in operation. The institutional specification of a private property market economy guided by price signals and disciplined by profit and loss accounting will steer self-interested behavior in the direction of social cooperation. The vast division of labor is

---

17. See Smith, *Wealth of Nations*, bk. v, 282–84.

coordinated throughout the world, and the most common products—from a woolen coat in Adam Smith's time to a pencil in Milton Friedman's—are made available to individuals who will never know who played a part in the production of that good, and who if required to produce this product all by themselves wouldn't know where to start.

This is just another way to state Smith's "invisible hand" proposition. Individuals pursuing their own self-interest within an institutional setting of property, contract, and consent will produce an overall order that, although not of their intention, enhances the public good. Absent that institutional setting, self-interest may very well not produce publicly desirable outcomes and, in fact, may produce the opposite. What matters for Smithian political economy is the institutional filter that individual actors work within, and which produces unique equilibrating processes.[18]

J.B. Say in his *Letters to Malthus* states that he revered Smith: "he is my master."[19] As I mentioned before, Say had such a strong affinity to Smith because of his exposition of the fundamental role of prices in coordinating economic activity. As Say argued, exchange and the market prices that emerged in the "higgling and bargaining" among individuals formed the cornerstone of Smith's political economy. Smith's economics was price theoretic economics, but it was also institutional economics. The link between the abstract function of price and the concrete role of institutions that Smithian political economy provides supplies the foundation for what endures in economics. However, in understanding the full implications of Smith's message about market theory, the price system, and the role of institutions, we also reveal why technocrats and meddlesome politicians find it unpopular.

Hayek has argued that Smith designed his political economy to be robust against both the stupidity and arrogance of actors within the system.[20] Smith and his contemporaries (e.g., Hume) sought to discover a system of governance in which bad men can do the least harm and which did not require for its op-

---

18. The emphasis on institutional filters and equilibrating processes is developed in Robert Nozick's discussion of invisible hand explanations in *Anarchy, State and Utopia* (New York: Basic Books, 1974), 18–22.

19. Say, *Letters*, 21.

20. F.A. Hayek, *Individualism and Economic Order* (1948; repr., Chicago: University of Chicago Press, 1996), 11ff.

eration that only the best and the brightest be in charge. They sought, in other words, a system of societal governance that treated men as they are—sometimes good, sometimes bad; sometimes intelligent, sometimes not so bright—and that would use their human variety to produce peace and prosperity. The classical political economists of the eighteenth and nineteenth century discovered that the private property market economy provided the basis for just such a system.

Smith had argued in *The Theory of Moral Sentiments* that the "man of systems" was wise in his own conceit, but perhaps his most biting passage on the arrogance of the politician is found in *The Wealth of Nations*. In the paragraph after the famous invisible hand passage, Smith argued the following:

> What is the species of domestic industry which his capital can employ, and which the produce is likely to be of the greatest value, every individual, it is evident, can, in his local situation, judge much better than any statesmen or lawgiver can do for him. The statesmen, who should attempt to direct private people in what manner they ought to employ their capitals, would not only load himself with a most unnecessary attention, but assume an authority which could safely be trusted, not only to no single person, but to no council or senate whatever, and which would no-where be so dangerous as in the hands of a man who had folly and presumption enough to fancy himself fit to exercise it.[21]

This passage anticipates the calculation/knowledge argument about government planning associated with Mises and Hayek, as well as the problem of arrogance and power that Hayek identified with the "pretense of knowledge" or "fatal conceit." In other writings I have argued that David Hume's dictum that when we design institutions of government we must assume that all men are knaves implies that we must watch out for both hubristic knavery of the kind that Hayek has emphasized as well as the opportunistic knavery of the kind that Buchanan and Tullock have emphasized in the development of public choice theory. Smith, in this passage, anticipates the core ideas in those modern critiques of government control over economic life and reveals another element of what is enduring in economics.

---

21. Smith, *Wealth of Nations*, bk. IV, 478.

What Is Enduring and What Is Not

When we teach principles of economics to our students, most teachers of economics introduce the concept of scarcity quickly. Individuals choose within constraints and do not make unconstrained choices. As a result, our choices always involve the assessment of trade-offs, and as such we need some tools to help us make those assessments. The price system provides those tools for us. More importantly, the price system translates our private assessment of trade-offs into publicly useful information for others to utilize in their own private assessment of trade-offs, and thereby establishes the terms of exchange on the market.

Economics explains exchange and the institutions within which exchange takes place. As Frank Knight often stressed, economic analysis must always begin with the recognition of the fundamental point that an exchange is an exchange is an exchange, and exchange is mutually beneficial, otherwise the trade would not have taken place. Economics is elementary, but the persistent and consistent application of the economic way of thinking to all walks of human life requires discipline and creativity. Economics is a deadly serious discipline about deadly serious topics, and economics is a joyous exploration of man in all his endeavors. In our capacity as teachers of economics, it is our responsibility to introduce our students to both sides of the economic way of thinking.

But one of the most valuable applications of the economic way of thinking may very well be in explaining why good economics more often than not conflicts with good politics under democracy. An economic analysis of democratic politics reveals that the process pits a vote-seeking political entrepreneur against rationally ignorant voters and voters with special interests. The logic of this situation produces a bias in which the vote-seeking political entrepreneur will seek to secure votes and campaign contributions by promising to concentrate benefits on the well-informed and well-organized special interest voters while dispersing costs on the unorganized and ill-informed rationally ignorant voters. Moreover, the election cycle will impact the timeframe and produce a short-sightedness bias to compound the concentrated benefits/dispersed cost logic.

This is good politics. To do otherwise risks not gathering the required votes to win election. A vote-seeking politician who cannot garner votes eventually is weeded out of the political marketplace. But do shortsighted policies that concentrate benefits on special interest groups and disperse costs on rationally ignorant (or rationally abstaining) voters produce good economics? We must conclude NO; they instead produce political externalities. Good economics instead would concentrate costs on decision makers but disperse the benefits widely on the population. This is, again, one way to think about the implications of Adam Smith's invisible hand postulate—individuals pursuing their self-interest within a system of private property and the competitive market system will bear the costs of their decisions but possess the opportunity to reap the benefits from mutual exchange, and these exchanges produce more generalized benefits to the society as a whole. As we can see in the spread of trading opportunities and gains from technological innovation, these benefits of modern commercial life are the gift that keeps on giving. In other words, the benefits are not short-term gains, but are long-term in nature and at the core of the explanation of the wealth of nations (and their poverty when the benefits from trade and the benefits from innovation are not regularly realized).

Good economics concentrates costs on decision makers in the short run and disperses benefits to the society as a whole in the long run, whereas good politics concentrates benefits on well-organized and well-informed interest groups in the short run, while dispersing costs on the ill-organized and ill-informed mass of voters (both rationally ignorant and rational abstainers) in the long run. Since the beginning of the discipline, economists have recognized the conflict between good economics and good politics.

In the wake of this realization, we must remember that our job as economic educators and scholars is neither to steer the ship of state in one direction or another nor to provide pleasant and popular news to the ears of politicians and the public about the possibility of enlightened government policy to provide a corrective to the social ills of this world. Instead, our job is the twofold task of (1) the pleasant job of presenting the basic principles of our discipline to our "students" and deploying those basic principles to make sense of the world around us, and (2) the unpleasant one of playing the social critic who demonstrates logically and empirically how the best intentions of policymakers go astray and produce outcomes that are worse than the conditions the policies intend to eradicate. As Knight stressed, we should not underestimate our role in providing *negative knowledge.*[22] Economics puts parameters on people's utopias, and the teachings of the principles of economics should inform as much on what *not* to do, perhaps even more than providing a guide to public action.

Implicit theories of post-scarcity worlds, theories that do not see a role for property, prices, and profit and loss, or theories that assume that the decision makers in policy are omniscient eunuchs (or more traditionally benevolent despots) should not endure in economic education. The vulnerability of such fragile analysis must be exposed and subjected to harsh criticism in our scientific journals, in our classroom lectures, in the policy papers we write or testimony before committees that we provide, and in our effort to reach the everyman with magazine articles, newspaper opinion editorials, Twitter and blog posts, and radio and television appearances. Arthur Marget supposedly used the analogy to the netman in the days of the gladiator to describe his intellectual endeavor. Carrying a net and a trident, the fighter would entrap his adversary in the net and then use the trident to strike the deathblow. Marget reportedly described his massive tome, *The Theory of Price* (1938–1942), as his effort to entrap all the Keynesian fallacies in his net, after which he would strike the deathblow with his analysis.

Amazingly, Keynesianism as a system of *political* economics displays resilience in the face of repeated efforts (intellectually successful from my perspective, I should add) to be ensnared in the net of economics as fallacious doctrine. I contend that political, rather than analytical, reasons explain its appeal, and so we must continue to fight this battle and expose the intellectual bankruptcy of politicized economics. Keynesianism is indeed a disease on the body politic in democratic society. An economic doctrine of technocratic arrogance, it suffers from the "pretense of knowledge" and gives scope to the opportunistic behavior of politicians who become unconstrained by Keynesianism in practice.

I have referenced J.B. Say as stressing the role of the price system in the self-regulation of the market, but his fellow Frenchman, Frederic Bastiat, should not be forgotten.[23] His infamous "petition," the classic economic satire, exposes the silliness of special pleading. What differs between the candlestick makers'

---

22. Knight, "Role of Principles," 365.
23. Bastiat, Frederic. 1964. "A Petition" in *Economic Sophisms,* Irvington-On-Hudson: Foundation For Economic Education, 56–60.

petition and the calls for bailouts, for protection from foreign competitors, for the establishment of public unions whose members are exempt from the vagaries of the marketplace, and so on? Not only must cold heads prevail over warm hearts; the arrogance as well as the loose reasoning must be continually exposed—no doubt first by careful theoretical and empirical analysis, but don't forget that ridicule and satire are also effective teaching tools.

Conclusion

This discussion of what is enduring in economics serves as a rally call for all of us who view our primary professional duty as that of economic educators. We have a job to do; we have to teach the basic principles of economics and cultivate an appreciation among our students of the teachings of the great political economists from Adam Smith and David Hume to F.A. Hayek and James Buchanan. Their message was clear: Not only is the private property market economy a self-regulating system guided through relative price adjustment and profit and loss calculus, but the market society forms the basis for a political order of free people. Efforts to intervene in the market order should always be checked for knavish efforts of either hubris or opportunism (or both). Even as we are staring the current situation of anti-economics knavery gone amok squarely in the face, let us, as economic educators, never lose sight of the core message and communicate it simply and clearly: When it comes to realizing the mutual gains from social cooperation, prices work, politics doesn't. The central message of the superiority of economic freedom compared to the tyranny of government control is what emerges from the study of the economic thinking that is valid for yesterday, today, and tomorrow.

PART I

On Teaching Economics

2

On the Tasks of Economics Education

Academic economics is primarily useful, both to the student and to the political leader, as a prophylactic against popular fallacies.

—Henry Simons[1]

Introduction

EACH FALL PARENTS across the country are saying goodbye to their kids who are setting off for college. Many of these students will travel great distances. Many of them will find living away from home to be a new experience. A subset of these fresh and eager young minds will find themselves sitting in an economics class. They will have purchased a textbook that costs close to $100 (or at least gained access to an online version of it).

Most likely the textbook will be written by Gregory Mankiw, though if the professor is of a certain age it might be written by Campbell McConnell. If the professor is of a certain ideological bent, the textbook might be written by James Gwartney and Richard Stroup, or perhaps E. K. Hunt, or Joseph Stiglitz. If the professor prides him- or herself on being a conventional center-left nonideological/technocratic professor of economics, the students might have to work through a textbook by William Baumol and Alan Blinder. If the students are very fortunate they will be asked to purchase the textbook by my colleagues Tyler Cowen and Alex Tabarrok, *Modern Principles of Economics*. If they are extremely fortunate (I am undoubtedly biased here) they will have

---

1. Henry C. Simons, *Simons' Syllabus*, edited by Gordon Tullock (Fairfax, VA: Center for the Study of Public Choice, 1983), 3.

that rare professor of good taste and judgment who assigns Paul Heyne's *The Economic Way of Thinking*.[2]

Of the thousands of students enrolling in their first economics class each fall, very few will have chosen how they would like to be taught economics, or by whom, or from what perspective. For the vast majority, enrollment in a particular class will be simply a random act or a decision based on scheduling trade-offs. Any given student might wind up with a dynamic economics professor, or more likely, to be honest, a boring dud. The professor might be very well informed about current affairs; then again, he or she might have no idea what is going on in the real world and might not care much about it either.

Because economics is often taught poorly, I find that, when people who discover that I am an economist, I can pretty much count on one of three reactions from them: (1) "Ugh! That was my least favorite class. How can you study that?" (2) "Oh, that's interesting. Do you know where interest rates are going?" (3) "Yea. I really enjoyed my economics class"—which remark is usually followed by a set of policy questions and, more often than not, a set of policy pronouncements randomly left, center, or right.[3] In the aftermath of 2008, I have often met people who, upon learning that I am an economist, blame my colleagues and me for the current financial crisis and insist that economists know absolutely nothing of value. Rarely, and I mean really rarely, do I encounter someone who says, "Oh, how exciting. I loved my economics teacher. He/she really changed my life and the way I think about the world." The few people who express an

---

2. Since Paul's untimely death in 2000, David Prychitko and I have revised and updated his textbook for the 10th, 11th, and 12th editions. Paul Heyne, Peter J. Boettke, and David L. Prychitko, *The Economic Way of Thinking*, 12th ed. (Upper Saddle River, NJ: Prentice Hall, 2010).

3. On a recent round of golf I was paired with a retired public school history teacher. When he found out I was an economics professor he asked me if I followed the teachings of Trotsky. I thought at first he was making a joke. But then he followed up with his theory of the Great Depression—"capitalism is immoral"—and the current crisis—"capitalists are thieves." I was then confronted with a choice: Try to hit a tee shot that didn't end up lost, or try to correct 50 years of bad thinking on the part of this man who had strong opinions that he was willing to share so easily. I chose to play golf and not debate him on the substance of economics and public policy. Sometimes, I thought to myself, you have to pick your battles.

attitude of that sort are apt to be graduate students, or perhaps other colleagues, if graduate school hasn't beaten all enthusiasm out of them. They are not apt to be people you just happen to meet in your neighborhood, at your church, or out in the community at large.

I have always been intrigued by this discrepancy. I had plenty of college classes outside of economics that to this day I remember with great fondness, for the professors' teaching and for the knowledge I gained.[4] But in economics it appears either that you get it or you don't. If you get it, you work in the field; if you don't, you hate what economists (as popularly imagined) stand for. Why?

I believe it is because we fail in our efforts to teach economics as an intellectually exciting and world-illuminating discipline. I often say that economics is a deadly serious discipline that tackles vital questions of wealth and poverty, of life and death; that it is an amazing framework for thinking about human behavior in the real world, including all human endeavors; and that is entertaining and downright fun.[5] Admittedly, there seems to be something strange and counterintuitive about economics. It is about freedom of choice, but within constraints; it is about human intentionality, but also the unintended consequences of human action. As Hayek has stated, "The curious task of economics is to demonstrate to men how little they really know about what they imagine they can design."[6] But it is also the case that economics in the hands of its finest practitioners is little more than applied common sense. As Frank Knight pointed out, "The serious fact is that the bulk of the really important things that economics has to teach are things that people would see for themselves if they were willing to see. And it is hard to believe in the utility of trying to teach

---

4. My education at Grove City College was outstanding. I remember very fondly my classes in philosophy, political history, religious studies, legal studies, and psychological theories. I even enjoyed my classes in business. I just assumed this was the common experience of my peers, but 25-plus years of subsequent experience in higher education have continually challenged my presumption.

5. Chris Coyne's *After War: The Political Economy of Exporting Democracy* (Stanford, CA: Stanford University Press, 2007) provides an example of the power of economic scholarship to address deadly serious matters; Peter T. Leeson's *The Invisible Hook: The Hidden Economics of Pirates* (Princeton, NJ: Princeton University Press, 2009) exemplifies scholarship brought to bear on unusual subject matter in a fascinating, entertaining manner.

6. Hayek, 1991, 76.

what men refuse to learn or even seriously listen to."[7] The tension between these two claims is largely a by-product of the way the discipline is taught and the way its teachings are applied to the realm of public policy in an inconsistent and ultimately ad hoc manner.[8]

Paul Heyne's basic approach to economic education was a combination of KISS (keep it simple, stupid) and a deep commitment to certain core principles of the discipline, both of which help to keep the message simple. But a professor who strives for simplicity and a sharp focus must also believe firmly that simple economics is *not simple-minded economics*. A professor who cannot genuinely believe that will be inclined to teach nuanced theoretical propositions acquired from graduate school courses, even when doing so is not appropriate. Even for those not uncomfortable with basic economics, the incentives faced in trying to balance teaching responsibilities with the demand for publication for professional advancement may cause a drift toward teaching the principles course as if it were a watered-down version of the courses they took in graduate school.

This approach to teaching economics fails to communicate basic principles effectively; it also pitches the principles of the discipline in the most inappropriate way for the audience intended. If you emphasize the exceptions to the principles at the principles level, the students learn the exceptions, not the principles. Thus, students walk away thinking about monopoly, externalities, public goods, income inequality, macroeconomic instability, and the corrective government policies launched to address each of these. They consider market failures to be the main lessons of economics, rather than the role played by private property, relative prices, and profit-and-loss accounting in an economic

---

7. Frank H. Knight, "The Role of Principles in Economics and Politics," *American Economic Review* 41, no. 1 (1951): 1–29, in *Selected Essays of Frank H. Knight*, edited by Ross Emmett, vol. 2 (repr., Chicago: University of Chicago Press, 1999), 364.

8. Hayek postulates as well that we are hardwired by our evolutionary past in small-group settings to have moral intuitions that are often at odds with the moral demands of the "Great Society"—the social cooperation under the division of labor that characterizes modern commercial society. Thus, economics can be applied as common sense, but its lessons are rejected as soon as they are heard for at least two reasons: (1) moral intuition based on the intimate order that is used to judge behavior in the extended order; and (2) interest-group politics that cuts against economic logic to pursue the political logic of concentrating benefits on well-organized and well-informed interest groups in the short-run, while dispersing costs on the unorganized and ill-informed voters in the long-run.

system (i.e., structuring incentives, generating information that guide decisions, inspiring innovation, and providing disciplinary feedback on decisions).

In short, following the watered-down PhD approach to teaching the principles of economics class doesn't cultivate an understanding among students of the gains from trade and the gains from innovation that explain the wealth and poverty of nations. Instead, it simply teaches a set of models and techniques of social control. The "worldly philosophy" of economics and political economy becomes the "dismal science of optimal" taxation, regulatory control, and macroeconomic fine-tuning. Both the science and its application are ill served by these lame attempts at teaching the economic way of thinking and demonstrating its relevance. Perhaps more importantly, the students are ill-served as the stuff of economics is presented in as boring and, ironically, as arrogant a manner as possible.

The Basic Economic Way of Thinking

One of the great joys of teaching basic economics is taking students who are completely innocent of the economic way of thinking and getting them to see that they are "all doing it, but none of them know they are doing it."[9] When I introduce the basic ideas of marginal benefit and marginal cost decision calculus to my introductory class, I draw the curves and label them correctly (marginal benefits declining, marginal costs rising), and then I ask, "How many of the young ladies in the room have been on a date?" Several hands are raised. I continue: "How many of you married that guy?" This is usually followed by some chuckles. I continue: "How many of you went on only one date with him?" Hands rise and the murmur in the room is audible. So I say, "OK, I see. The marginal costs of going out with 'Ed' another time exceeded the marginal benefits of another date with him." I elaborate: "Most guys are neither the guy

---

9. In his classic work, *The Common Sense of Political Economy: Including a Study of the Human Basis of Economic Law* (London: Macmillan, 1910), Wicksteed chose the actual quote from the German poet Goethe that I have paraphrased as the epigraph for his book. One way to read Tyler Cowen's recent book, *Discover Your Inner Economist: Use Incentives to Fall in Love, Survive Your Next Meeting, and Motivate Your Dentist* (Boston, MA: Dutton Adult, 2007), is as a modern example of this style of presenting economic reasoning to those who are largely innocent of the discipline.

you want to marry after one date, nor are most of them the guy you want to run away from for the rest of your life. Instead, with the guy in question, you probably go on three, five, or ten dates." Then I usually invoke a mythical break-up, "Look, you are a great guy; you are just not good boyfriend material." In such a case, her experiences with "Ed" reached a point of "optimality" at say, five dates; she chooses not to go on a sixth date because the marginal cost of the experience would exceed the marginal benefit. Neither my made-up couple nor my students are unique in this respect. When it comes to economic behavior, they are all doing it, but none of them know they are doing it. The economic way of thinking gives us a language to analyze their behavior in a systemic manner.

The economic way of thinking begins with understanding that human choice in all walks of life is always exercised against a background of constraints. The fundamental constraint is the fact of scarcity—not material or merely financial scarcity, but the logical fact of scarcity. Poverty and scarcity are not identical, and it is important to stress this point. Bill Gates must make choices just as you and I do; he also makes his choices against a background of constraints, and his choices reflect his trade-offs. But we do often identify the additional constraints that include financial constraints, technological constraints, time constraints, and resource constraints.

The reality of choice within constraints implies that we face trade-offs in making decisions. Substitutes abound. We are always choosing between alternative courses of action, and in making those choices we require various tools to aid us in assessing the trade-offs. We choose one path for an expected return, and we forgo an alternative with an expected cost. We need aids to assess the opportunity cost of our course of action. The exchange ratios established in the market come to us in the form of relative monetary prices that we can use to think about the alternatives. An introduction to monetary prices used in this way would emphasize, on the one hand, how the subjective assessment of trade-offs for some can become objective information about the market, which can then be used by others as they make their subjective assessments of trade-offs in economic decision making. An adequate introduction would also emphasize, on the other hand, the role played by property, prices, and profit/loss in coordinating economic decisions.

Both aspects of this subtle understanding need to be communicated to students if they are to understand market theory and the price system, the power of the market to coordinate the plans of buyers and sellers, the impossibility of rational economic calculation under collective ownership and the absence of a market for capital goods, and the economic instability of interventionist measures with price controls, regulations, and restrictions. Students must gain the same insight to understand their own participation in the market—buying and abstaining from buying as consumers; keeping alert to opportunities for mutual gain as traders and as entrepreneurs; and exercising creativity (in the discovery of innovative production processes, which provide cost savings, or in imagining new products, which better satisfy consumer demand) as entrepreneurs, managers, and enterprising business owners.

Basic economics teaches us that individuals, while not lightning-speed calculators of pleasure and pain, nevertheless are purposive actors who weigh costs and benefits in decisions and strive to do the best they can, given their situations (which include not only their constraints and specific contexts but also their cognitive limitations). This is, in short, what economists mean when they say that individuals engage in rational choice, or that individuals act in a self-interested manner. It does not mean that they are robotic in their choices, nor does it mean that they are atomistic, selfish actors. It does mean that they have ends and that they employ the means available to them to achieve those ends. They will pursue mutually advantageous exchanges with other economic actors. The prospect of great gains to be realized through specialization and exchange will guide them. They will focus on supplying goods and services they can produce at a low opportunity cost, and they will exchange their products for goods and services they could produce only at a high opportunity cost. In such exchanges, mutual gains from trade are realized, and the composition of the division of labor in society emerges.

The exercise of choice within constraints; the mutually beneficial aspect of exchange; the importance of property rights, incentives, prices, and information; the lure of profit and the penalty of loss; the spontaneous emergence of social cooperation under the division of labor—these basic principles comprise the core that beginning students must grasp as prerequisites for a more complete understanding of how a market economy works.

The great economist Henry Simons argued (as reflected in the epigraph to this chapter) that the primary purpose of economics as a discipline is to provide a prophylactic against popular fallacies. The insights needed to combat popular fallacies, Simons claimed, have to do with the role of prices and the adjustment of relative prices in bringing about the required adjustments that enable economic actors to realize mutual gains and push the economic system toward its market-clearing position (where all the gains from exchange and innovation at any point in time are realized). As Frank Knight often stressed, an exchange is an exchange is an exchange.[10] An exchange is mutually beneficial; otherwise it would not have been made. In a free market economy, economic interaction is a positive-sum game. That is, the interests of the players do not necessarily conflict; one player's gain does not entail another player's loss. Politics, on the other hand, is at best a zero-sum game, in which interests do conflict and one player's gain is another player's loss. (Politics can also be a negative-sum game, visiting mutual harm on the players, if the churning or rent-seeking state is unconstrained.)

Most popular fallacies are rooted in confusion over this basic point about exchange relationships. And a failure to understand the machinations of politics, even under democracy, leads many people to believe the opposite—that markets are zero-sum or negative-sum games, while politics represents a positive-sum game. From this perspective, politics is viewed as a corrective to market failures, operating through the basic legal framework it provides, the fiscal policy it enacts to stimulate aggregate demand, and the government policies it designs to promote economic growth and development. In this sense, government is the solution, while the market system is the problem.

These popular fallacies are a function of ignorance of the basics of economics; they are also fostered by the special pleading of interest groups. Teaching economics at the principles level will be effective to the extent that it communicates to the students the ubiquitous nature of trade-offs that individuals must negotiate, the role played by private property rights in structuring incentives, the role played by prices in communicating information to economic actors, the role played by the lure of profit in spurring innovation, and the role losses play in disciplining decisions and reallocating scarce resources to higher-valued uses. Sound economic policy embodies these basic principles; popular fallacies deny or ignore them.

---

10. Frank H. Knight, *Intelligence and Democratic Action* (Cambridge, MA: Harvard, 1960).

Tools Economic Actors Use,
and the Way Economists Understand Them

It is important to distinguish between economic actors and the economists who try to understand the behavior of economic actors. Here is a favorite thought experiment of mine—one I often share with my students. Imagine that you are in New York City or Washington, DC. What would have a greater impact on your life—if all the economists went on strike, or all the garbage men? The students immediately (and inevitably) get the point. Garbage men are more important for your day-to-day living than those of us who study the economy for a living. But the thought experiment also suggests a broader point. Economic life exists without economists. If there were no economists, there would still be trading, specialized production, constant seeking of economic advantage, and a strong desire to avoid losses. Individuals would want to buy low and sell high, and they would know they should avoid buying high and selling low. They would not need an economist to tell them this.

Economists came along after the existence of the phenomena they try to understand. In other words, economists emerged in a philosophic effort to understand an already existing practice. This point has broad implications for the nature of the discipline, even though we do not usually address them in introductory courses.[11]

In market economies, one vital activity economic actors engage in is rational calculation about alternative uses of scarce resources. Again, no economists were needed for this practice to evolve. All it took was private property and free pricing. Economic systems that do not permit private property and free pricing will distort the process of economic calculation and ultimately render it impossible for economic actors to engage in. This is the decisive objection to socialism as an economic system. It must forgo the intellectual division of labor in an economy by keeping economic actors completely in the dark about the fundamental questions of what is going to be produced, how it is going to be produced, and for whom it is going to be produced. Economists cannot

---

11. A simple way to understand the methodological differences between Mises and Hayek, on the one hand, and the mathematical and statistical approach to economics, on the other, is to emphasize this starting point of the discipline and the human dimension that permeates economic life.

answer those system-wide questions in the abstract, but the systemic study of economics helps us to understand how those questions are in fact answered as the by-product of thousands, hundreds, even millions of individuals who strive to improve their lot in life—pursuing opportunities for mutually advantageous exchange, channeling their creative energy in the pursuit of innovation in arts, commerce, and science. The "miracle" of modern economic growth and development did not spring from the brow of any genius; it was instead the outcome of a shift in the institutional environment, a shift that encouraged trade and enabled entrepreneurial ventures in arbitrage and innovation. As recently argued by economic historian Joel Mokyr, the critical point was the convergence of various philosophical and institutional changes that encouraged critical thinking and turned scientific innovations into commercially useful knowledge.[12] Advances in engineering science were translated into commercial innovations that satisfied consumer demands to a greater extent than had previously been imagined, and at lower cost. The "hockey stick" of economic growth—the upturn from a flat plane—that was experienced in the West is thus explained; and, by implication, so is the failure to experience comparable growth outside the countries of the West.

To reiterate, economists did not orchestrate the economic growth of the West. Where "economic planners" did make large-scale efforts to orchestrate growth—in the former Soviet Union, Africa, and Latin America—the results were not generalized prosperity; they were systemic poverty and political tyranny.[13] Conveying this history to beginning students in an intelligible manner is one of the vital tasks of the economics teacher. That a lot of bad thinking stems from a failure to understand this history is a central message in Deirdre McCloskey's fascinating *Bourgeois Virtues* (Chicago: University of Chicago Press, 2006) and *Bourgeois Dignity* (Chicago: University of Chicago Press, 2010).

Economists are not responsible for the wealth of nations, but they can be responsible for the poverty of nations. This is an ironic twist that students must

---

12. Joel Mokyr, *The Enlightened Economy: An Economic History of Britain 1700–1850* (New Haven, CT: Yale University Press, 2010).

13. See Peter J. Boettke, ed., *The Collapse of Development Planning* (New York: New York University Press, 1994).

come to understand. Economists err if they forget that economic life existed before them, and that it operates, for the most part, independently of them. Economists also err if in their work they keep realms of knowledge hermetically sealed in separate bins of scientific/philosophic exploration and market experimentation and innovation.

Again, this is a nuanced position that is not necessarily a suitable topic for basic economics courses, but the underlying point has been stressed by F.A. Hayek and Robert Lucas in their Nobel Prize–winning work, respectively. Hayek emphasized the difference between the knowledge embedded in an economy and the knowledge of the economist studying the economic system. A theoretical understanding of embedded economic knowledge does not necessarily mean that that knowledge will be available in a useable form to the economist or policy expert. Hayek's argument is that contextual knowledge in the possession of economic actors, and used by them, far exceeds (in importance and relevance to the coordination of economic activities) the abstract, theoretical knowledge that economists have at their disposal, derived from models of optimal control.

Lucas emphasized a slightly different point. He put a knowledge constraint on economists and economic actors. Hayek stressed the point that economists don't possess the contextual knowledge that economic actors possess; Lucas stressed the point that it is a methodological error to assume that economists have knowledge that is superior to that of economic actors. Whatever theoretical knowledge economists possess (e.g., the relationship between the quantity of money and the price level in an economy), economic actors will know it implicitly if not explicitly. Thus, policy designs are fundamentally flawed if they assume that economic actors are ignorant of theoretical formulations—formulations which are economically beneficial for them to know. This is, in essence, the rational expectations hypothesis and the core argument in the invariance proposition that led to the New Classical paradigm in macroeconomics.

Economic actors use the tools of reasoning the market economy provides for them: property rights provide incentives to economic actors; relative prices guide economic actors in their decisions; and profits and losses direct the uses of resources, encouraging innovation and spurring economic growth. The economist, on the other hand, possesses theoretical knowledge about how these tools are used by economic actors. Economists thus are best understood as *students* of society. Efforts to view them instead as *saviors* of society, armed with comprehensive plans and policy designs, more often than not result in frustrated efforts by governments to improve the economic welfare of their citizens.[14]

My teacher James M. Buchanan used to say to us, "It takes varied reiteration to force alien concepts upon reluctant minds." So perhaps I should be forgiven for repeating myself regarding the basic lessons of economics. Trade-offs abound; property, prices, and profits must do their job in coordinating economic activities; freedom of trade enables individuals to realize gains from systems of specialized production and exchange; and politics, while it provides a basic framework of law and order, is not to be viewed as a corrective for economic ills. One of the great ironies of economic knowledge is this: we do not need to *understand* economics in order to *experience* the benefits of freedom of exchange and production, but we may very well need to understand economics in order to *sustain and maintain* the institutional framework that enables us to realize the benefits that flow from freedom of exchange and production. Economic ignorance fueled by scientism and special interest pleading unleashed by unconstrained democracy have proved that economic liberalism is vulnerable to specious criticisms. Popular fallacies have substituted for basic economics in the public imagination. Our task as educators is to counter the ignorance and expose the special pleading for what it is. Since Henry Simons taught generations of students at the University of Chicago, our task as economic educators has grown more complicated rather than less.

Positive Economics, Normative Economics, and the Art of Political Economy

There is a science of economics. It is important that students come to understand this. Economics is not mere opinion. The economic way of thinking helps individuals reach informed opinions. The best way I have found to teach the scientific and objective nature of economic analysis is "the devil test." Using the example of minimum wage laws or rent control, I demonstrate to students that *the analysis* could be agreed upon by either an angel or the devil, but

---

14. See Peter J. Boettke and Christopher J. Coyne, "The Role of the Economist in Economic Development," *Quarterly Journal of Austrian Economics* 19, no. 2 (2006): 47–68.

the angel and devil would differ on the normative implications. In both instances of restrictions on market pricing to allocate resources (jobs and housing), the economic analysis demonstrates that the least advantaged are disproportionately made worse off. The angel, of course, finds this abhorrent, while the devil takes great pleasure in the outcome. But since the analysis of the situation is agreed upon by both, you know you are talking about an objective analysis and not the subjective policy preferences of the economist when you discuss the economics of price controls.

So that the students don't think I have pulled a trick on them, I often follow this up with the story of the good friends, and in many ways the co-founders of the study of political economy, David Hume and Adam Smith. I use the example of their "economic" analysis of state support of religion and religious education, and the seemingly counterintuitive results their analysis produces. Smith observed that in countries where religious institutions were strongly supported by the government, and religious leaders received salaries and operating funds from the government, the level of religiosity was lower than in those countries where religious institutions had to compete for funding from the believers. Smith reasoned that the incentives for religious leaders who were secure in their funding differed from the incentives for those who had to compete for funds. Religious competition would lead to more entertaining sermons, more pastoral engagement with parishioners—in short, more religiosity. Hume observed the same factual starting point and provided a similar analysis to explain the situation. However, Hume was a religious skeptic and desired less religiosity in society; therefore *he advocated state sponsorship of religion.* Smith was not a religious skeptic; therefore *he argued in favor of competition in religious activities.* Note that both analyzed the situation with the aid of rational choice theory and incentives, and a theory of competition and spontaneous order, but they differed in their normative assessments. The analysis provided by the economic way of thinking is independent of the normative position of the analyst. It is a mistake of significant proportions not to make this point clearly in introducing students to the economic way of thinking.

John Neville Keynes (the father of the more famous Keynes) divided economic knowledge into positive economics, normative economics, and the art of political economy. It is from the senior Keynes that we get the useful dichotomy between positive economics, as dealing with what is, and normative economics, as addressing what should be.[15] Welfare economics and concepts such as efficiency are (or at least can be) subtopics of positive economics; but when we engage in comparative assessment of states of affairs, the normative element almost by necessity comes into play. This is true whether we are talking about "rationality" as a benchmark concept (as is often the case in behavioral economics) or "competitive equilibrium" as a benchmark concept (as is often the case in conventional textbook economics and, in particular, in discussions related to industrial organization, antitrust legislation, and economic regulation).

The art of political economy emerges in the application of positive and normative economics to the realm of public policy. Political economy is, as the label implies, more art than science at this level. But it nevertheless makes use of scientific knowledge in applications ranging from mundane policy questions concerned with price controls, international trade, and macroeconomic instability to esoteric and ideologically charged questions associated with exploitation, injustice, and the choice between capitalism and socialism. To describe the intellectual interrelationship between economics and social philosophy, I try to show my students that political economy can become a value-relevant discipline only to the extent that economics can supply it with value-neutral analyses.

A common criticism of economics is that we economists know the price of everything but the value of nothing. This criticism, while it possesses a nice literary ring, doesn't really ring true.[16] Economists understand that human beings do not eat growth rates, and instead what matters is steady improvement along a variety of measures of human well-being. What is desired is the opportunity for individuals to live a flourishing life. Human flourishing takes into account subjective components of human choice as well as objective components that provide sound bases for making those choices. Ultimately, it becomes necessary to discuss the connection between the institutions of a free society and the individual's freedom to make choices. Still, in working with students, I find it important to stress that economic analysis per se is not a normative science, but a positive science. I repeat, over and over—economics cannot tell you whether

---

15. John N. Keynes, *The Scope and Method of Political Economy* (Cambridge, MA: C.J. Clay M.A. & Sons at the University Press, 1891).

16. See the concluding chapter and appendix to my *Calculation and Coordination* (New York: Routledge, 2001) for a documentation of the correlations between economic growth and various measures of human well-being.

profits are deserved or not, but economics can tell you the consequences of your answer to that question. The relevant analysis has evolved over centuries of economic thinking. It has yielded important empirical results relating to the "big questions" about wealth and poverty and human well-being. The analysis and the results to date are such that our introductory student should walk away from an economics course with a sense of what the state of play is in the discipline of economics.[17] Models are tools for economic reasoning, not the subject of economics. Too often students today walk away from an economics course in which they learned models, were tested on models, and now know a laundry list of models, but have no clue what economics as a subject is all about.[18] The models-intensive approach to teaching economics selects a certain type of student to pursue the serious study of economics and weeds out others.

The way we teach a subject is not neutral with respect to who becomes the next generation of students and teachers of the subject. The relationship of the instructional approach to the grooming of students and teachers creates a perpetual cycle. The current result, I contend, is that students, who have strong mathematical aptitude, and perhaps an engineering mentality (problem-solution), are selected into the discipline, while those possessed of a more interpretive aptitude, and a philosophical mentality (question-answer), are weeded out. As the cycle has progressed through the twentieth century, the worldly philosophy of political economy has been pushed aside in favor of the social physics of economics.

---

17. At NYU I taught an Honors Economics Principles course, designed for NYU's best and brightest students. It was a very elite group of students indeed, and their postgraduate careers have proven that assessment correct as they have moved on to significant careers in finance, law, and computer science. In this course I used Adam Smith's *The Wealth of Nations*, Alfred Marshall's *Principles of Economics*, and Joseph Stiglitz's *Economics*. My idea was to encourage the students to think about continuities and discontinuities in the history of the discipline of economics.

18. I recently learned of a large-section principles class at an elite institution of higher education where on the final exam the average score was 68 out of 200. The professor of the class was quite proud of his weeding-out powers but was apparently oblivious to the thought that if the average score among the best and brightest students is 34 percent, then of the three competing hypotheses—(1) the material is too difficult for the students; (2) the material was taught poorly; and (3) the test was ill-designed for the material taught—the least likely is that the material in a principles of economics class is too difficult for students, all of whom scored 1500 or higher on their SATs.

Exclusivity in either direction skews economic discourse, ultimately in an unproductive direction. In other words, economics and political economy require both logic and interpretation, an ability to grasp problems and offer solutions, and an ability to ponder deeper questions and offer tentative answers in an ongoing conversation that constitutes a progressive civilization. One of the really important lessons I try to get across to my students is the role that economics plays in the interplay between political economy and social philosophy. Economists must be willing to learn from and engage historians, philosophers, political scientists, sociologists, and other scholars. The economist must be a lifelong learner. There is nothing worse than an economist who knows only economics—except perhaps a moral philosopher who knows no economics at all.

Conclusion

I consider the teaching of economics to be a calling. In many ways the primary justification of our compensation as economists is the didactic role we play in society. It is not our job as teachers to impart a political ideology or even to cultivate a preference for a certain set of public policies. Instead, our task as economics teachers is to effectively communicate to our students the basic principles of economics so that those students may become informed participants in the ongoing process of democratic self-governance. Those basic principles are rooted in the logic of purposive human choice, in the exchange relationships that constitute the market economy, and in the spontaneous ordering of economic activity that results from leaving individuals free to choose within a private property market economy. If we are effective in our educational task, then economic literacy will be improved and we will have done our part in cultivating the capacities required for a self-governing citizenry in a society of free and responsible individuals. If we fail, then our theoretical and empirical efforts will be of little value to the enterprise of understanding, let alone improving, the human condition.

3

On Teaching Graduate Students in Austrian Economics

> Economics is not just a game to be played by clever people.
> —Gary Becker[1]

Introduction

THROUGHOUT MY CAREER I have consistently taught graduate students, and PhD students in particular. Teaching advanced students differs radically from attempting to excite young minds without any (or only minimal) background in the economic way of thinking. Both educational tasks are in essence open invitations to inquiry, but the level of presentation and subject matter under discussion changes. However, sometimes the advanced discussion leaves much to be desired because the focus tends to become more about what I call "blackboard" economics as opposed to the real economic activity that is going on "out the window." But the advanced student is both interested in learning the theories and approaches of other economists, and it is what is expected of them, whereas the beginning student is at best curious about the world they occupy.

It would help graduate level instruction and education if we focused more on "out the window" and less on the "blackboard." But the "blackboard" is fascinating as well. For those of us who choose to do economics for a living, not only is economic activity fascinating, but also economics as a discipline is the conversation we want to join. This chapter addresses what I have learned

---

1. This is taken from Becker's opening remarks at a dinner at the Dallas Federal Reserve Bank in 2003 to honor Milton and Rose Friedman. Becker argued that this was among the most important lessons he learned from Milton Friedman as a teacher of economics.

over the years from teaching PhD students how to join that conversation, while also pursuing an out of sync research and teaching agenda.

In the Classroom

In the classroom my courses at the PhD level are designed for students aiming to become scholars in the field of economics. A PhD is a research degree, and as such the teaching of PhD students must be done accordingly. It is not just an undergraduate course on steroids. Instead, the focus must be on helping the students find their research direction and encouraging them to take ownership of their research program. They must find their own voice, so to speak, and figure out how they will join the professional conversation.

This requires the students to be familiar with the necessary literature, to be able to intelligently discuss the literature, and to make their own contributions to the discipline. The class discussions are based around the relevant texts for the given class and not lectures exclusively. For example, my Austrian economics classes focuses primarily around Ludwig von Mises's *Human Action,* F.A. Hayek's *Individualism and Economic Order,* Israel Kirzner's *Competition and Entrepreneurship,* and Murray Rothbard's *Man, Economy, and State.*[2] These books expose students to the methodological arguments as well as economic issues such as monetary theory, capital theory, and market process theory developed by the Austrian school. Students also read modern scholars outside the Austrian tradition but whose ideas are in line with Austrian ideas. My classes focus on ideas, not on the personal histories and personalities of the different economists. And the main idea is to see what opportunities exist in the current conversation within economics and political economy for engagement from an Austrian perspective, as well as what opportunities exist in the current literature for mutual gains from intellectual exchange. I am trying to get the students interested in Austrian economics to see not only how they can advance the existing body of

---

2. Ludwig von Mises, *Human Action: A Treatise on Economics* (1949; Indianapolis, IN: Liberty Fund, 2010); F.A. Hayek, *Individualism and Economic Order* (1948; repr., Chicago: University of Chicago Press, 1996); Israel M. Kirzner, *Competition and Entrepreneurship* (Chicago: University of Chicago Press, 1978); Murray N. Rothbard, *Man, Economy, and State* (Auburn, AL: Ludwig von Mises Institute, 2009).

knowledge within the Austrian tradition within the contemporary scientific literature, but also what ways the contemporary literature could help improve the ideas that have traditionally been associated with the Austrian school of economics.

The advancement of a scientific research program requires at least three things: ideas, funding, and academic positions. When that research program is slightly out of sync with the mainstream of the current practice, the advanced PhD student must position him- or herself wisely within the scientific community or risk committing professional suicide. So as we move from the classroom to dissertation advising, my interactions with the students must also take into account these professional/career considerations.

The Placing of Graduate Students: The Role of Austrians in the Profession

The first thing I should state as a preliminary is that I know of no single instance of a successful stealth strategy in academics.[3] You are what you write and we compete with seriously skilled people; you cannot "fake out" the competition. Once you leave doing Austrian economics and classical liberal political economy, you leave it. The most successful people are those who make significant contributions to those areas and become known for the positions they take—Rothbard for anarcho-capitalism, Kirzner for entrepreneurship and market process theory, Lavoie for the critique of socialism, Caldwell for Hayek and methodology, Rizzo for law and economics and the philosophy of economics, Selgin and White for free banking, Garrison and Horwitz on macroeconomics, Wagner for public finance and fiscal sociology, Koppl for

---

3. Between pure careerism and pure isolationism an intellectual movement finds the way forward. Randall Collins's work *The Sociology of Philosophies* (Cambridge, MA: Belknap Press of Harvard University Press, 1998) is perhaps the best work on the intellectual movement characteristics that are progressive, retrogressive, and self-destructive. It is my belief that modern Austrian economics has had too much retrogressive and self-destructive tendencies and not enough progressive elements. It is my sincere hope that the individuals now emerging in their research and teaching careers and contributing to a contemporary Austrian school of economics have learned from the shortcomings of others and will have the mindset and requisite skills to bring about a wide-scale professional acceptance of the ideas first developed by Menger, Mises, and Hayek.

"Big Players," Stringham on anarcho-capitalism, Leeson on self-governance, Coyne on postwar reconstruction, Powell on sweatshops, etc.[4]

The second thing I should state clearly is what I mean by success in academia. I think we can all agree that our goal as professional economists is to publish path-breaking work that finds an outlet in high-profile professional journals and receives significant citations. Moreover, we can agree that our goal as teachers of economics is to have the opportunity to teach the best and brightest students of each generation. As Andrew Schotter, then department chairman at NYU, said to me when he hired me, "Look, you want to play for the New York Yankees not the Toledo Mud Hens, right?" When he said that to me in 1990 it made perfect sense, and it made perfect sense to me when I was sent back to "Toledo" in 1997 after being denied tenure and promotion.[5] And,

---

4. See for example: Murray N. Rothbard, *For a New Liberty: The Libertarian Manifesto* (Auburn, AL: Ludwig Von Mises Institute, 2006); Rothbard, *Man*; Kirzner, *Competition*; Israel M. Kirzner, *The Meaning of the Market Process: Essays in the Development of Modern Austrian Economics* (New York: Routledge, 1996); Don Lavoie, *National Economic Planning: What Is Left?* (Cambridge: Ballinger, 1985); Don Lavoie, *Rivalry and Central Planning* (New York: Cambridge, 1985); Bruce Caldwell, *Hayek's Challenge: An Intellectual Biography of F.A. Hayek* (Chicago: University of Chicago Press, 2004); Mario Rizzo, "The Problem with Moral Dirigisme: A New Argument against Moralistic Legislation," *NYU Journal of Law & Liberty* 1, no. 2 (2005): 790–844; George A. Selgin and Lawrence H. White, "How Would the Invisible Hand Handle Money?" *Journal of Economic Literature* 32, no. 4 (1994): 1718–49; Roger Garrison, *Time and Money: The Macroeconomics of Capital Structure* (New York: Routledge, 2000); Steven Horwitz, *Microfoundations and Macroeconomics: An Austrian Perspective* (New York: Routledge, 2000); Richard E. Wagner, *Fiscal Sociology and the Theory of Public Finance: An Exploratory Essay* (Northampton, UK: Edward Elgar Publishing, 2009); Roger Koppl, *Big Players and the Economic Theory of Expectations* (New York: Palgrave Macmillan, 2002); Edward P. Stringham, "The Extralegal Development of Securities Trading in Seventeenth Century Amsterdam," *Quarterly Review of Economics and Finance* 43, no. 2 (2003): 321–44; Peter T. Leeson, "Trading with Bandits," *Journal of Law & Economics* 50, no. 2 (2007): 303–21; Peter T. Leeson, *The Invisible Hook: The Hidden Economics of Pirates* (Princeton, NJ: Princeton University Press, 2009); Christopher J. Coyne, *After War: The Political Economy of Exporting Democracy* (Stanford, CA: Stanford University Press, 2007); Benjamin Powell, "In Reply to Sweatshop Sophistries," *Human Rights Quarterly* 28, no. 4 (2006): 1031–1042.

5. I left NYU in 1997 to teach at Manhattan College, an excellent undergraduate college that also had an MBA program. I maintained my affiliation with NYU and edited *Advances in Austrian Economics* out of my NYU office that academic year. But I learned a very important lesson that year and that was how much I missed teaching graduate

it still does make perfect sense to me today.[6] We want to make in the "major league"; nothing less will ultimately satisfy our scientific ambitions. Our goals and our reality are not aligned at the moment, which just means we have our work cut out for us. We must always remember what Frank Knight stressed— "to call a situation is hopeless is to say it is ideal." We are obviously far from ideal, so it is not hopeless.

The main thing that makes someone an Austrian is not the willingness to identify one's work with that label, but the substantive propositions in economics that an economist identifies with.[7] These substantive propositions relate to both questions of method and methodology in economics and political economy. And once we realize that it is not a label, but an approach you take and the positions you hold, then we have to admit that good economics and political economy are not the exclusive domain of those who are willing to label their work as Austrian.

---

students in economics, so when the opportunity to join a graduate faculty again at GMU was offered I jumped at it—forgoing an alternative offer as a chaired professor at Carthage College and a rather comfortable life at Manhattan College with a research affiliation at NYU. The experience taught me a lot and when I relocated to GMU, I did approach working with the graduate students differently than I had while at NYU as an assistant professor.

6. Michael Lewis's *Moneyball: The Art of Winning an Unfair Game* (New York: Norton, 2003) had a very significant impact on the way I have thought about building our department and centers of research at GMU. GMU is not analogous to the Toledo Mud Hens, but instead to the Oakland A's. Schools such as Chicago, Harvard, MIT, Princeton, and Stanford are analogous to the NY Yankees, Boston Red Sox, and LA Dodgers. In other words, how are small market teams to compete with the big budget teams in the majors? It requires a different hiring, retention, and promotion strategy than that followed by the major market franchises. As James Buchanan argued when he basically created the PhD program at GMU, you have to "dare to be different," or as Vernon Smith said when he made one of his academic moves to a department of lower rank by conventional standards, "any department that will support my work is by definition of first-class department in my eyes." GMU is a unique educational environment precisely because we have dared to be different and strike out in our own direction to support research and educational efforts in Austrian economics, experimental economics, history of economic thought, law and economics, public choice economics as well as conventional training in micro, macro, math, and econometrics.

7. See my 2008 essay on "The Austrian School of Economics" in David Henderson's edited *A Concise Encyclopedia of Economics* (http://www.econlib.org/library/Enc/Austrian SchoolofEconomics.html) and also my edited volume *The Handbook of Contemporary Austrian Economics*, Cheltenham, UK: Edward Elgar, 2010).

Instead, there are many economists and political economists from whom we can learn throughout the history of our discipline, and it would be intellectually ridiculous to not take advantage of that opportunity.

And we have no better intellectual role models in this endeavor of constantly learning from professional peers than Mises and Hayek. They both objected to being labeled, though they were both proud of their educational and intellectual heritage in Vienna; and yet it is generally recognized that they both contributed more to our self-understanding of modern Austrian economics than any other scholars. It is the work found in Mises's *Human Action* and Hayek's *Individualism and Economic Order* that set that agenda for the progressive development of Austrian economics and classical liberal political economy in the second half of the twentieth century and beyond.

My message to graduate students is to learn from Mises and Hayek in the way that they approached their research and teaching in economics and political economy. And that means that unless you are doing intellectual history work, your goal in writing papers should be to adopt arguments and make them your own and develop them in your unique intellectual context and engage your peers. It is not faithfulness in citation practices to the masters, and certainly not the number of block quotes you can provide from them, that makes a paper a worthy contribution to "Austrian" economics. It is instead the quality of the argument that you make, and its relevance to solving a significant problem in the economic and/or policy world. Deirdre McCloskey is right, every paper should be able to answer the "so what" question easily or perhaps it shouldn't be written.[8]

Advice to Austrian Graduate Students

Here are five points that I have found essential for getting Austrian graduate students on the right track to building successful research and teaching careers.[9]

1. What you emphasize in the phrase "Austrian economics" matters for how and whom you interact with. If you emphasize *Austrian* economics, then you are led to stress philosophical foundations and methodologi-

---

8. McCloskey, Deirdre. *The Writings of Economics* (New York: Macmillan, 1987). 19.
9. These can be applicable to succeeding in other fields of academia as well.

cal positions. If you emphasize Austrian *economics*, then you are led to stress substantive propositions in economic reasoning and applications. It is easier to communicate with your peers in economics if you do economics, and it is easier to talk to other social scientists and philosophers if you work on philosophy and methodology. And with historians it is 50/50. Bottom line—whichever side you come down on (Austrian or economics) strive to work with the best minds in the relevant disciplines. Don't spend your time talking only to those who share both the Austrian and the economics!

2. Academic life is too short and your professional colleagues are too interesting to emphasize differences, rather than commonalities. Constantly seek to find common ground from which to work with the purpose of tackling relevant problems. It is not the sins of commission that are most damaging for the advancement of economics, but the sins of omission.[10] Moreover, the intellectual inheritance of Mises and Hayek is too important in addressing the sins of omission to be appreciated only by a select few. Our task is one of engagement with our colleagues and our students, not isolation and insulation. If Mises and Hayek are as brilliant and as full of essential insights as we claim, then we should strive to make sure that every practicing economist and student of economics in the world comes to that same assessment of their work.

3. You need to absorb the basic logic of the economic way of thinking, and you need to learn the "language" of modern economics,[11] but you should not try to compete on that margin—that is not your comparative

---

10. This is the advice that was given to me by Mancur Olson over dinner one night after he had read my paper "Where Did Economics Go Wrong?" (See Boettke, "Where Did Economics Go Wrong: Modern Economics as a Flight from Reality," *Critical Review* 11, no. 1 (1997): 11–64); he strongly encouraged me to curtail my efforts at methodological evangelism and to concentrate on my work in comparative political economy. I have increasingly followed his advice in the years since, but I retain a strong intellectual commitment to methodology primarily because it is methodology that determines not only what are deemed good questions to pursue in economics but perhaps more importantly what are considered good answers to those questions.

11. I strongly encourage my students to teach intermediate price theory as graduate students and volunteer to teach intermediate price theory when they get their first university teaching job.

advantage. You as students need to "dare to be different" without being incompetent in the discipline. But you should also never forget why you got into economics in the first place and what that initial passion for the subject (a passion so strong that you decided to devote your life work to it) brings to the broader conversation in economics and political economy.

4. Pursue your passion, do not pursue what you think is fashionable in the literature at any moment. Look out the window; don't concentrate on what is on the blackboard. In pursuing your passion think like a Misesian, but write like a Popperian. In other words, thinking like an economist is all about the logic of choice and "invisible hand" explanations, but communicating with other economists often is best done in the language of theorems and propositions, hypotheses and tests, conjectures and refutations. Don't be afraid to put forth bold conjectures and to invite the criticism of your peers. Strive to always be in a room where you are learning from others in research settings, constantly having to clear a higher argumentative bar. Again, constantly stretch and test your comfort zone until you are able to converse with the best and the brightest minds currently practicing economics and political economy. In short, be wildly ambitious while also being wildly committed to truth tracking as you see it.

5. There is a basic formula for academic success. First, be the best student in your graduating class. Second, build your academic network by your third year (e.g., Association of Private Enterprise Education (APEE) is a natural network for Austrian economists; Society for the Development of Austrian Economics (SDAE) with its annual meetings at the Southern Economic Association). Third, every student I have taught who wanted an academic career who accomplished the following achieved such a career and in fact have had great success in that career:[12]

PhD in hand + publication in refereed journals
+ good teaching evaluations – lunch tax = quality job

Use the opportunities provided by various free market institutions and periodicals to learn how to write clearly and speak effectively early in your career.

---

12. See the list of my former students available on my web page (http://econfaculty.gmu .edu/pboettke/students.html) and their various appointments and follow the links to their own websites to see sample publications.

But do not stay in that comfort zone; strive to push out of it with your work and your presentations. Embrace your role as a teacher of economics and strive to excel in the classroom. Attend the professional meetings, and never ever be a "lunch tax" on either your friends or your foes.[13]

You will write as you read—read wisely; you will teach as you were taught—copy the best teachers you have ever had. Add to this that you strive to be a great colleague by commenting on the papers of your departmental colleagues in a timely and thoughtful manner, and be a good citizen to your college and university servicewise. If you do this you will become indispensable to your institution.

These five lessons I have tried to communicate to two generations of PhD students.

Conclusion

The economics profession has become more interesting in the 25 years I have been teaching. It is an amazingly exciting time to be doing economics and that excitement and enthusiasm should come out in your approach to this profession.

Finally, I truly believe that the teaching of economics is a higher calling for which we have been enlisted. Embrace your role as a teacher and scholar of economics. It simply is the greatest intellectual discipline (perhaps on some days I might say the only one) focused on the study of man. Economics can usefully be understood as a (1) deadly serious discipline focused on deadly serious subjects, and at the same time (2) the most illuminating intellectual framework for the study of man in all walks of life and in all historical circumstances. The fate of civilization is intimately tied to our ability to communicate the basic teachings of our discipline. There are laws of economics that cannot be violated without consequences for the fate of humanity. Appreciate economics as a discipline, and the essential contributions of Mises and Hayek will become obvious.

---

13. "Lunch tax" is shorthand for subtracting from, rather than adding to, collegiality. A little reflection on the various colleagues you have had over the years should convince you that there are many ways to be a lunch tax. Over-signaling, for example. Too many academicians act in such obnoxious and socially awkward manners because they believe it signals high intelligence. It doesn't; it just signals social awkwardness and escalates to "jerk" in the worst cases. It is simply best to avoid sending such signals, and instead be an enthusiastic teacher, a productive researcher, and a willing and able colleague.

4

Teaching Economics, Appreciating Spontaneous Order, and Economics as a Public Science

> Given the principle of freedom, as active freedom of association, the notion of scientific control of society is a palpable contradiction. . . . In a democracy, the notion of control is not merely unethical, it is excluded, ipso facto. . . . When a man or group asks for power to do good, my impulse is to . . . cancel the last three words, leaving simply "I want power"; that is easy to believe.
> —Frank Knight[1]

Introduction

JAMES BUCHANAN IS fond of telling the story that when he entered the University of Chicago PhD program in economics he was of socialist leanings, yet within six weeks of Frank Knight's price theory course, he was no longer a socialist. What was it that Knight taught that had such a transformative effect on Buchanan and several (but not all) of his classmates? This question has inspired, and vexed, Buchanan throughout his career as an economics professor.

Frank Knight taught economics students the basic principles of the discipline: the idea of scarcity, the necessity of choice, the role of relative prices in guiding adjustment to changing circumstances, and the importance of competition in the self-organization of the market economy. "Economic principles," Knight argued, "are simply the more general implications of the single principle

---

1. Frank H. Knight, "The Role of Principles in Economics and Politics," *American Economic Review* 42 (March 1951): 1–29, in *Selected Essays of Frank H. Knight*, edited by Ross Emmett, vol. 2 (repr., Chicago: University of Chicago Press, 1999), 361–91.

of freedom, individual and social, i.e., free association, in a certain sphere of activity."[2] The freedom of association that Knight is referring to is that of exchange, which serves as the basis of social order. As he would stress in *Intelligence and Democratic Action*, the elementary point that requires continual emphasis is that an exchange is an exchange is an exchange.[3] Exchange is voluntary, and it is mutually beneficial. Unless both parties benefit from the interaction, it would not be an exchange because it would not be voluntarily entered into and agreed to. It is exchange that gives rise to the division of labor, and it is exchange that guides production plans and satisfies consumption demands. The subject matter of economics is ultimately about exchange relationships among freely choosing individuals and the institutions within which those exchanges take place.

Unfortunately, the task of communicating that elementary point to students and the public is not always easy because of ignorance and vested interest. As Knight says:

> The serious fact is that the bulk of the really important things that economics has to teach are things that people would see for themselves if they were willing to see. And it is hard to believe in the utility of trying to teach what men refuse to learn or even seriously listen to.[4]

But we must, and do, find utility in trying to teach economics, even if it is only in our capacity to serve as an antidote to the poison being disseminated by the anti-economists that surround us in our schools and universities, in the churches and on the street, and in the courts and in the legislature.

Henry Simons in his class at University of Chicago, inspired by Knight's teachings, taught a generation of students that "economics is primarily useful, both to the student and to the political leader, as a prophylactic against popular fallacies."[5] Within a system of private property rights, freedom of contract, and monetary stability, the market economy will work through relative price adjustments and profit and loss accounting to guide individuals in their

---

2. Knight, "Role of Principles," 367.
3. Frank H. Knight, *Intelligence and Democratic Action* (Cambridge, MA: Harvard University Press, 1960).
4. Knight, "Role of Principles," 361.
5. Henry C. Simons, *Simons' Syllabus*, edited by Gordon Tullock (Fairfax, VA: Center for the Study of Public Choice, 1983).

economic decisions to take into account the relevant information about relative scarcities and exchange opportunities. Mutually beneficial exchange is wealth creating, and the market economy through relative price adjustments is self-correcting.

It is from Knight that Buchanan gained his understanding of the economic process; of how the market economy through the incentives and information of property, prices, and profit/loss is the prime example of a spontaneous order. And in those first six weeks at University of Chicago under Knight's tutelage, Buchanan moved from a passionate populist to a zealous advocate of the market order. As he has put it: "I was converted by the power of ideas, by an understanding of the model of the market. The experience shaped my attitude toward the use and purpose of economic instruction; if I could be converted so could others."[6]

It is this aspect of Buchanan's career—that of the economic educator in the broadest meaning of that term—that I what to explore. But my focus is not so much on his efforts at building research centers to encourage advanced study in the field of public economics and public choice at University of Virginia, Virginia Tech, and George Mason; nor will I focus on his role as a PhD supervisor to some forty-plus students who include significant and innovative scholars in fields such as experimental economics, law and economics, public finance, health economics, industrial organization, and, of course, public choice, and constitutional political economy; nor will I stress his role in organizing professional associations such as the Committee on Non-Market Decision Making, the Public Choice Society, and in the establishment of the scientific journals *Public Choice* and *Constitutional Political Economy*.[7] Instead, my focus is really on Buchanan's emphasis on elementary or basic economics, and the role of the "teacher" in communicating those principles to students and the general public,

---

6. James M. Buchanan, "Better than Plowing," in Buchanan, *The Collected Works of James M. Buchanan*, vol. 1 (1986; Indianapolis, IN: Liberty Fund, 1999), 15.

7. For an excellent discussion of Buchanan's institution-building efforts to professionalize graduate education and research in public choice and constitutional political economy see Steve Medema's discussion in *The Hesitant Hand* (Princeton, NJ: Princeton University Press, 2009), 125–59. Also see Richard Wagner's discussion of public choice as an academic enterprise and the experience at UVA, VPI and GMU, in "Value and Exchange," *Review of Austrian Economics* 20, no. 2–3 (2007): 97–103.

and how those principles can inform and improve the democratic process of collective decision-making.[8] To put it bluntly, James Buchanan argues that our primary purpose as economic educators, and the only justification for the public support of our efforts, is to teach our students (and the general public) the basic principles of economics and to cultivate in them an appreciation of the spontaneous ordering of economic activity, so that they in turn can become informed participants in the democratic process.

What Should Economists Do?

The economist looking out into the world of a commercial society is immediately struck with two primordial facts: individuals pursue their self-interest, and modern commercial society with its vast division of labor is orderly. It is not from the benevolence of the butcher, the baker, and the brewer that we get our dinner; despite the disparate purposes being pursued by economic actors in the market, "Paris gets fed." In short, the first task of the economist is to explain how these two facts of commercial life—self interest, and social order—are consistent with one another. If one cannot explain the consistency, then one has failed in the first task of being an economist.

---

8. This emphasis on basic principles also explains Buchanan's close affinity with the Austrian school of economics throughout his career. It is not just the thoroughgoing subjectivism of the Austrians that attracted Buchanan's intellectual interests, though as he argues in *Cost and Choice*, the problem with modern economists is that they too often "rush headlong into the intricacies of analysis while overlooking certain points of elementary economic logic" (in Buchanan, *Collected Works*, vol. 6). In this instance, Buchanan was stressing the consistent and persistent application of opportunity cost reasoning. In general it is important to remember throughout that Buchanan, besides being a subjectivist, is a methodological individualist social scientist; an exchange theorist in market and politics; an institutional theorist in law, politics and society; a spontaneous order theorist of the market; a positive political economist in public finance; and a social contract theorist in political science. But in all these endeavors, Buchanan demands that we come back to the elementary economic logic and pursue it consistently and persistently throughout the analysis. One of the empirical curiosities of the modern profession of economics, Buchanan notes, is that the Austrian economists seem to have a comparative advantage in communicating this elementary economic logic to students. See Buchanan's generally positive reaction to the revival of interest in Austrian economics that began in the 1970s (James M. Buchanan, "Politics without Romance," in Buchanan, *Collected Works*, vol. 1, 47–48).

It is important to stress that this does not commit the economist to the Panglossian fallacy. There can be much that is wrong in society that could benefit from collective action, and I will talk about that in the next section. But understanding the "invisible hand" proposition of economics is the first task that must be accomplished, otherwise all other questions cannot be addressed adequately.

Not only must the invisible hand or "spontaneous order" proposition be understood, but it has to be understood in a dynamic, rather than static, sense if it is going to be helpful. We must not understand the overall order in the economy as if a benevolent social planner is choosing the optimal allocation of resources for society. Instead, the order we are trying to understand is the composite outcome of a multitude of individuals each striving to realize their plans, often in conflict with one another, and reconciled through the exchange process.

The central message of Buchanan's classic paper "What Should Economists Do?" is that theory of exchange and not the theory of resource allocation should take center stage in economics.[9] Economists, Buchanan argues, have to face up to their basic disciplinary responsibility and understand their subject matter. That subject matter is "Man's behavior in the market relationship, reflecting the propensity to truck and to barter, and the manifold variations in structure that this relationship can take."[10] It is this particular form of human activity and the institutional arrangements that arise because of this activity that is the proper subject of the economist's study. The dominant allocation problem approach, on the other hand, misleads economists into viewing the economic problem in society as one of applied mathematics that can be addressed by social engineers entrusted with the policy levers of control.

But the economic problem of society is decidedly not one of allocating scarce means to obtain a defined end.[11] When elementary economics is taught in this

---

9. James M. Buchanan, "What Should Economists Do?" in Buchanan, *Collected Works*, vol. 1, 29. See the symposium in the *Review of Austrian Economics* for a contemporary treatment of this point, Wagner, "Value and Exchange."

10. James M. Buchanan, "What Should Economists Do?" 29.

11. See, e.g., F.A. Hayek, "The Use of Knowledge in Society," in *Individualism and Economic Order* (1944; repr., Chicago: University of Chicago Press, 1948), 77–78, 80, 82, 91. "The economic problem of society is thus not merely a problem of how to allocate 'given' resources—if 'given' is taken to mean given to a single mind which deliberately solves the problem set by these 'data.' It is rather a problem of how to secure the best use of resources known to any of the members of society, for ends whose relative importance only these

optimal allocation manner, the message is easily communicated to students that someone or some group must be in charge at the levers of social control and manage the economic system. Students are often taught that all economic systems must answer the questions of how, what, and for whom—how are goods going to be produced; what goods are going to be produced; and for whom are the goods going to be produced. Students are then taught that the market system—through the incentives of clearly defined and strictly enforced property rights, and the guiding force of prices and profit and loss accounting statements—answers these questions so effectively that exchange efficiency and production efficiency are simultaneously achieved. All the gains from exchange will be realized, prices will reflect the full opportunity cost of production, and the least cost technologies will be employed in production. No possible arrangement of economic affairs could improve the situation, unless, of course, there are imperfections in the market mechanism caused by monopoly, imperfect information, and/or externalities, which prevent the market from achieving an efficient allocation of resources. Gains from trade will go unexploited; price will not reflect opportunity costs; and production will not employ the least cost technologies.

Opportunities for social improvement abound but cannot be realized within the market due to the imperfections; the needed reform must come from outside the system. When confronted with such imperfections, the typical student is then taught that the economic role of government is to address the problems

---

individuals know. Or, to put it briefly, it is a problem of the utilization of knowledge which is not given to anyone in its totality." Hayek later stresses not only that the knowledge he is talking about is not abstract and technical knowledge, but "knowledge of the particular circumstances of time and place" that is revealed only within the context of the market process. Furthermore, he is quick to stress this knowledge is constantly changing to reflect the changing circumstances of economic life. The economic problem that society faces is not one that lends itself to representation in the optimal solution to a system of simultaneous equations. "It is, perhaps, worth stressing," Hayek states, "that economic problems arise always and only in consequence of change." The price system works its marvels in the context of responding to, reflecting, and ultimately guiding day-to-day adjustments. Hayek does not deny a useful role for equilibrium analysis in economics, but he does suggest that something is fundamentally wrong with an approach that "habitually disregards an essential part of the phenomena with which we have to deal: the unavoidable imperfections of man's knowledge and the consequent need for a process by which knowledge is constantly communicated and acquired."

of market structure and the conflicts over resource use through public policy. Government provides the corrective to the imperfections of the market economy. The structure-conduct-performance paradigm in antitrust economics is one such example of government as corrective, Pigovian welfare economics is another, and consumer protection is yet another still. The market economy, students are taught in most economics classes, is great when it works, but its ability to work is limited to situations where a set of highly restrictive assumptions hold. Where there are deviations from the ideal pattern in allocation, the government acts proactively to align prices with costs and align private and social costs in decisions.

A lot in this elementary tale of the economic system is important information for students to learn. For the spontaneous and complex coordination of market activity to be achieved, the induced variables of the market (prices and profit/ loss) and the underlying variables of the market (tastes, technology, and resource availability) must exhibit a strong tendency to dovetail, otherwise the "order" of the market would not be that orderly. In other words, the relationship between prices and costs and private and social costs are important to understand in talking about private and public choices. Social cooperation under the division of labor emerges as individuals within an economic system strive to realize the gains from trade and the gains from innovation guided by the ordinary motivations of men, and the informational signals provided by relative prices and profit and loss accounting. In the limit, when all those gains are in fact realized, resources would indeed at that precise moment be allocated to highest valued users and all least cost technologies would be employed. But "efficiency" is not the goal or purpose of the market. The market economy itself does not possess a teleology, though the individuals participating in the market have their own purposes and plans they are striving to achieve.[12]

---

12. For a more recent elaboration on the non-teleological nature of the market economy see James M. Buchanan and V. Vanberg, "The Market as a Creative Process," in Buchanan, *Collected Works*, vol. 18. It is critical to remember the phraseology highlighted by Hayek to capture spontaneous order—"of human action, but not of human design" ("The Results of Human Action but Not of Human Design," in *Studies in Philosophy, Politics and Economics* (Chicago: University of Chicago Press, 1967), 96–105. The order itself has no purpose, but the participants in the order have multiple purposes that they are pursuing. This is one of the key characteristics of spontaneous orders in the social world, as opposed to the physical world.

As Buchanan stresses: "The 'market' or market organization is not a *means* toward the accomplishment of anything. It is, instead, the institutional embodiment of the voluntary exchange processes that are entered into by individuals in their several capacities. This is all that there is to it. Individuals are observed to cooperate with one another, to reach agreements, to trade. The network of relationships that emerge or evolves out of this trading process, the institutional framework, is called 'the market.'"[13] The "order" of the market is defined within the process of its emergence. There is no order capable of being defined independent of the process itself. Neither allocation nor distribution are outcomes of an economic system that can be defined outside of the context of the trading behavior and exchange relationships that produce it.[14]

The constellation of relative prices that actors within the economy face in making decisions provide them with both an incentive and a signal that is essential in their assessment of the situation as they choose this path or that. The existing array of prices, in other terms, provide the *ex ante* information about relative scarcities that economic actors use to infer alternative use of resources and methods of production. The market price that is paid for the good or service, and the profit and loss statement revealed in the market from offering those goods and services, provide economic actors with an *ex post* assessment of the appropriateness or inappropriateness of the enterprising decisions made. And, the very discrepancy between the *ex ante* expectations and the *ex post* realization in the market, motivates the *discovery* or *learning* by economic actors of better ways to match their production plans with consumption demands. If this process of production and exchange doesn't take place, the knowledge and incentives required to produce the complex coordination of the market would not exist. It is not just that the information would be difficult to surmise; it is literally that it would not exist.

The fundamental point that Buchanan emphasizes on the emergent nature of the "order" of the market is that absent the market process there is no economic order to define. It is the buying and abstaining from buying, the haggling, the trucking, the bartering, and the exchanging that produce the market

---

13. Buchanan, *Cost and Choice*, 38.
14. See James M. Buchanan, "Order Defined in the Process of Its Emergence," in Buchanan, *Collected Works*, vol. 1, 244–45.

"order." In short, we must always come back to stress as economists that the subject matter of economics is exchange and the institutions within which exchange takes place.

The juxtaposition of the exchange approach to economics with the approach to economics that emphasizes optimal societal allocation and just distribution as products of a benevolent social planner sets the stage for Buchanan's distinction between economics and politics, as well as the emphasis on rules and the institutional framework. Questions of "just distribution" are never about particular distributions of resources but instead always about the choices over the rules of the game which engender a pattern of exchange, production, and thus distribution. Fairness is about rules, not outcomes; justice is about process, not end-states.

Similarly, the market economy is not competitive by assumption but becomes competitive.

> It is this *becoming* process, brought about by the continuous pressure of human behavior in exchange, that is the central part of our discipline, not the dry-rot of postulated perfection. A solution to a general-equilibrium set of equations is not predetermined by exogenously-determined rules. A general solution, if there is one, emerges as a result of a whole network of evolving exchanges, bargains, trades, side payments, agreements, contracts which, finally at some point, ceases to renew itself. At each stage in this evolution towards solution, there are *gains* to be made, there are exchanges possible, and this being true the direction of movement is modified.[15]

Economics as a science of exchange cannot yield precise predictions about exact points but instead yields pattern predictions about tendencies and direction of change. The market is a spontaneous order, and the consistency of that order originates within the process itself; thus any attempt to construct the order independent of that process is meaningless. We as economists have no way of knowing what the market will choose in advance of the process, it will choose, as Buchanan has put it, what it will choose.[16] Economics is about

---

15. Buchanan, "What Should Economists Do?" 37.
16. James M. Buchanan, "Social Choice, Democracy and Free Markets," in Buchanan, *Collected Works*, vol. 1, 101.

the social relations of freely contracting actors; politics, on the other hand, is about social relationships where individuals deal with one another in a coercive or potentially coercive manner. Buchanan's unique take on politics, however, is to stress the potential for changes in the rules of governance within the coercive or quasi-coercive institutions that can provide the basis for improvement in the economic-political game. The task of the economist is to study the exchange relationships that evolve within the market process; the task of the political economist is to propose changes in the rules that will yield greater gains from trade and from innovation within the ongoing market process. It is in this sense that Buchanan squares the entrepreneurial theory of the market with its emphasis on the continual evolution of the exchange process, with the contractarian theory of the state with its emphasis on the pre-constitutional level of choice among rules and the post-constitutional level of political activity within the given set of rules.

What Role for the Economist and Political Economist in Society?

The exchange paradigm that Buchanan advocates challenges the pretensions of social engineers. Economists must never pro-offer advice to politicians as if they were offering advice to a benevolent social planner, and they also must never assume the role of benevolent social planners themselves. The wisdom of classical political economy was to resist such delusions of grandeur.[17] As Adam Smith warned, politicians who attempt to control the economy would not only be operating without the knowledge of the local situation that businessmen and entrepreneurs possess, but would necessarily load themselves with a level of power over others in society that could not be safely trusted to any individual

---

17. My colleague David Levy argues that "saving ideas" was a significant motivation for the institution-building effort of James Buchanan and G. Warren Nutter at the University of Virginia and the Thomas Jefferson Center for Political Economy. Buchanan and Nutter had vowed to each other during their student days that if they ever had the opportunity to work together in the same department, they would in fact work to "save the ideas" of classical political economy. The UVA effort must be, judged on all conventional measures, a fantastic success. See James M. Buchanan, "Political Economy: 1957–1982," in Buchanan, *Collected Works,* vol. 19.

lawgiver or council or senate of lawgivers, and would nowhere be as dangerous as in the hands of those who "had folly and presumption enough to fancy himself fit to exercise it."[18] Smith's "man of systems," who is "wise in his own conceit" is the object of scorn in the Buchanan framework as it obviously was for Smith.[19]

Politics cannot be viewed as a process of achieving "truth judgment" unless we want to risk tyranny at the hands of the conceited "elite" who believe they are in possession of truth.[20] Much of twentieth-century economics and public policy developed to fit this progressive elite intellectual agenda. Consolidation of governmental units and centralization of bureaucratic entities combined with rule by trained experts defines the professionalization of modern governance and public administration.[21]

The role the economist plays in the progressive intellectual agenda must be that of a technical expert who is entrusted with the tools of social control. The "good society" results from exercising those tools of social control optimally. The economist *qua* social engineer follows naturally from the progressive intellectual and public policy agenda. And the way mainstream economics developed *after* the Great Depression and the post–World War II consensus on the neo-Keynesian synthesis feed directly into this progressive agenda often quite unconsciously, but at other times explicitly so. The invisible hand of the market was said to have been demonstrated to be a palsied hand, and thus in need of the visible hand of the state to accomplish the task of steering the economy. Economic regulators were to use the tools of the state to correct for microeconomic inefficiencies and fiscal and monetary policies that were going

---

18. Adam Smith, *An Inquiry into the Nature and Causes of the Wealth of Nations* (1776; repr., Chicago: University of Chicago Press, 1976), bk. IV, ch. 2, 478.

19. Adam Smith, *The Theory of Moral Sentiments* (1759; repr., Indianapolis, IN: Liberty Fund, 1982), 233.

20. See Buchanan's discussion of the debate between Knight and M. Polanyi (James M. Buchanan, "Politics and Science," in Buchanan, *Collected Works*, vol. 1, 234–37) and his further elaboration on the potential for tyranny in politics as science (James M. Buchanan, "The Potential for Tyranny in Politics as Science," in Buchanan, *Collected Works*, vol. 17).

21. See Vincent Ostrom, *The Intellectual Crisis in American Public Administration* (Tuscaloosa: University of Alabama Press, 1973). Aligica and Boettke provide an overview of the metropolitan reform debate in public administration and political economy in *Challenging Institutional Analysis and Development: The Bloomington School* (New York: Routledge, 2009), 5–51.

to be used to correct for macroeconomic instability. The perspective communicated in either Abba Lerner's *The Economics of Control* (London: Macmillan,
1946) or Paul Samuelson's classic text, *Economics* (New York: McGraw-Hill,
1948), saw the role of the economist as that of potential savior equipped with the
appropriate scientific/engineering tools to right social ills and guide the ship of
state. But, of course, such a perceived role of the economists makes sense, only
if the state is perceived as an active agent in the economy, and the discipline
of economics is more akin to engineering than philosophy. Such a view of the
economist as societal savior is subject to ridicule in a world where the government is seen as limited in scale and scope, just as the view of the economist as
a philosopher and student of society makes him or herself irrelevant in a world
where the state is expected to play an active role in the economic game. Table
4.1 may illustrate the situation:[22]

Table 4.1	State as Referee	State as Player
Economist as Student	Classical Liberalism	\<unstable\>
Economist as Savior	\<unstable\>	Activist Government

Buchanan's perspective is described by the upper left cell, and in that cell the
economist is not granted any privileged position in society. The economist is in
the much more humble position of being a student of society, a teacher of the
knowledge gleaned from his or her study, and at times a social critic of existing
practice in the citizen capacity. What he or she is never permitted to do is claim
to have a direct line to godlike truth, never mind godlike powers, which justify
imposing his or her vision on fellow citizens. Instead, as mentioned previously,
the primary role of the economist is to teach students the basic principles of
economics so that they may become informed participants in the democratic
process. Now remember that "teacher" in this context is being more broadly

---

22. See Peter J. Boettke and Steven Horwitz, "The Limits of Economic Expertise," annual
supplement, *History of Political Economy* 37 (2005): 10–39; Peter J. Boettke and Christopher J. Coyne, "The Role of the Economist in Economic Development," *Quarterly
Journal of Austrian Economics* 19, no. 2 (2006): 47–68; and Peter J. Boettke, Christopher
J. Coyne, and Peter T. Leeson, "High Priests and Lowly Philosophers: The Battle for the
Soul of Economics," *Case Western Reserve Law Review* 56, no. 3 (2006): 551–68, for a further elaboration on these ideas about the role of the economists in society.

defined to include a variety of activities that go far beyond the classroom proper, including the presentation of refined research to one's scientific peers, the presentation of policy analysis to decision makers, public commentary on current affairs in newspapers, and classroom instruction at a variety of levels from principles classes to advanced seminars for PhD students. In short, we are always engaged in "studying" and "teaching," but not "preaching" let alone "imposing."

The reformist thrust of economics is beyond the reach of the economist proper, though the political economist does have an important role in reform efforts even in the Buchanan framework of the humbled worldly philosopher.[23] Again, that role is far different from the one conceived of for the economist as savior. The political economist, Buchanan stressed, works at the level of rules, not at the level of active play within the rules. The subtle position Buchanan develops is laid out in his classic paper "Positive Economics, Welfare Economics, and Political Economy."[24] The intellectual dilemma that faces economics as a discipline, Buchanan argues, is that in the interest of the scientific stature of the discipline the pure economist must maintain strict value-freedom, limit their analysis to means-ends assessment, and the deriving of testable hypotheses. The professional economist has a very small role in the policy formation process. But, due to the nature of the discipline and its central importance in political debate, the profession will continue to attract young minds to its ranks who desire to assist the policy formation process, and to do so with the aid of the scientific discipline of economics.

The Buchanan restatement of political economy is an attempt to provide the solution to this intellectual agenda: to capture the imagination of young and ambitious social reformers, but to steer them toward an analysis of policies that do not violate the value-freedom strictures of positive economics. The critical step in this endeavor is the rejection of the omniscience assumption that

---

23. Humility is not to counsel despair. Buchanan's teacher Frank Knight would say that to call a situation hopeless is to call it ideal. Since the world is far from ideal, the situation must not be hopeless. Humility and political economy reform need not conflict with one another, but we always must be on guard for hubristic ambitions sneaking in if we want to avoid reform efforts being derailed by constructivism.

24. James M. Buchanan, "Positive Economics, Welfare Economics, and Political Economy," in Buchanan, *Collected Works*, vol. 1, 191–201.

is implicitly accepted in both old and new welfare economics.[25] The observing economist is not in a privileged position to judge the system from above against some idealized standard of "efficiency." Once the privileged position is rejected, the efficiency concept that the economist can discuss is one of voluntary agreement among the participants in the process. Nothing more, nothing less. To go back to Knight again, an exchange is an exchange is an exchange. So what then can the economist say?

As Buchanan puts it:

> The political economist is often conceived as being able to *recommend* policy A over policy B. If, as we have argued above, no objective social criterion exists, the economist qua scientist is unable to recommend. Therefore, any policy discussion on his part appears to take on normative implications. But there does exist a positive role for the economist in the formation of policy. His task is that of diagnosing social institutions and presenting to the choosing individuals a set of possible changes. He does not recommend policy A over policy B. He presents policy A as

---

25. In a brilliant passage that anticipated much of the subsequent development of the economic and political economy analysis of socialism and the social democratic welfare states, Ludwig von Mises argues that the inference that the state should be in control of the economy follows inescapably once intellectual perfection as well as moral perfection is attributed to government officials (*Human Action: A Treatise on Economics* (1949; repr., Indianapolis, IN: Liberty Fund, 2010), 692. Once we assume not only best of intentions, but omniscience, then it is obvious that the infallible state will do better than erring individuals in the conduct of business and ordinary life. One way to understand the relationship between Austrian economics as developed by Mises-Hayek-Kirzner was to challenge the assumption of omniscience in economic analysis while for value-freedom purposes leaving the assumption of benevolence in place. Much of the subsequent development of public choice theory in the 1950s and 1960s did the opposite, meaning that it left the neoclassical assumption of omniscience in place but challenged the benevolence assumption. As we see here in Buchanan's classic paper on the role of the political economist, he is challenging both assumptions and this is the analytical path that those working on developing robust political economy are following as well. See Peter J. Boettke and Peter T. Leeson, "Liberalism, Socialism and Robust Political Economy," *Journal of Markets & Morality* 7, no. 1 (2004): 99–111; and Peter J. Boettke and Christopher J. Coyne, "Best Case, Worse Case, and the Golden Mean in Political Economy," *Review of Austrian Economics* 22, no. 2 (2009): 123–25.

a hypothesis subject to testing. The hypothesis is that policy A will, in fact, prove to be Pareto-optimal. The conceptual test is *consensus* among members of the choosing group, not objective improvement in some measurable social aggregate.[26]

The policy task of the economist is to offer possible changes in the rules of the economic game that are acceptable to all parties and will produce Pareto improvement. Political economy, therefore, deals with a particular form of social change, that of collective action, or the deliberation among members of a social group over the rules that govern their interactions with one another in their attempt to live better together. The spontaneous adjustments that arise within production and exchange activity due to shifts in tastes, technology or resource availability are not the subject of collective action deliberation. These changes in the market guided by relative prices and profit and loss accounting occur constantly against the backdrop of an existing set of property rights rules and their enforcement. The economist qua economist is a student of this dynamic process of accommodating changes guided by relative prices and disciplined with feedback from profit and loss statements, a student of the spontaneous order of the market. The economist qua economist as a social critic can point out possible problems with the existing structure of property rights and/or government policies and how the existing rights and policy regime may in fact be preventing gains from trade to be realized or gains from innovation to be pursued due to incentive incompatibilities and/or distortions in the informational processing and feedback. And the political economists qua political economist on the basis of the scientific knowledge of spontaneous order and the analysis of means-ends that the discipline of economics provides can offer hypothetical changes to the rule structure that would yield Pareto improvements subject to the constraint of consensus among members of the collective action unit.

As we stressed earlier, the role of the economist is not as a savior to society; he or she is not a technical expert to be relied upon to fix ills through social engineering. No, the role of the economist is the far humbler one; that of a student of society and teacher of the basic principles of the discipline. His/her primary task is to communicate to students and the general public a basic appreciation of the spontaneous order of the market and the core ideas of choice

---

26. Buchanan, "Positive Economics," 195.

against constraints and mutually beneficial exchange. The knowledge of the discipline of economics is essential to helping his/her "students" become informed participants in the democratic process of collective choice.

Why Constitutional Craftsmanship Is Consistent with Spontaneous Order

Alexander Hamilton argued in *The Federalist #1* that the critical question that confronted his generation in America was whether good government can be a consequence of reflection and choice, or will it forever remain a consequence of accident and force.[27] This political question of Hamilton's remains an essential one to answer. In modern times, the exploration of the US constitutional experience became the research agenda of political economists such as F.A. Hayek and James M. Buchanan.[28] In their hands, it is an effort in developing a theory of "robust political economy" and it is synonymous with the development of the field of constitutional political economy.[29] To put it simply, can we take men as given with their ordinary motivations and their limited knowledge and find a set of rules that effectively ties the hands of the rulers in a way that allows them to govern, but not abuse the power so entrusted, creating the conditions under which members of society can freely engage in the complex coordination of economic activities to realize the gains from trade and innovation?[30]

---

27. Alexander Hamilton, *The Federalist Papers #1* (1787), http://thomas.loc.gov/home/histdox/fed_01.html.

28. F.A. Hayek, *The Constitution of Liberty* (Chicago: University of Chicago Press, 1960); see James M. Buchanan and Gordon Tullock, *The Calculus of Consent,* in Buchanan, *Collected Works,* vol. 3.

29. See Boettke and Leeson, "Liberalism, Socialism."

30. See F.A. Hayek, "Individualism: True and False," in *Individualism and Economic Order* (1946; repr., Chicago: University of Chicago Press, 1996), 11–14 where he argues that "the main point about which there can be little doubt is that Smith's chief concern was not so much with what men might occasionally achieve when he was at his best but that he should have as little opportunity as possible to do harm when he was at his worst." The Scottish Enlightenment philosophers searched for a "social system which does not depend for its functioning on our finding good men for running it, or on all men becoming better than they are now, but which makes use of men in all their given variety and complexity, sometimes good and sometimes bad, sometimes intelligent and more often stupid. Their aim was a system under which it should be possible to grant

As points of emphasis in their respective works, Hayek concentrated on the limits on man's knowledge at the abstract level and the contextual nature of the knowledge residing in the economy at the concrete level, while Buchanan stressed the institutional/organizational logic of politics and the systemic incentives that different rule environments generate. In both, however, the central message (same players, different rules produce different games) is seen throughout their work in comparative political economy. To Hayek the puzzle was how to limit the rationalistic hubris of men, to Buchanan the puzzle was how to limit the opportunistic impulse of men. Both found hope in what they called a "generality norm" embedded in a constitutional contract—no law shall be passed, or rule established, which privileges one group of individuals in society.[31] Hayek seemingly relies on an evolutionary process of trial and error in rule regimes that selects for those rules that enable group success and weeds out those that derail group progress,[32] while Buchanan proposes a constitutional "convention" that employs a "veil of ignorance" construct to ensure fairness in the social contract and strives for a social contract that exhibits conceptual unanimity. In actual practice, we do not see either evolution or social contract in pure form, but instead, some combination where constitutional contracts are based on evolved social norms if they are to "stick" in any given society.[33] What we see is an interaction between creative constitutional craftsmanship and codification of existing norms into formal law. The subordinate state of constitutionalism finds its legitimacy in the inhibited state of cultural norms and methods of social

---

freedom to all, instead of restricting it, as their French contemporaries wished to, to 'the good and the wise." The great intellectual discovery of these eighteenth-century political economists and social philosophers was that "the system of private property did provide such inducements [to direct the ordinary motivations of men to pursue their self-interest by contributing to the betterment of others] to a much greater extent than had yet been understood." Man with his ordinary motivation of self-interest and with his limited cognitive capacities is nevertheless directed toward pursuing actions which result in the common good through the institutional setting of private property and freedom of competition in the marketplace.

31. See the fascinating interview between Hayek and Buchanan from 1978, now available online in video at http://www.hayek.ufm.edu/index.php/James_Buchanan.

32. Hayek, *Constitution of Liberty*.

33. See Peter J. Boettke, Christopher J. Coyne, and Peter T. Leeson, "Institutional Stickiness and the New Development Economics," *American Journal of Economics & Sociology* 67, no. 2 (2008): 331–58.

sanction; if the formal rules of governance are not grounded in the informal rules embedded in norms and social conventions, then the cost of enforcement would be prohibitive.[34]

The normative thrust of classical political economy is to craft rules that both bind government power and establish an environment that promotes social cooperation under the division of labor. In thinking about the constitutional contract, it is useful to use Buchanan's distinctions between the protective state (law and order), the productive state (public goods), and the redistributive state (rent-seeking), and to see the basic conundrum as to whether or not we can find a set of rules of governance that enables the protective and the productive state without unleashing the redistributive state.[35]

Rules must bind the behavior of politicians even though they don't transform human nature. In other words, men remain presumed to be knaves,[36] but the rules of good governance within which men interact with one another discipline their knavery to such an extent that knavish behavior is held in check to the point of nonexistence. Rules of good governance can also limit the rationalistic hubris of politicians that is evident in their efforts to exercise command and control over the economy.

The important point to stress for our present purposes is that there is no conflict between the exercise of constitutional craftsmanship and the appreciation of the spontaneous order within a market economy with clearly defined and enforced property rights and freedom on contract, and the recognition of the socioevolutionary processes that occur in any society to produce norms and mores that enable individuals in groups to cooperate with one another

---

34. See Peter J. Boettke, "The Political Infrastructure in Economic Development," in *Calculation and Coordination* (1994; repr., New York: Routledge, 2001), on the infrastructure of economic development; and also the work of Claudia Williamson, "Informal Institutions Rule," *Public Choice* 139, no. 3 (2009): 371–387, on informal and formal institutions.
35. James M. Buchanan, *The Limits of Liberty: Between Anarchy and Leviathan*, in Buchanan, *Collected Works*, vol. 7.
36. David Hume counseled that when political economists design rules of governance, and propose constitutional constraints and checks and balances they should do so under the working assumption that all men are knaves. This way the rules would work in such a manner that bad men can do least harm (*Essays Moral, Political, and Literary* (1758; repr., Indianapolis, IN: Liberty Fund, 1985). Also see Geoffrey Brennan and James M. Buchanan, *The Reason of Rules*, in Buchanan, *Collected Works*, vol. 10, 53–75.

even sometimes in very difficult circumstances. Constitutional craftsmanship, properly understood, cannot step outside of history and propose imaginary scenarios of completely new rules. Buchanan's strictures against omniscience in political economy cut against the constructivist impulse, just as his work on the relevance of the status quo in political economy gives us the guideline for where the exercise in constitutional craftsmanship must begin.

The status quo in Buchanan's framework possesses no normative weight, but it does possess analytical weight. It is what it is. We begin from the here and now, and not from some imaginary start state where the problems that plague the existing structure of rights could be safely assumed away. The task of the political economist in constitutional craftsmanship remains that of proposing hypothetical rule changes that must generate agreement among the members of the collective action unit, including those who currently benefit from the status quo. Politics as exchange seeks to find the Pareto improving deals that can produce agreement, and the compensation principle is a significant guide in that process of collective choice.

That constitutional craftsmanship begins with the here and now means it is constrained by history, but it doesn't mean it is a slave to history. The relationship between culture and political economy is a nuanced one; culture is neither perfectly rigid nor perfectly malleable. But culture is omnipresent and cannot be escaped. To use Eric Jones's phrase, we see cultures merging throughout history with respect to institutional change and economic growth.[37]

When Hayek included his appendix "Why I Am Not a Conservative," the message he was trying to communicate was that like Hamilton he was unwilling to acquiesce to accident and force, when proper reflection and choice could be employed to improve the human condition.[38] *The Constitution of Liberty*, as part of a larger project in Hayek's mind concerning "The Abuse of Reason,"[39] did attempt to disabuse intellectuals of their hubris. Hayek sought to "use reason to whittle down the claims of Reason" as he put it. But, again, the point of the book

---

37. Eric Jones, *Cultures Merging* (Princeton, NJ: Princeton University Press, 2006). See also Peter J. Boettke, Review of Eric Jones's *Cultures Merging*, *Economic Development & Culture Change* 57 (January 2009): 434–37.

38. Hayek, *Constitution of Liberty*.

39. See Bruce Caldwell, *Hayek's Challenge: An Intellectual Biography of F. A. Hayek* (Chicago: University of Chicago Press, 2004), 232–60.

was to persuade others that a change in rules—both general rules over the nature of government and particular rules, such as monetary policy or labor policy, were needed if western civilization was going to continue to advance along a trajectory of peace and prosperity. Hayek's main insight, and a point that Buchanan would develop even further, was that the particular rules of policy must be consistent with the general rules of governance if we are to make progress. Government was to be bound by rules, not run by interests.

But in coming to this critical assessment, Hayek conceded an important epistemological point in the effort to get sound social change of the rules of good governance. While the social scientist should be critical of all social conventions and existing patterns of social rules, he or she cannot be critical of all of them at the same time. To take the critical rationalist stance, Hayek argued, one must hold as given a host of existing behaviors and not criticize root and branch all of social rules. The rational constructivist proposes root and branch social transformation; Hayek argues that such an effort is hubristic and doomed to frustration and failure. On the other hand, Hayek—despite how some (including Buchanan at various times) have interpreted him—does not counsel that constitutional craftsmanship is doomed to such frustration and failure. Far from it, otherwise how could he have written such works as *The Constitution of Liberty*, let alone the third volume of *Law, Legislation and Liberty*.[40] Freedom to Hayek, as it is to Buchanan, is found in the constitutional contract that binds the hands of the rulers and yet establishes the institutional framework that enables us to live better together; it is the institutional framework provided by the constitution that turns situations of social conflict into opportunities for social cooperation.

Buchanan confronted this Hayekian epistemic problem in social change in his reflections on post-socialist political economy.[41] The "tacit presuppositions of political economy," Buchanan argued, had to be explicitly recognized and examined in light of the radically different historical experience of the people under socialist regimes. History matters in doing institutional analysis; as Buchanan

---

40. See F.A. Hayek, *Law, Legislation and Liberty*, vol. 3 (Chicago: University of Chicago Press, 1979).
41. James M. Buchanan, "Asymmetrical Reciprocity in Market Exchange," in Buchanan, *Collected Works*, vol. 12, 409–25.

puts it: "History, and the historical imagination that it shapes, matters."[42] It is the lived history of a people that forms the status quo from which social change through constitutional craftsmanship must be accomplished.

Root and branch constitutional construction is to be rejected as suffering from the "fatal conceit," but constitutional craftsmanship from within an existing status quo, and negotiated within an ongoing process of collective action is an intricate part of establishing a liberal order.[43] And it is through this ongoing process that an appreciation of spontaneous order not only doesn't conflict with constitutional craftsmanship, but gives economic content to the rule structure toward which our efforts at craftsmanship must strive if citizens want to live better more meaningful and self-directed lives.[44] There may indeed be many ways for individuals to live, but there are actually few ways for them to live together and simultaneously achieve individual autonomy, peaceful social relations, and generalized prosperity.[45]

---

42. Buchanan, "Asymmetrical Reciprocity," 422.

43. As Buchanan states: "Hayek's strictures against the rational constructivists are directed at those putative scholar-reformers who would ignore the boundaries established by these culturally evolved abstract rules for behaviour, who would, quite literally, seek to make 'new men,' who would overturn the eighteenth century discovery of the essential uniformities of human nature upon which any understanding of, and hence prospect for reform of, social interaction must rest ("Cultural Evolution and Institutional Reform," in Buchanan, *Collected Works*, vol. 18, 317).

44. I argue that not only must the rules be binding, they must signal specific content if they are going to produce social change in the direction of peace and prosperity. Peter J. Boettke, "Institutional Transition and the Problem of Credible Commitment," *Annual Proceedings of the Wealth & Well-Being of Nations* 1 (2009): 41–51.

45. In *One Economics, Many Recipes: Globalization, Institutions, and Economic Growth* (Princeton, NJ: Princeton University Press, 2007), Dani Rodrik may want to insist that there is "one economics with many recipes," but if recorded human history is the guide there is actually "one economics and few recipes for peace and prosperity." Private property, freedom of trade, freedom of contract, monetary stability, and fiscal responsibility are the basic recipe ingredients. Of course, this recipe has to be adopted and modified according to local conditions rather than being imposed from afar by Washington technocrats, and in that sense Rodrik's central point is not off mark. The only path to reform is an indigenous one, but not all indigenous paths are productive ones to pursue. The development debate, like all modern economic policy debates, was adversely impacted by the "Keynesian divergence" and continues to suffer from this intellectual legacy of aggregate analysis and policies of social control.

Conclusion

We have seen that James Buchanan puts great emphasis on the economist's role as student of society and teacher of basic principles of economics. The task of the economist and political economist is never conceived as that of the so-cial engineer in command of the levers of social control in the polity and over the economy. As our epigraph from Knight argued, such a conception of the role of the economist is at odds with the very notion of democratic governance and within a democratic system actually is unethical. Who actually agreed to privilege the economist in the political discourse? Instead, the economist and political economist has the far humbler, yet essential role to play in a free soci-ety. As economists we teach students (broadly defined) the basic principles of our scientific discipline so that they may in fact become informed participants within the democratic process. As Buchanan explicitly states:

> I have often argued that there is only one principle in economics that is worth stressing, and that the economists' didactic function is one of conveying some understanding of this principle to the public at large. Apart from this principle there would be no basis for general public support for economics as a legitimate academic discipline, no place for economics as an appropriate part of a liberal educational curriculum. I refer, of course, to the principle of the spontaneous order of the market, which was the great intellectual discovery of the eighteenth century.[46]

The political economist, on the other hand, as we have argued, proposes hypothetical changes in the structure of rules that are subjected to the test of consensus of others within the collective choice arena. Order is not imposed, order results from agreement.

The order of the market is spontaneous and emerges from the exchange be-havior of individuals within a preexisting structure of property rights and rules of engagement and mechanisms of enforcement. It is an ongoing process within rules. At a different level of analysis, there is the choice over the rules that frame this process and help that order continually define and redefine itself as a con-sequence of conscious deliberation. Buchanan's great contribution to political

---

46. James M. Buchanan, "Law and the Invisible Hand," in Buchanan, *Collected Works*, vol. 17, 96.

economy and social philosophy was to reconcile the emphasis on economic processes and the strategic behavior of individuals within the economic game, and the choice over the rules of the game, the enforcement of those rules, and in general the constitutional level of analysis. In so doing, Buchanan demonstrates how only through the utilization of a value-neutral science of economics can we construct a value-relevant vision of political economy and social philosophy. To put this another way, economics focuses on the play within any given set of rules; while social philosophy reflects on questions of justice and the "good society." Political economy insists that questions of justice and the "good society" cannot be addressed independently from the recognition that politics is never about particular distributions of resources but always about rules of the social game that engender a pattern of exchange, production, and distribution. Questions of "fairness" and "justice" are not about distributional outcomes and end-states, but about rules and the process of social interaction within those rules. Ultimately, social philosophers may be asking "what is a good game?" but it is the science of economics that answers the question of "how players play the game given the rules of the game."

Political economy as a discipline is about the tacking back and forth between the rules and the strategies, and the recognition that the answer to "what is the good game?" cannot be provided unless we examine how the players are going to play that game given those rules. Economics provides necessary (not sufficient) information to social philosophy, without which social philosophic discourse will prove irrelevant for answering the questions asked concerning the "good society."

Economics is a public science in two senses. If the knowledge produced by the discipline results in better laws, rules, and institutions, then the public appellation is justified. But, Buchanan stresses, there is another sense in which economics is a public science. It is an educational endeavor where the transmission of the basic knowledge of the discipline improves the ability of the students to be informed participants in the ongoing democratic process of selecting the parametric constraints within which economic interaction takes place.[47]

---

47. See James M. Buchanan, "Economics as a Public Science," in Buchanan, *Collected Works*, vol. 12, 48.

In both senses of economics as public science, spontaneous order theorizing is not at odds with the intellectual exercise of constitutional craftsmanship. In fact, rather than in contradiction, they exist in a symbiotic intellectual relationship to one another. The spontaneous order of economic play within the market is structured by the established framework of law and order, and the self-sustaining framework of law and order is legitimated in the history and culture of a people. As Hamilton suggested, it does come down to us to see our constitutions as a product of reflection and choice rather than accident and force. But history and culture do matter. As Buchanan has recognized in a variety of different contexts, it is history and culture that represent the status quo from which all political negotiation must begin. The "here and now" is what it is; no normative weight attributed to it, it just is. But that means that all bargaining must begin there and not at some mythical start state.

Constitutional craftsmanship begins with this recognition of the previous evolution and proposes rules that hypothetically will enable us to live better together, subject to the agreement of parties to the collective action, and so established will realize the hypothesized Pareto improvements by creating an economic environment where the spontaneous ordering of the market realizes the gains from trade and realizes the gains from innovation that follow from promoting social cooperation under the division of labor. Not only is there freedom in constitutional contract, there is also the promise of peace and prosperity. That is an important lesson that economics has to offer to our fellow citizens as they engage in the ongoing practice of democratic self-governance. And, it is a lesson that is taught perhaps clearer than in any other writer in the history of our discipline by the work of James M. Buchanan.

PART II

On Teachers of Economics

5

Relevance as a Virtue

Hans Sennholz

ADVANCED STUDY IN economics is devoted to learning how other economists think, the language they use, the models they create, and the evidence they provide. Very little of your economic education is devoted to studying the actual economy and the appropriate policy response to given problems. In short, you study the writings of other economists, not really the economy per se.

As a teacher of economics, I have often thought about my own educational experience at Grove City College, and why I ultimately chose to become an economist and professor of economics. I have realized that the power behind Dr. Sennholz's approach was the relevance he conveyed about economics for understanding the real world. We spent little time on Keynes, less on Marx, and some on Friedman. For the most part Dr. Sennholz devoted his energy to applying the economic insights of the Austrian School to explaining the economic history of the Industrial Revolution, the Great Depression, the operation of a gold standard, and the failure of socialism, fascism, and interventionism. The benefits of free trade were extolled and the vices of protectionism were laid bare.

The Austrian School of economics, in Dr. Sennholz's lectures, was the most consistent and articulate advocate of the private property, free enterprise system. But the Austrian School was prone to irrelevance just as other schools of economic thought trapped within the academy. Dr. Sennholz described the contemporary Austrian School to me, circa 1983, when I had started to lean toward the career of becoming a professional economist, in the following way: Kirzner was a methodologist who while engaging other scholars failed to seriously engage the world; Lachmann wrote a good book on capital but nothing else; Rothbard was content with being a radical libertarian which was irrelevant for the practical world of public policy; but the Sennholz branch of the Austrian School was constantly fighting the public policy battle in Washington (or "Washin" as he would pronounce it). At that time (and to this day) my sympathies were already with Rothbard's libertarianism so I tended to dismiss Sennholz's characterization as too conservative. And, as I delved more into the scholarship of the contemporary Austrian School I disagreed with his assessment of Kirzner and Lachmann and put more weight on the pure scholarly contributions of these individuals than their policy stance. But now in the middle of my career, I am coming to appreciate Dr. Sennholz's demand for continuous engagement with the world of public policy more than I have at any time since I was his student 30 years ago. We economists should be mindful of our relevance to public policy debates. We do better economics when the work we do is relevant to addressing real-world problems. Of course, science and philosophy matter and truth should be our ultimate goal. But we hope that truth yields better insight into how the world works, and on the basis of that correct understanding we should be able to engage the world more directly. We must avoid the economist's (Austrian or otherwise) vice of focusing our attention exclusively on other economists rather than on the economy.[1]

Dr. Sennholz's Own Scholarship as an Example of Striving for Relevance

The most significant contributions Dr. Sennholz made in his career were undoubtedly in the classroom and lecture hall. A dynamic public speaker (who knew how to use his German accent to highlight points), Sennholz spoke to thousands of college students and lay audiences over his years at Grove City College and then as President of the Foundation for Economic Education (FEE). He wrote continuous commentaries of the world of public policy. Many of these pieces are not what one could refer to as scholarship but are instead exercises in

---

1. On the important role that economists can play in society see Dan Klein, ed., *What Do Economists Contribute?* (New York: New York University Press, 1999), and Dan Klein, *A Plea to Economists Who Favour Liberty: Assist the Everyman* (London: Institute for Economic Affairs). For the classic statement see W.H. Hutt, *Economists and the Public* (1936; repr., New Brunswick, NJ: Transaction Publishers, 1990).

economic journalism. Some actually are more moral sermons than economics—sermons on the private property order and sound monetary policy. In addition to this commitment to almost daily engagement in contemporary public policy issues, Sennholz did publish books intended to be more lasting contributions. Characteristic of his intellectual interests, however, each of these books are devoted to public policy issues—European development after World War II in the 1950s, the problems of inflation in the 1970s, the issue of unemployment in the early 1980s, the looming problem of debts and deficits in the late 1980s, and a proposal to restore monetary freedom.[2]

In each of these books, Sennholz sought to use the important insights of the Austrian School of economics, and in particular those of his teacher Ludwig von Mises, to expose the failings of government policy to manage the economic system. Mises, along with Wilhelm Röpke, were the economists who influenced Sennholz the most and this shows in his emphasis on the security of private property, open trade, free labor, sound money, and fiscal responsibility. The utilitarianism of Mises shows in the consequentialist arguments Sennholz provides against government intervention and Röpke's moralism shows through in the ethical dimension that Sennholz rarely leaves out of his work. The basic message in all of Sennholz's writings is that the free market economy is not just efficient, but morally correct. Government interference in the natural workings of the economy is not just ineffective, but an evil that must be resisted. Inflationary policies not only distort economic calculation but also represent a fundamental breach of trust between the government and its citizens. Unions do not just impede the labor market, but legal barriers that favor unions and thwart the freedom of contract introduce conflict into a market which otherwise would tend toward harmony of interests through voluntary choice. Debts and deficits do not just dissipate future productivity by crowding out private investment, they destroy the fiscal discipline required to keep government in check and ward off the entitlement mentality that is inherent to democratic processes and which brings with it social and racial conflict.

---

2. In order, see Hans F. Sennholz, *How Can Europe Survive?* (Princeton, NJ: D. Van Nostrand, 1955); Hans F. Sennholz, *Age of Inflation* (Belmont, MA: Western Islands, 1979); Hans F. Sennholz, *The Politics of Unemployment* (Spring Mills, PA: Libertarian Press, 1987); Hans F. Sennholz, *Debts and Deficits* (Spring Mills, PA: Libertarian Press, 1987); and Hans F. Sennholz, *Money and Freedom* (Spring Mills, PA: Libertarian Press).

Sennholz makes these arguments in plain language with a minimal use of the jargon of professional economists. His audience is primarily the interested layman, not other economists. However, he does pepper his discourse with commentary on the work of other economists, in particular figures such as John Maynard Keynes, A.C. Pigou, and Milton Friedman. His reference to the evolution of economic ideas within the economics profession is always in the context of his broader mission of exposing the popular misconceptions that underlie erroneous public policy. The economist's role, Sennholz insists, requires a courageous stance against the "putative guardians of the common good pointing in the wrong direction."[3]

The basic message that Sennholz attempted to convey to his readers was consistent from his first book to his most recent writings. To give an example, consider an extended excerpt from his first book, *How Can Europe Survive?*

If all the world were interventionist, peaceful coexistence of sovereign nations would also be impossible. Government interference with the operation of the market economy favors certain producers to the detriment of other producers and consumers. This "favor" and "protection" usually takes the form of influencing and regulating prices, which in turn is based upon the restriction of imports and exports. Import and export restrictions, however, are measures of economic nationalism and cause international economic conflict. Inflationary policies together with arbitrary parity regulations bring about foreign exchange shortages, which in turn lead to further restrictions on foreign trade. Numerous other forms of government intervention and protection—restriction of competition and investment, control of quantity and quality of goods produced, supervision of the methods of production employed, taxation that consumes capital and drives liquid capital elsewhere, and protection of numerous trade and professional organizations—are either direct acts of economic nationalism or depend upon supplementary acts of economic nationalism. No matter how we may analyze the system of interventionism, its inherent international aspect is the disintegration of the division of labor. Each act of economic nationalism requires painful adjustments on the part of those countries that deal with the offending country. In the

3. Sennholz, *Age of Inflation*, vii.

final analysis, the structure of production in all countries, interdependent through foreign trade, is forced to make adjustments because of a single act of economic nationalism. Only the system of individual liberty and the unhampered world economy can provide the enormous advantages of the international division of labor and provide the milieu for nations to live in peace.[4]

The theme of how one intervention begets another intervention that undermines the peaceful market order is repeated again and again in Sennholz's books, articles, and lectures. The imagery that he evoked in his lectures still rings in my ears 20 years later; for example, he described the modern welfare state as a giant circle with all of us having our hands in the pockets of our neighbors. But Sennholz did not just effectively use rhetoric and imagery to excite young minds about economics and the political economy of a free society; as the previous excerpt demonstrates, his analysis had a lasting relevance. What he wrote in 1955 is as relevant today as it was then. In the wake of the Asian crisis of 1998 many economists, most notably Joseph Stiglitz, called for the imposition of capital controls.[5] But as Sennholz points out, restrictive policy on capital consumes capital today and drives liquid capital elsewhere. His argument also remains relevant (largely as a warning) to the contemporary formation of the European Union. Rather than create an environment of freedom of capital and labor throughout Europe, industrial special interest groups and labor unions wield political power to maintain restrictions. But as Dr. Sennholz argued in the 1950s, the establishment of freedom of trade and movement of men and capital is the most important policy move that the people of Europe could adopt. Unification would be acceptable if the majority of Europeans were classical liberals in political inclination, but with the majority of Europeans leaning toward interventionism and socialism, the promise of an economically unified Europe will go unfulfilled. Unification assumes free movement of labor, whereas the welfare state requires immigration laws and limiting labor supply to

---

4. Sennholz, *How Can Europe,* 31.

5. Stiglitz won the Nobel Prize for Economic Sciences in 2001 for his contributions to information economics. However, he has become somewhat infamous in 2002 for publishing a book critical of recent globalization efforts and challenging market-oriented policy. See Joseph Stiglitz, *Globalization and Its Discontents* (New York: Norton, 2002).

maintain wages above market clearing levels for privileged labor groups. Unification assumes that individual governments will abolish all barriers to entry from foreign competitors with domestic firms to ensure that these firms are constantly striving for cost minimization in production to compete effectively. The welfare state, on the other hand, raises the costs of doing business in order to ensure that security and social objectives are met. This means that domestic firms must be protected from foreign competitors otherwise their competitive position will be endangered. In short, the welfare state breeds protectionism. Unification presumes a stable currency, whereas the welfare state leads to credit expansion to finance social democratic policies. Unification requires free migration of capital, but the welfare state requires government control of capital investments and capital movements. As Sennholz argued, "It is obvious that the welfare state is incompatible with interstate unification, which requires the European nations to make a momentous decision. They must choose between government welfare and interstate unification. They cannot have both."[6]

In addition to his deployment of the economic analysis of interventionism and credit expansion, a consistent theme in Sennholz's writings is, as I have said previously, that the moral element should not be forgotten. Only a change in private and public morality will result in the necessary changes. "Significant reforms," he argues, "in the final analysis, are moral reforms, changes in the perception of right conduct."[7]

Conclusion

The economic "sermons" I was subjected to at Grove City College redirected my life. There is not a day that goes by that I don't remember fondly the style and substance of Dr. Sennholz's lectures. As a teacher of basic economics to hundreds of students each year, I borrow generously from those memories to try to convey the principles of economics and their implications for a free society. I am not as comfortable with introducing the moral element into the discussion in my classes, but I fundamentally believe that Dr. Sennholz is right that lasting reform requires a change in morality. The difficulty within the transition econo-

---

6. Sennholz, *How Can Europe*, 318.
7. Sennholz, *Debts*, 163.

mies over the past decade in establishing a free market economy highlights the intricate institutional matrix required for a price system to function properly. Independent of even the transition experience, political economy in principle necessitates, at a certain level of analysis, the adoption of a moral stance.[8]

Dr. Sennholz successfully blended his knowledge of the science of economics with a deep commitment to the moral principles governing a society of free and responsible individuals. It was this message that was conveyed clearly in his writings and lectures. To those students who were open, Sennholz's message was transformative. During the dark days of the twentieth century, when socialism had seemed to grab the higher moral ground, there remained a vital few who resisted that intellectual trend. Some of them devoted their energies to pure scholarship—Nobel Prize winners, such as F.A. Hayek, Milton Friedman, George Stigler, James Buchanan, Ronald Coase, and Douglass North, pushed economics in new directions and provided new ammunition for the defense of the free market economy. Some among these, notably Milton Friedman, also rose to celebrity status as public intellectuals. Others such as Murray Rothbard pursued a mixed strategy of scholarship and political activism, while Israel Kirzner attempted to create a purely academic Austrian movement. But as the history of the Austrian School in the mid- to late-twentieth century is written, the contributions of Dr. Hans Sennholz as a teacher and popular writer must be accounted for as well. He provided scores of young people with the opportunity to learn the teachings of the Austrian School of economics at a time when Mises's name was no longer recognized by economists. From his position at a rural liberal arts college in Pennsylvania, Dr. Sennholz conveyed in a consistent and forceful manner the principles of freedom and free enterprise for over 30 years.

---

8. See Peter J. Boettke, *Calculation and Coordination: Essays on Socialism and Transitional Political Economy* (New York: Routledge, 2001), 7–28.

6

The Forgotten Contribution

*Murray Rothbard on Socialism
in Theory and in Practice*

MURRAY N. ROTHBARD made a significant contribution to our understanding of the theory and practice of socialism in the Soviet Union. Rothbard, writing in the 1950s and 1960s, anticipated *all* the major subsequent developments in the economic analysis regarding the problems of the Soviet economy and *all* the major works in comparative political economy for real-existing socialism in the Soviet Union.

> [T]he extent of socialism in the present-day world is at the same time underestimated in countries such as the United States and overestimated in Soviet Russia. It is underestimated because the expansion of government lending to private enterprise in the United States has been generally neglected, and we have seen that the lender, regardless of his legal status, is also an entrepreneur and part owner. The extent of socialism is overestimated because most writers ignore the fact that Russia, socialist as she is, cannot have full socialism as long as she can still refer to the relatively free markets existing in other parts of the world. In short, a single socialist country or bloc of countries, while inevitably experiencing enormous difficulties and wastes in planning, can still buy and sell and refer to the world market and can therefore at least vaguely approximate some sort of rational pricing of producers' goods by extrapolating from the market. The well-known wastes and errors of this partial socialist planning are negligible compared to what would be experienced under the total calculational chaos of a world socialist state.[1]

---

1. Murray N. Rothbard, *Man, Economy, and State,* 2 vols. (Princeton, NJ: D. Van Nostrand, 1962), 830–31.

It has become commonplace for economists to insist that the collapse of the communist bloc in 1989 is a defining moment in twentieth-century political economy. It is also almost obligatory for these economists to insist that nobody predicted the collapse of communism. But this humility is self-imposed by the intellectual straitjacket that many economists wear. Murray Rothbard refused to be so confined by the methods and methodology of the dominant lines of economic thought during his lifetime. He rejected the formalism of Walrasian price theory, the positivism of econometrics, and the aggregation of Keynesianism. But make no mistake, historically Rothbard was a member in good standing in the mainstream of economic thought, and this orthodox strain in economics would not have to be so humble in the face of the collapse of communism in the late 1980s. These economists warned of the problems that deviations from a private property regime and attempts of government control of the economy would bring well before the socialist revolutions of the twentieth century.

The puzzle that economists of Rothbard's ilk must confront is how socialism could have persisted in practice for such a long time given all the problems they identified with the theoretical system. Fortunately, Rothbard was not silent on this "black box" of real-existing socialism. In short, he was able to demonstrate in his work why the socialist economy was theoretically impossible and how socialism in practice muddled through. In *Man, Economy, and State*, Rothbard not only provided the reader with a thorough presentation of the basic principles of economic and political economy, but gave the serious student a framework for the analysis of real-existing socialism in the Soviet Union that was far superior to the framework that dominated Sovietology and the field of comparative economic systems at the time and, if truth be told, to this day. Like in most other areas of economics and political economy, Rothbard let the logic of the argument take him wherever it led without regard to conventional opinion.

One must remember the intellectual context in economics and the social sciences with regard to socialism in the 1950s and 1960s. While there were critics of socialism, the majority of scholars thought not only that socialism was a moral ideal, but that socialist economic planning had the potential to outstrip capitalism in terms of economic growth. Many recognized the atrocities committed against humanity by the Soviet regime, but that was not due to any inherent difficulties with socialist planning. The problems with the Soviet Union were due to the lack of a democratic political system. The Soviet economic system had avoided the Great Depression, stimulated the industrial investment that afforded the defeat of Hitler, achieved significant economic growth in the post–World War II period according to official figures, and beat the U.S. in the technology race for conquering space with the launching of Sputnik in 1957 and then Yuri Gagarin in April 1961. When Khrushchev banged his shoe on the podium at the UN General Assembly, he was not referring exclusively to military superiority.

Rothbard's analysis of the Soviet system in practice challenged all these presumptions. Where popular opinion among economists saw economic growth, Rothbard argued that it is unsustainable growth; where popular opinion saw economic efficiency, Rothbard argued that there are inefficiencies; where popular opinion saw collective property and central planning, Rothbard saw attenuated property rights, world pricing, and black market activity. Outside of the writings of less than a handful of economists, it took until the 1990s for research in comparative economic systems to catch up to the analysis Rothbard had laid out in *Man, Economy, and State*. And, as we will indicate throughout this chapter, even as more and more scholars come to understand the conceptual issues that underlie Rothbard's analysis, the full implications of the argument remain largely hidden from the vast majority of economists who work with these concepts.

Theoretical Contributions on the Problems with Socialism

The starting point of Rothbard's analysis is the demonstration by Ludwig von Mises that economic calculation within a socialist commonwealth was, strictly speaking, impossible. Absent rational economic calculation, economic production would be reduced to merely stabs in the dark. In choosing between production project A or production project B, economic planners would be left without any economic criterion in making their decision. To put this in more practical terms, imagine a socialist planner confronted with the task of deciding whether railroad track should be made of platinum or steel. Platinum is the technologically superior metal for the task of ensuring long-lasting and smooth train rides. In a capitalist economy, the market for capital goods would reflect the alternative uses of platinum and thus give the investor some guidepost by which to make the decision in terms of cost effectiveness. But under the assumptions of socialism, the market for the means of production would be abolished. Under full socialism all reference to world markets and memory of previous market allocations would be abolished. Planners would be confronted with a situation where the price system, being abolished, could no longer serve as a relative scarcity indicator that provides the necessary knowledge input into the calculation of decision makers. In short, economic criterion would be out. The inability to engage in rational economic calculation means that socialist *economy* is impossible.[2]

Rothbard makes this point concisely: "Mises, who has had the last as well as the first word in this debate, has demonstrated irrefutably that a socialist economic system cannot calculate, since it lacks a market, and hence lacks prices for producers' and especially capital goods."[3] Rothbard actually argues that, paradoxically, the Misesian criticism of socialism does not turn on the issue of collective property per se (despite the problems that this scheme has for agent incentives), but because that institutional arrangement necessitates one agent to direct the use of all resources within an economy. Rothbard presents the Misesian argument in the context of a natural tendency within a capitalist economy toward increasing vertical integration of business enterprises and thus monopoly power in a market economy. Critics of the free market often argued that the natural tendency was for the economy to evolve toward one big cartel which would control all productive assets in the economy. But a market economy, Rothbard argued, cannot tend in this direction because firms cannot vertically integrate without facing the problem of calculation. The laws of economic science establish limits to the size of any particular firm on the market and that limit is established by calculational limits.[4]

---

2. This insight of Ludwig von Mises's is *the* most significant contribution to political economy made in the twentieth century. See Peter J. Boettke, "Economic Calculation: The Austrian Contribution to Political Economy," *Advances in Austrian Economics* 5 (1998): 131–58, for an examination of why this Austrian insight into the impossibility of economic calculation under socialism is the contribution to modern political economy. Also see Peter J., Boettke, ed., *Socialism and the Market: The Socialist Calculation Debate Revisited* (London: Routledge, 2000), for a nine-volume reference collection on the debate over socialism and the introduction to those volumes for why Mises's contribution is central to the entire debate.

3. Rothbard, *Man, Economy, and State*, vol. 2, 548.

4. Rothbard's development of this argument is discussed in detail in Peter Klein, "Economic Calculation and the Limits of Organization," *Review of Austrian Economics* 9, no. 2 (1996): 3–28.

Suppose a firm attempts to vertically integrate and thus eliminates the external market for producer goods. Rothbard points out the following:

> In that case, it would have no way of knowing which stage was being conducted profitably and which not. It would therefore have no way of knowing how to allocate factors to the various stages. There would be no way for it to estimate any implicit price or opportunity cost for the capital goods at that particular stage. Any estimate would be completely arbitrary and have no meaningful relation to economic conditions.[5]

Rothbard's discussion anticipated the work that would later be done on the internal organization of the firm, the problems of transfer pricing, and the evolution of the multidivisional firm to overcome these difficulties with centralization.[6] The important issue to stress is that Rothbard saw the problem of economic calculation as actually increasing in magnitude the more advanced the social system of exchange and production became. Rothbard wrote:

> Economic calculation becomes ever more important as the market economy develops and progresses, as the stages and the complexities of type and variety of capital goods increase. Ever more important for the maintenance of an advanced economy, then, is the preservation of *markets* for all the capital and other producers' goods.[7]

This last point is crucial because it relates to the claim that Marxists made concerning the goal of socialist economic planning. In Rothbard's later writing, he makes the seemingly obvious, but very perceptive, observation that "The key to the intricate and massive system of thought created by Karl Marx (1818–83) is at bottom a simple one: *Karl Marx was a communist.*"[8] Marx was a millenialist who argued that communism would bring an end to the suffering of mankind.

---

5. Rothbard, *Man, Economy, and State*, vol. 2, 547.
6. See the work of Frederic Sautet, *An Entrepreneurial Theory of the Firm* (New York: Routledge, 2000), 85–132, for a discussion of the problems of centralization within the internal organization of the firm. Also see Peter Lewin, *Capital in Disequilibrium: The Role of Capital in a Changing World* (New York: Routledge, 1999), 134–74, for a discussion of the implications of Austrian capital theory on the organization of business enterprises.
7. Rothbard, *Man, Economy, and State*, vol. 2, 548.
8. Murray N. Rothbard, *An Austrian Perspective on the History of Economic Thought: The Classical Economists* (Cheltenham, UK: Edward Elgar, 1995), 317.

Crucial to this argument is that the future communist society would be a post-scarcity world. All economic problems would fade away and there would be no need to address the question of the allocation of scarce means among competing ends. The rationalization of production under communism would lead to a burst of productivity and thus make it possible to move from the "Kingdom of Necessity to the Kingdom of Freedom."[9] As Rothbard details in his discussion of Marx, the promise was that the higher stage of communism would eradicate the division of labor and man would be freed from all limitations.[10]

Against this Marxist claim Mises's demonstration of the impossibility of economic calculation under socialism is devastating. The collectivization of the means of production will not result in rationalization, but in chaos. Rather than superabundance, production will come to a standstill and starvation will ensue. We do not intend to go through the various attempts by Marxist and other social scientists to address Mises's calculation argument here.[11] However, it is important to report Rothbard's interpretation of the socialist calculation debate because it anticipated the reinterpretation of that debate that gained currency in the writings of Karen Vaughn, Peter Murrell, and Don Lavoie in the 1980s, concluding that the Austrians had indeed won the calculation debate.[12] The

---

9. One of the clearest discussions of how this ideological presupposition formed the aspirations of the Bolshevik revolution can be found in A. Walicki, *Marxism and the Leap into the Kingdom of Freedom: The Rise and Fall of Communist Utopia* (Stanford, CA: Stanford University Press, 1995).

10. Rothbard, *Austrian Perspective*, 323ff.

11. See David Ramsey Steele, *From Marx to Mises* (La Salle, IL: Open Court, 1992), for a summary of all the traditional attempts to address Mises's argument. For more recent attempts to address the Mises challenge to socialism, see Pranab Bardhan and John Roemer, "Market Socialism: A Case for Rejuvenation," *Journal of Economic Perspectives* 6, no. 3 (1992): 101–16; F. Adaman and Pat Devine, "The Economic Calculation Debate: Lessons for Socialists," *Cambridge Journal of Economics* 20, no. 5 (1996): 523–37; and Allin Cottrell and W. Paul Cockshot, "Calculation, Complexity and Planning," *Review of Political Economy* 5, no. 1 (1993): 73–112. For rejoinders from a Mises-Hayek perspective to some of these attempts to reformulate the argument for socialism, see Steve Horwitz, "Money, Money Prices and the Socialist Calculation Debate," *Advances in Austrian Economics* 3 (1996): 59–77; and Bruce Caldwell, "Hayek and Socialism," *Journal of Economic Literature* 35, no. 4 (1997): 1856–90.

12. Karen I. Vaughn, "Economic Calculation under Socialism: The Austrian Contribution," *Economic Inquiry* XVIII (1980): 535–54; Peter Murrell, "Did the Theory of Market Socialism Answer the Challenge of Ludwig von Mises? A Reinterpretation of the

following quotes show how Rothbard's presentation in 1962 already implied the failure of equilibrium economics to adequately address the issues in the socialist calculation debate that was stressed in later contributions by Vaughn (1980), Murrell (1983), and Lavoie (1985).

> A curious legend has become quite popular among the writers on the socialist side of the debate over economic calculation. This runs as follows: Mises, in his original article, asserted "theoretically" that there could be no economic calculation under socialism; Barone proved mathematically that this is false and that calculation is possible; Hayek and Robbins conceded the validity of this proof but then asserted that calculation would not be "practical." The inference is that the argument of Mises has been disposed of and that all socialism needs is a few practical devices (perhaps calculating machines) or economic advisers to permit calculation and the "counting of the equations."
>
> This legend is almost completely wrong from start to finish. In the first place, the dichotomy between "theoretical" and "practical" is a false one. In economics, all arguments are theoretical. And, since economics discusses the real world, these theoretical arguments are by their nature "practical" ones as well.
>
> The false dichotomy disposed of, the true nature of the Barone "proof" becomes apparent. It is not so much "theoretical" as irrelevant. The proof-by-listing-of-mathematical-equations is not proof at all. It applies, at best, only to the evenly rotating economy. Obviously, our whole discussion of the calculation problem applies to the real world *and to it only. There can be no calculation problem in the ERE because no calculation there is necessary.* Obviously, there is no need to calculate profits and losses when all future data are known from the beginning and where there are no profits and losses. In the ERE, the best allocation

---

Socialist Controversy," *History of Political Economy* 15, no. 1 (1983): 92–105; Don Lavoie, *Rivalry and Central Planning* (New York: Cambridge University Press, 1985). The standard view in the 1970s was that the Austrians had been involved in the calculation debate but that the Austrians had been defeated. Vaughn, Murrell, and Lavoie are often credited for reinterpreting this event but upon reading Rothbard, it is clear that his work anticipated their reinterpretations by two decades.

of resources proceeds automatically. For Barone to demonstrate that the calculation difficulty does not exist in the ERE is not a solution; it is simply a mathematical belaboring of the obvious. The difficulty of calculation applies to the real world only.[13]

The equilibrium economics of Taylor-Lange-Lerner was unable to grasp the nature of economic calculation because it solves the problem by assumption, which in fact is no solution at all. As we have already seen in Rothbard's discussion of the economic organization of the firm, economic calculation is vital for the maintenance of investment projects in an advanced economy. The problem of the coordination of the capital structure that makes up an advanced economy is a problem of the real world. This is a world of factors of production that are neither purely specific nor purely nonspecific. In a world of purely specific factors these goods could be used to produce only one product, and in a world of purely nonspecific factors these goods could be used to produce any product.[14] The capital structure coordination problem exists because capital goods have multiple-specificity and must be allocated among competing investment projects. Economic actors must decide where to allocate scarce capital goods to produce final products that meet consumer demands. Production plans of some must mesh with the consumption demands of others. If these plans don't mesh, resources will be misallocated and thus wasted—people will produce things that nobody wants and want things that nobody produces. It is this real world of heterogeneous capital goods with multiple-specificity where the ability to engage in rational economic calculation is vital to the success or failure of the economic system. Without the guideposts of market prices and profit and loss accounting, economic planners would be set adrift on the sea of possibilities.

These Rothbardian insights into the magnitude of the problem of economic calculation for a modern economy are hidden from view in the circular flow model of Knight, the Arrow-Hahn-Debreu model of general competitive equilibrium, the income expenditure Keynesian model, and the ISLM model of neo-Keynesianism. In short, all the established models of the economy in the period in which Rothbard wrote were ill suited to address the question of

---

13. Rothbard, *Man, Economy, and State*, vol. 2, 549–50.
14. Rothbard, *Man, Economy, and State*, vol. 1, 280–84.

economic calculation. *These models all assumed the problem of calculation away by construction.*

One final theoretical point that Rothbard raised in *Man, Economy, and State* that is relevant to the analysis of socialism in theory and practice is his discussion of collective or public ownership.[15] Rothbard argues that "the important feature of ownership is not legal formality but actual rule, and under government ownership it is the government officialdom that controls and directs, and therefore 'owns,' the property."[16] But while government officials possess ownership in terms of control rights, they do not possess full cash flow rights and the rights they do possess are not secure in the long run.

> Hence government officials will tend to regard themselves as only transitory owners of "public" resources. . . . In short, except in the case of the "private property" of a hereditary monarch, government officials own the current use of resources, but not their capital value. But if a resource itself cannot be owned, but only its current use, there will rapidly ensue an uneconomic exhaustion of the resource, since it will be to no one's benefit to conserve it over a period of time, and yet to each owner's advantage to use it up quickly.[17]

In *Man, Economy, and State*, Rothbard was able to persuasively present not only Mises's argument about the impossibility of rational economic calculation under socialism, but the conceptual incoherence of the very idea of collective property.[18] It is not just that rational economic calculation is impossible, but that the very idea of socialism is impossible. The idea is intellectually bankrupt from the get-go.

---

15. Rothbard, *Man, Economy, and State*, vol. 2, 828–29.
16. Rothbard, *Man, Economy, and State*, vol. 2, 828.
17. Rothbard, *Man, Economy, and State*, vol. 2, 828–29.
18. Yoram Barzel in his influential book on property rights economics put this point as follows: "The claim that private property has been abolished in communist states and that all property there belongs to the state seems to me to be an attempt to divert attention from who the true owners of the property are. It seems that these owners also own the right to the terminology." *Economic Analysis of Property Rights* (New York: Cambridge University Press, 1989), 104n.

The Analysis of Soviet Reality

Rothbard was not content in just laying out the theoretical case against socialism. As previously quoted, Rothbard argues that all theoretical arguments are practical arguments and thus he used the teachings of economics to analyze the Soviet reality of his time and lay bare the false premises about the system that were promulgated at the time. Again, it is important to remember the 1950s and 1960s context in which *Man, Economy, and State* was written. The conversation in the economics profession on the Soviet Union at this time was divided into three distinct literatures: (1) theoretical models of planning, (2) empirical models on economic growth, and (3) conservative economists who criticized the Soviet system. The conservative critique mainly focused on the distorted incentives in the Soviet system that produced inefficiencies. At the time of *Man, Economy, and State*, there were few conservative critics of socialism in economics. Frank Knight, although critical of socialism, did not criticize it from the point of view of economics. In fact, he argued that socialism did not have any economic problems, only political problems.[19] Milton Friedman had criticized Abba Lerner's *The Economics of Control* in the 1940s, but Friedman's scholarship was primarily focused on technical issues in microeconomics and empirical issues in macroeconomics.[20] His full-blown commitment to classical liberalism would become more evident in his writings after *Capitalism and Freedom* was published in 1962. G. Warren Nutter's work on the Soviet system was published in 1962, and James Buchanan and Gordon Tullock's development of public choice would also have to wait until the 1960s. Free market economists

---

19. See Peter J. Boettke and Karen I. Vaughn, "Knight and the Austrians on Capital and the Problems of Socialism," *History of Political Economy* 34, no. 1 (2002): 155–76, for a discussion of Knight on the problem of socialism and its relationship to the argument against socialism as presented in the body of work by Mises and Hayek.

20. Friedman's criticism of Lerner is perceptive in that he attacks Lerner for developing his theory in an institutional vacuum. Thus, Friedman recognized that the mid-century desire to derive an institutionally antiseptic theory of the economic process would run aground and eventually would lead to the counter-reaction in economics that resulted in the literature that now goes under the heading of New Institutional Economics. Milton Friedman, "Lerner's Economics of Control," *Journal of Political Economy* 55, no. 5 (1947): 405–16.

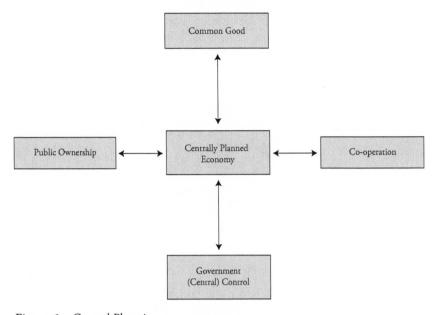

Figure 6.1. Central Planning
Source: http://www.cssd.ab.ca/tech/social/tut9/lesson 7.htm

were in short supply and in a general state of ill repute within the profession in the 1950s and early 1960s.

The economic critics of socialism were essentially limited by the 1950s to Mises and Hayek and their followers, and the profession proceeded as if Mises and Hayek had been soundly defeated in the socialist calculation debate— "the curious legend" Rothbard alludes to in the quote cited earlier. Having dispensed with these naysayers, the economic literature divided into either the microanalytics of planning, or the macroeconomic estimates of growth rates. On the theoretical plane, Soviet planning was said to follow a materials balance approach to economic planning. A simplistic rendering of the ideal of the Soviet centrally planned economy is captured in Figure 6.1.

The material balances approach to economic planning was supposed to ensure that the various stages of planning were coordinated and that resources would be allocated in a way to maximize their use in meeting the objectives of the plan. The planning process that was supposed to operate in the Soviet system is depicted in Figure 6.2.

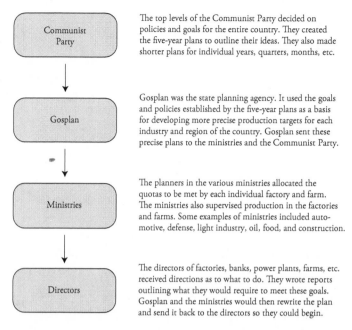

Figure 6.2. Soviet Planning as It Was Supposed to Work
Source: http://www.cssd.ab.ca/tech/sohttpcial/tut9/lesson 21.htm

Of course, reality deviated significantly from this picture of top-down and coordinated planning of the economic system.[21] Planning could not be coordinated so efficiently even under ideal real-world conditions because of the problem of economic calculation. Moreover, once we recognize the "slack" in the system, we have to reorient the way we understand the operation of the Soviet-type economy.

If not an example of the ideal central planning economy, then how would one characterize the Soviet system? Here Rothbard was way ahead of his peers in the economics profession by pointing out the essential elements of a market economy that persisted within the Soviet system and kept it afloat. The work of Paul Craig Roberts, who developed a polycentric understanding of the Soviet system in contrast to the central planning interpretation, serves to

---

21. I discuss the contrast between how the system was supposed to operate in theory with how the system actually operated in practice. Peter J. Boettke, *Why Perestroika Failed: The Politics and Economics of Socialist Transformation* (New York: Routledge, 1993), 57–72.

illustrate Rothbard's anticipation of those who would write later.[22] Unfortunately, Roberts's work, much like Rothbard's insights, was largely ignored by the profession.[23] The important point for our present purposes, however, is that just as Rothbard anticipated the main lines of argument developed by Lavoie in his critique of the theoretical literature, Rothbard's analysis of real-existing socialism anticipated the main elements in the Roberts understanding of the role of black and different colored markets in Soviet economy.

Rothbard clearly recognized the incentive problems present in the production process. The absurdity of measuring outputs in terms of gross aggregates and not market value provided the incentive to produce larger amounts and quantities of output with no concern for the allocation of resources. Despite the severity of these problems with incentives, the problems with the Soviet economic system were even deeper. The economic planning system attempted to adjust to accommodate for these structural problems and in effect produced a system entirely different from the one the textbooks were attempting to model.[24]

Rothbard's discussion of real-existing socialism points to three factors that are essential for understanding the Soviet economic reality as deviating significantly from the textbook model of central planning. The first factor is the existence of world market prices upon which Soviet planners could rely in

---

22. Paul Craig Roberts, *Alienation and the Soviet Economy* (New York: Holmes & Meier, 1971).

23. Roberts's work served as the foundation for my work on Soviet history and the collapse of communism (see Peter J. Boettke, *The Political Economy of Soviet Socialism: The Formative Years, 1918–1928* (Boston, MA: Kluwer, 1990); Boettke, *Why Perestroika Failed*; Peter J. Boettke, *Calculation and Coordination: Essays on Socialism and Transitional Political Economy* (New York: Routledge, 2001)). To the extent that Rothbard anticipated Roberts's work, he also anticipated my own work in this area.

24. It is not that incentive distortions do not matter, they do. But as Mises pointed out the problem was deeper than the incentives faced by managers. In *Human Action: A Treatise on Economics* (1949; repr., Indianapolis, IN: Liberty Fund, 2010), 708. Mises wrote:

> Our problem does not refer to managerial activities; it concerns the allocation of capital to the various branches of industry. The question is: In which branches should production be increased or restricted, in which branches should the objective of production be altered, what new branches should be inaugurated? With regard to these issues it is vain to cite the honest corporation manager and his well-tried efficiency. Those who confuse entrepreneurship and management close their eyes to the economic problem.

formulating their plans. A socialist country existing within a sea of market established prices could buy and sell in, and refer to, the world market. This in turn enables economic planners to "vaguely approximate some sort of rational pricing of producer goods."[25] It is this ability to rely on world prices that prevents any current attempt at comprehensive central planning from collapsing into total calculational chaos.

But the Soviet system did not exist on the basis of world prices alone. The production failures and consumer frustration gave rise to internal markets as well. As Rothbard put it:

> Another neglected factor diminishing the extent of planning in social-ist countries is "black market" activities, particularly in commodities (candy, cigarettes, drugs, stockings, etc.) that are easy to conceal. Even in bulkier commodities, falsification of records and extensive graft may bring some sort of limited market—a market violating all socialist plans—into existence.[26]

The importance of the black market for understanding the Soviet economy would remain largely neglected until after the system was visibly collapsing. In the late 1980s, the leading textbooks in the field still gave little more than a few pages to the discussion of the black market despite the evidence of its extensive use both internal to the plan to attempt to meet output targets and external to the plan to satisfy consumer demands. And the existence of graft and corruption as a crucial part of the operation of Soviet economy would only be discussed after models of the shortage economy were worked out in detail in the 1980s and early 1990s, even though we can find references in the literature that "blat" was higher than even Stalin.[27]

---

25. Rothbard, *Man, Economy, and State,* vol. 2, 831.
26. Rothbard, *Man, Economy, and State,* vol. 2, 831.
27. There was a window of opportunity for more "on the ground" research by Western scholars in the wake of the Khrushchev 1956 thaw, and a team of graduate students in political science and economics wrote breakthrough PhD theses taking advantage of this opportunity. In economics, this work is represented by Joseph Berliner, *Factory and Manager in the USSR* (Cambridge, MA: Harvard University Press, 1957), and David Granick, *Management and the Industrial Firm in the USSR* (1954; repr., Westport, CT: Greenwood Press, 1980), on the organization of Soviet firms. Despite the important em-pirical findings available in these works, the authors lacked the appropriate theoretical

How much Rothbard anticipated the advances in the field that would occur some 20 years later is evidenced by his discussions of the centrally prohibited economy, the lack of innovation in the Soviet system, and the fallacy of Soviet growth rates. Rothbard's discussion of why the Soviet system is not really a centrally planned one is worth quoting at length:

> Moreover, it should be noted that a centrally "planned" economy is a centrally *prohibited* economy. The concept of "social engineering" is a deceptive metaphor, since in the *social* realm, it is largely *people* who are being planned, rather than the inanimate machinery of engineering blueprints. And since every individual is by nature, if not always by law, a self-owner and self starter—i.e., self-energizer, this means that central orders, backed up, as they must be under socialism, by force and violence, effectively *prohibit* all the individuals doing what they want most or what they believe themselves to be best fitted to do.[28]

The Soviet system was in essence a prohibition economy writ large. In analyzing a prohibition economy, we can stress one of two things—the force and violence that must be used to attempt to enforce the decrees of the authorities, or the failures of enforcement to stop individuals from finding ways to pursue their plans and how the prohibition environment impacts that pursuit. On the one hand, we have force and violence, and on the other hand, we have black markets and graft as individuals assume the risk of arbitrary punishment by authorities to pursue their plans and realize their desires. People within this prohibition environment still pursue their plans, but they are forced to do so in a

---

framework to make full sense of the findings. As a result, when the window was closed and opportunities for on the ground research were lost, the main insights from this period were dissipated and optimal planning models and/or statistical estimates of growth rates dominated the literature on the Soviet economy. The emigré work of scholars such as Gregory Grossman would point out how the Soviet system really worked and how it deviated significantly from the model of central planning, but this was not incorporated into the textbook treatment ("The 'Second Economy' of the USSR," in *The Soviet Economy,* ed. Morris Bornstein (1977; repr., Boulder, CO: Westview, 1981)). Even the widely accepted work of Janos Kornai on overadministration and the shortage economy, while providing concepts which could be found in all textbooks (e .g., storming), would not change the basic textbook model of central planning (*The Political Economy of Communism* (Princeton, NJ: Princeton University Press, 1992)).

28. Rothbard, *Man, Economy, and State,* vol. 2, 831.

manner that is different from what would take place in an unhampered market environment. Prohibition in the 1920s did not curtail alcohol consumption, but it did create an environment that gave rise to bathtub gin and Al Capone. Similarly, the prohibition of the market throughout Soviet Russia did not curtail market exchange—it just forced it underground.[29]

One of the most damaging consequences of this prohibition environment for the long-term performance of the Soviet economy, Rothbard pointed out, was the detrimental impact on invention and innovation that the attempt at central planning produced. "[I]nventions, innovations, technological developments, by their very nature, by definition, cannot be predicted in advance and therefore cannot be centrally and bureaucratically *planned*."[30] Leaving room for the unforeseen possibilities is not in the nature of planning exercises. In a free market society, what will be invented, when it will be invented, and who will do the inventing remains hidden from us until after the fact.[31] The central

---

29. See Rothbard's discussion of triangular intervention for a discussion of these effects (*Man, Economy, and State*, 785–91). Of the many important insights Rothbard has into the economic consequences of interventionism, he anticipated the rent-seeking theory of the Soviet economy developed in the 1990s by Gary Anderson and Peter J. Boettke ("Perestroika and Public Choice: The Economics of Autocratic Succession in a Rent-Seeking Society," *Public Choice* 75, no. 2 (1993): 101–18; "Soviet Venality: A Rent-Seeking Model of the Communist State," *Public Choice* 93, nos. 1–2 (1997): 37–53); David Levy ("The Bias in Centrally Planned Prices," *Public Choice* 67 (1990): 213–26); and Andrei Shleifer and Robert Vishny (*The Grabbing Hand* (Cambridge, MA: Harvard University Press, 1998)) when he states that: "The direct beneficiaries of product control, then, are the government bureaucrats who administer the regulations: partly from the tax-centered jobs that the regulations create, and partly from satisfactions gained from wielding coercive power over others" (*Man, Economy, and State*, 785–86). The inevitable emergence of "black markets" in the wake of the prohibition also generates a situation where the control, paradoxically, "is apt to serve as a monopoly grant of privilege to the black marketers. For they are likely to be very different entrepreneurs from those who would have succeeded in this industry in a legal market" (*Man, Economy, and State*, 786). Rothbard's analysis also addresses the short-term time horizon of investment that black markets generate due to the need to maintain secrecy to avoid legal detection.

30. Rothbard, *Man, Economy, and State*, vol. 2, 831.

31. In *The Constitution of Liberty* (Chicago: University of Chicago Press, 1960), 29, Hayek states:

> If there were omniscient men, if we could know not only all that affects the attainment of our present wishes but also our future wants and desires, there would be little case for liberty. And, in turn, liberty of the individual would, of course,

planning task, if it is to be coherent, would require knowing in advance and planning for technological innovation. Planned innovation, however, is a classic oxymoron. And once we recognize that central planning cannot plan technological innovations, the claims to economic rationalization must be abandoned completely. Rothbard concludes:

> Clearly a centrally prohibited economy, irrational and inefficient enough for given ends and *given* means and techniques at any point of time, is all the more incompetent if a flow of inventions and new developments are desired in a society. Bureaucracy, incompetent enough to plan a stationary system, is vastly more incompetent at planning a progressive one.[32]

In the early 1960s, it was commonplace to dismiss known Soviet crimes against humanity and alleged Soviet economic inefficiencies because the central planning apparatus was said to have achieved economic growth such that a largely peasant society was transformed into an industrial society in less than a generation, and this transformation was responsible for the defeat of Hitler in World War II. Soviet economic growth justified whatever sacrifices were made in terms of human rights and consumer frustration. Rothbard did not want to address in full the "hullabaloo that has been raised in recent years over the supposedly enormous rate of Soviet growth."[33] But his short comments anticipated the main line of argument that was later put forward by critics of Soviet growth and effectively challenged the empirical record. The bottom line is that growth was measured incorrectly and the inputs to production were counted while the value of output was not. Nutter was one of the first to try to put forth a realistic analysis of Soviet economic performance but he had little success in reducing the exaggerated numbers and his own estimates

---

make complete foresight impossible. Liberty is essential in order to leave room for the unforeseeable and unpredictable; we want it because we have learned to expect from it the opportunity of realizing many of our aims. It is because every individual knows so little and, in particular, because we rarely know which of us knows best that we trust the independent and competitive efforts of many to induce the emergence of what we shall want when we see it.

32. Rothbard, *Man, Economy, and State,* vol. 2, 832.
33. Rothbard, *Man, Economy, and State,* vol. 2, 835.

were eventually shown to be high by Roberts.[34] Rothbard, clearly realizing the exaggerated growth data, noted:

> Curiously, one finds that the "growth" seems to be taking place almost exclusively in capital goods, such as iron and steel, hydroelectric dams, etc., whereas little or none of this growth ever seems to filter down to the standard of living of the average Soviet consumer. The consumer's standard of living, however, is the be-all and end-all of the entire production process. *Production* makes no sense whatever except as a means to *consumption*. Investment in capital goods means nothing except as a *necessary way station to increased consumption*.[35]

The Soviet system was one of "conspicuous production" where government investment, rather than producing tangible benefits to consumers, "turns out to be a peculiar form of wasteful 'consumption' by government officials."[36]

The scarce capital goods that are allocated based on government compulsion according to some central plan are either wasted or dissipated because the investment is not based on consumer demand and profit-and-loss signals on the market. These investments are malinvestments, and if government subsidization ceased it is unlikely that the investment would be sustained. Rothbard sums up the Soviet situation as follows:

> Capital is an intricate, delicate, interweaving *structure* of capital goods. All of the delicate strands of this structure have to fit, and fit precisely, or else malinvestment occurs. The free market is almost an automatic mechanism for such fitting; and we have seen throughout this volume how the free market, with its price system and profit-and-loss criteria, adjusts the output and variety of the different strands of production, preventing any one from getting long out of alignment. But under socialism or with massive government investment, there is no such mechanism for

---

34. G. Warren Nutter, *The Growth of Industrial Production in the Soviet Economy* (Princeton, NJ: Princeton University Press, 1962); Paul Craig Roberts, "My Time with Soviet Economics," *Independent Review* 7, no. 2 (2002): 259–64.
35. Rothbard, *Man, Economy, and State,* vol. 2, 835–36.
36. Rothbard, *Man, Economy, and State,* vol. 2, 836.

fitting and harmonizing. Deprived of a free price system and profit-and-loss criteria, the government can only blunder along, blindly "investing" without being able to invest properly in the right fields, the right products, or the right places. A beautiful subway will be built, but no wheels will be available for the trains; a giant dam, but no copper for transmission lines, etc. These sudden surpluses and shortages, so characteristic of government planning, are the result of massive malinvestment by the government.[37]

Thus, Soviet economic growth was at the same time both overestimated and unsustainable. Surprisingly, the gross exaggeration of the Soviet economic performance continued into the late 1970s and beyond.[38] In fact, one could still find a positive discussion of the Soviet economy as late as 1989 in Samuelson and Nordhaus's best selling textbook.[39]

When one looks at the best modern analysis of real-existing socialism by Andrei Shleifer and Robert Vishny and the best historical scholarship by Paul Gregory, it is readily apparent to the reader that these authors are building on Rothbardian themes, even if unacknowledged.[40] Shleifer and Vishny's analysis focuses on the "grabbing hand" and the bias within the planning system for shortages. Gregory has dug deep into the archives and used the framework of modern political economy to provide a coherent and comprehensive interpretation of the political economy of Stalinism. In both instances, Shleifer and Vishny and Gregory use concepts first developed by Rothbard. However, these authors (as is the near universal condition) are unaware of Rothbard's groundbreaking analysis from the 1950s and 1960s. When one realizes that it took the economics profession more than 30 years to realize and accept what Rothbard had penned in *Man, Economy, and State*, the true greatness of his contribution to political economy becomes evident. Unfortunately, even when these ideas are recognized, they are rarely if ever attributed to Rothbard.

---

37. Rothbard, *Man, Economy, and State*, vol. 2, 836–37.
38. Roberts, "My Time," 260.
39. Paul A. Samuelson and William D. Nordhaus, *Economics*, 13th ed. (New York: McGraw-Hill, 1989).
40. Shleifer and Vishny, *Grabbing Hand*; Paul Gregory, *The Political Economy of Stalinism* (New York: Cambridge University Press, 2003).

Conclusion

As we have seen, Murray Rothbard's *Man, Economy, and State* was able to not only present the theoretical critique of socialism, but also extend that analysis through the application to understand the failings of the real-existing Soviet economy. Rothbard in the early 1960s anticipated *all* the major developments in the analysis of socialism in theory and practice that would be made during the 1980s and 1990s. Rothbard first suggested the reinterpretation of the socialist calculation debate, later championed by Lavoie, which emphasized the dynamic market process as opposed to preoccupation with equilibrium.[41] Rothbard also clearly stated the critique of the idea of collective property rights by indicating that such a notion fails to not recognize the control rights that must reside with those entrusted with decision-making power.[42] Similarly, Rothbard challenged the very idea of comprehensive central economic planning and introduced the idea of the prohibited economy as opposed to the planned economy.[43] The combination of Rothbard's identification of the "owners" in a supposedly collective property regime and his clarification of the main benefactors from the prohibited economy anticipated the rent-seeking interpretation of Soviet planning developed in the public choice literature.[44] Rothbard also challenged the interpretation of Soviet growth and argued that it was simultaneously overestimated and malinvested.[45]

Given the textual evidence we have provided, there should be little doubt that Rothbard was ahead of his time in terms of articulating the failings of the Soviet system. His analysis is so fresh that we must remember that it was written in the 1950s and *Man, Economy, and State* was not extensively revised when it was republished over the years. But even if we recognize that he anticipated the subsequent developments in the literature, we are left with the question of whether his analysis could have aided the post-communist period? The answer to this question must be an unequivocal yes. One of the biggest problems with the transition period has been a misspecification of the original system. Textbooks

---

41. Rothbard, *Man, Economy, and State,* vol. 2, 549.
42. Rothbard, *Man, Economy, and State,* vol. 2, 828.
43. Rothbard, *Man, Economy, and State,* vol. 2, 831.
44. Rothbard, *Man, Economy, and State,* vol. 2, 786.
45. Rothbard, *Man, Economy, and State,* vol. 2, 835.

described the Soviet-type system as one where nobody possessed property rights in the current status quo. Of course, the reality of the situation was as Rothbard described—the main benefactors of the system were those in political leadership. In addition, the Soviet investment structure was malinvested. Thus, the policy implications of Rothbard's analysis would have led to two major themes: (1) homesteading and eliminating government prohibitions to market activity, and (2) eliminating all government restrictions on market adjustments to weed out the malinvestment and reallocate capital into more appropriate uses. In short, the policy advice Rothbard presented in *America's Great Depression* (Princeton, NJ: D. Van Nostrand, 1963) in the wake of the boom-bust cycle is the same advice that one would get in the wake of the post-Soviet bust.[46] In addition to extending the policy implications from *America's Great Depression*, Rothbard also provided a blueprint for transition economies in "How and How Not to Desocialize."[47] In that article, Rothbard provides ten "do" and "don't" guidelines for transitioning from socialism to markets. Unfortunately, the political coalitions across the former Soviet type economies resisted many of these policy prescriptions put forth by Rothbard.

Rothbard's *Man, Economy, and State* is a recognized landmark in Austrian economics. Alongside Ludwig von Mises's *Human Action*, Rothbard's book stands as the only systematic treatise in the field. Rothbard guides the reader from the basic principles of the discipline to the refined interpretation of the economic consequences of interventionism. A prime example of the intellectual power of this work is his treatment of the theoretical problems of socialism and the application of the understanding of those theoretical insights to analyze Soviet reality.

---

46. See Boettke ("Why Perestroika Failed," 106–31) for a wholesale adoption of Rothbard's policy prescription for the post-Soviet period.
47. Murray N. Rothbard, "How and How Not to Desocialize," *Review of Austrian Economics* 6, no. 1 (1992): 65–77.

7

Mr. Boulding
and the Austrians

The real world is a muddle. And if the real world is a muddle,
it is a great mistake to be clear about. —Kenneth E. Boulding.[1]

Introduction

KENNETH E. BOULDING was undoubtedly one of the most
prolific economic and social thinkers of the twentieth century. Boulding published close to forty books and hundreds of articles in his academic career. His
scholarship, which ranged from technical issues in capital theory to peace research and defense economics to evolutionary social theory, was also one of the
most interesting among that of academics. Boulding was a bold social thinker,
who not only tried to construct a unified theory of social science, but of knowledge in general.

He was an eclectic thinker who defied classification. In a very real sense
he was his own school—sadly a school of all master chefs and no cooks. His
classic principles text, *Economic Analysis* (New York: Harper & Brothers, 1941),
established Boulding firmly within the mainstream of economic thought. The
revised versions of this text were among the first attempts to introduce Keynesian ideas into the pedagogical mainstream of economics. Yet Boulding was not
a traditional Keynesian, despite the fact that he accepted the label.[2] Boulding

---

1. Lecture notes from Boulding's course, Great Books in the History of Political Economy (George Mason University, September 10, 1985).
2. See, for example, his acceptance and reservations about Keynesianism expressed in
the preface to the first edition of *A Reconstruction of Economics* (New York: John Wiley
& Sons, 1950), ix. Also see *The Skills of the Economist* (Cleveland: Howard Allen, 1958), 5,

was also influenced to some extent by Joseph Schumpeter, whom, in fact, he had first met on the boat coming to America and with whom he worked at Harvard in 1932. He studied capital theory with Schumpeter and apparently discovered a fundamental flaw in Boehm-Bawerk's theory.[3]

Boulding often expressed surprise at the pigeonhole others tried to fit him into. As he states in the introduction to the first volume of his *Collected Papers*:

> In spite of the fact that I see myself as not much of a radical, being close to the "main line" of economic thought that goes from Adam Smith to Ricardo, Mill, Marshall, and Keynes, in terms of the reception I feel much closer to the heretics, especially in the American institutionalists— to Veblen, Wesley Mitchell, and especially to John R. Commons, who has achieved the remarkable distinction of being perhaps the most influential and most neglected American thinker of the twentieth century.[4]

We do not seek in this chapter to offer the reader another classification for Boulding. He was at one and the same time mainstream economist and radical critic, classic theorist and modern technician, scientist, and mystic. Our purpose is, instead, to call attention to those features of Boulding's lifework that suggest that he is one of the most important (let alone creative) post-Knightean American subjectivists.

One of the influences, which is often overlooked with regard to Boulding, is his deep affinity to the Austrian or subjectivist tradition in economic analysis.

---

where Boulding refers to himself as a classical economist on the one hand (though he learned a great deal from institutionalism and historicism), and a moderate Keynesian on the other (though he must admit that Mises and Hayek raise important and disturbing questions).

3. Boulding remarked: "I worked with him (Schumpeter) on capital theory, and discovered what I thought was a fundamental flaw in Boehm-Bawerk, I cannot quite now remember what it was, and I seem to have lost my paper." ("My Life Philosophy," *The American Economist* 29 (Fall 1985): 6). It seems that Boulding's paper probably didn't influence Schumpeter, as there is no reference to Boulding's criticism in Schumpeter's discussion of Boehm-Bawerk in *The History of Economic Analysis* (New York: Oxford University Press, 1954).

4. Kenneth E. Boulding, "Introduction," In *Collected Papers*, vol. 1 (Boulder: Colorado Associated University Press, 1971), viii.

His early technical papers, for example, were explorations of Austrian and Fisherian capital theory.[5] Moreover, this influence continued when he moved from technical economics to broader issues in the social sciences. *The Image* (Ann Arbor: University of Michigan Press, 1956), especially, represents a neglected classic in the subjectivist tradition.

A basic theme that Boulding shares with subjectivists of all stripes is that the social world is a messy and complex system, not amenable to neat and monocasual explanations. In fact, formally elegant explanations which purport to provide objective knowledge and tight predictability are an illusion, if not a dogma. Such deterministic views of the social system, Boulding argued, can be quite disastrous since we can be led "to neglect of adaptability, tentativeness, and that constant willingness to revise images, which are necessities of survival in an uncertain world."[6]

Background on Boulding

Boulding was born in Liverpool, England, in 1910. He attended New College, Oxford, on a science scholarship beginning in 1928, intending to study chemistry. But Boulding did not find science as interesting as he initially believed, and decided to focus on social problems instead. In June 1929, Boulding recounts, he went to visit Lionel Robbins—who was just leaving Oxford for a professorship as the London School of Economics. Boulding wanted to find out what he should read for the summer if he wanted to study economics. Robbins provided a list that included Alfred Marshall's *Principles* and Philip Wicksteed's *Common Sense of Political Economy*. Upon returning to Oxford in the fall of 1929, Boulding scored an almost perfect score on his economic examination, and he was able to retain his science scholarship despite enrolling in the honors school of politics, philosophy, and economics.

---

5. See, for example, Kenneth E. Boulding, "The Application of the Pure Theory of Population Change to the Theory of Capital," *Quarterly Journal of Economics* 48 (August 1934): 645–66; Boulding, "Time and Investment," *Economica* 10 (May 1936): 196–220.
6. Kenneth E. Boulding, "Systems Research and the Hierarchy of World Systems," *Systems Research* 2 (1985): 11.

Boulding published his first professional paper—an examination of the theoretical role of "displacement costs"—as an undergraduate in *The Economic Journal* (which Keynes edited at the time). After he graduated from Oxford, Boulding secured a Commonwealth Fellowship (the British equivalent to a Rhodes Scholarship) and left to study economics in the United States, first for a brief period at Harvard with Joseph Schumpeter, and then at the University of Chicago with Frank Knight. In fact, Boulding's explorations in Austrian capital theory so irked Knight that it led the latter to publish a paper entitled "Mr. Boulding and the Austrians," from which we obviously borrowed the title for our present purposes.

Boulding never completed his PhD in economics; an experience he often said would have killed him. Boulding often attributed the professional opportunities he received despite not receiving his academic "union card" to two factors: his Oxford education, and the scientific "endorsement" of Frank Knight.[7]

Boulding's teaching career included posts at Edinburgh, Fisk, Colgate, Iowa State, McGill, Michigan, and Colorado. After retiring from Colorado in 1980, he taught as a visiting professor at several universities throughout the 1980s. Boulding's contribution as a scholar were vast. As mentioned previously, his book, *Economic Analysis*, was one of the leading textbooks in economics in the 1940s. Along with Ludwig von Bertalanffy, Boulding founded the Society for General Systems Research in the 1950s and served as the association's first president. He basically invented the field of defense economics and conflict resolution, and his *Conflict and Defense* (New York: Harper & Row, 1962) is considered a classic in the field.

Boulding became restless with standard economics early in his career. In *A Reconstruction of Economics*, for example, he wrote that there was no such thing as economics, just social science applied to economic problems (vii). Boulding's disillusionment with standard economics stemmed from a profound discomfort with the assumption of perfect knowledge, perfect markets, and static equilibrium. The requirements of technical economics actually forced economists into an intellectual straightjacket and failed to offer significant gains that outweighed the loss of creative and critical analysis. The benefits of modern economic tech-

---

7. Boulding was deeply impressed with Knight despite their disagreements in technical economics. In fact, Boulding's description of Knight as "an engine of creativity without a clutch" may also be just as appropriate a label for himself.

nique were there to be had, but the cost to human understanding, Boulding emphasized, should not be overlooked.[8]

It would be mistaken, however, to assume that Boulding was against formalism in economics. During his youth, he was as technically sophisticated as the best of them. What he sought to do, beginning with his first articles on capital theory, but especially with *A Reconstruction of Economics*, was to supplement the techniques of a Newtonian world-view with the formal tools appropriate for a dynamic and heterogeneous world.

In addition to his unorthodox economic views, Boulding was a devout Quaker and pacifist. He was a deeply spiritual man in a profession of rationalists. His critical attitude toward modern economics and his deep spirituality made Boulding an iconoclast.

Despite his outsider status, Boulding was bestowed with many honors during his career. In 1949 he won the John Bates Clark Medal from the American Economic Association, an award that is given every two years to the economists under the age of 40 judged to have made the most significant contribution to economic thought. After the Clark award Boulding drifted further away from mainstream economics and more into the interdisciplinary social science and social philosophy. Nevertheless, in 1968 he was elected President of the American Economic Association.[9]

---

8. See, for example, Boulding's review of Paul Samuelson's *Foundation of Economic Analysis*. Logic and judgment are necessary for scientific purposes, according to Boulding, but mathematical skill does not help us with judgment. Rather, it is only an aid to logic. As Boulding states: "Conventions of generality and mathematical elegance may be just as much barriers to the attainment and diffusion of knowledge as may contentment with particularity and literary vagueness. . . . It may well be that the slovenly and literary borderland between economics and sociology will be the most fruitful building ground during the years to come and that mathematical economics will remain too flawless in its perfection to be very fruitful." ("Samuelson's *Foundations*: The Role of Mathematics in Economics," *Journal of Political Economy* 56 (June 1948): 247). Also see Boulding, *Economics as a Science* (New York: McGraw-Hill, 1970), 115, where he argues that mathematical reasoning can be a wonderful servant, but a very bad master.

9. Boulding, we believe, set a record for serving as the president of major scholarly societies. Besides the American Economic Association, he served as the president of the American Association for the Advancement of Science, International Studies Association, Peace Research Society, Society for General Systems Research, and the Association for the Study of the Grants Economy.

Subjectivist Themes in Boulding's Economics

Since its first systematic presentation in Carl Menger's *Principles of Economics*,[10] subjectivist economics had been distinguished from other schools of thought by the emphasis placed on question of knowledge, time, and process. In a very limited sense all of neoclassical economics embraced the subjective theory of value. But in an important respect the neoclassical revolution represented a victory of marginalism rather than subjectivism. Alfred Marshall's *Principles*, for example, quickly reintroduced an untenable objective cost side into the analysis of market behavior.[11]

A fundamental theme in the subjectivist view of knowledge is that the social world is nothing more (or less) than a social construction of reality. It is individual values, perceptions, and expectations that guide judgment about alternative courses of action. In other words, our world is fragmented into multiple realties and value systems. The knowledge embedded in the social system is dispersed among the various participants. To the subjectivist, both the conflict of values and dispersal of knowledge focus scholarly attention on the institutions and practices that enable participants to coordinate their activities with one another in a reasonable manner. It is precisely these institutions and practices which provide the bridge from solipsism to social order that economists and social scientists seek to explain.[12]

As opposed to the standard Newtonian conception of time, subjectivists view time in a Heraclition manner. Time is irreversible and represents an unending flow of consciousness. "So far as men are concerned, being" as G.L.S.

10. Carl Menger, *Principles of Economics* (1871; repr., New York: New York University Press, 1981).

11. Alfred Marshall, *Principles of Economics*, 9th ed. (New York: Macmillan, 1961). This is a point that Wicksteed made clear in his critical address to the British Economics Society in 1914. Rather than two blades of a pair of scissors, Wicksteed explained, supply and demand are made of the same stuff—the subjective evaluations of consumers. See Philip Wicksteed, "The Scope and Method of Political Economy in Light of the 'Marginal' Theory of Value and Distribution," in *The Common Sense of Political Economy*, 2 vols. (1914; repr., London: Routledge, 1938).

12. See, for example, Georg Simmel, "How Is Society Possible?" in *On Individuality and Social Forms*, edited by Donald N. Levine (1908; repr., Chicago: University of Chicago Press, 1971), for a discussion of the motivating question of social theory.

Shackle has put it, "consists in endless fresh knowing."[13] Time viewed in this manner involves the acceptance of an inherent uncertainty of the future which defies reduction to mathematical formalization.

The concern with knowledge and time leads to a vision of the social world as complex and dynamic. Subjectivists have traditionally argued that process and evolutionary analysis are the most appropriate methods for making sense of the interdependencies of dynamic systems and structures of reality.[14] Standard equilibrium models, at best, provide a useful heuristic for explicating tendencies of mutual adjustments of behavior.

Throughout the vast corpus of Boulding's work, these themes are repeatedly stressed. Even when Boulding was at his most mainstream (in terms of technique and style of argument) his formal analysis—both graphical and in systems of equations—sought to examine period by period adjustments, whereas his verbal analysis often stressed the evolutionary dynamics underlying systems. Boulding never exclusively concentrated on equilibrium states. In fact, his recognition of the possibility of multiple equilibria and, even more important, the necessity of disequilibrium foundations of equilibrium economics led Boulding from the earliest period in his professional development to look to formal models of population theory and ecological interaction developed in the biological sciences to aid his social research. For instance, both *A Reconstruction of Economics* and *Conflict and Defense*, which were highly technical works (especially given their time), reflect Boulding's concern with process analysis and evolutionary dynamics.

The basic thesis of *A Reconstruction* was that a balance sheet approach to the study of economics would examine the sequence of states rather than the particular states of affairs which traditional equilibrium models are limited to analyzing. In the standard theory of the firm, Boulding argued, it appears to be impossible to introduce the essential concept of uncertainty. Maximizing theories are based on certain knowledge of the future. This approach cannot examine the asset structure of the firm. An analysis of the preferred structure of the

---

13. G.L.S. Shackle, *Epistemics and Economics* (Cambridge: Cambridge University Press, 1972), 156.
14. Process analysis examines the adjustments and changes of behavior within any existing set of parameters, whereas evolutionary theory examines consequences of changes in the parameters themselves.

balance sheet, and especially the liquidity and flexibility of assets, is not possible without introducing uncertainty from the start. The uncertainty of the future, and the defenses against uncertainty, are built into the asset structure of the firm. If we try to build an elegant theory of the profit-maximizing firm in the absence of uncertainty, then, Boulding feared, we will never be able to fit uncertainty back into the analysis, and our theory of the firm will be woefully deficient.[15]

Moreover, in *Conflict and Defense* Boulding employs the concept of Richardsonian processes to examine the multiple equilibria that emerge in the face of conflict (these are processes which generate self-justifying and unproductive emulation.) His purpose was to develop a theory of conflicting and its resolution in order to demonstrate that "conflict processes are neither arbitrary, random, nor incomprehensible."[16] It was his hope that in understanding the logic of conflict, humankind would find solutions to the problems of human betterment and welfare in a nuclear age. The positive analytical point that we wish to highlight is simply that Boulding was concerned with processes and movements between equilibria, and not the theoretical fiction of equilibrium per se.

As Boulding grew even more diverted from the mainstream of economic thought, he ultimately saw the task of the social sciences as explaining the evolution and progress of human knowledge.[17] Equilibrium economics was a case in point of the misallocation of intellectual resources in economics.[18]

---

15. Boulding, *A Reconstruction*, 26–38.

16. Boulding, *Conflict*, 328.

17. A few of Boulding's famous quips relate his growing disillusionment with mainstream economics. When asked why in the mid-twentieth century logical positivism took hold of economics, Boulding simply replied: "Of course nobody opposed logical positivism because no one wanted to be consider an illogical negativist." In addition, Boulding often referred to Walras as a "total disaster for economics because he had no concept of the food-chain." In other words, the concept of evolutionary dynamics was completely foreign to mainstream equilibrium analysis. Finally, Boulding also would state that the main problem with modern economists was that they were employing seventeenth-century mathematics to solve twentieth-century problems, and they thought they were sophisticated. This discussion was drawn from our lecture notes from Boulding's Great Books in the History of Political Economy course at George Mason University (Fall 1985), and personal conversations.

18. Boulding argued that intellectual resources could be misallocated because in the absence of a working capital market in ideas we do not have reliable information on the rates of return on the use of intellectual resources. Instead, information concerning intellectual resource use is provided (a) from the grants economy, and (b) from the in-

The individual in the subjectivist tradition is neither a lightning calculator of pleasure and pain, nor completely blind. Rather, the individual muddles through somewhere between alluring hopes and haunting fear. *The Image* was Boulding's attempt to communicate with his fellow social scientists just how much is absent from analysis when uncertainty, ignorance, and dynamic change are left out of the analysis due to the acceptance of certain operational assumptions, such as perfect knowledge and perfect markets. Rather than perfect, our "relational image is faulty at the best. Our image of the consequences of our acts is suffused with uncertainty to the point where we are not even sure what we are uncertain about."[19] Traditional economics had dealt with this problem of uncertainty by assuming that human decision making consists of choosing between alternatives that are presents to the chooser with a known utility tag and probability distribution. This enables economists to calculate the expected value of their choices with great agility. But this does not explain human decision making in the face of uncertainty, nor does it help us understand how our images adjust to guide behavior and coordinate our actions with those of others.

The calculative wizard of mainstream economics provides the foundation for the doctrine of perfect markets. In the analysis of perfect markets, individual decision makers need only rely on price information in order to adjust behavior appropriately. Once imperfections are introduced into the market, however, price information is not the only relevant information. Now, information concerning quantities, quality, reputation of the dealer, and so on, provide vital feedback. The decision maker must choose his course of action in an environment where he can only dimly see the possibilities in front of him.

"The process of reorganization of economic images through messages," Boulding argued, "is the key to the understanding of economic dynamics."[20]

---

tellectual fashions. As Boulding saw it, the real problem was that the power structure of the modern university system (and especially the system of doctoral education) could serve to generate a tyranny of fashion, and it was not clear that there were "forces" in the system that would provide the necessary feedback to "correct" misallocations. See Kenneth E. Boulding, "The Misallocation of Intellectual Resources in Economics," in *Collected Papers,* vol. 3 (Boulder: Colorado Associated University Press, 1973). Also see Kenneth E. Boulding, *The Impact of the Social Sciences* (New Brunswick, NJ: Rutgers University Press, 1966), 102–14.

19. Boulding, *Image,* 84.
20. Boulding, *Image,* 90.

Economic life is governed by the reorganization of our images through the transmission of knowledge. The explanation of the use of knowledge in any social system, thus, becomes the key scientific question for understanding the evolutionary dynamic.

Evolution proceeds largely through the ability of "know-how" to instruct and thus, guide human decisions. "Know-how" is embedded within our images. "The evolutionary vision," Boulding writes, "is unfriendly to any simple reductionism or materialism. It sees the essence of the evolutionary process in the field of information, know-how, programmed instructions, and so on, leading the human race to consciousness and a great expansion of know-how through the development of 'know-what'—that is, consciously knowledge."[21] This transference of "know-how" to "know-what" is only possible because of the capacity of individuals to communicate via language. "Know-how" is embedded in the gene structure of animals—a chicken egg, for example "knows how" to become a chicken—but human progress includes both "know-how" and "know-what."

A key question for economists, then, falls well outside the confines of neoclassical equilibrium theory: How are people within complex, advanced society generally able to convert "know-how" into "know-what" when, in fact, there is no central authority or data bank through which this knowledge flows? "A very important principle of economic production is that the know-how which is the foundation of it is not held in any single mind," argued Boulding, "but is scattered among many minds and has to be coordinated through processes of communication."[22] This has been one of the guiding questions of subjectivist economics from Menger to Hayek, and Boulding's approach (if not always his conclusions) was consistent with that research program. On the other hand, neoclassical general equilibrium models, beginning with Walras, basically ignore the question by assuming perfect information. Even the models of imperfect information introduced into economics within the last generation assume an objective knowledge of the statistical distribution of possibilities. Real uncertainty remains untractable even in the most advanced models of information economics. In a fundamental sense, this is because mainstream models can

21. Kenneth E. Boulding, *Ecodynamics* (New York: Sage, 1978), 20.
22. Kenneth E. Boulding, *Evolutionary Economics* (New York: Sage, 1981), 186.

only incorporate "know-what"—objective data—and must remain silent on "know-how."

The confidence with which neoclassical economists assert the efficiency of the market system seems to rise and fall with external events. After the Great Depression and World War II, economic theory often stressed how the real-world market economy failed to live up to the ideal of the model of perfect competition. In other words, imperfections in the objective data failed to guide resource use efficiently, and thus, corrective government measures were necessary. Recently, and especially with the collapse of socialism in Eastern Europe and the former Soviet Union, neoclassical economists have tended to emphasize the comparative ability of the decentralized price system to generate efficient outcomes. In either case the similarity to the subjectivist questions concerning the use of knowledge is only superficial.

Boulding was too sharp to accept fully the formal neoclassical arguments on either the strengths or weaknesses of the price system. It is not so much that neoclassical economics is wrong when it cautions about the pathologies of the price system or champions the strength of the market economy to generate efficient outcomes, as much as the theory says too little about how the system accomplishes what it does, and how other social systems are also employed within society to coordinate people's plans and images.[23]

> Boulding emphasized a more interdisciplinary approach and identified at least three systems that coordinate individuals within society—prices, politics, and preachments—his so-called three Ps.[24] The coordination of complex societies requires more than market prices. Political systems (systems of law, protection of property rights, the power of threat) as well as integrative systems (systems of morals, ethics, love, and kinship) are just as crucial to legitimate economic institutions and provide a trust in

---

23. This was part of Boulding's critique of the Whig theory of the history of economic thought, i.e., the belief that all that was good in the ancients has been incorporated in the moderns. On the contrary, Boulding argued that earlier writers, such as Adam Smith, may have contained wisdom which our modern techniques overlook. See Kenneth E. Boulding, "After Samuelson, Who Needs Adam Smith?" *History of Political Economy 3* (Fall 1971): 225–37.

24. Boulding, *Ecodynamics,* 2–24; Boulding, *Evolutionary Economics,* 177–80.

both face-to-face and more socially anonymous interaction. His *Three Faces of Power* (New York: Sage, 1990) is a primer to a social theory that attempts the difficult intellectual feat of integrating the interdependent, but conceptually distinct, coordinating systems of modern society.

Boulding the Disciplinary Trespasser: A Conclusion

Few scholars in the twentieth century had Kenneth Boulding's remarkable ability to speak across disciplines, from economics and biology to sociology and ecology to mathematics and systems research, and to say something sensible and insightful. Few people will.

One of the methodological threads that ties much of Boulding's far-reaching analysis together was his radical subjectivism, germinating early in his technical economics articles in the 1930s and 1940s, surfacing in *The Image* in the 1950s, and flourishing, both implicitly and explicitly, throughout most of his later social analysis. We hope that this chapter properly places Boulding within the American branch of modern subjectivist economics and, moreover, that it might encourage others in the tradition critically to explore further the fruits of Boulding's theoretical contributions.

8

Putting the "Political"
Back into Political Economy

Warren Samuels

WARREN SAMUELS HAS spent his scholarly career examin-
ing the intellectual history and internal logic of arguments concerned with
the economic role of government. He has been quite eclectic in his approach
and has studied deeply the thought of the classical economists and modern
economists such as Pareto, Knight, Hayek, Coase, and Buchanan, as well as
those scholars working within the institutionalist tradition of economic and
political economy scholarship. While he has cast a rather wide net for study, his
basic message has been rather consistent. Samuels emphasizes the irreducible
embeddedness of all economic processes in the political and legal nexus. This
is a significant point to emphasize, especially when we remember the post-
1950s effort by economists to develop an institutional antiseptic theory of the
economic process. By emphasizing the framework within which all economic
activity takes place, Samuels has sought to put the political back into political
economy and as such, he surely deserves to be recognized as one of the foremost
scholars responsible for resurrecting political economy in the second half of
the twentieth century.

To illustrate the Samuels contribution to the research program of modern
political economy, I will examine his engagement with James M. Buchanan in
the 1970s. The debate took place not only in their exchange in *Journal of Law
and Economics*, but in private correspondence between these two scholars that
was subsequently published in the *Journal of Economic Issues*. I am quite sympathetic to Samuels's position as articulated in the article and correspondence
with regard to the embeddedness of economic action within a political and
legal nexus, and I appreciate his point about the essential nonneutrality of all
state action (including action associated exclusively with pursuing a so-called

laissez-faire policy). However, I do not go all the way with him in terms of the implication of the argument. Here, I will pick up a point stressed by Buchanan on the relative position of the status quo in political economy analysis, which Samuels does not fully appreciate in the exchange with Buchanan. This is a point of analytical economics that has normative implications and not a normative endorsement of whatever exists at the beginning of our analysis. After laying out the positions, I will illustrate this Buchanan-inspired caveat to the Samuels position by reference to a discussion of transitional political economy in the former Soviet Union.

Samuels does not like school labels and I appreciate his resistance to this intellectual habit more and more as my career matures. I considered a subtitle to this chapter that read "Lessons from an Old Institutionalist to a New Austrian," which conveys some vital information, for Samuels's contribution is an *institutionalist* critique of orthodox political economy. But it goes beyond those earlier arguments found in writers such as Commons and Hale, though it has intellectual roots in those arguments. On the other hand, I am the most closely associated with work in the Austrian tradition of economics and the Virginia School of Political Economy, though perhaps someday we can just talk about political economy without the labels and still be able to understand each other. The Samuels exchange with Buchanan demonstrates how two honest and reasonable scholars coming at fundamental questions from radically divergent perspectives can nevertheless find common ground. Despite my only according to Samuels two cheers in his exchange with Buchanan, as opposed to the full three cheers, I want this common ground to be recognized. There is much that a student of Hayek and Buchanan can learn from a student of Commons and Hale, and I have taken advantage of that opportunity.

Samuels was never my teacher in the formal sense of the term, but I came under his guiding influence in my first year of graduate school, even though I was in Fairfax and he was located in East Lansing. That influence has been with me ever since. We met through a paper I had written as a first-year graduate student on the relationship between the Austrians and the institutionalists, and specifically the common ground between these two often-antithetical schools on the importance of evolutionary change for economic understanding. In writing that paper I had read a similar working paper by Samuels on the topic. These papers were eventually published with commentary by others in the annual *Re-*

search in the History of Economic Thought and Methodology.[1] But our contact was more than those papers: he came to present a paper at GMU, and we exchanged letters and met at HES meetings and discussed an entire range of topics over the years. When I took my first teaching job at Oakland University in Rochester, Michigan, Samuels got me involved with his weekly workshop at Michigan State (a rather short drive from Rochester) and he came and gave presentations at Oakland University and then later also at NYU when I moved there after two years in Michigan. Much of my thinking has been shaped by Samuels, in terms of both style (including professional attitude toward those with whom you have intellectual disagreement, the values of scholarship that are required to advance the dialogue in political economy, and the generosity shown to junior colleagues starting out in the professional discourse) and substantive propositions in economic theory, methodology, and political economy. He has not shaken me of some of my cherished beliefs, but he has made me aware of how much some of those beliefs are more acts of faith than of reason. The current chapter attempts to provide some good reasons why incorporating the Samuels lesson on embeddedness can nevertheless reinforce some of those cherished beliefs about private property, permanence and predictability in the law, and the contractual nature of realist reform.

Cedar Rust and Apple Orchards

Samuels chose the case of *Miller et al. v. Schoene* to examine the essential nonneutrality of limited government because it is a simple illustration of the basic principles of the interdependence of the economic, the legal, and the political.[2] The case concerns the constitutionality of legislation enacted in Virginia in 1914 and was heard before the Supreme Court in 1928. The case involves red cedars and apple trees and their respective owners. Red cedars were vulnerable to developing a plant disease called cedar rust. While cedar rust was harmless to the host cedar trees, the fungus was fatal to apple trees. In 1914, the state

---

1. Warren J. Samuels, "Austrians and the Institutionalist Compared," *Research in the History of Economic Thought & Methodology* 6 (1989), 53–72.
2. Warren J. Samuels, "Interrelations between Legal and Economic Processes," *Journal of Law & Economics,* in *Essays on the Economic Role of Government: Volume 1—Fundamentals* (1971; repr., New York: New York University Press, 1992), 139–55.

legislature of Virginia passed as statute that empowered apple tree owners to employ the state legal apparatus to uphold their rights with respect to the destructive force of the red cedar fungus. The plaintiffs in the case, *Miller et al.*, argued that the legislature had unconstitutionally "taken" their property to the benefit of the apple orchard owners. Private property, they argued, had been taken without compensation not for public use, but to benefit another group of private owners.

Samuels argues that this case illustrates the necessity of government to make a choice to support one set of rights at the expense of another. If the legislature had not enacted the statute which enabled apple growers to appeal to the state entomologist to investigate red cedars within a two-mile radius of their orchards, then the law would have been favoring the owners of red cedars at the expense of the apple orchard. The court ultimately ruled that when such a choice is of necessity, the state is not overstepping its constitutional powers by deciding to destroy the property of one class of owners in order to save another class of property owners. The outcome of this particular case is not Samuels's concern. Instead, as he puts it, it is "the ineluctable necessity of choice" that the case highlights that is relevant for exploring the fundamentals of political economy. "The state had to make a choice as to which property owner was to be made not only formally secure but practically viable in his legal rights."[3] Without state action to protect the apple growers against the lost value of their destroyed trees, the existing property law would have disadvantaged the apple growers in respect to the red cedar owners. In other words, one group is going to be protected in their rights, the other is not, and the state must choose which. The generalizable proposition that Samuels wants the reader to walk away with is that it is never the case that the choice is between government or no government, intervention or laissez-faire. Laissez-faire, in a fundamental sense, is conceptually bankrupt. "Market forces emerge and take on shape and slope only within the pattern of, *inter alia*, legal choices as to relative rights, relative exposure to injury and relative coercive advantage or disadvantage."[4] Once we move away from ideologically charged discussion, we can dispassion-

---

3. Samuels, "Interrelations," 142.
4. Samuels, "Interrelations," 144.

ately recognize that government is omnipresent as the basic framework against which all economic activity takes place. In this particular case, "it is a matter of which interest government will be used to support."[5]

Samuels' point is well taken and his emphasis on the embedded nature of all economic activity with the political and legal setting is an important point which was not always explicitly recognized in the public choice and law and economics tended to emphasize how the tools of economic reasoning (maximizing and equilibrium) could be used to address questions in the political and legal nexus. The examination (from the other direction) of how the political and legal shape of economic outcomes was not yet part of the research agenda. Political economy at the time was either a term deployed to describe Marxian scholarship, or a nascent (but growing) rational choice approach to political, legal, and sociological scholarship. Thus, Samuels's emphasis on the embeddedness of economic activity within the political and legal nexus represented an important alternative vision of political economy and served as a corrective to the idea of disembodied economic processes. The Nobel Prize committee has recognized James Buchanan (politics) and Ronald Coase (law) as being pioneers in the development of this rational choice approach to political economy. Ironically, while both men are correctly identified with the founding of both the public choice and law and economics movements, they both had (and continue to have) serious reservations about the way the fields have developed. And the reservations of both come from the crowding out of the embeddedness side of the research program that Samuels emphasizes. I will restrict my comments to Buchanan's exchange with Samuels on the *Miller et al. v. Schoene* case, emphasizing their common ground with regard to embeddedness, but readers interested in the case of Coase are recommended to read Steve Medema's intellectual biography, *Ronald Coase* (London: Macmillan, 1994).

Negotiated Solutions and the Status Quo

James Buchanan chose to respond to Samuels's interpretation of the *Miller et al. v. Schoene* case because in Buchanan's mind, Samuels's position reflected

---

5. Samuels, "Interrelations," 145.

the "received wisdom" of the early 1970s, which resulted in the "omnipresent hand of the state in all our lives."[6] Whereas Samuels had chosen the case because he thought it was "not a case with which one can get readily emotionally or ideologically involved,"[7] to Buchanan the account of Samuels is grounded in a different vision of the social order. Buchanan contends that Samuels's account does not adequately account for the exchange opportunities that would arise in the wake of exogenous changes in the environment. Once the interdependence between the red cedars and apple trees became apparent with the introduction of cedar rust, in Buchanan's language, "potential gains from exchange should have existed that would have allowed this new interdependence to be eliminated."[8] Rather than placing his trust in the exchange process, Buchanan argues that Samuels's story places faith in the legislative/judicial process that can presumably measure the superior benefits of a new arrangement of property rights which is to be imposed without the necessity of compensation. Buchanan's subjectivism does not allow him to follow this argument.

It is important to recognize, however, that Buchanan does not deny that economic processes always take place against the backdrop of some set of property rights. As he says "The principle to be emphasized, however, is that *some* structure, *any* structure, of well-defined rights is a necessary starting point for the potential trades that are required to remove the newly emergent interdependence."[9] The necessary embeddedness of economic action within a legal and political setting is a position shared by both Buchanan and Samuels. They diverge on the role accorded to trading behavior in the resolution of conflict between parties. Buchanan follows the general rule that negotiating away conflicts to internalize costs and benefits is preferred to adjudication; adjudication in a way to clarify the property rights arrangement to ease exchange opportunities is preferred to legislation; and finally, if legislation is to be pursued, it should be limited to situations where public goods problems persist even after efforts at negotiating a

6. James M. Buchanan, "Politics, Property and the Law," *Journal of Law and Economics*, in *Freedom in Constitutional Contract* (1972; repr., College Station: Texas A&M University Press, 1979), 94–109.

7. Samuels, "Interrelations," 139.

8. Buchanan, "Politics," 97.

9. Buchanan, "Politics," 97.

solution have been attempted.[10] But as Buchanan points out, even in such cases where the public goods situation justifies collective interference, the question of how collective action is to be organized is an open one. Buchanan, as is now well understood, relies on the Wicksellian principle of unanimity, which is the collective choice analog to mutual beneficial exchange in the private choice setting. In other words, the principle of mutual agreement remains the criterion for collective action as it did in private action. Rather than seeing the resolution of conflicting claims as being resolved through the state apparatus and the rule of experts relied upon in the *Miller et al. v. Schoene* case as described by Samuels, Buchanan's analysis invokes mutual agreement. Resolution is not being done through either/or, but through compromise and agreement. Both interests agree to adjust their expectations and behavior after the exogenous change in the social setting, which brought about the interdependencies that previously had not been a problem.

By appealing directly to the state, the apple growers truncated the process by which exchange opportunities could have resolved the conflict between the apple orchard and the red cedars. Instead the state was required to assess the value of the damage to the apple trees from cedar rust infestation relative to the damage to the cedar trees from cedar rust infestation relative to the damage to the cedar trees from premature cutting. In the particular case of *Miller et al. v. Schoene*, the state relied on the expert opinion of a Virginia entomologist to make that determination. There are some important points to consider. First, an entomological determination is not necessarily an economic determination, but from the economic point of view we are concerned with approximating a Pareto solution. Second, it should be recognized that the generalizability of the *Miller et al. v. Schoene* case breaks down when the expert is introduced. As Buchanan puts it: "In most economic interdependencies there are no 'experts,' and there are likely to be major errors in any cost-benefit estimates."[11]

---

10. Buchanan argues that the legislative process—an instrument for reconciling separate interests—must be viewed as fundamentally distinct from the judicial process—an instrument for clarifying ambiguities in the existing rights structure. This distinction, Buchanan contends, is absent from the Samuels' discussion. "Politics," 103.

11. Buchanan, "Politics," 98.

Of course, as pointed out previously, Buchanan admits that in the face of a genuine public goods problem (e.g., perhaps the removal of cedar rust in large number situations would qualify) or high transaction costs, the collective decision making of the state legislature might have to substitute for the reconciliation of interests through negotiation. Buchanan points out that the Virginia Cedar Rust Act might have, in fact, recognized the large number problem by requiring a petition of at least ten freeholders before the state entomologist was empowered to act.

Buchanan and Samuels both argue that economic activity is inexorably embedded within political and legal settings. But their approach diverges from this fundamental starting point. Descriptively, Samuels challenges the myth of neutrality of the state in liberal thought. The state is necessarily protecting one set of rights against another whether a decision to intervene is made or not. Samuels is not making a normative judgment here; he does not give us reason to believe he favors apple growers or red cedar growers. It is an exercise in pure description and the analytical implications of such a description of politics, property, and law. To Buchanan this description must be qualified. No doubt the state is invoked to favor one interest over another, but Buchanan wants to ask on what grounds such a decision is made. Since no persuasive metric is offered, Buchanan's suggestion is to circumscribe state action. Neutrality (or nondiscriminatory) state action is not a description in Buchanan, but a goal which the institutional design should be set up to accomplish if it is at all possible.

This is where the position of the status quo enters into Buchanan's analytical system. "There is an explicit prejudice in favor of previously existing rights, not because this structure possesses some intrinsic ethical attributes, and because change itself is undesirable, but for the much more elementary reason that only such a prejudice offers incentives for the emergence of voluntarily negotiated settlements among the parties themselves."[12]

It is the relative status of the status quo as laid out in this passage that to a large extent became the focus of the exchange of thoughtful letters between Samuels and Buchanan that were eventually published by them as "On Some

---

12. Buchanan, "Politics," 109.

Fundamental Issues in Political Economy: An Exchange of Correspondence."[13] Samuels accuses Buchanan of privileging the status quo as a normative ideal for conservative purposes, while Buchanan counters that it is actually Samuels who is the defender of the status quo. Samuels responds that it is true that both he and Buchanan have subjective perceptions of the world, but Buchanan has a built-in presumption for the status quo, while he is only providing a descriptive starting point for the critical discussion of the status quo. The correspondence between them on this issue begins in 1972, ends in 1974, and contains 13 letters.[14] There is some inevitable talking past each other, but there is also the further clarification of respective positions that comes with reiteration of an argument. However, to this reader the issue of the status quo is never satisfactorily addressed because the positive, the normative, and the pragmatic are conflated in the exchange.

The status quo in Buchanan's work has elements of the positive, the normative, and the pragmatic to it. But the normative enters into the analysis not as Samuels suggests. There is no normative weight to be accorded to the status quo position. Instead, the status quo serves primarily as positive—this is the world in which we find ourselves—and pragmatic—real reform cannot begin but from the existing status quo. In other words, Buchanan emphasizes in various writings, that realism in political economy (what he terms "politics without romance") must begin with the "here and now" and not some imaginary ideal that the analyst would like to impose on the system. In the case of the red cedar growers and the apple tree growers, Buchanan's analysis begins with the existing property law prior to the Cedar Rust Act because it is that arrangement that needed to be adjusted. Samuels comes to understand this point in his correspondence with Buchanan, but he insists that "the problem is that there is no agreement on the mechanism of change." But it is on this point that the pragmatic value of the status quo is not completely appreciated. Samuels insists, correctly to my mind, that Buchanan often attempts to "simulate with logic

---

13. Warren J. Samuels and James M. Buchanan, "On Some Fundamental Issues in Political Economy: An Exchange of Correspondence," *Journal of Economic Issues*, in *Essays on the Methodology and Discourse of Economics* (1975; repr., New York: New York University Press, 1992), 201–30.

14. Samuels and Buchanan, "Fundamental Issues," 205.

what is *in reality* a function of power, knowledge and psychology."[15] This move in Buchanan is most evident in his work on the basic social contract derived behind a veil of ignorance (or uncertainty). But even here, isn't it really the case that Buchanan's point is a pragmatic one rather than a justificatory one? I choose to interpret the Buchanan point as not denying the function of power, knowledge, and psychology, but instead as beginning with that existing reality as the necessary starting point of analysis. Buchanan does not, to go back to the specific case, deny that under older property arrangement the introduction of cedar rust presents us with a conflict between the different owners. The presence of the new interdependency is what drives the exchange opportunity between the two parties to negotiate away their conflict. In other words, Buchanan denies two levels of "either/or" propositions that are contained in Samuels—the either/or choice at the level of the analysis between the two parties to the exchange, and the either/or choice at the level of social theory. Thus, Samuels's claim that "so long as anarchy without social control is repugnant, the problem boils down to what (whose) system social control"[16] has different implications for Buchanan. Social "control" in terms of the establishment of the rules of the game is a major theme in all of Buchanan's writings, but within that framework of rules the driving force of the analysis from one state of affairs to another state of affairs is the vehicle of mutual agreement—either through the mechanism of economic exchange or democratic consensus building through the unanimity principle.

It is the compensation principle that is at the core of Buchanan's analysis of the transitional path. We begin with existing rights claims and the social arrangement of power, knowledge, and psychology not because that situation is normatively desirable, but because it represents the "here" that must be transformed to get "there" if that is so desired. It is, as I said above, a blend of the positive (to accurately describe the "here"), the normative (to posit why the "there" would be a "better" situation), and the pragmatic (to analyze potential paths from "here" to "there"). Samuels contends that this position is ultimately confusing; as he says in the correspondence, the Buchanan argument

---

15. Samuels and Buchanan, "Fundamental Issues," 209.
16. Samuels and Buchanan, "Fundamental Issues," 209.

is hard to follow because "Part is against change and part is for change and the part that is for change is against all but contractual change thereafter."[17]

In defense of his position, Buchanan responds to Samuels in the following manner:

> But my defense of the *status quo* stems from my unwillingness, indeed inability, to discuss changes other than those that are contractual in nature. I can, of course, lay down my own notions and think about how God might listen to me and impose these changes on me, you and everyone else. This seems to me what most social scientist do all the time. But, to me, this is simply wasted effort. And explains most of the frustration. It seems to me that our task is really quite different, that of trying to find, locate, invent, schemes that change command unanimous or quasi-unanimous consent and propose them. Since persons disagree on so much, these schemes may be a very limited set, and this may suggest to you that few changes are possible. Hence, the *status quo* is defended indirectly. That *status quo* has no propriety at all save for its existence, and it is all that exists. The point I always emphasize is that we start from here and not from somewhere else. And, as an economist, all I can do is try to talk about and explain ways of changing that are conceptually contractual, nothing more. This does allow me to take a limited step toward normative judgments or hypothesis, namely to suggest that the changes seem to be potentially agreeable to everyone. Pareto efficient changes, which must, of course, include compensations. The criterion in my scheme is agreement, and I cannot stress this too much. My approach is strictly Wicksellian here.[18]

Samuels, in response, correctly points out that while Buchanan's approach might posit that the status quo does not have any propriety save its existence, the unanimity criterion does privilege the existing situation. "Change or continuity of the *status quo* is a normative matter and your approach builds in the continuity of the *status quo*."[19] It seems to me that Samuels is right here; there

---

17. Samuels and Buchanan, "Fundamental Issues," 213.
18. Samuels and Buchanan, "Fundamental Issues," 215.
19. Samuels and Buchanan, "Fundamental Issues," 217.

is a "conservatism" built into the analysis as Buchanan develops the approach. But what is the alternative? We have to begin somewhere in our analysis, and realism in political economy demands that we begin with the existing set of arrangements. Furthermore, what exactly would be the alternative to the mutual agreement model in politics, and why would it have any normative weight? A mutual-consent-driven model does not have to deny Samuels's points about either the nonneutrality of affairs or the necessity of choice between rights claims as points of fact, but it does suggest that we can strive to minimize the impact of nonneutrality (a goal rather than a description) and we can provide an environment within which negotiated solutions to conflicts between agents can be pursued as much as humanly possible.

Implications for Transitional Political Economy

The former Soviet-type economy is often portrayed as a centrally planned economy. This description misses out on the de facto organizing principles of that social system of production by focusing exclusively on the de jure pronouncements of economic organization. However, we must also be willing to peer underneath given institutions and explore the practices which govern economic life in a society. In a fundamental sense, markets existed throughout the long history of Soviet planning, they just were pushed into a sub rosa level of existence. The basic institutions of a Western market society, for example, do not accord well with the lived experience of the Soviet peoples with markets. Within the Soviet underground setting the institutions of pricing and bargaining took concrete form. But they did so within an environment of black (and other colored) markets without well-defined or enforced property rights, and with a shortage of goods and lack of alternative supply networks. If we just look at the simplest depiction of this shortage economy situation, then we can start to see the problem for transitional political economy that must be addressed. See Figure 8.1.

This very simple supply and demand configuration brings to the forefront the basic fact that in a shortage situation, the real price of obtaining the good in a shortage economy is higher than the official price. There is a gap between quantity demanded and the quantity supplied which creates a situation where there are nonmonetary costs to buyers associated with acquiring the good.

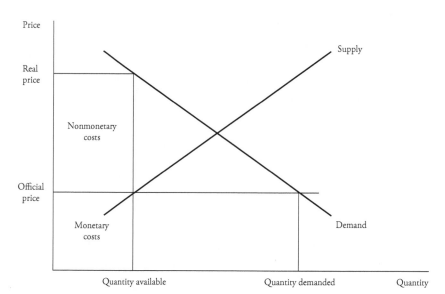

Figure 8.1. Basic Supply and Demand Analysis

Under "normal" market conditions, the costs to buyers are simultaneous benefits to sellers. But in the artificial shortage situation (caused by administered pricing), the nonmonetary costs are not immediate benefits to the sellers, so the seller has a strong incentive to transform those nonmonetary costs to buyers into benefits (monetary or nonmonetary) for themselves. In other words, what this simple diagram reveals is the "rents" that are to be had by those who can exploit the shortage situation—rents that took the form of monetary "bribes," "black market profits," and nonmonetary "privileges" to those in special favor with the ruling elite.

Changing this situation is not just a matter of freeing prices so they can adjust to the market clearing level. "Getting the prices right" is not enough. Those who have been in a position to convert the nonmonetary costs to buyers into benefits for themselves basically have a "property right" in the existing arrangement. By analogy we can say that the nomenklatura was in a position similar to the red cedar owners in the *Miller et al. v. Schoene* case discussed by Samuels and Buchanan.

In Samuels's interpretation of the case, the state is required to make a choice either to support the existing arrangement, which benefits the red cedar growers, or a new property rights system, which supports the apple orchard. The older property rights arrangement was nonproblematic until the exogenous shock of cedar rust introduced an interdependency that had not previously existed. In Buchanan's interpretation, the existence of the interdependency provides an opportunity for mutually beneficial exchange, but this option was not pursued because recourse to the state for resolution was pursued rather than negotiation.

Running through these arguments about changing property rights in the post-Soviet context, I believe, highlights the importance for political economy of Buchanan's status quo. In the case of *Miller et al. v. Schoene*, Buchanan objects to the legislative change in property rights because it didn't follow the compensation principle. Samuels counters that this prejudices Buchanan's position to the status quo—in this case, the preexisting property statutes, which favored the red cedar growers over the apple orchards. In the post-Soviet case, the Buchanan analysis would also suggest the use of the compensation principle as the guide for reform. Begin the analysis by recognizing that some members in that society possess a property right in the rent (the box in Figure 8.1 labeled "Nonmonetary costs"). In other words, they have control over an asset (position) and guard that asset to make sure they receive benefits that accrue from that ownership claim. They will only agree to give up that property right for compensation (in the limit of the present value of the future income stream of their property right).

There is nothing desirable about the preexisting Soviet situation from the point of view of my analysis, nor am I postulating anything desirable about compensating the nomenklatura for giving up their privileged positions. The point is, and it is the same point suggested by Buchanan, that reform in a manner which does not privilege the will of one over the will of others can only be accomplished following the compensation principle. This move is sometimes quite costly—in fact, if you look at Figure 8.1 closely, you can see that it might cost more to compensate the preexisting rent-holder for their loss of the future income stream than will be the benefits received by buyers as a result of eliminating the artificial scarcity, depending on the slope of the supply and demand curves. Moreover, high transaction costs may prevent such a deal from being brokered successfully. These concerns are important, but they are secondary to the main point to be stressed—that realism in reform must begin with the existing rights and talk about how to make moves to assure the transition from one set of arrangements to another.

If the compensation principle is not followed in the wake of an exogenous shock (e.g., introduction of the fungus cedar rust, or the collapse of the communist system), then what will the new existing property owners expect when they are confronted with the next exogenous shock? If their expectations are formed on the basis of their previous experience, then they will expect that their property rights could be reassigned without consent or compensation. Accordingly, they will shorten the time horizon of investment and by thwarting the expansion of the market limit the opportunities for specialization and exchange. In short, further opportunities for mutual benefit will be undeveloped and thus unexploited.

This quasi-abstract discussion took on concrete form in the recent privatization debates in the former Soviet Union. The argument I laid out for privatization in my book, *Why Perestroika Failed: The Politics and Economics of Socialist Transformation* (New York: Routledge, 1993), was for privatization by the nomenklatura. The position was influenced by the Buchanan (and Tullock) argument concerning the relative position of the status quo and the problems of reforming the rent-seeking society. Given the rather high transactions costs associated with a lump sum transfer to compensate the preexisting "property owners," I argued that the Russian government should simply formally recognize these de facto owners, and then commit to a policy of free entry and zero subsidies. I argued that this would effectively buy out the existing owners by compensating them by formally giving them the cash flow rights to firm assets in addition to their existing control rights over those assets. At the same time, the threat of domestic and foreign entry would ensure that the existing system was not privileged, and instead would lead to a changing structure of rights enacted through mutual agreement and evolutionary adjustment as new opportunities presented themselves along several dimensions.

This argument was too optimistic. The counterargument at the time took on two forms—either postpone privatization or pursue it without recognizing the preexisting owners. Neither of these arguments were (are) persuasive in my opinion. The over-optimism concerned the desire of the post-Soviet government to create conditions of entry. The compensation principle was followed to some extent during the mass privatization, but the second round of entry and zero subsidies was not. Basically, the same subsidization of the Soviet economy continued in the post-Soviet period.[20] Entry was discouraged with regard to large-scale industry, and discriminatory taxation and burdensome regulation have directed new entry in smaller-scale production into an underground existence. The above-ground economy is concerned with restructured (or half-restructured) former state industrial enterprises and the rents that are still possible to garner through political action. As a result, Russia is still a far way from moving along the path toward a private property market economy.

My particular diagnosis of the Russian reform effort is not the point of this detour. Instead, I hoped to highlight the issues that are in the Samuels and Buchanan exchange. Samuels makes much sense when he emphasizes that economic actions are embedded within the political and legal nexus. Moreover, he makes great sense when he insists that the state is an institution, which can be, and will be, used by some to exploit others. The state, in this sense, is nonneutral at the core. But, Buchanan's concern that reform must begin here and now also seems right to me. Furthermore, the emphasis on how, beginning in the here and now, the compensation principle must guide the move from here to there unless we want to resort to means beyond mutual agreement is compelling.

Conclusion

Samuels has raised our level of understanding of the political, legal, and social embeddedness of the economy. In fact, he has emphasized not just the interrelations between these separate spheres of social control, but their essential bondedness. They produce and reproduce each other through their operation. The economy takes concrete shape only in relation to the legal and political setting; change the structure of rights and the economy is reconfigured.

Samuels has also raised our awareness of the issue of power within society, including in the economy. In social construction, he has argued, the key policy question is always about whose interests are to count and whose can be ignored. The answer to that question is always defined within the political-legal process

---

20. B. Ickes and Clifford Gaddy, "Russia's Virtual Economy," *Foreign Affairs* (Fall 1998). vol. 77 (5), 53–67.

and is shaped by existing power relations found in government, in the economy, and in society. Samuels has further advanced our understanding of these issues by highlighting the role of ideology and belief systems in social systems and modes of analysis. As Samuels puts it:

> Rights are not produced in a black box called government; and the economy does not operate on its own. A legal-economic nexus is formed by the process in which both are simultaneously (re)determined. At the heart of society and of social (including legal) change is control and use of the legal-economic nexus, and at the heart thereof is the exercise of government, power and belief system. The fundamentals of the legal-economic nexus are not as simple and obvious as contemplated by views that maintain that the polity and economy are pre-existent, self-subsistent spheres.[21]

One must appreciate the deep insights that Samuels has given us on the nature of the political economy and the contribution he has made throughout his distinguished career to our discourse on that subject. But I fear that his concern with institutions of mutual coercion has often (though not always) directed his attention away from the institution of mutual consent. It is not that Samuels does not appreciate the power of the human imagination to realize the mutually advantageous opportunities in the market place, in science, and in cultural transmission. It is just that his work does not emphasize this aspect of human social interaction. In the analysis of legal change, as in the *Miller et al. v. Schoene* case, a blind eye to opportunities for mutually advantageous moves lead to a bias in favor of state action over resolution of conflict through negotiation. But if Samuels is correct in his positive description of the embeddedness of the economy and the power of existing interests, then it seems to me that his analysis must be supplemented with a recognition that the discussion of the transition from one situation to another must begin with the here and now. The status quo must be accorded its appropriate place, not because it is anything special, but simply because it *is*. And once that is incorporated

---

21. Warren J. Samuels, "The Legal-Economic Nexus," *George Washington Law Review*, in *Essays on the Economic Role of Government: Volume 1—Fundamentals* (1989; Repr., New York: New York University Press, 1992), 162–86.

into the analysis, the compensation principle becomes the guiding method by which we are able to make whatever improving moves (however small or great) we can make in this world. In short, Samuels's descriptive analysis of social control can be (perhaps must be) the beginning of our analysis, but it is not enough of an analytical framework to address the issue of the political economy of social change. Power, knowledge, and belief systems must be at the core of our analysis, but continuity, predictability, and compensation must be as well. The resulting Buchanan/Samuels hybrid framework provides a blend of the descriptive, the pragmatic, and the normative to forge a political economy worthy of our classical predecessors.

9

Maximizing Behavior and Market Forces

Gordon Tullock

Introduction

GORDON TULLOCK'S CONTRIBUTIONS to political economy have been well documented. Concepts such as "logrolling," "the vote motive," and "rent-seeking" that were explored in detail by Tullock are now part of the common language of economists and political economists. As James Buchanan has argued, Tullock is a "natural economist."[1] The natural economist, like a "natural" in athletics, exhibits outstanding attributes for the field before formal training. In the case of athletics this is usually seen in terms of explosive speed, great agility, and amazing hand-eye coordination. In economics, the attributes are different and usually are associated with an ability to penetrate analytical puzzles and offer logically sound arguments quickly.[2] The natural economist thinks like an economist without thinking about it. In other words, natural economists see individuals in all contexts as rational actors facing trade-offs in their decisions and choosing the utility-maximizing path. Ethical and moral precepts do not cloud the analysis. By taking this perspective so consistently, even in arenas where this approach was unknown, Tullock revealed new terrain in law, politics, science, and sociobiology that even today is only partially explored. Individuals in nonmarket settings, as well as their counterparts in the

---

1. James M. Buchanan, "The Qualities of a Natural Economist," in *The Collected Works of James M. Buchanan: Ideas, Persons, and Events*, vol. 19 (Indianapolis, IN: Liberty Fund, 2001), 95–107.

2. After a seminar at George Mason University several years ago, Gordon asked me what I thought was the answer to an empirical puzzle that he raised in the seminar, I replied that I was not that quick on my feet. Tullock in characteristic fashion pointed to the chair next to me and said, "Sit down then." He wanted an answer.

competitive market economy, follow the same motivational-behavioral model and thus the economist can predict patterns of behavior across a variety of activities and environments.

Tullock's creative applications of the economic way of thinking often follow the analytical path of inferring intentions from outcomes. Where does this leave the so-called unintended consequences of human action? The concept of unintended consequences is at the core of the economic analysis of the "invisible hand" or "spontaneous order." If the "rents" that flow to special interest groups are a product of deliberate design, does this mean that Tullock's economics has little to do with unintended consequences?

It is my task to argue that Tullock's economics is grounded in a deep appreciation of invisible hand explanations. As Nozick argues, invisible hand explanations require the explicating of *filtering processes* and *equilibrium processes*.[3] The motivational-behavioral model of self-interest alone cannot provide such an explanation. It may be a necessary component, but it is certainly not sufficient. The natural economist will prove to be not such a natural unless he or she understands that context matters and that there is a gap between the choices of individuals and the social outcome that is a function of the institutional environment of choice. The institutional environment provides the filtering process, and the combination of the motivational-behavioral model with an identification of the filtering mechanism produces an understanding of processes of adjustment that generate an equilibrium state, if no other changes are introduced.

Tullock's insistence on applying the economic way of thinking far beyond the realm of market competition and monetary calculation has resulted in a deeper appreciation of the conditions that produce social cooperation or social conflict. Within an institutional environment of private property and freedom of exchange, self-interested behavior can result in public good (the invisible hand). On the other hand, outside of the private property setting, the filtering processes and equilibrium processes at work will steer self-interested behavior in directions that produce public "bad" (tragedy of the commons). Another way to view this is that the social game is always played by self-interested actors, but Tullock's work argues that the rules of that game will determine whether

---

3. Robert Nozick, *Anarchy, State and Utopia* (New York: Basic Books, 1974), 18–22.

we are playing positive sum, zero sum, or negative sum games. That insight, I would argue, is just as important to identifying the natural economist, as the motivational-behavioral assumption they make about humanity.

Simons' Syllabus and the Cultivation of an Economist

As a matter of personal biography, Tullock received very little training as an economist as he is quick to tell anyone. But the training he did receive was of the highest level one could get. Tullock was a student at the University of Chicago School of Law and he took the basic economics course from Henry Simons. This course, as Tullock readily admits, changed his life. It instilled in him a curiosity for the discipline and gave him enough background so that he could teach himself to be a professional economist.[4] What did one learn from Simons' course in economics? First, that "economics is primarily useful, both to the student and to the political leader, as a prophylactic against popular fallacies."[5] Second, that economic analysis began with the systematic exploration of the debates over government policy. Third, that the first task of economics is to understand the operation of the market economy and that analysis proceeds by assuming private property, freedom of contract, freedom of choice, and a monetary system. And, it is important to stress that the demonstration of the social order that emerges under those assumptions is not a normative exercise in apology of the capitalist system, but a positive analysis of how the system works. Fourth, that economic analysis necessarily makes simplifying assumptions, but that the goal is to streamline the analysis without making it irrelevant. And, finally, assuming an institutional environment of private property, freedom of contract, freedom of choice and the monetary system, the price system will guide production and consumption in a way that results in an allocatively

---

4. In his preface to *Simons' Syllabus*, Tullock describes the "dramatic conversion" that resulted from his experience in Simons' class. Tullock states simply that the course "clearly changed my life." Gordon Tullock, preface to *Simons' Syllabus,* by Henry C. Simons (Fairfax, VA: Center for the Study of Public Choice), v. He also states that while he may be the only student he knows who became an economist simply by taking Simons' course, he knew several prominent economists who got their introduction to economics through Simons.

5. Simons, *Simons' Syllabus*, 3.

efficient equilibrium, and any departure from that equilibrium will set in motion forces which will equilibrate the system. In fact, Tullock learned from Simons that the fundamental task of price theory is that of explaining the *equilibrium adjustment process* guided by relative price movements.

Economic change in the model that Simons taught resulted from either (a) change in terms of adjustment to given conditions or (b) changes to the underlying conditions, such as tastes, technology and resource ownership. The equilibrium adjustments to given conditions are guided by relative price movements and profit/loss signals. But this method, Simons argued, would also enable the economist to predict reasonably well the consequences of a particular change in the underlying conditions (say as a result of a change in legislation) provided other variables don't change. "Thus, the static analysis, together with a little judgment, may enable us to assert with confidence that, by virtue of particular changes, economic conditions will be different in specified respects from what they otherwise would have been."[6] The static assumptions, as Simons understood them, were not confining, but necessary intellectual tools for helping the student understand the social complexities of the market economy and political economy.

Tullock was convinced by Simons' approach to the economic way of thinking and its influence on him can be seen throughout his teaching and scholarly career. Under competitive conditions, price movements guided a complex and intricate interdependency in economic life that served to coordinate production plans and consumption demands.[7] In *Simons' Syllabus*, while market forces under competitive conditions are the primary focus of analysis, deviation from those conditions are explored in terms of monopoly and cartel situations.[8] The main lessons that Simons stressed in his lectures were (1) that in the real world, unless protected by governmental decree, monopolies face a difficult time exploiting their advantageous situations because of (a) the danger from adverse legislation and/or hostile public opinion in the form of consumer boycott, and (b) the costs of maintaining monopoly power against potential competitors; and (2) that in theory the analysis of monopoly power is important because it demonstrates in

---

6. Simons, *Simons' Syllabus*, 6.
7. Simons, *Simons' Syllabus*, 17–18.
8. Simons, *Simons' Syllabus*, 42–50.

a straightforward manner the losses to the community as a whole of restrictions imposed on market competition by special interest group pleading.

Arguably Tullock's most famous paper in economics "The Welfare Costs of Monopolies Tariffs, and Theft" is a fuller (richer) exploration of these propositions by Simons concerning the problem of monopoly and government policy.[9] In "Entry Barriers in Politics," Tullock builds on the propositions that Simons lays out dealing with potential competitors and anticipates many of the arguments later associated with the theory of contestable markets in the field of industrial organization and applies them to understand the puzzles and paradoxes of politics.[10] In both instances, Tullock's genius was to pursue the argumentative structure developed in basic price theory and apply that style of reasoning to render intelligible phenomena outside the market realm. As we will see, this is arguably true of Tullock's contributions across the board in dealing with market and nonmarket decision making. It is price theory from start to finish in his work, even when the questions are outside the realm of the market economy and there are no prices per se to examine.

Understanding Market Forces, Illuminating Nonmarket Phenomena

Armed with this understanding of the market forces at work in a competitive economy and how the self-interest of the individual can be guided by relative prices and the lure of profit to generate a complex and intricate web of social cooperation, Tullock set out to explain the empirical world in which he found himself early on in the Department of State. Tullock lived in a world of bureaucracy and politics, not in the world of market forces. The same motivational-behavioral model was to be deployed, but within an alternative institutional environment. Rather than through price movements, coordination was obtained through voting, bureaucratic rules, or philanthropic impulse in the environments Tullock chose to explore. The simple question is, what are the filtering processes and equilibrium processes in operation in these institutional environments?

---

9. Gordon Tullock, "The Welfare Costs of Monopolies, Tariffs, and Theft," in *The Selected Works of Gordon Tullock: Virginia Political Economy,* edited by C.K. Rowley, vol. 1 (Indianapolis, IN: Liberty Fund, 2004), 169–79.

10. Gordon Tullock, "Entry Barriers in Politics," in Tullock, *Selected Works,* vol. 1, 69–77.

A classic example that captures Tullock's style of argument is his answer to the apparent result that seatbelts and air bags counterintuitively do not increase highway safety.[11] Reckless driving can account for a large percentage of automobile accident–related deaths. On the road with reckless drivers are also conscientious drivers. Unfortunately, the mandating of seatbelts and air bags lowers the private costs of reckless driving but raises the social costs. The argument is simple. In weighing the expected costs and benefits of driving fast, making U-turns where not allowed, switching lanes, etc., drivers don't only consider the potential cost of the accident, but the benefits of getting to their destinations sooner. In short, recklessness can be modeled as the outcome of a rational deliberation just as conscientiousness is. Safety devices reduce the probability of death and injury from an accident. When government makes these safety devices mandatory, it reduces the expected cost of an accident to those in the car. By reducing the costs associated with reckless driving, the mandate actually increases the probability of accidents (holding other things constant). If the goal of government policy is to reduce recklessness and thus reduce the probability of accidents, then perhaps a more effective government policy would be to mandate that a dagger be mounted on the steering wheel pointed right at the driver's chest. The driver in that situation would clearly have a strong incentive to drive safely.

This example illustrates the ruthlessness with regard to the persistent and consistent application of the logic of economics to the problems of policy. It also reflects Tullock's keen observation that self-interest is not sufficient to explain social outcomes in economic terms. Self-interest is a motivational-behavioral assumption that cuts across observed outcomes, but the outcomes are the result of that motivational-behavioral assumption conjoined with specific institutional contexts that provide a structure of costs versus benefits. Ensuring an environment of safety within the vehicle induces rational choosers to behave one way, while increasing the costs of recklessness via an unsafe environment within the vehicle induces rational choosers to behave differently. The counterintuitive irony in Tullock's narrative is how internal vehicle safety results in more dangerous driving, while a certain lack of internal vehicle safety will result in more conscientious driving. Tullock's discussion of how self-interested behavior, when the

---

11. R. McKenzie and Gordon Tullock, *The New World of Economics* (Homewood, IL: Irwin, 1989), 39–42.

costs are borne by that driver, yields a better social outcome is reminiscent of the style of reasoning that one finds in Adam Smith's discussion of how it is the self-interest of the butcher, the baker, and the brewer that produces our dinner.

Driving, dating, voting, giving at church, and childrearing are just examples of rational deliberation within specific contexts. In deciding whether or not to vote, for example, the individual will consider not only the benefits associated with voting, but the costs of engaging in the act of voting. Well-known propositions in public choice theory concerning rational ignorance, rational abstention, and special interest voting all follow from the persistent and consistent application of economic logic to settings outside of the market economy. *Self-interest is omnipresent, competition is omnipresent, but the way self-interest and competition manifest themselves is institutionally contingent.* Within the context of a market economy with clearly defined and strictly enforced private property rights, Tullock reasons in fairly conventional fashion (as defined by Simons and the Chicago School price theory of 1940s and 1950s), that self-interested behavior will result in lower cost, higher quality products as producers pursue profit by satisfying the demands of consumers. The filter mechanisms in operation in the market economy are the lure of profit and the penalty of loss—which continually reshuffle the pattern of resource use and ownership and spur innovation by entrepreneurs. The path to equilibrium proceeds through relative price adjustments and entrepreneurial arbitrage that push the system toward the optimal conditions when all the gains from trade are realized.

The challenge that Tullock faces in his extension of the logic of economics outside the realm of the market is to identify the alternative filters and equilibrium processes that are in operation in the realm of politics, law and order, human sexuality, and the behavior of nonhuman biological life. Property, prices, and profit/loss do not exist in these realms to discipline actors and channel effort in a direction that aligns private interests and public benefit as they do in the market economy.[12] Individuals still weigh marginal costs (MC) and marginal benefits (MB) in making decisions and will pursue activities provided that MB

---

12. Tullock is not blind to "market failures" and in fact much of his work begins with an admission of deviations from ideal that lead to demands for political and philanthropic solutions. But in examining the filter and equilibrium processes in the proposed solutions, Tullock often provides the pessimistic conclusion that the "cure" of government and philanthropic corrections may be worse than the market "disease" they set out to address.

> MC, but the position and slope of the MB and MC lines are functions of the institutional environment within which choices are being made.

Reconciling Spontaneous Order and Public Choice

A core presumption of public choice economics is that we can infer intentions from outcomes.[13] If legislation is passed to raise the minimum wage above the market wage, and as a result low-wage workers are displaced as economic theory would predict, public choice economists boldly infer that higher wage workers and the legislature must have conspired to pass legislation intended to reduce competition from lower wage workers. Politics is about concentrating benefits on the well-organized and well-informed interest groups, and dispersing costs on the unorganized and ill-informed masses. Stigler put the public choice presumption of inferring intentions from outcomes as follows:

> The announced goals of a policy are sometimes unrelated or perversely related to its actual effects, and the *truly intended effects should be deduced from the actual effects.* This is not a tautology designed to gloss over a hard problem, but instead a hypothesis on the nature of political life. Policies may of course be adopted in error, and error is an inherent trait of the behavior of men. But errors are not what men live by or on. If an economic policy has been adopted by many communities, or if it is persistently pursued by a society over a long span of time, it is fruitful to assume that the real effects were known and desired. Indeed, an explanation of a policy in terms of error or confusion is no explanation at all—anything and everything is compatible with that "explanation."[14]

On the face of it, it seems that this relentless pursuit of linking intentions and outcomes cuts against spontaneous order theorizing of unintended consequences.

---

13. R. Wagner, *To Promote the General Welfare* (San Francisco: Pacific Research Institute, 1989), 56.

14. George Stigler, *The Citizen and the State* (Chicago: University of Chicago Press, 1975), 40.

But this conflict is only apparent. Adam Smith detailed the power of invisible hand processes to channel self-interest into public benefits. But he also recognized that the hidden hand of the sophistry of the merchants can, in concert with government officials, result in special privileges for a few that undermine the prosperity of the general population. Tullock's work in microeconomics and political economy are rooted firmly in this Smithian tradition.

Some critics of spontaneous order theorizing mischaracterize the position arguing that intentionality is absent from the analysis. Hayek's phraseology, some need to be reminded, was of human action though not of human design. As we saw with Nozick, invisible hand explanations begin with the individual deliberating a course of action; proceeding through particular filter processes that are defined by the context of choice, and the pattern of behavior and interaction that results exhibit equilibrium properties. Adam Smith's presentation of the invisible hand proposition followed the same argumentative structure. Smith, it is important to stress, did not presume that acting self-interestedly was enough to ensure a benevolent social order. On the contrary, it is self-interest that guides the statesmen to overburden himself; it is also what leads Oxford dons into not satisfying the educational demands of their students, and teachers of religious doctrine into being less zealous and hard-working in the state-supported religious sects as compared to those sects that rely solely on voluntary contributions.[15] Self-interest also leads the businessman to conspire with his competitors to set price, and to seek out protection from foreign competitors.[16] It is self-interest that is behind the sophistry of the merchants and the manufacturers in the quest for monopolistic status, just as it is self-interest among professors and preachers when they seek secure incomes and protection from competitors in the instruction of philosophy and religious doctrine.

Self-interest is also what drives the refinements in the division of labor, the coordinative activities of an economy guided by relative price movements, and the innovations of the entrepreneur. Self-interest is not unique to laissez-faire,

15. Adam Smith, *An Inquiry into the Nature and Causes of the Wealth of Nations* (1776; repr., Chicago: University of Chicago Press, 1976), bk. IV, ch. II, 478; Smith, *Wealth of Nations,* bk. V, ch. I, 284; Smith, *Wealth of Nations,* bk. V, ch. I, 309.
16. Smith, *Wealth of Nations,* bk. I, ch. 10, 144; e.g., Smith, *Wealth of Nations,* bk. IV, ch. 2, 489–90.

but a regime of laissez-faire (within the specified institutions of natural liberty or what Hume called the system of "property, contract and consent") will channel self-interest in a direction that will maximize the likelihood of a social order of peace and prosperity. When the institutions of natural liberty are absent, or government attempts to thwart their development, Smith's claim was that tyranny and poverty would result.

Tullock's work in spontaneous order theorizing is similar to that of other modern political economists who studied nonmarket decision making, e.g., Thomas Schelling, and often stresses unintended yet undesirable consequences of human action.[17] Whereas most work in the tradition of economics focuses on the market system (with its readily existing carrots and sticks to reward and discipline individual behavior) and the counterintuitive proposition that self-interest can generate public benefit, those scholars that focus on nonmarket decision making tended to show that either self-interest can lead one astray, or that public spiritedness can result tragically in undesired outcomes. There is a dark side to the logic of unintended consequences as well as a bright side, and which direction the system will go will be a function of the institutions in which individuals pursue their self-interest.

A classic example of Tullock's appreciation of spontaneous order in the conventional benign sense of that term can be found in his paper "Adam Smith and the Prisoners' Dilemma."[18] Tullock demonstrates how the discipline of repeated dealings in the market induces cooperation among anonymous strangers and promotes cooperation and trade. The cost of not cooperating is too high because of the market for reputation. As Tullock sums up the argument, if you choose not to cooperate you may soon find that you have no one to noncooperate with. The prisoners' dilemma is thus transformed into a positive-sum game of trade and wealth creation through the filter mechanism of reputation as de-

---

17. Thomas Schelling, *Micromotives and Macrobehavior* (New York: Norton, 1978). Hayek, on the other hand, tends to stress the unintended yet desirable consequences of human action. See, e.g., F.A. Hayek, *The Constitution of Liberty* (Chicago: University of Chicago Press, 1960); Hayek, *Law, Legislation and Liberty*, 3 vols. (Chicago: University of Chicago Press, 1973).

18. Gordon Tullock, "Adam Smith and the Prisoners' Dilemma," in *The Selected Works of Gordon Tullock: Economics without Frontiers*, edited by C.K. Rowley, vol. 10 (Indianapolis, IN: Liberty Fund, 2006), 429–37.

veloped through repeated dealings and a thickening of information flows across markets. Absent that filter, the prisoners' dilemma situation would exhibit an equilibrium tendency to the non-cooperative solution. Politics as rent-seeking can be either a zero-sum or a negative-sum game that leads decision makers to pursue paths of action that reflect self-interest, but results in undesired social outcomes as wealth is either merely redistributed or in the worst case destroyed.

The failures in politics, from this perspective, result not from ignorance and perverse incentives alone, but to the absence of institutions that would work to ameliorate the problems of ignorance and the existence of institutions that instead often exacerbate the perversity of the incentives that actors face in making decisions. Political institutions possess their own filter processes and equilibrium properties, and as such the less-than-ideal patterns that emerge have strong survival characteristics. Recognizing this leads directly to the "constitutional" perspective identified usually with James Buchanan, but to which Gordon Tullock contributed greatly in his own work in political economy. Successful reforms are a consequence of alternative constitutional rules, not in providing better information, or selecting better politicians. An important illustration of this can be seen in Tullock's work on how an appropriate federalist system, characterized by decentralization and competition among government (and empowering the principle of citizens voting with their feet) can improve the public policy choices of government.[19] There is self-interest being followed, there is an institutional environment in place, and there are filter processes at work and equilibrium properties exhibited in his narrative of how competition among government jurisdictions produces a better mix of public policies to satisfy widespread citizen demands. Tullock again exhibits the Smithian style of reasoning about emerging outcomes that he first learned from Henry Simons in his one and only formal class of economics.

Conclusion

The great Chicago economist Frank Knight often remarked that "To say a situation is hopeless is to say it is ideal." Gordon Tullock's work in public choice political economy is not obviously reformist in bent the way that his colleague

---

19. Gordon Tullock, *The New Federalist* (Vancouver: Fraser Institute, 1994).

James Buchanan's work is. But Tullock is not really a pessimist nor an optimist; he is instead a realist. People are what they are; politics is what it is. Markets work because they take people as they are and utilize their base motivations to illicit cooperative behavior from them. Politics, despite the rhetoric of improving mankind and ennobling him through public service, operates on the basis of self-interest no less than markets. But the institutional environment within which political choices are made is radically different from the context of private property, freedom of contract, and profit-and-loss accounting. Due to the altered structure of rewards and penalties, self-interest manifests itself differently than it does in the market economy. But it is self-interest nevertheless that drives human action, and because of that we can as political economists reasonably identify how changing the institutional structure will steer behavior in this or that direction.

In analyzing politics with the same analytical tools that one uses to examine the market order, Tullock was able to make significant and lasting contributions to our understanding of the spontaneous forces that emerge from human action. The patterns of exchange that emerge in our relations in the market, in the courtroom, in the halls of Congress, and, yes, even in the bedrooms of husband and wife were all illuminated with great and nontrivial insight by Gordon Tullock. He tended to emphasize the dark side of the hidden hand of political manipulation by special interests, rather than the bright side of the "invisible hand" of market processes.

But in his analysis Tullock persistently and consistently applied rational choice theory across all walks of human (and nonhuman) life, identifying the filter processes in operation, and the equilibrium properties that are exhibited in the social settings he was studying. When we speak of the twentieth-century heirs of Adam Smith and his invisible hand style of reasoning, Tullock's rich contributions to the field of political economy earned him the right to have his name alongside those of Hayek and Buchanan.

10

Methodological Individualism, Spontaneous Order, and the Research Program of the Workshop in Political Theory and Policy Analysis

Vincent and Elinor Ostrom

Introduction

ONE OF THE MOST exciting developments in the twentieth century in social sciences is the rapid expansion of the style of reasoning and techniques of measurement common in economics into other disciplines. History, law, political science, and sociology were transformed in the 1950s and 1960s through what has become known as the "rational choice" revolution. The earliest developments along these lines were simply focused on the notion that the human actor had to find a central role in any analysis of social life. In other words, the adoption of *methodological individualism* was the crucial step taken by the original scientific revolutionaries. This was in direct contrast to the way the social sciences were carved up at the end of the nineteenth century and beginning of the twentieth century. As areas of study, history focused on the past, anthropology the exotic, law the courts, politics the state, and economics the market. Durkheim, in the face of this intellectual division of labor, decided that sociology would trump all these disciplines by insisting that the "social" was in everything. In the process, he transformed sociology from a general science of human action (which is what it was in the hands of Spencer, Weber, and Simmel) to a discipline focused on the social forces that underlie social reality. Whatever merits the Durkheim approach could be said to have, the consequence of this system of thought was to lose sight of the human actor, the incentives he or she faces, the information he or she must process, and his or her ability to adapt to changing circumstances.

The success of *methodological holism* never impacted economics as a discipline. In the early part of the twentieth century, there were heterodox voices that challenged the methodological individualism of the marginal revolution, and certainly, the Keynesian hegemony from 1940s to 1970s rejected the methodological individualism of economics. But throughout this time, microeconomic analysis never disappeared from its dominant place within the discipline, and thus methodological individualism never lost its strong foothold in economics. The other social sciences were not in the same situation. The reintroduction of methodological individualism to those disciplines was seen as part and parcel of the movement that would be termed "economic imperialism."

By the time the original "imperialists" were either exporting (in the case of James Buchanan) or importing (in the case of William Riker or James Coleman) the basic economic model, the nature of the discipline of economics had transformed itself such that working with the economic model meant not just methodological individualism but an approach to modeling and measuring in the social sciences. Modeling the individual meant optimizing behavior and measuring meant finding statistical significance. Critics of economic imperialism focused on three targets, which are not necessarily interconnected: (1) inappropriateness of methodological individualism, (2) the unrealism of the maximization model as a description of human behavior, and (3) the (a) empirical failure of the maximizing model in terms of statistical tests, and (b) inappropriateness of tests of statistical significance in disciplines hoping to generate *understanding* as opposed to prediction. Many of these criticisms may indeed be valid.

There are at least three problems with this critical tack toward economic imperialism. First, it is unclear that methodological individualism necessarily commits a scholar to maximization models and tests of statistical significance. Second, as compared to existing methodological collectivist explanations, even the most obnoxious maximization and statistical modeling exercise might be superior. In other words, the parsimonious explanation will defeat the more complicated analysis that includes all the social forces that impact the situation under examination. Third, perhaps an empirical approach to the social sciences can be found that both deploys a model of human action in a broader context than maximization models do and focuses on issues of human meaning and understanding the context of choice rather than prediction.

We show that in the first half of the twentieth century a vision of the social sciences was unified—where the human actor was central and the goal was understanding and not prediction—and that this vision was promoted by economists such as Mises, Knight, and Hayek. In the second half of the twentieth century, this research program would be picked up most identifiably in the work of Buchanan and the development of the Virginia School of Political Economy. This imperialism is of a different sort than that practiced by the Chicago School, which is often forgotten in an effort to homogenize all the attempts to work with the economic way of thinking outside the realm of the market. For example, Ronald Coase has rejected the imperialism reflected in Richard Posner's brand of law and economics while most people credit Coase with leading that revolution in legal scholarship. Douglass North finds himself in a similar predicament with regard to cliometrics and scholarship in economic history.

One of the best examples of the methodological individualist research program of the early twentieth century being pushed in a new direction and developed further is the work of Vincent and Elinor Ostrom and the Workshop in Political Theory and Policy Analysis at the University of Indiana. The "Bloomington School" is recognized as one of the three main schools associated with the development of public choice theory—the other two are Rochester (Riker) and Virginia (Buchanan and Tullock). The workshop was founded in the 1970s and, as the name suggests, is grounded in the intellectual commitment to collaborative scholarship between faculty and graduate students and emphasizes the interconnection between problems in theory and the practical problems in public policy. Building on early work done by the Ostroms on the polycentric nature of municipalities and of public goods provision, the workshop has pursued research on federalism, common-pool resources, and the institutional analysis of development. In each of these endeavors, we will argue, the Ostroms' research builds on and refines the approach to the social sciences laid out by Mises, Knight, and Hayek in terms of methodological individualism and spontaneous order.[1] In so doing, they usefully deploy and expand the economic

---

1. Our exercise is actually one of the archaeology of knowledge, as the influences are not direct in terms of pedagogical lineage nor are they always evident in the citation patterns. We are trying to unearth an underlying set of themes. In fact, one could argue that in the archaeology of knowledge one could find a source that influenced the ideas in Knight, Mises, and Hayek that independently influenced the Ostroms' project, such as Tocqueville. As an aside, it has been told to us by an historian of the Mont Pelerin Society that Hayek originally toyed with the idea of naming the Mont Pelerin Society the Tocqueville–Acton Society, but Knight, among others, objected to name the society in this manner due to the Catholicism of Tocqueville and Acton.

way of thinking beyond its traditional boundaries while avoiding most of the criticisms of economic imperialism.

Intellectual Predecessors

Thorstein Veblen was one of the first major critics of the neoclassical conception of the maximizing man. Veblen argued that the anthropological foundations of modern economics were ill-founded and failed to account for the complexity of human choice in a dynamic world. Economics had yet to take an appropriate evolutionary turn in its analysis. Instead, in one of the most famous criticisms of economics penned by an economist yet, Veblen charged that

> The hedonistic conception of man is that of a lightening calculator of pleasures and pains who oscillates like a homogeneous globule of desire and happiness under the impulse of stimuli that shift him about the area, but leave him intact. He has neither antecedent nor consequent. He is an isolated, definitive human datum, in stable equilibrium except for the buffets of the impinging forces that displace him in one direction or another. Self-imposed in elemental space, he spins symmetrically about his own spiritual axis until the parallelogram of forces bears down upon him, whereupon he follows the line of the resultant. When the force of the impact is spent, he comes to rest, a self-contained globule of desire as before. Spiritually, the hedonistic man is not a primer mover. He is not the seat of a process of living except in the sense that he is subject to a series of permutations enforced upon him by circumstances external and alien to him.[2]

Veblen found himself in an awkward position with regard to the Austrian economists and, in particular, Menger. He argued that the discussion of marginal utility and subjective valuation must be seen as an appropriately evolutionary approach to the problems of human choice. Unfortunately, Veblen argued that the Austrians' faulty conception of human nature derailed the project. But what was Veblen's alternative?

---

2. Thorstein Veblen, "Why Is Economics Not an Evolutionary Science?" in *The Portable Veblen*, edited by M. Lerner (1899; repr., New York: Viking Press, 1948), 232–33.

Herein lies the problem with all nonmethodological individualist models of social interaction. If the focus of our analytical attention is to be a dynamic theory of social change, then we must have agents of social change. Unless we fail to focus on these agents of change and instead concentrate on social forces beyond the individual's control, then we will not be able to develop a theory of social change. Veblen's institutionalism, like the caricature of neoclassical economics he penned, does not provide a theory of the process of living but must see change as forced upon us by external and alien circumstances.

The question of the alternative framework must always be considered in these methodological discussions because the real determining factor in the social sciences is not so much truth-value but pragmatic value of the approach. We might not have the true explanation of phenomena, but we might have a useful explanation. The criticism of the homogenous globule engaged in a hedonistic calculation of pleasure and pain should not be directed at descriptive accuracy of whether we have behaved or will behave in such a fashion. The question, instead, is one of whether viewing men in this manner serves our scientific purpose. And clearly for many purposes it does not.

This was recognized by economists such as Mises, Knight, and Hayek, all of whom reject in some form or another the fiction of "economic man." On the other hand, all three are committed methodological individualists and, as we will argue, were the founding fathers of the universal applicability of rational choice theory across the disciplines.

Knight agitated for many years at the University of Chicago for an educational and research program that would blend elements of neoclassical economics with institutional economics. This program never got off the ground in an institutional sense, but Knight's influence on his students was immense. Knight, however, was conflicted on the issue of economics as a science and the broader discipline of political economy. In his essay, "What Is Truth in Economics?" Knight defends the logical foundations of economics against the positivist charge: "The fundamental propositions and definitions of economics are neither observed nor inferred from observation in anything like the sense of the generalizations of the positive natural sciences or of mathematics, and yet they are in no real sense arbitrary."[3] The methodology of the natural sciences

---

3. Frank H. Knight, "What Is Truth in Economics?" *Journal of Political Economy* 48 (1940), 5.

is not applicable to the human sciences, yet the human sciences are capable of generating knowledge of reality. What ensures scientific progress are not positivistic methods, but good scientists. As Knight points out, "Without a sense of honor (as well as special competence) among scientists—if, say, they were all charlatans—there could be no science."[4] Reasoned debate among competent economists is what produces "truth" in economics.

At the core of economic discourse is the economizing human actor. Knight wrote:

> All discussion of economics assumes (and it is certainly "true") that every rational and competent mind knows that (a) some behavior involves the apportionment or allocation of means limited in supply among alternative modes of use in realizing ends; (b) given modes of apportionment achieve in different "degrees" for any subject some general end which is a common denominator of comparisons; (c) there is some one "ideal" apportionment which would achieve the general end in a "maximum" degree, conditioned by the quantity of means available to the subject and the terms of allocations presented by the facts of the given situation.[5]

Knight even goes on to argue that we *know* these economic propositions better than we know any natural science propositions that are derived through observation. We possess knowledge, as it were, from "the inside" because we ourselves are economic actors. Just as we know we are writing rather than just making black markings on a white surface or reading rather than just seeing dark markings, we know the core propositions of economics by living in the world.

Technical economics is limited in scope in Knight's view and largely consists of what could be termed *negative knowledge*—informing on what is wrong with the current situation or a line of thought. Comprehensive social control of individual economic action through the techniques of science is both impossible and abhorrent to humane thinking. Economics cannot serve as a tool for social control, but instead serves as a tool for critical thinking. To move beyond the negative role of economics, the social thinker moves into the realm of value judgments. In order to make such a move legitimately, Knight argues, what is

---

4. Knight, "What Is Truth," 7–8.
5. Knight, "What Is Truth," 16.

needed is "an interpretative study (*verstehende Wissenschaft*) which, however, would need to go far beyond any possible boundaries of economics and should include the humanities as well as the entire field of the social disciplines."[6]

Mises, building on Knight and Weber as well as Menger, attempted to develop a framework for *verstehende Wissenschaft* grounded in the logic of individual action. He entitled the discipline *praxeology*, for the simple reason that the discipline of sociology had, between the time of Weber and Mises, been dominated by methodological collectivism. In this intellectual atmosphere, the economic and sociological perspective that Mises was developing would be met with incomprehension. Instead, as an action-oriented approach to the social sciences, he thought praxeology better captured his disciplinary and methodological intent. "Out of the political economy of the classical school," Mises argued, "emerges the general theory of human action, *praxeology*. The economic or catallactic problems are embedded in a more general science, and can no longer be severed from this connection. No treatment of economic problems proper can avoid starting from acts of choice;[7] economics becomes part, although the hitherto best elaborated part, of a more universal science, praxeology."[8]

Mises argued forcefully for methodological individualism. "Nobody ventures to deny that nations, states, municipalities, parties, religious communities, are real factors determining the course of human events. Methodological individualism, far from contesting the significance of such collective wholes, considers it as one of its main tasks to describe and to analyze their becoming and their disappearing, their changing structures, and their operation. And it chooses the only method fitted to solve this problem satisfactorily."[9] In short, Mises is a methodological individualist and a rational choice social scientist, but he emphatically rejects the mechanical version of rational choice, *homo*

---

6. Knight, "What Is Truth," 31.

7. This starting point for Mises is essential on several grounds, but for our present purposes, we want to highlight that we begin with an individual chooser because it is at the level of the individual that we can attribute meaning to human action in terms of purposes and plans. On the nonarbitrary nature of this starting point for praxeology, see Ludwig von Mises, *Human Action: A Treatise on Economics* (1949; repr., Indianapolis, IN: Liberty Fund, 2010), 39.

8. Mises, *Human Action*, 3.

9. Mises, *Human Action*, 42.

oeconomicus.[10] Instead, Mises insists that, "Economics deals with real actions of real men. Its theorems refer neither to ideal nor perfect men, neither to the phantom of a fabulous economic man (*homo oeconomicus*) nor to the statistical notion of an average man (*homme moyen*). Man with all his weaknesses and limitations, every man as he lives and acts, is the subject matter of catallactics. Every human action is a theme of praxeology. The subject matter of praxeology is not only the study of society, societal relations, and mass phenomena, but the study of all human action."[11]

Hayek, building on these ideas of Knight and Mises, developed an argument for the uniqueness of the human sciences, methodological individualism, and the compositive method in order to study complex phenomena.[12] For the social scientist,

> The problems which they try to answer arise only insofar as the conscious action of many men produce un-designed results, insofar as regularities are observed which are not the result of anybody's design. If social phenomena showed no order except insofar as they were consciously designed, there would indeed be no room for theoretical sciences of society

---

10. Mises, *Human Action*, 62.

11. Mises, *Human Action*, 651.

12. The exemplar of the compositive method is the explanation of the origin of a common medium of exchange. Mises is often read as stressing the logic of human action, while Hayek is read as stressing the spontaneous emergence of social phenomena. However, this reading underestimates Mises's appreciation of spontaneous order and underestimates Hayek's appreciation of the logic of choice as an essential building block in the compositive method of analysis. See Mises, *Human Action*, 405, where he states that, "Carl Menger has not only provided an irrefutable praxeological theory of the origin of money. He has also recognized the import of his theory for the elucidation of fundamental principles of praxeology and its method of research." Also see Hayek's *Individualism and Economic Order*, where he discusses how the logic of choice is a necessary, but not sufficient component to the development of a theory of the market process. The complement to the logic of choice is to be found in an empirical examination of the epistemic properties of alternative institutional arrangements. Empirical knowledge of how actors learn, and how effective that learning is with regard to coordinating their plans with others and utilizing scarce resources in the most efficient manner possible within different social settings, constitutes the complementary scientific knowledge that is able to translate the mere tautologies of the logic of choice into empirically meaningful statements. F.A. Hayek, *Individualism and Economic Order* (1948; Repr., Chicago: University of Chicago Press, 1996), 33–56.

and there would be, as is often argued, only problems of psychology. It is only insofar as some sort of order arises as a result of individual action but without being designed by any individual that a problem is raised which demands a theoretical explanation.[13]

The goal of the social scientist is twofold according to Hayek. First, social phenomena must be rendered intelligible in terms of the purposes and plans of individuals in striving to serve their own interests (methodological individualism). Second, the unintended consequences of those actions must be traced out (spontaneous order). While methodological individualism was at the core of his research project, Hayek rejects the atomism often associated with methodological individualism. And, like Mises, Hayek rejects the *homo oeconomicus* model of man.

Instead, what we get from Hayek is a research program in the social sciences and political economy that is grounded in an analysis of rational choice as conducted by human actors (and not robots) where beliefs, norms, and habits guide the choosing actor.[14] The program, however, is not content with the examination of the situational logic that the actor pursues. The unintended consequences of those actions generate the social order that is the object of study. The most important examples resulting from human action, but not from human design, that Hayek gives in his work of social phenomena are language, cultural norms and mores, money and markets, and law. Social cooperation under the division of labor emerges when the norms and mores of a society support and reinforce the formal institutions of property and contract that enable the expansion of a market economy. Modernity and civilization itself are products of the development of a market economy. In this regard, Hayek is the twentieth-century representative of a line of thought that can be traced back to eighteenth-century figures like David Hume and Adam Smith.

---

13. F.A. Hayek, *The Counter-Revolution of Science* (1952; repr., Indianapolis, IN: Liberty Fund, 1979), 68–69.

14. For an overview of Hayek's research program, see Peter J. Boettke, "Which Enlightenment, Whose Liberalism: F.A. Hayek's research Program for Understanding the Liberal Society," in *The Legacy of F.A. Hayek: Politics, Philosophy, Economics*, edited by Peter J. Boettke, vol. 1 (Cheltenham, UK: Edward Elgar Publishing, 1999) xi–lv. For a more detailed analysis of Hayek's research analysis, see Bruce Caldwell, *Hayek's Challenge: An Intellectual Biography of F.A. Hayek* (Chicago: University of Chicago Press, 2004).

Municipalities, Development, and Self-organization

This basic Humean and Smithian project in the social sciences is what animates the Ostroms' joint project in political economy and public policy. Vincent Ostrom has often complained about social theorists who work in broad-brush categories: market versus planning, free market versus government intervention, civil society versus state, private versus public, and so on, but the characterization of classical political economy as working with such broad brushstrokes is, of course, a mistake. The Scottish enlightenment thinkers were not blunt, but complicated theorists, who understood the complexities of social intercourse. Modern neoclassical economics might be guilty of being unsubtle, but not Hume and Smith, who understood the multidimensionality of human motivation, the institutionally contingent nature of social cooperation, and the law of unintended consequences in human affairs.

Vincent Ostrom recognized that this more subtle approach to political economy is required for a viable research program in public choice. "Neoclassical economic theory relies on a 'model' presuming a perfectly competitive market economy in which fully informed actors participate as buyers and sellers when a price equilibrium is achieved at a point where demand at that price equals the supply offered at that price."[15] But this "model" of human interaction has its problems and limitations in social settings, mainly being divorced from reality. The problem of "model-thinking" is a serious one that often leads to free-floating abstractions rather than engaging in the examination of the realities of human affairs.[16] The absurdities that can result from the pristine economic model

---

15. Vincent Ostrom, *The Meaning of Democracy and the Vulnerability of Democracies* (Ann Arbor: University of Michigan Press, 1997), 98.

16. To criticize "model-thinking," Vincent Ostrom draws on the work of both W. Euken, *The Foundations of Economics* (1940; repr., Chicago: University of Chicago Press, 1951); and H. Albert, "*Modell-Denken und historische Wirklichkeit*," in *Ökonomisches Denken und soziale Ordnung*, edited by H. Albert (Tübingen: J.C. B Mohr, 1984), 39–61. Mises was a major critic of the "model-thinking" of modern economics as well. We suspect that he is not mentioned in the Ostroms' work because many people interpret Mises's methodology as closing off the empirical side of social science, but this is actually a fallacious interpretation. It is true that Mises rejects the positivist epistemology of falsifiability, but this does not mean that his system is blind to empirical reality. "All theorems of economics are necessarily valid in every instance in which all the assumptions presupposed are given. Of course, they have no practical significance in situations where the conditions

are perhaps best exemplified when the model is extended beyond the realm of market exchange to questions in politics, religion, sociology, and law.[17] "Continuing to adhere to an orthodox way of applying 'economic reasoning' to nonmarket decision-making does not allow for learning to occur. An openness to uncertainty, social dilemmas, anomalies, and puzzles as presenting problematics, allows for learning, innovation, and basic advances in knowledge to occur."[18]

The framework of analysis that was developed at the workshop was grounded in an examination of the incentive structures that individuals face in different decision-making contexts, or action arenas. In addition to incentives, the framework also seeks to highlight the knowledge and information that actors acquire and utilize within these different decision contexts. Vincent Ostrom argued that contextualizing the human condition enabled the scholar who wanted to analyze policy to steer a course between the abstractions of economic theorists and the approach that defined German historicists and American institutionalists: compiling facts upon facts without a theoretical language to sort through them. Instead, by developing a framework for institutional analysis, the scholars associated with the workshop were able to bridge the gap between free-floating abstractions and momentary concreteness.

---

are not present" (Mises, *Human Action*, 66). In other words, the criteria is not falsifiability, but applicability; either a theory is applicable or not, and that is a function of empirical information that the scientist knows. There has been great misinterpretation about the Austrian position as laid out by Mises over the years, including by some of his closest followers, but it could be clarified by recognizing that there are three levels of analysis in Mises's system: pure theory, applied theory (or institutionally contingent theory), and economic history. The pure logic of choice is a necessary foundation of all economics, but the institutionally contingent is what translates exercises in pure deduction into practically relevant propositions, and the use of both pure theory and applied theory to provide an interpretative framework for doing history is in fact the purpose and entire justification for doing theory.

17. It is important to note, however, that neither Vincent nor Elinor Ostrom rejects the applicability of methodological individualism in the analysis of market and nonmarket settings. The question is whether a rigorous model is specified. They prefer the term "framework" rather than "model" to describe the approach that guides their analysis. A model is more closed by definition in their system of thought. See Elinor Ostrom, *Governing the Commons: The Evolution of Institutions for Collective Action* (New York: Cambridge University Press, 1990), 214–15; and V. Ostrom, *Meaning of Democracy*, 105–14.

18. V. Ostrom, *Meaning of Democracy*, 99.

The first applications of this evolving framework were in the field of public good provision by municipalities, such as water supply.[19] Theoretically, the framework had to refine the definition of institutions in order to develop. Institutions have three separate meanings in the literature: (1) institutions as equilibrium strategies, (2) institutions as rules of the game, and (3) institutions as norms.[20] We do not see why there should be any reason why a structure induced equilibrium style of reasoning cannot absorb all three meanings into a framework of analysis.[21] First, the most productive definition of institutions is probably as the formal and informal rules of the game that are in operation in any decision context. These rules dictate the equilibrium behavior that actors exhibit, not the other way around. Second, we must also address the question of enforcement of the rules of the game. In a world where the informal rules (norms) legitimate the formal rules, the costs of enforcement will be lower, and in a world where

---

19. See Ostrom, "Water and Politics California Style" 31, in *Polycentric Governance and Development: Readings from the Workshop in Political Theory and Policy Analysis,* edited by M. McGinnis (1967; repr., Ann Arbor: University of Michigan Press, 1999), 31; Ostrom and Ostrom, "Legal and Political Conditions of Water Resource Development" in *Polycentric Governance and Development: Readings from the Workshop in Political Theory and Policy Analysis,* edited by M. McGinnis (1972; repr., Ann Arbor: University of Michigan Press, 1999).

20. See Crawford and Ostrom, "A Grammar of Institutions" in *Polycentric Games and Institutions: Readings from the Workshop in Political Theory and Policy Analysis,* edited by M. McGinnis (1995; repr., Ann Arbor: University of Michigan Press, 2000).

21. It is not our purpose here, but we believe there is confusion in the literature with regard to Menger and Hayek. Following Schotter's *The Economic Theory of Social Institutions* (New York: Cambridge University Press, 1981), many have claimed that Menger and Hayek view institutions as equilibrium behavior. We disagree with that; institutions are what brings forth the equilibria, that structure incentives, dictate the use of information, and the discovery of new knowledge. Clearly, there is an ambiguity in the writings of Menger and Hayek because the concept of institutions as guide posts to action in a world of uncertainty and ignorance is somewhat ambiguous, but in reading Hayek, we believe, you can parse out the following: full coordination results from the perfect dovetailing of individual plans—this is what is referred to as equilibrium (mutual plan consistency); social order can emerge that tends toward coordination but is not there at one point in time, and that state of affairs is defined by mutually reinforcing sets of expectations; finally, there is a general framework of rules to provide the context within which actors pursue their plans, and it is this framework that generates the social order (mutually reinforcing expectations) that enables actors to coordinate their plans with one another (equilibrium).

the informal and formal rules are in conflict, the costs of enforcing the formal rules may often be prohibitive.

In examining the decision rules within municipal governments, Vincent Ostrom (first in joint work with Tiebout and Warren and then on his own) developed the concept of polycentricity in the organization of government. "Polycentric connotes many centers of decisionmaking that are formally independent of each other."[22] (The organizational arrangements and the performance of polycentricism are again a function of rules of the game at the "constitutional level." At any point in time, a framework of analysis must respect the nested games that are in operation and the strategic interactions each game sets in motion. Competition among the different decision centers can stimulate individuals within the system to tend toward "efficiency" in production and exchange. "With the development of quasi-market conditions in production, much of the flexibility and responsiveness of market organization can be realized in the public service economy."[23] But scholars must be cognizant of the possibilities for pathology that exist even within a polycentric system of public goods delivery. Without full property rights and a free market pricing system, the problems of economic calculation will present perversities in the production and exchange of goods and services.

> Several difficulties in the regulation of a competitive public service economy can be anticipated. Economic pricing and cost allocation are dependent upon the development of effective measurement of municipal services. Since the preferred states of affairs in a community cannot be converted to a single scale of values such as dollar profits in a private enterprise, it may be more difficult to sustain an objective competitive relationship in a public service economy.[24]

---

22. Ostrom, Tiebout, and Warren, "The Organization of Government in Metropolitan Areas: A Theoretical Inquiry," in *Polycentricity and Local Public Economies: Readings from the Workshop in Political Theory and Policy Analysis,* edited by M. McGinnis (1961; repr. Ann Arbor: University of Michigan Press, 1999), 31–32.

23. Ostrom, Tiebout, and Warren, "The Organization of Government in Metropolitan Areas: A Theoretical Inquiry," 45.

24. Ostrom, Tiebout, and Warren, "The Organization of Government in Metropolitan Areas: A Theoretical Inquiry," 45. This problem of the pricing of public goods was recognized by the Italian public finance theorists who greatly influenced the research program

Polycentrism emerges because a unified hierarchy organizing the public services of a large metropolitan area is grossly ineffective (e.g., the problems of incentives and calculation would be compounded in such a hierarchical arrangement). But as we have seen, the polycentric system has its own pathologies that must be addressed. Vincent Ostrom saw the path to a solution to these problems at the constitutional level of analysis, through general rules.[25]

> Polanyi's emphasis upon a general system of rules as providing a framework for ordering relationships in a polycentric system is an issue that was seriously neglected in Ostrom, Tiebout, and Warren. . . . The task of formulating a general system of rules applicable to the conduct of governmental units in metropolitan areas and of maintaining institutional facilities appropriate to enforce such rules of law is a problem we failed to treat. *Whether the governance of metropolitan areas can be organized as a polycentric system will depend upon whether various aspects of rule making and rule enforcing can be performed in polycentric structures.*[26]

At this point, it is important to highlight the connection between the notion of spontaneous order and polycentrism. It is critical to recall that the notion of spontaneous order does not jettison purposeful action on the part of individual actors. In stark contrast, a spontaneous order is the outcome of purposeful behavior. At the highest level, it is clear that no central planner could purposefully design a complex system of polycentric governance to function in the way that it does in fact operate. The notion of spontaneous order is not intended to mean that a system arrives at some fixed equilibrium in the absence of purposeful human action. Rather, the main idea is that there are unintended consequences to purposeful human action. These unintended consequences play a significant role in constituting the overall order of the system. As a result, what is needed is a set of institutions that allow individuals to act purposefully and make adjustments to the unintended consequences of those actions.

---

of Buchanan. The pricing problem has its roots in the analysis of the problem of factor pricing within a socialist economy that was identified by Mises in the 1920s.

25. Ostrom, "Polycentricity (Part 1)" in *Polycentricity and Local Public Economies: Readings from the Workshop in Political Theory and Policy Analysis,* edited by M. McGinnis (1961; repr. Ann Arbor: University of Michigan Press, 1999).

26. Ostrom, "Polycentricity (Part 1)," 58 (emphasis in original).

One can envision two kinds of order in society. There is what Hayek called "organization," which is actions that are consciously thought out and implemented. The second type of order is spontaneous in that it is independent of anyone's oversight or direction. It is critical to keep in mind that the claim being made is not that all complex phenomena must be spontaneous. Rather, the more complex the order, the more we will have to rely on spontaneous forces to generate that order.

Given this dichotomy of the types of order, one can see that polycentric systems of governance clearly display both types of order. Within the overall system, there are complex rules and institutional mechanisms that facilitate social interaction and conflict resolution. The stock of local and tacit knowledge of "how to get things done" within the polycentric system can be seen as a spontaneous order that is continually changing. What can be called the cultural aspects of the social order, how to interact with others, how to solve problems, and so on, can be characterized as a spontaneous order. Individuals purposefully interact with others, but the set of norms that evolve are an unintended result of those purposeful interactions. In stark contrast to the idea that a spontaneous order is some static equilibrium that is generated in the absence of purposeful behavior, it is precisely because we cannot know all future situations that we need an institutional environment that is malleable and can handle ever-changing circumstances. In sum, the very notion of spontaneous order expunges any notion of a static equilibrium and requires an emphasis on the mechanisms that allow individuals to deal with unique situations that arise. The emphasis on these mechanisms for dealing with unintended consequences pervades the Ostroms' work on polycentric systems of governance.

It is within this context that one can make a connection with Vincent Ostrom's notion of public entrepreneurship. Public entrepreneurship involves the ability of individuals to engage in joint problem solving. The need to deal with new conflicts is precisely an outcome of the fact that there are unintended consequences of purposeful action that cannot be known in advance. If future situations were known in advance, the notion of public entrepreneurship would be vacuous.

An essential ingredient in the research program of the workshop is a demand to connect real-world problems with the human condition. To gain access to these problems, fieldwork, experiments, and detailed case studies are utilized. Water supply, irrigation systems, police, indigenous institutions addressing common-pool resources, and the process of economic development in less developed economies have all been the focus of institutional analysis by scholars associated with the Bloomington school. In order to engage in this analysis, the emphasis has been first on identifying the organization and the social mechanisms in operation without addressing their performance. The assessment of performance and the sustainability of the existing system are conducted after clarifying exactly the organizational structures in operation in any given societal context.

The analysis proceeds from context to the action arena to incentives to patterns of interactions to outcomes, which are evaluated and, in turn, influence the interactions. The context is defined by the physical and material conditions existing in a society, the attributes of the community in question, and the rules that are in use in that society. The different action arenas generate incentives that, in turn, engender a pattern of social interactions. The pattern of interactions results in outcomes that either reinforce the context of choice or conflict with it.

This has been an extremely productive research program and has successfully challenged the artificial division of the disciplines in the social sciences in terms of both the positive institutional analysis of existing social interactions, identifying dysfunctional situations and suggesting policy changes to affect social change. Public choice, positive political economy, and new institutional economics are interwoven in the work of scholars associated with the workshop under the rubric of comparative institutional analysis. However, unlike much of the work in these research programs, the scholars associated with the Bloomington school are more engaged in empirical work, and in particular, in close-up case studies derived through fieldwork, in which multiple forms of evidence including in-depth interviews and surveys are placed on the table. As a result, the richness of the details in the institutional analysis is able to unearth not just the formal rules that are in operation, but the informal norms and rules that govern social intercourse.

In her work on common-pool resource problems, Elinor Ostrom has been able to demonstrate how local customs and knowledge in less-developed countries (LDCs) provide solutions to the common problems without adopting the formal rules present in more developed economies. An important implication of this analysis is that the search for one true model that fits all situations must be abandoned. Another implication is that formal models such as the prisoners' dilemma and the tragedy of the commons do not have the universal applicability that is often attributed to them. We know this because of the empirical reality as evidenced with experiments and fieldwork. But while local customs and knowledge may provide solutions to social dilemmas, they possess other imperfections that must be accounted for and that make them vulnerable and limited in promoting social order beyond certain limits. Someone may counter that these customs are more robust than what might be first thought of as demonstrated by their longevity. However, the alternative interpretation, which stresses the pathological nature of customary solutions to prisoners' dilemma (PD) games and common problems, is that the solution only works within small group settings of relatively homogenous agents, and such institutional settings are limited in their ability to generate wealth creation and generalized development in any society.

There are major dilemmas of governance that the workshop research project excites in a scholar's imagination. Primary among these is the problem of self-enforcement. A free society works best when the need for a policeman is least, that is, when contracts are largely self-enforcing and the benefits of association outweigh any gains from deviant behavior. But as a modern society expands beyond small group settings of relatively homogeneous agents, the focus shifts from self-enforcement to formal rules of the game which police social intercourse effectively so individuals can realize the gains from association. Following Tocqueville, the Ostroms have sought to develop a science and art of association so that they realize the mutual gains from exchange and production within a diverse society.[27] The legal framework adopted in a society either reinforces or conflicts with the self-governing associations that take place outside the realm of the state, but once society recognizes that the law can buttress the existing self-governing associations in operation, the question remains as to how to protect the arena of self-governance from being perverted by the formal rules that give coercive power to the state.

---

27. Part of our purpose in this paper is to highlight the similarities of the research project of the Ostroms and scholars such as Knight, Mises, and Hayek. We would like to point the reader to the core chapter in Mises's *Human Action* on what he terms "Ricardo's Law of Association." Sympathy and friendship are the fruits of social cooperation, not the cause of it. See Mises, *Human Action*, 143–76.

Since rules are not self-applying and self-enforcing, any system of constitutional rule depends upon a knowledgeable use of the prerogatives of government and citizenship to maintain and enforce limits inherent in a system of constitutional law. Knowledge, both of techniques and design criteria, is thus essential to the conduct of the American experiments in constitutional rule. This knowledge provides the appropriate criteria to evaluate performance and methods that can be used for officials to check and limit one another, and for citizens to maintain proper limits in their relationships with officials. Any such structure of relationships is vulnerable to the development of coalitions that attempt to dominate all decision structures. The viability of a system of constitutional rule depends, in turn, upon awareness of these exposures and the willingness of others to resist such usurpations of authority."[28]

There are two important points that this passage highlights. First, the political economist must appreciate the vulnerability of any social system that requires the introduction of the coercive power of the state to overcome the breakdown of self-enforcement to maintain social order. In building the political institutions that will address the situation beyond self-enforcement, the theorist must seek to minimize the vulnerability.[29] The Tocquevillian answer lies in civil associations that are self-governing; the Madisonian answer lies in political structures that pit ambition against ambition. A free society must have both in a wide scope for nongovernmental social associations and political and legal institutions that minimize the domination of some by others by making the competition between the interest groups checkmate one another.[30]

---

28. Ostrom, "A Forgotten Tradition: The Constitutional Level of Analysis," in *Polycentric Governance and Development: Readings from the Workshop in Political Theory and Policy Analysis,* edited by M. McGinnis (1967; repr., Ann Arbor: University of Michigan Press, 1999), 164.

29. Hayek puts it this way in describing the classical liberal political economy of Hume and Smith: "the chief concern was not so much with what man might occasionally achieve when he was at his best but that he should have as little opportunity as possible to do harm when he was at his worst" (Hayek, *Individualism*, 11).

30. See Ostrom, *Meaning of Democracy,* 273.

Conclusion

The research program of the Workshop in Political Theory and Policy Analysis is both sophisticated and relevant to the analysis of real-world problems. With a multiplicity of insights from across disciplines, a framework is forged that enables the theorist to engage in a comparative institutional analysis that is rich in details and historical context. Moreover, the analysis is capable of generating evaluation and designing institutional remedies to the pathologies and perversities that exist in any given structure.

It is important to stress that the analysis is grounded in methodological individualism and the economic way of thinking. In contrast to the model-thinking of mainstream neoclassical economics, an archeology of knowledge perspective reveals that the research agenda of the Ostroms draws significantly from the ideas developed in the first half of the twentieth century by Knight, Mises, and Hayek.

The methodological importance of the Ostrom approach cannot be underestimated. The landscape of the social sciences can be categorized as follows (Figure 10.1).

The missing cell in the social sciences was an attempt to combine the logical structure of economic reasoning with the rich institutional details of history and anthropological and sociological analysis. The Workshop in Political Theory and Policy Analysis has bridged the gap between the free-floating abstractions of mainstream economists and the naive empiricism of historicism and older institutionalism, but these scholars have also steered clear of the pseudo-scientific

Figure 10.1. The Landscape of the Social Sciences

	THIN	THICK
DIRTY	Analytic Narrative Approach to Political Economy of Weingast/Bates, etc., and the Institutional Analysis of Policy Approach of the Ostroms	Anthropology and Sociology
CLEAN	Mainstream Economics	Statistical Political Science

sophistication of tests of statistical significance unaided by a theoretical framework. The data does not speak itself, but this also does not mean that the data should never be allowed to speak at all.

Through their own work and the collaborative work of generations of scholars, Vincent and Elinor Ostrom have pursued a research program that has had the effect of reinvigorating a tradition in political economy that can be dated from Hume and Smith down to Knight, Mises, and Hayek. The Ostroms have given this research program both empirical content and a normative thrust grounded in a respect for the self-governing properties of civil associations. These civil associations empower citizens by helping constrain the power of the state to grant special privileges to some at the expense of others and by enabling diverse individuals to realize the mutual benefits from exchange and production so that wealth is created and social cooperation, rather than conflict, characterizes the societal order. The classical liberals from Smith to Tocqueville understood that a society of free and responsible individuals simultaneously achieves individual liberty, wealth creation, and peaceful cooperation. The work of Vincent and Elinor Ostrom have elaborated on that grand intellectual tradition and enriched its scientific content.

11

Is the Only Form of "Reasonable Regulation" Self-Regulation?

Elinor Ostrom

Introduction

ELINOR "LIN" OSTROM, the 2009 Nobel Prize winner in economic science, has made significant contributions throughout her career to the disciplines of political economy and public choice. Her most widely recognized contributions relate to the work on common-pool resources. She has discovered a diversity of institutional arrangements that serve in various human societies to promote cooperation and avoid conflict over resource use. Where a strict interpretation of theory would predict overuse and mismanagement, she found collective action arrangements that proved effective in limiting access and establishing accountability. Many of the effective tools of governance she found resided not in the formal structure of government, but instead in the informal, and sometimes even tacit, rules that communities live by.

I would like to push Ostrom's argument a bit, and ask whether the foundation of an effective system of regulation must be found first and foremost in the rules of self-regulation that communities adopt and their citizens abide by, rather than in well-designed regulatory statutes by efficiency experts. Efforts to regulate human activities to suppress our most crass desires, to discipline our wildest whims, and to harness our self-interest exist throughout the world. Most of our intellectual efforts as economists and political economists have been directed at studying the formal regulations established and implemented by agencies within government. Ostrom, on the other hand, studied the political economy of everyday life and the self-regulation of behavior, rather than the political economy of government exclusively. What do we learn from her work about the relationship between these two forms of the regulation of behavior in human societies?[1] Thus my question, "is the only form of 'reasonable regulation' self-regulation?"

The Paradox of Governance
and the Elusive Quest for "Reasonable Regulation"

Several years ago I was at a conference celebrating the work of P.T. Bauer at the London School of Economics. Anne Krueger summed up (I am paraphrasing her) what we learned about economic policy during the last quarter of the twentieth century with a statement to the effect: "Yes, Bauer is right. Free markets outperform government central planning and government intervention. But we also know that completely unfettered markets are unrealistic. We can all agree that what we need is to establish *reasonable regulation that is not capturable by special interests*." I was immediately struck by Krueger's phraseology because it seemed, well, so reasonable. Who could be against "reasonable regulation" that wasn't captured by special interest groups? Nobody in their right mind would argue for unreasonable regulation dominated by interest group politics. Anne Krueger, as she so often does, had hit the nail on the head. But I had a nagging thought, so I raised my hand. "What if," I said, "that set of regulations is a null set?" My question was never seriously entertained that day, but I think it should be.

One of the grand dilemmas of political economy is the recognition that when we turn to government to solve our problems we necessarily create a new set of problems that previously did not exist, but that must now be addressed. I am not saying a priori that the costs of addressing these problems always outweigh the benefits of turning to government, but only that we need to be conscious of the fact that we have in fact created a new set of problems to contend with and contending with it entails costs that must be taken into account. We turn to government in the first place to provide security in our daily lives—protection of property, the guarantee of contracts, etc. In short, we turn to government

---

1. See also Peter J. Boettke, "Why Culture Matters: Economics, Politics, and the Imprint of History," in *Calculation and Coordination: Essays on Socialism and Transitional Political Economy* (New York: Routledge, 2001), 248–65; Peter J. Boettke, Christopher J. Coyne, and Peter T. Leeson, "Institutional Stickiness and the New Development Economics," *American Journal of Economics and Sociology* 67, no. 2 (2008): 331–58.

because we are concerned about the threat of private predation. Unfortunately, as soon as we establish a government body to provide for our protection we become vulnerable to the threat of public predation. So we have to engage in costly measures to protect us against the predatory behavior of government. As James Madison explained the basic dilemma in *The Federalist Papers*, we have to empower the state and then constrain the state. This is, in essence, the constitutional project in forming a workable government.

The desire to institute reasonable regulation that is not captured is laudable, but implementing such a desire in practice is a question of positive political economy. By what means can we establish such regulations through the political process, and how are we going to enforce them and hermetically seal them from capture by interested parties?

The positive political economy of regulation leads us to question theories of regulation that postulate either a public interest origin (not to deny, but certainly to question) and a benevolent despot idea of enforcement. Instead, a common practice in positive political economy is to dig into the data both to infer intentions from outcomes and to follow the money trail and always ask who benefits at whose expense. Regulation may indeed be introduced to address some perceived market failure, but we cannot assume that the government regulation will costlessly correct for the problem. This demand for comparative institutional analysis, of course, was one of Ronald Coase's main points in both his 1959 paper on the FCC and his 1960 paper on social cost.

In the Federal Communications Commission paper, Coase argued that:

> Quite apart from the malallocations which are the result of political pressures, an administrative agency which attempts to perform the function normally carried out by the pricing mechanism operates under two handicaps. First of all, it lacks the precise monetary measure of benefit and cost provided by the market. Second, it cannot, by the nature of things, be in possession of all the relevant information possessed by the managers of every business which uses or might use radio frequencies, to say nothing of the preferences of consumers for the various goods and services in the production of which radio frequencies could be used. . . .
>
> The operation of the market is not itself costless, and if the costs of operating the market exceeded the costs of running the agency by a

sufficiently large amount, we might be willing to acquiesce in the mal-allocation of resources resulting from the agency's lack of knowledge, inflexibility and exposure to political pressure.[2]

In other words, attempts to replace the price system with government administration of allocations run into the problems of calculation, dispersed knowledge, and political interest groups, and these problems not only distort existing arrangements but curtail the entrepreneurial discovery procedure of new and potentially better ways to arrange affairs and allocate resources.

In "The Problem of Social Cost," Coase explains further that we must "start our analysis with a situation approximating that which actually exists, to examine the effects of a proposed policy change and attempt to decide whether the new situation would be, in total, better or worse than the original one."[3] It would be desirable, Coase adds, if policy reform were costless and we could guarantee that proposed changes would work as planned so we gain more than we lose.

> But in choosing between social arrangements within the context of which individual decisions are made, we have to bear in mind that a change in the existing system which will lead to an improvement in some decisions may well lead to a worsening of others. Furthermore, we have to take into account the costs involved in operating the various social arrangements (whether it be the working of a market or of a government department), as well as the costs involved in moving to a new system.[4]

Coase's argument is not that the laissez-faire market is ideal (unless that is merely definitional), but instead that the quest for "reasonable regulation" is elusive. In other words, it is not so unreasonable to question the ease with which we find in existence (let alone design, implement, and sustain) "reasonable regulation" of markets by government.

Recognizing the elusive question doesn't change the fact that human beings are imperfect and their passions need to be tamed. Governance is required. We

---

2. Ronald Coase, "The Federal Communications Commission," *Journal of Law & Economics* 2, no. 1 (1959), 18.
3. Ronald Coase, "The Problem of Social Cost," *Journal of Law & Economics* 3, no. 1 (1960), 43.
4. Coase, "Problem of Social Cost," 44.

humans must be disciplined for a peaceful and prosperous social order to emerge. But how precisely do we tame those human passions, and what mechanisms do we employ in the taming? Hirschman argued that throughout the intellectual history of the West, the taming of the passions was the object of various systems of beliefs.[5] The passions, Hirschman argues, could be repressed by authority and force, they could be suppressed by religious conviction, they could be harnessed, or they could be held in check by the countervailing force of pitting passion against passion. Economic theory, in fact, could be said to have been born in the effort to see how the passions are harnessed through commercial interest so that our private vices would be transformed into public virtue. And, it was through refinements in the classical theory of political economy, and the historical practice of constitutional craftsmanship by the American founding fathers that led to an appreciation of the countervailing forces in society.

The mechanism for the harnessing, as well as the checking, of the passions identified by the classical political economists was private property and the price system and the rule of law and constitutional order.[6] Competition in the pursuit of profit, as well as the penalty of loss, would discipline men so that they would orient their behavior to realize the gains from trade and the gains from innovation in the most effective way possible given tastes, technology, and resource availability. Profits encourage risk taking by economic actors, while losses encourage prudence in decision making. The market economy was a clear example of a self-regulating system where risk and prudence were balanced against each other.

Participants within a market economy are incentivized to seek out mutual advantageous exchange and discover least-cost methods to realize those gains from exchange. Humanity would be better served by "truck, barter, exchange" than by pursuing "rape, pillage, plunder," provided that the institutional environment within which individuals act ensured that mutually advantageous trade, rather than violent taking, was the more economically rewarding activity. The passions would be harnessed and they would be held in check, and peace

---

5. A.O. Hirschman, *The Passions and the Interests* (Princeton, NJ: Princeton University Press, 1977).
6. See F.A. Hayek, *Individualism and Economic Order* (1948; repr., Chicago: University of Chicago Press, 1996), 11–14.

and prosperity would follow from the establishment of a system of "property, contract, and consent."

The main intellectual debate in political economy since the eighteenth century has been whether social order is a function of the taming of the passions by central authority (Hobbes) or through the "invisible hand" of the market economy (Smith). Enter Elinor Ostrom in the late twentieth century, not so much to resolve the debate as to transcend it. Ostrom has persuasively argued that this traditional way of looking at things has proven ineffective in addressing situations as diverse as understanding the organization of local public economies to the plight of underdevelopment, and the management of forestry and fisheries in between. One way to think of her contribution to the economics of governance is to view her work as arguing that there were Smithian (spontaneous order) answers to Hobbesian (constructivist) questions. But that really doesn't quite capture the essence of her argument, which drills deeper into the form and function (and enforcement) of the rules of governance that are in operation in a diversity of human societies.

From Municipal Public Goods to Community-Based Resource Management

In the debate over local public economies, Lin Ostrom and her husband Vincent challenged the conventional wisdom in public administration by arguing that efficient administration was not a function of consolidation and centralized administration, but a by-product of polycentric processes of local communities competing for residents through the provision of public goods and services in exchange for local taxes and fees.[7] What looked chaotic to the rationalistic mind of modernist public administration was, in fact, the orderly organization of local public economies that emerged from citizen participation and community engagement. Decentralized mechanisms were in operation that generated a more responsive and adaptable municipality to satisfy the demands of its citizens

---

7. See, e.g., M. McGinnis, ed., *Polycentricity and Local Public Economies: Readings from the Workshop in Political Theory and Policy Analysis* (Ann Arbor: University of Michigan Press, 1999).

than the efficiency experts in modern public administration were recognizing. The "scientific" consensus for centralization of administration was mistaken and where followed would lead to a worsening (rather than an improvement) in the performance of the basic functions of governance in urban areas.

But what was true of managing public administration of police, schools, and utilities in large urban environments was also true, the Ostroms argued, for management of common-pool resources from fisheries to forestry to irrigation systems in rural and underdeveloped environments.[8] Efforts by the efficiency experts to centralize administration of resource allocation ran into the problems of malallocation (as Coase had also identified) due to the inability to engage in economic calculation, the inability to mobilize the dispersed knowledge in society, and the failure to ward off the destructive influence of special interest groups. However, there is a flip side to the Coasean framework that must be recognized. The proponents of modern public administration often made arguments claiming not only that the decentralized forces at work were inefficient compared to centralized administration, but that local actors couldn't negotiate their way around the inefficiencies no matter how hard they might try. Coase asked instead for economists and policymakers to look at where the deals (often hidden) were being made that enable people to transform situations of conflict into opportunities for cooperation. Similarly, the Ostroms looked at the agreements on the rules of governance and mechanisms of enforcement that local people crafted (or stumbled upon) that turned situations of potential conflict into opportunities for cooperation. Lin Ostrom's work showed that the people she has studied dealing with common-pool resources in a variety of contexts don't face a "tragedy of the commons" as much an "opportunity of the commons" and that the conflict situation presents an opportunity to find the right rule systems to ensure a well-governed commons and the possibility of peaceful cooperation.[9]

---

8. See, e.g., M. McGinnis, ed., *Polycentric Governance and Development: Readings from the Workshop in Political Theory and Policy Analysis* (Ann Arbor: University of Michigan Press, 1999).

9. Alex Tabarrok, "Elinor Ostrom and the Well-Governed Commons," *Marginal Revolution*, October 12, 2009, accessed 20 January 2010, http://www.marginalrevolution.com/marginalrevolution/2009/10/elinor-ostrom-and-the-wellgoverned-commons.html.

We can, and do, in short, find ways to live better together. As Shivakumar put it, the Ostroms work points us in the direction of a "new science of politics" for understanding democratic civilization in the twenty-first century, a science that "draws on the human capacity to craft the rules of self-governance through reflection and choice. Indeed, human beings possess the potential to improve their well-being by devising rules governing their association with each other."[10]

Summing Up the Lessons from Lin

So what does this work mean for the future of public choice and political economy? Much of the history of public choice has been defined by the economic examination of politics and formal government. The work of the Ostroms certainly isn't blind to formal government. But their work asks us to think more broadly about governance—the formal and informal rules of the social game that tame, harness, and check our passions, and the mechanisms of enforcement that ensure effective governance even in the most unexpected environments. How good governance actually works in situations when it shouldn't and how individuals in these societies develop the capacities necessary to be self-governing citizens are the questions their work forces us to consider.

I would argue that the first enduring lesson from Lin Ostrom's work is that individuals in their local situation are more effective at knowing the right rules and actions to avoid conflict and promote cooperation than are government officials removed from the daily life of the community. Trust in the people to craft the right rules rather than experts from afar who promise rational solution to social ills. This conclusion can be interpreted either as a caution to would-be reformers to respect local traditions and customs prior to efforts at imposing change in governance structures (let's call this caution optimism), or as a sanction against all such efforts at reform from afar and an embracing of the conclusion that the only path to reform in an indigenous one (let's call this pessimistic). Ostrom would not deny the possibilities of improvements in governance coming from foreign experts, but she does stress that these reform efforts must respect

---

10. S. Shivakumar, *The Constitution of Development: Crafting Capabilities For Self-Governance* (New York: Palgrave, 2005), 131.

the incentives that recipients of the assistance face and the nested games that are being played throughout the policy process.[11]

Lin, and Vincent in particular, often pointed to Hamilton's quote from *The Federalist Papers* for inspiration: "whether societies of men are really capable or not of establishing good government from reflection and choice, or whether they are forever destined to depend for their political constitutions on accident and force."[12] They are cautiously optimistic that man can establish good government through reflection and choice, and not forever be knocked about by the rough seas of history. However, it is important to stress where the Ostroms found their reasons for optimism. Hope, in their writings, is not to be found in rationalistic reforms of government planners informed by the modern science of public administration, but in the "science and art of association" as practiced by a self-governing citizenry. It is people and their capacity to embrace (rather than shirk from) the troubles of thinking and the cares of living, not the machinations of politics, that give rise to hope that constitutional craftsmanship will produce a social order of peace and prosperity.

I want to emphasize a reading of her (and Vincent's) research that nudges this argument a bit further and emphasizes the consistent and full implications of what we have learned from the various studies emerging from the research at the Workshop in Political Theory and Policy Analysis for the "science and art of association." The rules that are binding are the rules that people live by already. Lin Ostrom has found, in the field of collective action, the equivalent of finding the Coasean trades in private markets that were already struck to resolve conflicts over property and resource use. Beekeepers and apple growers, Cheung showed, worked out deals that addressed the potential externality issues even though market failure theorists had pointed to the example in textbooks and papers as a prime example of an externality that would result in market failure.[13]

---

11. See, e.g., Elinor Ostrom et al., *Aid, Incentives, and Sustainability: An Institutional Analysis of Development Cooperation* (Stockholm: Swedish International Development Cooperation Agency, 2002).

12. Vincent Ostrom, *The Meaning of Democracy and the Vulnerability of Democracies* (Ann Arbor: University of Michigan Press, 1997), 10.

13. S. Cheung, "The Fable of the Bees: An Economic Investigation," *Journal of Law & Economics* 16, no. 1 (1973): 11–33.

Economic life practices defied what the pure logic of the theory predicted, and what that tells the analyst is that the solution to the puzzle is found in the institutional details in the arrangements worked out by people in their everyday life. In the case of beekeepers and apple growers, it was contractual deals that internalized the externalities; in the case of mountain grazing in Switzerland and irrigation systems in Spain, it was internal rules and monitoring arrangements that disciplined temptations to violate community rules and ensured a robust conformity to those rules of governing the common-pool resource.[14]

The major insight that Ostrom's work on common-pool resource management emphasized was the evolved rule systems that emerged to provide accountability and effective mechanisms of punishment for those who violate the rules. Community-based rules and community engagement found ways around the conflict-ridden situation of the commons, just as beekeepers and apple growers found ways around the situation of the externality, to realize the possibility of mutually advantageous social cooperation. These local systems of self-governance to preserve and protect the common-pool resource, she found in a diversity of human societies, persisted through time—in some instances for a century, in other instances dating back as far a millennium. She has been quick to point out that she is not saying that these rule systems reflect the optimal form of governance imaginable given the circumstances, but she does not hesitate in labeling them as successful systems of governance either.

This leads to the second major lesson from Ostrom's work—in examining systems of governance, it is the "rules in use" (the lived practice of everyday life) that matter for social cooperation, not so much the "rules in form" (on the books). I would add that there is also the discussion of the function of rules. In the basic economics of property rights, the rules surrounding property rights provide economic actors with incentives that guide their behavior. Property rules determine who owns what and what they can do with what they own. Private property rights delineate ownership, provide accountability, and encourage stewardship. Without clearly defined and enforced property rights, incentives become distorted and decisions over resource use are made with less care. Thus, when due to technological difficulties or other impediments, the

---

14. Elinor Ostrom, *Governing the Commons: The Evolution of Institutions for Collective Action* (New York: Cambridge University Press, 1990), 58–102.

establishment of private property rights over a resource is "impossible," traditional theory would predict poor management demanding either privatization or extensive regulation or government ownership. Ostrom's detailed studies of the management of common-pool resources should make us think twice about these well-worn classifications of ownership rights. What she has demonstrated is not only that the "rules in use" determine practice, but that the same function of rules can be served by a diversity of forms of rules.[15] In short, the function that private property rights has served in terms of providing incentives for accountability and responsibility in resource use has been served by a variety of community-based rule systems. These rules in use employ various methods to limit access to the resource, assign accountability to those who use it or are entrusted with its care, and establish methods of punishment for those who violate the community rules (ranging from monetary fines to social sanctions such as shaming and shunning).

The work demonstrates that people are capable of devising systems of self-regulation in a variety of circumstances. To get to the theme from my title, we see in the varied experience of common-pool resources in Western societies as well as non-Western societies, and across historical epochs and stages of development, self-regulation systems work to discipline the passions of man and turn situations of potential conflict into a reality of social cooperation. And, since the self-regulation systems in these varied environments and across time are operating outside of the formal realm of politics, they do not face the problem of protecting against unwanted influence of politically empowered special interest groups. Governance without government can, and does, happen in the lived world in which we study as political economists, even in the least favorable of circumstances.[16] "Reasonable regulation," as I defined here (from Anne Krueger), becomes not elusive but realized in the examples provided in Ostrom's works on self-regulation. No longer defined as the null set, we now find a variety of examples of effective systems of rules that govern an individual's social interactions by taming human passions and harnessing them in the direction that produces peaceful social cooperation under the division of labor even in situations (such

---

15. Elinor Ostrom, *Understanding Institutional Diversity* (Princeton, NJ: Princeton University Press, 2005).

16. See, e.g., Peter T. Leeson, "The Laws of Lawlessness," *Journal of Legal Studies* 38, no. 2 (2009): 471–503.

as with the management of common-pool resources) that we should be most pessimistic about voluntary ordering of human affairs.

There are two additional lessons from Ostrom's work that are essential for the future of public choice scholarship. The third lesson I would stress is her intellectual curiosity and methodological openness to a variety of techniques and approaches to learning. She studied at UCLA, where she learned economics from Armen Alchian as an undergraduate. She pursued a degree in political science, where she studied local public economies and was influenced by the idea of Tiebout competition in public economies. She was a major contributor to public choice and modern political economy, in fact a pioneer in these fields, focusing her work on puzzles of the tragedy of the commons, prisoner dilemmas, and the logic of collective action. She engaged in detailed case studies but also looked to abstract game theory to help her understand the dynamic play between rules and strategies in the political economy of everyday life. She also turned to the lab and experimental economics to test out her theories of common-pool resources, as well as experiments in the field to learn about the applicability of her ideas to different contexts. In her presidential address to the American Political Science Association, Ostrom described her own approach as "A Behavioral Approach to the Rational Choice Theory of Collective Action."[17] And, when you unpack that description it somehow fits perfectly. Finally, she understood that her work on rule systems represented the study of complex phenomena and not simple phenomena. In order to study complex phenomena, she sought to gain additional insight from the field of social complexity and computer modeling of complex systems. It is arguable, that not since Kenneth Boulding[18] have we seen any social scientist allow sheer curiosity about the world to take him or her on such a methodological journey of so many different approaches to get at the phenomena he or she wants to understand—the rules of self-governance that are

---

17. Elinor Ostrom, "A Behavioral Approach to the Rational Choice Theory of Collective Action" (presidential address, American Political Science Association 1997), *American Political Science Review* 92, no. 1 (1998), 1–22, in *Polycentric Games and Institutions: Readings from the Workshop in Political Theory and Policy Analysis*, edited by M. McGinnis (1998; repr., Ann Arbor: University of Michigan Press, 2000).

18. See, e.g., Peter J. Boettke and David L. Prychitko, "Mr. Boulding and the Austrians," in *Joseph Schumpeter, Historian of Economics,* edited by L. Moss (New York: Routledge, 1996), 250–59.

in operation in the lived lives of a diversity of people that result in cooperation and avoid conflict.[19] At the same time, Ostrom has a unity in her research methods as well—rational choice as if the choosers were human, and institutional analysis as if history mattered.

The final lesson from Lin Ostrom, and one that certainly deserves to be highlighted, is her (and Vincent's) motivation for their life project as scholars and educators in the policy sciences. They view their vocation as one of cultivating a self-governing citizenry and the characteristics necessary for such a citizenry. In an interview for my book with Paul Dragos Aligica, *Challenging Institutional Analysis and Development: The Bloomington School*, Lin Ostrom states of their joint work at the Workshop that one of their "greatest priorities" has always been that their research and education efforts are geared toward cultivating citizens that have the capacity for self-governance. "Self-governing, democratic systems are always fragile enterprises," Lin points out. "Future citizens need to understand that they participate in the constitution and re-constitution of rule-governed politics. And they need to learn the 'art and science of association'. If we fail in this, all our investigations and theoretical efforts are useless."[20]

Those are very inspiring words and deeds.

---

19. A. Poteete, M. Janssen, and Elinor Ostrom, *Working Together: Collective Action, the Commons, and Multiple Methods in Practice* (Princeton, NJ: Princeton University Press, 2010).

20. P. Dragos Aligica and Peter J. Boettke, *Challenging Institutional Analysis and Development: The Bloomington School* (New York: Routledge, 2009), 159.

12

The Matter of Methodology
Don Lavoie

DON LAVOIE, the David and Charles Koch Professor of Economics in the School of Public Policy at George Mason University, passed away in November 2001. In his tragically short life, he published three original books, edited two others, and published scores of articles in the field of Austrian economics, Marxian economics, the history of economic thought, comparative economics, computer software design, computer simulation studies, educational theory, libertarian political theory, and the methodology of the social sciences. As this sample of fields he worked in demonstrates, he was a wide-ranging scholar. His background was fittingly wide—trained in computer science, he wrote some of the early programs for computers to teach themselves music; and then while working in the field of computer science, he earned his PhD in economics at NYU. While completing his PhD (where he concentrated not only in Austrian economics, but also Marxian economics), Lavoie was able to publish papers in journals on the history of economic thought and methodology. In 1981, after completing his PhD, Don joined the faculty at George Mason University, which was starting a new PhD program. Along with Karen Vaughn, Richard Fink, and Jack High he started the Center for the Study of Market Processes, a research and education center which in the 1980s produced more PhD students interested in Austrian economics than had been produced at anytime since the 1920s in Vienna. Lavoie was at the intellectual center of this productive research and education group as he published more articles and supervised more theses than any other faculty member in the unit. He was particularly focused on making students publish their dissertations as books, rather than as the then-emerging practice (and now dominant practice) of publishing three essays. He was amazingly successful in this endeavor as is evidenced by his track record in this regard with the books by Roy Cordato, David Prychitko, Steve Horwitz, Emily Chamlee-Wright, Howard Baejter, and myself.

As a scholar Lavoie was best known for his work on the theoretical debate over socialism, *Rivalry and Central Planning* (New York: Cambridge University Press, 1985). In 1985, he also published *National Economic Planning: What Is Left?* (Cambridge: Ballinger, 1985). Like Hayek before him, Lavoie was led to focus on methodological questions because of the problems he saw in communicating the Austrian points in this debate to mainstream economists. The points he stressed in his interpretation of the debate, and his own development of the line of argument, about rivalry, dispersed information, local knowledge, and the tacit domain were simply unintelligible to most economists wedded to formalism and positivism. Lavoie's philosophical tour in search of an answer to this conundrum went from postpositivist philosophy of science to philosophical hermeneutics to postmodernism. Starting in the mid-1980s, Lavoie's work increasingly took the form of methodological issues. He appreciated the postmodern critique of science, while distancing himself from the deconstructivist position of epistemological relativism. He found his philosophical comfort zone between objectivism and relativism and in the teachings of philosophical hermeneutics and in particular the writings of Hans-Georg Gadamer.

Lavoie's study of Gadamer led him to reconstruct the philosophical basis for the Austrian School of Economics. For those of us close to Lavoie, there was a logic to his position that many critics simply did not understand. First, it is important to recognize that Austrian economics is embedded within a continental philosophical tradition, and not an analytic one. Second, one must be familiar enough with Mises's writings to realize that he divided the social sciences into theory and history and argued for unique epistemological positions for each—theory or conception would result from pursuing the phenomenological method of analysis as laid out by the early Husserl, while history or understanding would result from adopting a hermeneutical or interpretive stance as developed by Dilthey. Once this history is understood—which few readers did, even those sympathetic to the Austrians—then the appeal to Gadamer by Lavoie is not a radical break with his Austrian roots, but a natural evolution. Gadamer's position of philosophical hermeneutics could be relabeled (and in fact was labeled by Gadamer) as phenomenological hermeneutics. Gadamer was a student of both Husserl and Heidegger and he attempted a synthesis between these two figures of German philosophy. Lavoie in a fundamental sense was simply tracing out the footnotes from Mises's work and updating philosophical underpinnings of the Austrian school.

One of Gadamer's most important insights is the idea of the fusing of horizons between the author and the reader. We read one another not to indict each other, but to learn from each other. To become something different than before we experienced the words of one another. Lavoie was a man of deep ideological commitment, yet his respect for the values of scholarship trumped that and forced him to be open to the point of view of others. He constantly sought to learn from those who did not share his ideological or methodological perspective. Around 1990, he became persuaded that there was more room for learning if he was in an environment where people agreed on the basic philosophical stance and thus he eventually left the economics department at George Mason and started a new program in the School of Public Policy. He also worked with PhD students in the cultural studies department. A dedicated teacher, he was twice honored by GMU with the teacher of the year award and was an innovator in regard to the electronic classroom and distance learning.

Don Lavoie's life was cut tragically short by disease. He never did get to write his book on methodology that was to challenge the presumptions of our discipline and make the case for a hermeneutical approach to political economy and the social sciences. That task has now been passed to his many students who were fortunate to have Don as a teacher, mentor, and friend.

Invitation to Political Economy

*Peter Berger and the Comedic Drama
of Political, Economic, and Social Life*

PETER L. BERGER is one of the most influential social scientists of the twentieth century. A citation study of his work published in 1986 that studied the decade between the early 1970s to early 1980s demonstrated that his citation count during this time (1052) put him in the company of other thinkers such as Dewey, Whitehead, and Marcuse. His contributions to the sociology of knowledge, sociology of religion, and the sociological/cultural analysis of capitalism are well known and widely discussed. They are not without controversy however. In fact, it might be safe to say that Peter Berger marched to a beat of a different drum within his chosen field of sociology. Paul Samuelson once remarked that in economic science we compete for the only coin worth achieving, the applause of our peers. Peter Berger saw things differently and pursued a more subversive agenda in the social sciences. The pursuit of truth and the coming to an understanding of the society in which we dwell, as well as that which remains exotic, required a skeptical (and often comical) stance.

A certain level of irreverence to the task of social understanding is to be encouraged. This is not to undermine the seriousness of the task of sociology, but to recognize that self-effacement is a sign of intellectual maturity. We often have the hardest time gaining an understanding of that which is closest to us in terms of familiarity. Those who are in professional academic disciplines dwell within university settings (and the politics of everyday academic life) and the disciplines themselves (with specialized language and expectations). But precisely because we are embedded in these worlds, it is hard for us to have the critical distance that is often required to gain understanding.

Ironically, Berger makes this clear to the uninitiated in his introduction to the field. His *Invitation to Sociology* (New York: Doubleday, 1963) sold approximately 670,000 copies in the 25-year period (1963–1988) since it was published and was translated into sixteen different languages by that time as well. The book was widely adopted throughout the United States for "Intro to Sociology" classes. As one commentator observed, given the extensive used book market for college texts, Berger's book has probably been assigned to well over a million students over that period. Yet the professional reviews were mostly weak, and the student feedback hasn't been all that encouraging. On the other hand, graduate students in the discipline, as well as older professors, are said to have been particularly impressed with the work. This presents a puzzle. Undergraduates find the book intimidating. Sociologists currently working in the field find the book too glib. But graduate students find the book refreshing as it reminds them of what they wanted to do when they first started studying sociology; and older professor find the book appealing because it discusses (in clear language) what they had hoped for the discipline, only to see it lost.

Berger is a humanistic sociologist and sees the discipline as humanistic. But the social sciences, especially in the United States after World War II, moved in unison toward a more scientistic stance. That scientism actually hinders scientific progress is one of the great puzzles of twentieth-century social thought. Unfortunately, due to the tight grip of scientism on the minds of social scientists, they don't see this; they mistake perilous progress for real progress. In a characteristic passage, Berger sums up this point as follows: "sociologists, especially in America, have become so preoccupied with methodological questions that they have ceased to be interested in society at all. As a result, they have found out nothing of significance about any aspect of social life, since in science as in love a concentration on technique is quite likely to lead to impotence."[1] Disciplines can, in fact, lose themselves in methodological quagmires. Given the inferiority complex in relation to natural sciences, the sciences of man are particularly susceptible. Mimicking the methods appropriate for the study of nature has embarrassingly been the habit of those who study human beings because they fear being accused of engaging in a nonscientific intellectual enterprise.

A simple example might get this point across. The natural sciences matured by purging all forms of anthropomorphism from their explanations. Lightening doesn't come from the anger of the gods; the change in seasons is not a

---

1. Berger, *Invitation to Sociology,* 13.

consequence of divine command. Instead of understanding these physical phenomena by reference to the purposes and plans of gods, scientific thought was advanced by finding the underlying physical explanation. But the sciences of man differ from the sciences of nature. When we purge purposes and plans from the social sciences, we actually purge the subject matter for our study. A human is not a rock, and rocks cannot speak to us. Concepts such as intentionality and meaning have no role in the natural sciences, but they are the substance of the social sciences. Berger states his concern with confusing the two distinct sciences as follows: "Sociology will be especially well advised not to fixate itself in an attitude of humorless scientism that is blind and deaf to the buffoonery of the social spectacle. If sociology does that, it may find that it has acquired a foolproof methodology, only to lose the world of phenomena that it originally set out to explore."[2]

Berger's concerns echo those of other social scientists. Kenneth Boulding was concerned that the flawless precision of mathematical modeling would prove less fruitful than less precise literary methods for understanding the messy social world in which we live.[3] F.A. Hayek is perhaps identified as the most vocal critic of scientism in the study of man, warning that the scientistic path led not only to a false picture of man and society, but also gave the impression that social science could be an effective tool for social control.[4] My intent, however, is not to make a methodological assessment of these arguments. Instead, I want to see how, given these positions, one offers an invitation to others to study man in various walks of life and social situations. Berger, as well as the others mentioned above, warns the reader about viewing the social sciences in a certain way but also promises insight to those who study human beings in another way. The invitation to study promises enlightenment, but it also contains a warning of the limits. This is what I want to explore. As Berger highlights, the sociologists meets up with the economists in some social space, and the political scientist in others.[5] Thus, how one views the sciences of man when studying economy,

---

2. Berger, *Invitation to Sociology*, 165.
3. Kenneth E. Boulding, "Samuelson's *Foundations*: The Role of Mathematics in Economics," *Journal of Political Economy* 56 (June 1948): 187–99.
4. F.A. Hayek, *The Counter-Revolution of Science* (1952; repr., Indianapolis, IN: Liberty Fund, 1979).
5. Berger, *Invitation to Sociology*, 19.

polity, and society is what I am exploring and, in particular, how one offers an invitation to this conversation. In other words, what is the topic of the conversation and who is invited to converse? Berger is explicit that this conversation is a "royal game" and "one doesn't invite to a chess tournament those who are incapable of playing dominoes."[6] On the other hand, we are offering an open invitation to those in our classroom and beyond who are "intensively, endlessly, and shamelessly interested in the doings of men."[7]

An Invitation to Inquiry

I compare and contrast two books that are intended as invitations to their respective disciplines: Berger's *Invitation to Sociology* and Thomas Mayer's *Invitation to Economics* (New York: Wiley, 2009). While Berger's is a classic, Mayer's is recent and not as widely known. Berger and Mayer both come from a German language background (Austria) but received their graduate educations in the United States after World War II (and both in New York City; Berger, born in 1929, received his PhD from the New School in 1954; Mayer, born in 1927, received his PhD from Columbia in 1953). And both take a rather irreverent look at current practice of the discipline they are asking students to join while, at the same, seeing great opportunity for the advancement in thought if the discipline is practiced correctly. After comparing and contrasting these invitations, I show what is common to both invitations concerning the subject matter to which understanding is hoped for.

Comparison to Invitations to Economics

The great strength of Berger's invitation to students is thinking of society as an unfolding drama and man's various roles as that of actors on the stage. But the script is not as deterministic as that imagery might imply and the concept of play extends far beyond the confines of the stage. Our identity is wrapped up in the range of roles we play. The rules we accept are a function of the games we play. Society shapes us, but through our actions in various social situations,

---

6. Berger, *Invitation to Sociology*, vii.
7. Berger, *Invitation to Sociology*, 18.

we shape it as well. Berger argues, in fact, that it is impossible to understand culture and society unless we look at it from the perspective of play and playfulness.[8] Along the way, each situation in the play is sustained by the fabric of shared meanings that is woven out of the actions of individual participants. The social world constitutes an order that is the result of human action, but not necessarily of human design.

The great strength of Mayer's invitation is his emphasis on the intuitive yet logical structure of economic arguments. He tells his readers from the beginning that good economics begins with recognizing the trade-offs that individuals face in making decisions, and continues with an examination of unintended consequences. As Mayer argues, his approach is a human centered approach because it deals "with the way human beings spend much of their time."[9] The "tragic vision" of life that recognizes scarcity defines the situation in which humans find themselves, but the analysis of trade-offs and unintended consequences (or indirect effects) defines thinking like an economist. But Mayer also suggests that this way of thinking is really just an exercise in applied logic. "It is amazing how far common sense, accompanied by a critical attitude and a willingness to think about a problem instead of jumping at an emotionally satisfying conclusion, can carry you in economics."[10]

Both books put humans at the center of the analysis, recognize the constraints individuals must confront in acting, and stress both the intentionality and consequences of those intended actions that go beyond those intentions. Both see economics as embedded in a broader context of politics and society, where that all three (economy, polity, society) are embedded in the broader fields of philosophy and history. Yet both books also promise their reader that isolating their respective disciplines has its benefits as a "fruitful and convenient research strategy."[11] By looking closely at both invitations, it is my hope to show the commonality one can see in a humanistic sociology and a humanistic economics, to suggest that a positive RSVP to the party is warranted, and that the goings-on at the party will consist of a focus on human intentionality, the unintended consequences of human action, and the dramatic comedy that is the story of

8. Berger, *Invitation to Sociology,* 140.
9. Mayer, *Invitation to Economics,* 3.
10. Mayer, *Invitation to Economics,* xiv.
11. Mayer, *Invitation to Economics,* 7.

humankind. The jokes at the party will be plenty; and, while often cutting, they will always be about capturing truth in the human realm.

Perhaps the most important aspect of both books is that if the invitation is accepted the reader will be taught with candor the tools of reasoning to detect "bullshit" in the arguments and social explanations offered in the popular press, by politicians and others in authority, as well as by other social thinkers. While both books present themselves as invitations to a discipline, they are really invitations to inquiry and critical thinking. In the case of Berger, the sociologist takes a subversive stance as he or she transforms the meaning of the familiar through critical analysis. To Mayer, again starting from our observations of the "ordinary course of living," the aspiring economist is advised to pursue common-sense reasoning and critically ask "is this really so" and "under what conditions is it true?"[12] Berger looks at the interaction between intentionality and social structure; Mayer looks at trade-offs and unintended consequences; both look at the systemic forces that produce and reproduce social order.

Spontaneous Sociability and the Two Disciplines

There can be little doubt that part of the economist's effort to intellectually seduce the reader would be a discussion of the spontaneous order of the market economy. Adam Smith's "invisible hand" style of reasoning has been the main intellectual pull of economic theory since the seventeenth and eighteenth centuries, and the phenomena of the spontaneous order of the market place is the central theoretical puzzle of the discipline. Mayer refers to this discovery as "The Crown Jewel of Economics."[13] The price system permits an extensive division of labor in society by coordinating the exchange and production activities in a society. The market system is a complex web of interconnected activities guided through price adjustments and disciplined by profit and loss accounting. The production plans of some are led to mesh with the consumption plans of others in a manner that tends to simultaneously answer the questions of what is going to be produced, how it is going to be produced, and for whom is it going to be produced. A free market economy accomplishes this by marshaling incentives

---

12. Mayer, *Invitation to Economics*, 311.
13. Mayer, *Invitation to Economics*, 115–55.

and mobilizing information while continually alerting economic actors to potential gains from exchange and gains from innovation. Interference in this economic process only distorts the pattern of exchange and production by not allowing prices to tell the "true story" about relative scarcities, underlying tastes and preferences, and technological possibilities. The important point to stress for our purposes is that this system is neither mechanical nor dehumanizing, but intimately human-centered throughout. It begins with people and it ends with people, consisting entirely of their everyday doings.

Many representations of economic person and the market economy do present the material in a machinelike fashion with human actors reduced to flawless rational agents and the market system as perfectly competitive. But such presentations of the economic way of thinking and the logic of the marketplace need not be, nor have they been, the dominant representations. Adam Smith and David Hume, for example, both had a more complicated understanding of man and a more dynamic understanding of the competitive processes that make up the market economy. In short, there is a way to see the complex interdependencies of economic relations guided through price adjustments that is initiated at each step of the analysis by *humanly* rational actors.

These two pictures of the market economy—one human the other mechanical—can also be seen in depictions of society in general. Functionalism, for example, could be seen as the sociology equivalent to the mechanical rendering of the market economy in textbook models of maximizing behavior and perfect competition. Berger points out that, to Durkheim, society was an objective constraint that individuals had to confront.[14] Society confronts us as whole and cannot be reduced to its constituent parts. Rather, it has an objective existence outside of us. "Society, as objective and external fact, confronts us especially in the form of coercion. Its institutions pattern our actions and even shape our expectations." Society has reward structures when we conform to our expected role, and sharp penalties when we deviate from that path. From ridicule to actual deprivation of liberty, society has its way of disciplining its members. Society, in this picture, both precedes us, and will live beyond us. Society, Berger concludes from this Durkheimian perspective, "is the walls of our imprisonment in history."

---

14. Berger, *Invitation to Sociology*, 91–92.

This grim picture of our fate corresponds nicely to the picture that modern textbook economics paints as well. The individual is of measure zero in the model of perfect competition, and the "choice" problem is reduced to an exercise in applied mathematics as the individual maximizes his utility subject to constraints. In fact, Berger is alert to the similarity in the picture drawn by functionalism in sociology with that of functionalist formalism as drawn in economics and argues that perhaps the imagery of society as a forbidding prison could replace the economics picture of constrained optimization in the face of scarcity as the true practitioner of the dismal science. However, there is also evidence of another picture drawn in both disciplines: the spontaneous order of the market and sociability as captured in the law of unintended consequences. In the disciplines of economics and sociology as represented by Mayer and Berger, the invitation to inquiry is twofold—first to see the dilemma of human choice and understanding of the individual's place in society and second to examine the by-product of those choices as both intention driven but not intention limited. The outcomes of the choices individuals make and the interactions they choose to engage in go well beyond the motivations that give rise to those choices in the first place, and the outcomes can be both more desirable than originally imagined or more problematic. The invitation from Mayer and Berger respectively is to study the systemic reasons why actor intentions are channeled in directions where the total benefits of their interactions are greater than the sum of the individual transactions in some instances, and in other instances the total benefits is actually less than the sum of the parts. To put this in economic language, both invisible hand outcomes and tragedy of the commons outcomes are arrived at using the same intellectual tools of spontaneous order analysis.

Examples of Filters and Equilibrium Properties

The tools of spontaneous order analysis postulate a behavioral motivation, examine the institutions within which individuals act and interact for the incentives and information provided to decision makers and establish the penalty and reward structure in the specific environment. Only then can the properties of the resulting order be considered. Again, economics as a discipline provides the most refined set of tools for thinking along these lines about social order. The individual actor does not act in a vacuum but instead within a specified institutional environment defined by law (e.g., property rights) and cultural history (e.g., beliefs) that serve as a "filter" in shifting and steering behavior in this or that direction depending on the incentives, information, and rewards. As action is filtered it comes out the other side exhibiting strong tendencies toward equilibrium states that have "properties" that can be attributed to the respective order. With respect to the overall society, some orders are beneficial; others, less so. To Berger and Mayer, the Scottish Enlightenment phraseology "of human action, but not of human design" aptly explains the massive social structure we find ourselves in whether it be the norms of middle-class suburbia or the array of prices we confront at the supermarket. Social order doesn't just happen; it is composite of the behavior of multitudes of individuals who create and sustain it. In this process, however, Berger and Mayer permit some individuals (the charismatic in the social realm, the entrepreneurial in the market realm) to have bigger roles than others without granting determinant control.[15]

To see the spontaneous order style of reasoning at work in the different disciplines I am going to draw on examples primarily from Berger's discussions that analyze the social structure as it exists in the "world-taken-for-granted" that he was writing in: academia and scientific values. I have steered clear of religion, though of course it is perhaps the realm of human life that Berger is most famous for analyzing, but religion could be used as a shining example of spontaneous order theorizing as it was in Smith and Hume. Consider, for example, the shared analysis though differing normative judgment in Smith and Hume's analysis of state-sponsored religion. Both Smith and Hume observed lower levels of religiosity among the population (as measured by attendance) in states with a publicly supported monopoly of religion. In states where religious service and education was not sponsored by the government, on the other hand, religious diversity and religious fervor among the population was characteristic. Both reasoned that this was due to the incentives that religious leaders faced under the different institutional conditions (i.e., the filter in place). In the state-sponsored monopoly environment, religious leaders felt no special need to attract parishioners to their church and be observant to the teachings of the church. But in situations where the religious leader had to raise the operating expenses for the church through donations from parishioners, incentives led to more entertaining

---

15. Berger, *Invitation to Sociology*, 127–29; Mayer, *Invitation to Economics*, 157–59.

sermons and activities directed at persuading parishioners of the benefits of religious practice. Both less religiosity in the one instance and more in the other were equilibrium properties of the institutional filter of competition (or lack thereof) in the context of religious services. Despite agreement in the analysis, however, their normative positions differed substantially. Smith, who felt that religiosity was desirable, advocated the abolition of state monopoly on religion; Hume, who felt differently about religion, concluded that state-sponsored religion was the more desired policy.

The analysis does not entail a normative stance, nor does even the "normative" welfare conclusion entail the adoption of a normative position. But the application of the analysis to the world of policy does require a normative judgment be made. At the level of the invitation, however, what is seductive to the reader are not the normative policy conclusions in Berger or Mayer, but the astute observations of the world that follow from the analysis. It is very much an intellectual, analytical seduction these authors are engaged in—not an ideological, policy-oriented seduction. In both cases a sort of sophisticated distance is adopted while using the analysis to question familiar institutions and practices. In both instances, readers are invited to develop their critical faculties and be alert to the nonsense that often passes as analysis in the media, among politicians, and certainly among their peers.

Academia

Consider their respective treatments of contemporary academia and scientific values of their respective disciplines. Both describe the incentive structure within academia, the "filter mechanism" of tenure and promotion, and the "equilibrium tendency" of the research and publication practices in the fields of economics and sociology. In both instances, the picture is not pretty. To Berger, the structure of American academic life has encouraged research in sociology that has decidedly rejected theory and instead is preoccupied with "little studies of obscure fragments of social life, irrelevant to any broader theoretical concern."[16] Mayer, on the other hand, sees the incentives of modern academic economics as steering young economists into the all-too-common practice of writing papers

---

16. Berger, *Invitation to Sociology*, 9.

with "many unnecessary citations to papers by colleagues in the hope they will reciprocate."[17]

Part of Berger's and Mayer's appeal to their respective invitees is that they offer distance from the current practice but an intellectual promise of what the appropriate practice of the discipline can in fact deliver to those brave souls who choose to accept the invitation as offered and join the party. Let me reiterate. Berger is clear that not everyone is invited—"one doesn't invite to a chess tournament those who are incapable of playing dominos."[18] Mayer is more inviting, suggesting that anyone can come to the party provided they are willing to engage in "systematically thinking about a problem in a commonsensical way."[19] You can be your own teacher of economics by never taking statements as given but always scrutinizing them by asking, "Is this so?" and "Under what conditions?"—never forgetting to ask not only what the immediate effects of a policy will be, but also demanding that the long-run and indirect effects be explicitly considered. You can train your economic intuition by constantly seeking to explain the reason why the ordinary behavior you see occurring everyday. In short, to be seduced by economics proper (i.e., not scientism or a toolkit for social engineering) is to enable oneself to be amazed at the miracle of the mundane.

Again we see here common ground in the invitation, an appeal to the "world-taken-for-granted" and then subjected to critical analysis which then changes our perception of the familiar in economic and social life. We get to see spontaneous sociability through the lens of sociology, and spontaneous market efficiency through the lens of economics. But we also see how that spontaneous sociability can break down and how the economic order can be inefficient. In the context of academia and scholarship—the "world-taken-for-granted" for the students and faculty who are the primary readers of the *Invitation to Sociology* and *Invitation to Economics*—the structure of incentives for faculty tenure and promotion, as well as everyday academic politics and the sociology of knowledge, produce results which should disabuse one of the notion that this is a game consisting of pure truth-seeking scientists pursuing only the lofty goals of philosophical wisdom and historical accuracy. However, despite the troubles, both Berger

---

17. Mayer, *Invitation to Economics,* 76.
18. Berger, *Invitation to Sociology,* vi.
19. Mayer, *Invitation to Economics,* 311.

and Mayer affirm that the process of scholarship and critical dialogue produce, albeit as a by-product, improved understanding of both the underlying social and economic relationships and empirical reality.

The Curse of Scientism

Another surprising common ground in the two invitations is how they see the curse of scientism both distorting the respective disciplines and ultimately transforming the disciplinary practice to such an extent that the invitation offered is no longer interesting to those invited to the intellectual party. In other words, though emphasizing different issues, Berger and Mayer can be read as arguing that scientism kills science. To clarify, it is not that scientism produces less insightful work; it is that it kills the ability to actually derive insight. A grim humorlessness takes over the discipline. Not only do we lose the miracle of the mundane, and the mystery of everyday life, but we are also left unable to appreciate the buffoonery of humanity in social settings.

Economic man is reduced by formalism and positivism to a lightening calculator of pleasure and pain, rather than a creature forever caught between alluring hopes and haunting fears that must embrace the challenge of their freedom and is compelled to cope with the imperfections of their knowledge. Similarly, the foolproof methodology of formalism and positivism fits well with a certain form of functionalism in sociology. The individual's struggle with identity, association, and community are ignored as outside the realm of the appropriately scientific. "Freedom," Berger writes, "is not empirically available."[20] While we experience freedom every day in our lives, "it is not open to demonstration by any scientific methods." Freedom is thus elusive to the scientific mind. But, Berger warns, such a positivistic understanding of the sociologist's task produces a form of "intellectual barbarism."[21]

Ironically, for our purposes, Berger sees the solution to the problem of freedom within the framework developed by Max Weber for his interpretative sociology. Subsequent developments in sociology would accuse Weber's sociological

---

20. Berger, *Invitation to Sociology*, 122.
21. Berger, *Invitation to Sociology*, 124.

theory of being "voluntaristic." While Durkheim emphasized the external and objective nature of society, Weber emphasized human intentionality and the subjective meanings of social action. In this rendering of the perspectives we are presented with what might be called a pure externalist point of view and a pure internalist point of view. But, as Berger points out, this misconstrues the Weberian (and Schutzian) sociological project. (Recall that Schutz wrote his doctoral dissertation under Ludwig von Mises, who also attempted to build upon Weber's project in the science of human action.) Weber recognized not only the intentions of the actors in society, but also the unintended consequences. Weber's point was simply to stress that in the social sciences, the "subjective dimension must be taken into consideration for an adequate sociological understanding."[22] Social order cannot be viewed purely from the outside. The social actors' interpretations of meanings run throughout and the social order is sustained by "the fabric of meanings that are brought into it by the several participants." Any "scientific" methodology which precludes our ability to gain access to this world of social meanings ultimately undermines the scientific enterprise. There can be coherence to a purely externalist perspective, but it hides from view what is most human about social life. On the other hand, a purely internalist perspective would deny the social reality of others and the reality that we are born into a social world that defines and shapes us from birth. Our scientific methods must make room and legitimize dialogue that enables us to come to grips with what Berger calls the paradox of social existence: "That society defines us, but is in turn defined by us."[23]

Berger uses the metaphor of theatre to explain the subject of the human sciences. Individuals are performing in drama and comedies. They are playing a role in a play, but also improvising on stage. Society appears to the actor as precarious, uncertain and unpredictable. At the same time, the institutions of society constrain us and channel our behavior. It all sounds very much like the economic way of thinking as influenced by Mises, Hayek, Lachmann, Kirzner, and Lavoie. As it should, since it also finds its roots in Weber's *verstehen* sociology, and its methods of scientific procedure represent positive social

22. Berger, *Invitation to Sociology*, 126.
23. Berger, *Invitation to Sociology*, 129.

science prior to positivism (i.e., ends are treated as given and the analysis is limited to the efficacy of chosen means in terms of satisfying those ends).

Mayer is not an Austrian school economist, though he was born in Austria. He is instead a rather conventional macroeconomist trained midcentury. Nonetheless, he possesses unusual sensibilities about methodological and philosophical questions. Mayer rejects naïve positivism and the difficulties that the empirical project in economics must confront.[24] On the other hand, he is a strong advocate for careful empirical economics and especially sophisticated statistical analysis. However, he does believe that the efforts at demarking science from other forms of human knowledge have not been successful. The search for a demarcation criterion, he argues, may in fact be futile. There is no reliable way to draw the line between science and nonscience, but we can distinguish between sense and nonsense. Mayer embraces the German language distinctions between subjects such as the humanities, the natural sciences, and the social sciences. The disciplined study of an area of human knowledge—*Wissenschaft*—is modified by "*Naturwissenschaften*" or "*Sozialwissenschaften*" as we get the only demarcation points we can humanly achieve. Scientific thought progresses when those practicing it are able to evaluate arguments and evidence in a disinterested way, willing to abandon previous beliefs when logic and evidence persuade us otherwise, and, "in general, be more interested in establishing truth than in building their reputations."[25]

Berger makes the compelling argument that once we take the humanistic turn in social thought, the students and practitioners of the discipline so conceived must be in continuous communication with other disciplines that explore the human condition. In Berger's *Invitation*, he ignores economics, and rightfully so because the economics he sees being practiced in the 1960s is the technical economics of textbook maximizing man and perfect competition in microeconomics, or the mechanical exercises of social control with the hydraulic Keynesianism of aggregate demand management in macroeconomics. There is simply nothing very human to either of these intellectual exercises. In fact, this style of economics aligns quite nicely with the pure externalist perspective of some forms of functionalism and, as such, completely purges the

---

24. Mayer, *Invitation to Economics*, 227–310.
25. Mayer, *Invitation to Economics*, 55.

human actor with his purposes and plans from the analysis. But Berger does mention philosophy and history as the most important disciplines to keep the social theorist engaged humanistically.[26] For those who are critical of formalism and positivism in economics, the same disciplines are called upon to keep the humanistic economist grounded in the concern for the human condition.

Mutual Seductions

As pointed out, Berger's *Invitation to Sociology* has had a curious history. In terms of sales it has been an amazing success; in terms of reviews by peers, less so. The reason for this paradox is simple. Berger offers a staggering criticism to the dominant sociological approach within the academic milieu at the time of publication and up through today. Yet, as he notes, if a more humanistic sociology is going to be practiced, it will have to be practiced in the academy.

Berger excites his readers by informing them that they must be curious and "be a person that is intensively, endlessly, shamelessly interested in the doings of men."[27] The sociologist must be willing to study man in "all the human gathering places of the world, wherever men come together." And "his consuming interest remains in the world of men, their institutions, their history, their passions." The sociologist must not only be drawn to understand man in "moments of tragedy and grandeur and ecstasy," but also be "fascinated by the commonplace, the everyday."

I have argued that Berger's *Invitation to Sociology* has many striking similarities to Mayer's *Invitation to Economics*. Both attempt to seduce the reader through a combination of critical irreverence as well as a stunning appreciation for the mystery of our mundane existence. The human being with purposes and plans, as well as foibles and fears, is at the center of both invitations to inquiry. The institutions of society both define us and are shaped by us in both the story offered by Berger and by Mayer. Dynamic individuals break the lock hold of social structure—the charismatic in society, the entrepreneur in the economy. And the notion of play—in its many different meanings—and the rules that define the realm of play make an appearance in both invitations. And for our

---

26. Berger, *Invitation to Sociology*, 168.
27. Berger, *Invitation to Sociology*, 18.

present purposes, the central theme of the play is the spontaneous ordering of society: sociability in the form of identity, associations, and community in Berger's story; and firms, organizations, and patterns of trade in Mayer's. The law of unintended consequences is one of the core ideas offered to readers of both invitations as a critical tool of reasoning and social understanding.

Jon Elster has recently described Tocqueville as one of the first great social thinkers.[28] In a book published that same year, Richard Swedberg describes Tocqueville's political economy.[29] In a recently published book, Dragos Aligica and I pick up on Vincent Ostrom's ruminations on Tocqueville and democracy and lay out the modern project for the science of association and the cultivation of a people well prepared to accept the "troubles of thinking and the cares of living."[30] But, actually, Berger beat us to the punch (except for Tocqueville, of course) when he concludes that much can be learned from the metaphor of a puppet theatre as society. The logic of the situation comes into sharp focus in such a theater and we can see ourselves in such a play. The pure externalist perspective may even lead us to think of ourselves as puppets dancing at the end of the strings. "But then we grasp a decisive difference between the puppet theatre and our own drama. Unlike the puppets, we have the possibility of stopping in our movements, looking up and perceiving the machinery by which we have been moved. In this act lies the first step towards freedom. And in this same act we find the conclusive justification of sociology as a humanistic discipline."[31]

In so concluding his *Invitation to Sociology*, I suggest, Peter Berger not only demonstrated throughout the work the seductive intellectual project of spontaneous order studies—the critical frame of mind that can result from examining sociability as the product of human action, but not of human design—but also forged the indispensable link between the humanistic project in sociology and

28. Jon Elster, *Alexis de Tocqueville: The First Social Scientist* (New York: Cambridge University Press, 2009).

29. Richard Swedberg, *Tocqueville's Political Economy* (Princeton, NJ: Princeton University Press, 2009).

30. P. Dragos Aligica and Peter J. Boettke, *Challenging Institutional Analysis and Development: The Bloomington School* (New York: Routledge, 2009); Vincent Ostrom, *The Meaning of Democracy and the Vulnerability of Democracies* (Ann Arbor: University of Michigan Press, 1997).

31. Berger, *Invitation to Sociology*, 176.

the understanding of the freedom of the individual in society. If our methods make us blind and deaf to the buffoonery of human society, they will also steer us away from a true understanding of the human condition. Peter Berger fought constantly and continues to fight so that we may see how a human being lives, and that we may hear an individual tell, in all his or her glory (and silliness), the story of a free human actor in the unfolding drama (and comedy) which constitutes our social world.

14

Was Mises Right?

Introduction

THE AUSTRIAN SCHOOL'S unique methodological stance separates it from the rest of the economics profession. Methodological subjectivism, recognition of radical uncertainty, and the notion of markets as processes are often cited as defining characteristics of the Austrian approach.[1] Due to its controversial status, less frequently noted in the modern literature is *methodological apriorism*. Indeed, throughout the history of the Austrian school, many of its adherents have attempted to distance themselves from Menger's exact laws and Mises's *apriorism*, while at the same time building on the theoretical insights of these thinkers. Several of Mises's students from the Vienna years—Fritz Machlup, for example—attempted to accomplish this two-step maneuver.[2] But to the Austrian economists who trained with Mises during his

---

1. See, e.g., Gerald P. O'Driscoll and Mario J. Rizzo, *The Economics of Time and Ignorance* (New York: Basil Blackwell Publishers, 1985); Karen I. Vaughn, *Austrian Economics in America* (New York: Cambridge University Press, 1994); Peter J. Boettke, ed., *The Elgar Companion to Austrian Economics* (Aldershot, UK: Edward Elgar Publishing, 1994); Peter J. Boettke and Peter T. Leeson, "The Austrian School of Economics, 1950–2000," in *The Blackwell Companion to the History of Economic Thought*, edited by Warren J. Samuels, Jeff E. Biddle, and John B. Davis (Oxford: Basil Blackwell Publishers, 2003).
2. Alfred Schutz and Felix Kaufmann were students of Mises who attempted to critically reconstruct Mises's methodology through the philosophy of Husserl (Schutz) and positivism (Kaufmann) and develop a general methodological stance for the social sciences. See Alfred Schutz, *The Phenomenology of the Social World* (Evanston, IL: Northwestern University Press, 1967); Felix Kaufmann, *The Methodology of the Social Sciences* (London: Oxford University Press, 1944).

New York University period (1944–1969), like Murray Rothbard, adherence to methodological *apriorism* is *the* distinguishing characteristic of the Austrian school, and alternative methodological positions are interpreted as undermining Mises's strong claim about the nature of economic reasoning.[3]

The Austrian position has long been associated with a bifurcation of knowledge—deductive versus historical method, *apriorism* versus positivism, etc. We suggest that these blunt divisions fail to capture the subtle position that was developed by Menger, Boehm-Bawerk, and Mises in the attempt to carve out a unique niche for the human sciences. For most economists, economics was a science located between the natural sciences and the cultural discipline of history. For these Austrians, however, economics was a human science that could derive laws that had the same ontological status as the laws derived in the natural sciences, yet accounted for the complexity of the human experience. Mises did not originate the Austrian position but inherited it from Menger and Boehm-Bawerk and sought to provide an updated philosophical defense of that position.[4]

---

3. See, for instance, Murray N. Rothbard, "In Defense of Extreme Apriorism," *Southern Economic Journal* vol. 23:3 (1957), 314–20; Rothbard, "Praxeology: The Method of Austrian Economics," in *Foundations of Modern Economics*, edited by E. Dolan (1972; repr., Kansas City, KS: Sheed & Ward, 1976). In "In Defense," Rothbard, however, defends *apriorism* on slightly different grounds than Mises. He maintains that while the starting point of economic theory—the proposition that all humans behave purposively—may be known via introspection (per Mises), it can also be defended as *aprioristic* if it is learned by appealing to "broad empirical" observation. In this way, Rothbard introduces what he calls an "Aristotelian" derivation of the action axiom's *aprioristic* status. Also on this issue, see Smith who defends the view of an ontological a priori—a "deep-lying a priori dimension on the side of the things themselves" (B. Smith, "In Defense of Extreme (Fallibilistic) Apriorism," *Journal of Libertarian Studies*, 12:1 (Spring 1996): 179–92). In *Ludwig von Mises* (Wilmington, NC: ISI Books, 2001), Israel Kirzner recounts a story in which Mises allegedly told him that the action axiom was derived from "experience" as well. In his first book and doctoral dissertation written under the direction of Mises, however, Kirzner maintains the traditional Misesian argument that we know humans act by way of introspection (Kirzner, *The Economic Point of View* (Princeton, NJ: Van Nostrand, 1960)).

4. See, e.g., Ludwig von Mises, *Epistemological Problems of Economics* (1933; repr., New York: New York University Press, 1981).

While Menger and Mises resorted to epistemological argument, Boehm-Bawerk put his argument in more common-sense terms.[5] Here the deductive method is justified on the grounds that in the act of arranging the array of historical facts to construct a meaningful story, the historian must arrange according to some criteria of priority. The criteria, Boehm-Bawerk argued, are provided by theory. The purpose of theory is to aid in the act of historical investigation—not to fight against it. In making this argument, which was (is) the Austrian argument, Boehm-Bawerk carved out a niche where the advancement of human knowledge in the discipline of political economy was neither a product of pure deduction nor empirical induction, but a blending of both.

On this basis we propose a tripartite division of economic inquiry: pure theory, institutionally contingent theory, and economic history and statistical analysis. Each realm of economic inquiry serves different purposes and the knowledge claims being made in each constitute different epistemological moments.[6] Just as we must recognize the empirical component of economic inquiry, we must also recognize the importance of pure theory, which is constructed through logical deduction.

---

5. See E. Boehm-Bawerk, "The Historical versus the Deductive Method in Political Economy," *Annals of the American Academy of Political Science* I, in *Classics in Austrian Economics*, edited by Israel M. Kirzner (1891; repr., London: Pickering & Chatto, 1994), 109–29.

6. Boehm-Bawerk divides price theory into a first part, which is pure theory of exchange and price, and a second part which incorporates into that analysis different individual motivations, differing empirical circumstance, and alternative concrete institutions.

> The amount of attention devoted by economists to each of these two parts of the theory of price has varied with the prevailing phase in methods of research. As long as the abstractly deductive phase characteristic of the English school was in the ascendancy, the first part of the price problem was almost the only one to be treated, and much too nearly to the complete exclusion of the other. Later on, the historical method, originating in Germany, took over the lead. It was characterized by a fondness for emphasizing not only the general, but the particular as well, for noting not only the influence of broader types, but also that of national, social and individual peculiarities.

E. Boehm-Bawerk, *Capital and Interest*, 3 vols. (1884–1921; repr., South Holland, IL: Libertarian Press, 1949), vol. II, 212–13. While Boehm-Bawerk saw his own main contributions to the area of pure theory, he argues that "I acknowledge that what I am offering indubitably calls for complementary treatment of the second part of the theory of price . . ." (*Capital*, vol. 2, 213).

In a science dominated by what many have called "physics envy," Austrian school writers who have insisted on the *aprioristic* nature of pure economics have often endured a greater marginalization of their status in the eyes of the profession than those economists who have distanced themselves from the *aprioristic* approach. We contend that this is a serious error born out of the confusion over the different realms of knowledge that constitute economic inquiry.

This chapter explores methodological *apriorism* as laid out by its most recognizable defender, Ludwig von Mises. We argue that his position is more philosophically sophisticated than either friend or foe has cared to admit. Mises's position is explained as grounded in the practical problems of economic inquiry and a common-sense rendering of these problems as we have just attributed to Boehm-Bawerk. We provide evidence to show how Mises was influenced in his attempt to justify pure theory by the philosophy of Immanuel Kant and also demonstrate that Mises's *application* of this idea to the science of economics moves beyond Kant. Specifically, we contend that building upon these developments, Mises eschewed the traditional analytic/synthetic dichotomy, successfully both revealing the illegitimacy of the positivist approach and defending the empirical relevance of "mere tautologies" in economic science. Finally, we discuss the relevance of Mises's methodological position for modern economic science.

Kant on *Apriorism*

The idea of the synthetic a priori is most famously connected with Immanuel Kant's *Critique of Pure Reason*.[7] Building on a distinction between the appearance of things and things in themselves, Kant argued that the transcendental deduction of concepts is the most important intellectual exercise for our understanding. Human cognition can be divided into those concepts we come to understand completely independent of experience and those that we come to understand only through experience. Kant argued that the problem that arises in human understanding is how our subjective conditions of thinking could obtain objective validity. This problem, he maintained, is solved through transcendental deduction.

---

7. Immanuel Kant, *The Critique of Pure Reason*, translated by N.K. Smith (New York: St. Martin's Press, 1958), B1–30.

The extreme rationalism of philosophers like Leibniz, Wolff, and Baumgarten, Kant maintained, was wrong. By itself reason cannot teach us anything about the actual world. Without the data of experience, pure logic is at a loss to impart information to us regarding the reality we live in. Similarly, the empiricism defended by scholars like Locke, Berkeley, and Hume was also incorrect. Facts of the world are never presented to the mind tabula rasa. They can only be understood with the aid of concepts that exist in our mind prior to any experience. In response to both (pure) rationalism and (pure) empiricism, Kant develops the notion of a class of knowledge held by individuals that while known to us a priori nonetheless imparts information about the real world.

Kant contended that a priori axioms known to us apart from experience are embedded in us as categories of the human mind. These a priori concepts are necessary to use the human faculty of judgment to understand objects in the world. Indeed, understanding of the world is impossible except through these categories that enable us to make sense of our experiences. According to Kant then, our understanding of objective reality has objective validity via the employment of concepts known a priori. At the basis of all empirical cognition are a priori concepts, without which objective validity would be denied to us. As Kant argued, we do not derive concepts from nature, but interrogate nature with the aid of these concepts. He held that through introspection we are able to realize what our minds already know and can come to discover the a priori categories that shape our thinking and perceptions of the world.[8]

This brief and elementary statement of Kant's position is not meant to be complete and clearly does not do justice to the many and complicated nuances of his philosophy. Instead it is meant merely to sketch a crude outline of Kant's epistemology as a means of analyzing the context in which Mises develops his position concerning the nature of economic science—a task we take up in the following section.

Similarly, it is often argued that Kant's argument was motivated by a desire to provide the metaphysical foundation for Newtonian science. We have no particular interest in this question. Nor do we have any comments to offer on whether the effort was one to legitimate science while leaving room for morality

---

8. Kant, *Critique*, A95–130.

and religious faith. Recognizing the Kantian background to Mises's defense of the nature of economic thought is our primary focus. Kant developed his argument concerning human action by reference to Locke's discussion of how belief gives rise to action. Locke argued that our understanding of human action arises only through our experience with nature. While Kant admits that empirical study may enable us to understand the occasional cause by which the pure categories and forms of intuition are brought into application, he argues for their strict a priori nature. It is this focus on the a priori categories of human action that would occupy Mises's philosophical attention.

Mises and the Nature of Economic Science

For most of his career Mises found himself in a methodologically uncomfortable position.[9] As a German-language economist, the discipline he was educated in was dominated by historicism. As a Viennese intellectual, Mises began to mature as a thinker within the philosophical culture of Wittgenstein and the Vienna Circle. When he published his first major statement concerning his methodological views, logical positivism was starting to spread in economics.[10] As Mises conceived it, logical positivism denied the existence of a priori knowledge and rejected all nonempirical forms of analysis.[11] According to this view, if economics is to progress as a science, indeed, if it constitutes a science at all,

---

9. And we should add that Mises was ideologically uncomfortable as well. Put the two together, and his claim to intellectual legitimacy was hard to maintain during the majority of his career. He was held to be both methodologically and ideologically suspect. But we argue that Mises's position (both methodologically and ideologically) is actually much more in line with the mainstream of political and economic thought historically contemplated than anyone cared to admit during his lifetime.

10. Mises, *Epistemological Problems*. Apriorism was not alien to economics at this time as was evident in Lionel Robbins, *Essay on the Nature and Significance of Economic Science* (London: Macmillan, 1932), and Frank H. Knight, "What Is Truth in Economics?" *Journal of Political Economy* 48 (1940): 1–32. However, by the time Milton Friedman published his *Essays in Positive Economics* (Chicago: University of Chicago Press, 1953), it was standard for economists to argue that economic science required submitting falsifiable hypotheses to empirical test.

11. See P. Greaves, *Mises Made Easier: A Glossary for Ludwig von Mises's* Human Action (New York: Free-Market Books, 1974).

it must follow the methods of falsification employed by the physical sciences.[12] Truth about the world, positivists maintain, is only accessible through experience. The sterile objectivity that truth demands cannot permit "non-facts" to pollute it. The positivist program thus aimed at purging subjective influence from the pure facts of the world. The brute facts, they maintained, untainted by the scientist's preconceptions, could only be arrived at through the scientific method. According to this view, value-freedom is entirely procedural in the sense that objective truth is a function of following the scientific procedure.[13] While it is possible to disagree with this formulation of logical positivism, this is clearly how Mises conceived of it, and it is with his conception that we are concerned.[14]

It was against this view of positivism, as well as the view of the older German historicists like Gustav Schmoller and later, his student, Werner Sombart, that Mises developed his argument for methodological *apriorism*. The historicist and positivist programs, Mises pointed out, were fatally flawed from the outset in their failure to appreciate the necessarily theory-laden nature of all "facts."[15]

---

12. T.W. Hutchison was the most ardent supporter of this position (*The Significance and Basic Postulates of Economic Theory* (1938; repr., New York: Augustus M. Kelley, 1965). It is also important to remember that, as his work indicates, the vehemence with which positivism was presented in economics was in large part *ideologically motivated*—to be used as a philosophical hammer with which to defeat ideological systems such as Marxism and Nazism from intruding into the realm of science as they had in the 1930s.

13. Contrast this with the position developed by Max Weber and Ludwig von Mises for assuring value-free analysis. Weber and Mises were prepositivistic positive economists and their position is important to articulate as an alternative to the positivistic notion of value-freedom. For discussions of Weber's development of his argument, see Richard Swedberg, *Max Weber and the Idea of Economic Sociology* (Princeton, NJ: Princeton University Press, 1997) and Bruce Caldwell, *Hayek's Challenge: An Intellectual Biography of F.A. Hayek* (Chicago: University of Chicago Press, 2004). Also see Peter J. Boettke, "Why Are There No Austrian Socialists? Ideology, Science and the Austrian School," *Journal of the History of Economic Thought* 17 (Spring 1995): 35–56; and Boettke, "Is Economics a Moral Science?" *Journal of Markets & Morality* 1, no. 2 (1998): 212–19.

14. See, e.g., Ludwig von Mises, *The Ultimate Foundation of Economic Science* (Kansas City, KS: Sheed & McMeel, 1978), 38, 120–24, 133; Mises, *Epistemological Problems*, 7–12; Mises, *Human Action: A Treatise on Economics* (1949; Repr., Indianapolis, IN: Liberty Fund, 2010), 4, 30, 59. See also Greaves, *Mises Made Easier,* who compiled a glossary of terms including "logical positivism" as a companion to Mises's *Human Action*, which Mises oversaw and approved.

15. Mises's point about the impossibility of unambiguous tests of theory can be understood as anticipating the more refined Duhem-Quine thesis which stated that the truth

This insight is not new to Mises but was emphasized by Goethe who stated: "everything in the realm of fact is already theory."[16] Mises employed a version of this argument when he pointed out that empiricists are "able to believe that facts can be understood without any theory only because they failed to recognize a theory is already contained in the very linguistic terms involved in every act of thought. To apply language, with its words and concepts to anything is at the same time to approach it with theory."[17] The choice is never between theory and no theory; it is between articulated and defended theory and unarticulated and nondefended theory.

The unavoidability of theory-laden facts renders impossible the procedural value-freedom put forth by the positivists. If "pure" facts are required for objectivity, then objectivity is impossible. Objectivity in the social sciences, Mises argued, was ensured by restricting analysis to the assessment of the effectiveness of chosen means for given ends. The radical subjectivism of Mises with regard to the ends individuals pursue enabled the objectivity of economic analysis.

To Mises, the theory-laden nature of the "facts of the social sciences" implied that we should strive to articulate theory and defend it in a clear and logical fashion. But this did not mean that theory was immune from criticism. The economist "can never be absolutely certain that his inquiries were not misled and that what he considers as certain truth is not error. All [he] can do is submit all his theories again and again to the most critical reexamination."[18] Nor did it deny the fundamental importance of empirical work for understanding the social world. In fact, in Mises's system the entire purpose of theory was to aid

---

or falsity of a theoretical statement cannot be determined independently of a network of statements. See Peter J. Boettke, "Ludwig von Mises," in *The Handbook of Economic Methodology*, edited by J. Davis, D. Wade Hands, and U. Maki (Cheltenham, UK: Edward Elgar Publishing, 1998), 534–40.

16. Johann Wolfgang von Goethe, *Scientific Studies* (Princeton, NJ: Princeton University Press), 307.

17. Mises, *Epistemological Problems*, 28.

18. Mises, *Human Action*, 69. On the issue of fallibility in Mises's methodology see also our discussion of B. Smith, "Aristotle, Menger, Mises: An Essay in the Metaphysics of Economics," *History of Political Economy*, Annual Supplement to Volume 22 (1990): 263–88; Smith, "Aristotelianism, Apriorism, Essentialism," in *The Elgar Companion to Austrian Economics*, edited by Peter J. Boettke (Northampton, MA: Edward Elgar, 1994), 33–37; Smith, "In Defense"; evolution; and Mises later in this section.

the act of historical interpretation. He divided the realms of knowledge into conception (theory) and understanding (history), due to the separate epistemological issues involved in both endeavors.[19] Although this position is frequently overlooked by his critics, it is clear in Mises's writings that historical understanding was the vital goal towards which the theoretical construct of economics was to be employed. Economic theory was the servant of empirical work; aprioristic theory and the interpretation of historical phenomena are intertwined.[20]

Mises leveled another criticism at the logical positivists who championed methodological monism in the sciences. He pointed out that what distinguishes economics from other sciences is that our science deals with conscious actors. Unlike the unmotivated subject matter of the physical sciences, the subjects of economic study are rational, conscious agents with certain desires and beliefs about how to achieve them. In the physical sciences the ultimate causes of matter's "behavior" can never be known. This fact is due to the relationship between the physical scientist and his subject of study, which differs radically for social scientists and their subject of study.

The physical scientist must remain an outside observer of his subject. He can never "get inside" the object of his inquiry and so can never have direct, intimate knowledge of the source of his subject's primary properties. Indeed, by repeatedly observing his object of inquiry externally under varying conditions the physical scientist attempts to get closer to knowledge of the object under observation. While this process can bring him closer, his unalterable status as external observer prohibits him from ever having final knowledge of his subject's ultimate cause.[21]

The social scientist, on the other hand, is in a relatively better position, for qua human beings, he or she is the very subject of study. This fortunate posi-

---

19. See Ludwig von Mises, *Theory and History* (New Haven, CT: Yale University Press, 1957).

20. Mises, *Human Action*, 66.

21. Austrian writers from F. von Wieser (*Social Economics* (New York: Adelphi, 1927)) to Mises (*Human Action*) to F.A. Hayek ("The Facts of the Social Sciences," in *Individualism and Economics Order* (1943; repr., Chicago: University of Chicago Press, 1996), 57–76) have emphasized "knowledge from within" as a distinct characteristic of the human sciences.

tion allows him or her to get inside the mind of the subject. Thus, in the social sciences, the scientist *begins* with knowledge of the ultimate causes driving the subject's behavior. And it is in this sense that the social scientist is in a better position for the study of his or her field than the physical scientist in terms of understanding *causation*. This fundamental difference between the relationship of the physical scientist to his or her subject of inquiry and social scientist to his or her subject of study suggests a fundamental difference in the epistemological status of their insights and implies a methodological dualism in the realm of science.

Our understanding of the natural world improved tremendously when explanations of physical phenomena by way of "purpose" were replaced with explanations that discussed the physical laws of nature. Explanations that appealed to the whims of the gods to explain the changing seasons, for instance, were replaced by one which discussed the earth's rotation around the sun. The purging of anthropomorphism in the natural sciences thus led to the advancement of knowledge of the physical universe. But as Mises recognized, in attempting to mimic the natural sciences, if we purge human purposes and plans from the human sciences, we purge our very subject matter.[22] "Praxeological reality is not the physical universe," Mises argued, "but man's conscious reaction to the given state of this universe. Economics is not about things and tangible material objects; it is about men, their meanings and actions. Goods, commodities, and wealth and all the other notions of conduct are not elements of nature; they are elements of human meaning and conduct."[23]

Additionally, in contrast to the natural sciences, Mises argued that there are no constant relationships in human action. As such no universally valid *quantitative* laws are possible in the realm of human affairs. Standing between the claims of methodological monism on the one side and historicism on the other side, Mises sought to carve out a niche for the science of human action—one that agreed with the cultural critics of methodological monism that the human sciences were unique yet resisted the implication of these critics that there were no nomological laws possible in the human realm. Mises's position was that

---

22. Besides Mises, see also Hayek's classic work *The Counter-Revolution of Science* (1952; repr., Indianapolis, IN: Liberty Fund, 1979) on this point.
23. Mises, *Human Action*, 92.

while the science of human action (praxeology) was different from the natural sciences for the reasons enumerated above, it generated nomological laws that had the same ontological claim on our attention as that of the natural sciences.

Economics' epistemological status had to be different by the nature of the subject of study, but scientific discovery and advance were indeed possible. While quantitative laws could not be derived, qualitative counterparts could be derived and were, in fact, essential to the enterprise of understanding social reality and public policy.

> The experience with which the sciences of human action have to deal is always an experience of complex phenomena. No laboratory experiments can be performed with regard to human action. We are never in a position to observe the change in one element, only, all other conditions of the event being equal to a case in which the element concerned did not change.[24]

Thus we cannot, "holding the rest of the world constant," change price to determine its relationship to quantity, as the scientific method touted by positivists requires.[25] But this does not mean that we cannot understand the relationship between price and quantity. We can derive pattern predictions or explanation of the principle even if we cannot derive point predictions subject to refutation. These fundamental differences between the physical and human sciences, Mises tells us, require that we be methodological dualists.

Mises's methodological dualism established the framework for his *apriorism*. If historicists are wrong and economic laws are indeed evident and can be understood through scientific investigation, what must follow? And, if the positivists are wrong and the methods of the natural sciences are ill-suited to elaborate the laws of economics, what method must economics follow? In response to this question Mises, like Kant, uses the notion of (a) a priori axioms

---

24. Mises, *Human Action*, 31.
25. Economic laws are deduced from the axiom of action *aprioristically* with the aid of the ceteris paribus assumption that enables a sort of controlled mental experiment. And theoretical progress in the human sciences, according to Mises, occurs by way of these mental experiments. Mises goes as far as to say that the method of praxeology is the method of imaginary constructions (*Human Action*, 237–38).

and logical categories of the human mind that are (b) known to individuals through a process of introspection, which (c) act as the means through which we understand the world, and then applies this idea to the science of economics.

According to Mises our nature as actors—beings who purposefully act—is known through introspection. Reflection on what it means to be human reveals that purposeful behavior is our primary and distinguishing feature. This knowledge is *aprioristic*. We do not become aware of our uniquely human characteristic through experience because we cannot, in fact, "experience" without purpose. Thus, "man does not have the creative power to imagine categories at variance" with the category of action.[26] In taking action as the starting point for all of economic theory, Mises roots the logic of choice in the broader logic of action he calls praxeology.

In the course of laying out his argument, Mises moves beyond Kant. Critics of the notion of a synthetic a priori worried that such a view would give license to any set of theories. According to these critics, by arbitrarily postulating any given axiom as *aprioristic*, any number of erroneous conclusions can be arrived at. A related line of criticism points out that even if we could agree on what axioms are truly known *aprioristically*, how are we to choose among the axioms to employ when different axioms yield differing or even contradictory results?

In response to criticisms about the alleged arbitrary selection of starting axioms Mises argued that the deductive procedure does not begin with an arbitrary choice of axioms, but that rather with reflection on the essence of human action. As he stated it: "The starting point of praxeology is not a choice of axioms and a decision about methods of procedure, but reflection about the essence of action."[27] In our efforts to understand reality *we do not choose* the axiom we wish to begin with so much as it is *chosen for us* by the world in which we live. The axiom of action is in a sense imposed on us by the world. As the "filter" through which we make sense of our surroundings, we must necessarily begin our understanding processes with the concept of purposeful action. It is the only means available to us for this purpose, as we cannot help but see the world through the "lenses" conditioned by the unavoidable structure of our minds.

---

26. Mises, *Human Action*, 35.
27. Mises, *Human Action*, 40.

If we desire to ground economics in the reality of the world, Mises maintained, we have no choice but start with the axiom of action. No other starting point can yield theory that illuminates the behavior of real individuals.

It is true, economic theory could begin with another axiom and the laws thus deduced would be valid if no errors were made in the process of deduction and the assumptions posited corresponded to the circumstances at hand. But because for Mises economics is both *aprioristic* and interested in illuminating the real world, its starting axiom must be both known without reference to experience and fundamentally connected to the world of man. The action axiom fits both of these descriptions. In contrast, the competitive equilibrium world of Arrow-Hahn-Debreu is derived *aprioristically* but eschewed by Mises because unlike theory deduced from the axiom of action, it remains largely unconnected to the real world.[28]

Like Kant, Mises suggests that action implies certain prerequisites of action—categories of the mind, which are also known a priori. He indicates six such categories without which purposeful behavior is impossible: temporality, causality, uncertainty, dissatisfaction, an imagined preferred state of affairs, and beliefs or expectations about the means available for satisfying wants.

In examining the a priori nature of these logical categories, Mises offers a speculative history as to how they evolved as part of the human mind in *Human Action* and *Ultimate Foundation*. According to Mises the a priori categories evolved along with humans in a Darwinian fashion. We have the categories of the mind that we do today precisely because they were best able to impart

---

28. This is why Cowen and Fink's suggestion that the evenly rotating economy (ERE) is an inconsistent construct and that Arrow-Hahn-Debreu's model of general competitive equilibrium serves as a better model can be challenged. See Tyler Cowen and R. Fink, "Inconsistent Equilibrium Constructs: Mises and Rothbard on the Evenly Rotating Economy," *American Economic Review* (September 1985): 866–69. It depends on the purpose for which the model construct is being used. Furthermore, Caldwell's criticism in "Praxeology and Its Critics" that among competing a priori theories one is left powerless to choose between them must also be challenged. Criteria of choice are provided by relevance for the task the scientist hopes to put the thought experiment toward. Note the difference here between our response to Caldwell, which utilizes what Smith (in "In Defense") calls the Kant–Mises "subjectivist" *apriorism*, and Smith's own response, which is closer to Rothbard's position and overcomes Caldwell's criticism by pointing to an "objectivist" *apriorism*—"an a priori in the real world" ("In Defense," 191).

accurate information about the real world to us necessary for our survival. The categories are subject to future evolution as improved variations enable us to better understand the world or the underlying reality as the world itself changes. This hypothesized evolutionary process helps explain the necessary connection of the starting point of action, and the categories that it implies, to the real world. If they were not connected in this way to the world, humans possessing them could not have evolved as they have. There is a mutually interactive process between our minds and the world, forming a feedback loop between the evolution of our a priori mental categories that determine the world we experience, and the reality of the world that conditions our way of thinking and understanding reality.

Barry Smith's important work defends "extreme, *fallible*, apriorism," on the grounds that there are "*a priori* structures" in the world itself.[29] He distinguishes between "impositionist" *apriorism*, which is subjectivist in its approach and maintains that individual actors impose structures on the world that give rise to knowledge, and "reflectionist" *apriorism*, which maintains that "we can have *a priori* knowledge of what exists, independently of all impositions or inscriptions of the mind, as a result of the fact that certain structures in the world enjoy some degree of intelligibility in their own right."[30]

While Smith views Mises as being of the subjectivist or "impositionist" variety, our argument places Mises in neither camp, or perhaps more accurately, as having one foot in both. On the one hand, as discussed above, like Kant, Mises clearly believed in logical categories of the mind that actors use to understand the world and was thoroughly subjectivist in this regard. As Mises put it: "He who wants to deal with [economics] must not look at the external world; he must search for them in the meaning of acting men."[31]

On the other hand, his evolutionary explanation of the emergence of these categories, which conditions them on the reality of the world, suggests a "reflectionist" view since a priori knowledge evolves over time with the evolution of individuals' mental categories. In this sense, there is a Smith-like "falliblistic"

29. See Smith, "Aristotle, Menger, Mises"; "Aristotelianism, Apriorism, Essentialism"; and "In Defense."
30. Smith, "Aristotle, Menger, Mises," 275.
31. Mises, *Human Action*, 92.

element to Mises's conception of a priori knowledge, which, though "true" for acting man at the present may ultimately be revealed to be mistaken (i.e., inconsistent with objective reality) with further developments in the evolution of the human mind.

From these categories implied in the axiom of action, Mises contends we can deduce the pure logic of choice. The theories thus arrived at, because they represent the elucidation and teasing out of the implications of the fact that man acts "are, like those of logic and mathematics, a priori."[32] If no logical error has been made in the process of deduction from the axiom of action, the theories arrived at are *aprioristically* true and apodictically certain. Their *aprioristic* quality, however, does not render them irrelevant to the real world. "The theorems attained by correct praxeological reasoning are not only perfectly certain and incontestable, like the correct mathematical theorems. They refer, moreover with the full rigidity of their apodictic certainty and incontestability to the reality of action as it appears in life and history. Praxeology conveys exact and precise knowledge of real things."[33]

Of course, Mises points out, while in principle all of economic theory can be logically spun out of the axiom of action in this fashion, for practical purposes we limit our activities to elucidating those theories that are relevant for the world in which we live. We could, for instance, imagine all possible states of the world and develop theories that logically follow from the assumptions posited. Such theories, assuming no errors were made in the process of deduction, would accurately describe processes and outcomes whenever the assumptions posited actually held. For example, we could imagine a world in which instead of labor bringing about disutility, it brought about joy. The labor theory deduced from this assumption would be correct but hold only in a world in which labor brings about joy. However, since our purpose is to understand the world in which we actually live, we observe the conditions of our world (in our example the disutility of labor) and use this empirical subsidiary postulate to circumscribe the bounds of our theorizing.[34] As Mises put it, "the end of [economic] science is

---

32. Mises, *Human Action,* 32.
33. Mises, *Human Action,* 39.
34. It should be noted that such use of empirical subsidiary postulates does not alter the *aprioristic* nature of the theories thus arrived at.

to know reality. It is not mental gymnastics or a logical pastime. Therefore praxeology restricts its inquiries to the study of acting under those conditions . . . which are given in reality."[35]

Mises's *apriorism* implied an important insight regarding the possibility of value-freedom. The deductive logic entailed in examining economic chains of events must always take ends as given. The role of the economist is to employ a priori theory in evaluating the efficacy of the means chosen in light of the stated ends. The economist then has nothing to say about the ends themselves but is instead in the position of commenting upon the coherence of various means towards the achievement of those ends. As Mises put it: "The ultimate judgments of value and the ultimate ends of human action are given for any kind of scientific inquiry; they are not open to any further analysis. Praxeology deals with the way and means chosen for the attainment of such ultimate ends. Its object is means, not ends."[36] Thus, in contrast to the procedural value-freedom of positivist methodology, *aprioristic* methodology is *analytically* value-free.[37] Means-ends analysis in light of *aprioristically* deduced economic law both avoids the fatal positivist failure to recognize that all facts are theory-laden and avoids the importation of value judgments into economic elucidation.

Mises points out that the *aprioristic* character of the pure logic of choice implies that economic theory can never be empirically validated or invalidated. The laws of economics "are not subject to verification or falsification on the ground of experience and facts."[38] Attempts to empirically *test* economic theory are not only fruitless, but indicate the wrong-headedness of the scientists who attempt to do so. Such scientists are in the same position as those who believe that they can validate or invalidate the Pythagorean theorem by measuring right triangles in the real world. Both fail to grasp the *aprioristic* nature of the theory they try in vain to test. Like the laws of mathematics, the laws of economics "are both logically and temporally antecedent to any comprehension of

35. Mises, *Human Action*, 65.
36. Mises, *Human Action*, 21.
37. On the Austrian argument for value-freedom see Boettke ("Ludwig von Mises," and "Is Economics").
38. Mises, *Human Action*, 32.

historical facts."[39] This fact in conjunction with the impossibility of controlled experiments in the real world makes it impossible to empirically test economic theory as positivist philosophers of economics claim one should.[40]

The critics of Mises are quick to point to this as evidence of his denial of the importance of empirical work and the real world. As we noted earlier however, though typically ignored, Mises is explicit in asserting that a priori economic deduction is to be the servant of empirical examinations of the world. Thus, in Mises's eyes, Carl Menger's institutionally contingent historical explanation of the emergence of money accurately represents the "fundamental principles of praxeology and its methods of research."[41] We are interested in economic theory because it illuminates the world outside the window. The institutional arrangements of the world that frame the rules within which the logic of choice in human decision making operates are the fundamental elements toward which economic theory is aimed. Thus, every argument in Mises, from the impossibility of rational economic calculation under socialism to the movement of the business cycle, is institutionally embedded and contingent.

The function of *aprioristic* theory in these analyses is to put parameters on people's utopias. So while an examination of the emergence of money is necessarily an empirical inquiry into the institutional features that enable or disenable its emergence, the demand for money always slopes downward. In this fashion a priori theory bounds our behavioral possibilities while making it possible for us to examine real features of the empirical world. "Theory and the comprehension of living and changing reality are not in opposition to one another" but rather

---

39. Mises, *Human Action*, 32.

40. We think it is important to distinguish between philosophers of economics (such as Hutchinson, Blaug, Hausman, Rosenberg, etc.) and practicing economists. As has been pointed out by several scholars, most notably McCloskey, the practice of economists is quite divorced from the official rhetoric of economics. Some philosophers of economics, e.g. Rosenberg, believe this reflects the intellectual failing of the discipline of economics, while others, e.g. McCloskey, believe it demonstrates the intellectual bankruptcy of prescriptive methodology by the philosophers. If the positivist philosophers' advice cannot be followed in practice in the discipline of economics because the subject matter cannot be so treated, then the use of positivistic criteria to demarcate science from nonscience is a nonstarter. In the case of someone like Mises, his methodological writings have been misunderstood by friend and foe precisely because of the mischaracterization of the philosophical misconceptions that he eschewed.

41. Mises, *Human Action*, 405.

enjoy a symbiotic relationship.[42] Viewed this way, rather than hypertheoretical, Mises's *apriorism* is actually radically empirical.[43] The pure logic of choice is a necessary component of economic explanation, but not sufficient.

Mises's critics were also fond of pointing out that if he is correct, the pure logic of choice is "mere tautology." Traditionally, philosophy distinguished between analytic and synthetic propositions. While the former were purely tautological, the latter, it was held, conveyed to us information about the real world. Kant's notion of a synthetic a priori—a class of knowledge known to us apart from experience that nonetheless imparts information about the real world shattered traditionally held beliefs about necessity of a priori claims as analytic truths. Kant thus accepted the traditional analytic/synthetic distinction but argued that some a priori truths formerly thought to be analytic could in fact be synthetic. Although Mises can be understood as building upon Kant, he ultimately goes beyond Kant by rejecting the traditional analytic/synthetic distinction altogether.

According to Mises it is true that like the laws of geometry, the pure logic of choice is entirely tautological. Nevertheless these "mere tautologies" have incredible empirical significance. Who would deny, for instance, that the *aprioristic* propositions of geometry are applicable to the real world? All architectural structures from bridges to buildings rely on these tautological propositions to be effectively constructed. Similarly, in economics we rely upon the law of demand for instance—which is tautological at its foundation—to analyze the coherence of various means for the attainment of various ends. Just because observation cannot falsify this law does not mean that the law is empirically irrelevant. Like all *aprioristic* propositions derived from the axiom of action, it is extremely empirically relevant. Indeed, without it we would be entirely unable to understand the functioning of the economy. The application of the aprioristic laws of economics to the real world yields empirical, institutionally contingent propositions about economic reality. Thus, Mises points out, tautologies deduced from an axiom inextricably linked to the real world are no vice. On the contrary, they are the indispensable mental constructs that make it possible for us to understand the real world.

---

42. Mises, *Human Action*, 38–39.

43. Theories are not refuted or failed to be refuted by empirical analysis; they are either applicable or inapplicable—relevant or irrelevant to the task of empirical interpretation.

The Relevance of Mises's Position for Modern Economics

Mises's radical methodological and epistemological positions have been the source of considerable criticism. With the rise of positivism and empiricism the desire to imitate the methods of the physical sciences in the social sciences has largely proved too strong to resist for the profession of economics. Influential economists from Paul Samuelson to Milton Friedman argued that in order for economics to have the status of a "real" science it needed to take a formalist and quantitative turn. Others, like T.W. Hutchison, pushed for a purely positivistic approach. Over time the lures of mathematical elegance and the desire for precise predictive power won over the hearts of most economists. As a result Mises was largely viewed as out of step with the times. This is what led the well-known historian of economic thought and methodologist, Mark Blaug, to dismiss Mises's methodological position as "cranky and idiosyncratic."

Nonetheless, it is worth noting that for many years a more or less methodological *apriorism* as described by Mises was common among economists. In fact a deductive "common sense" approach was the dominant way of doing economics for quite some time. As Mises put it, "We do not maintain that the theoretical science of human action should be aprioristic, but that it is and always has been so."[44] Nassau Senior, Destutt de Tracy, J.B. Say, John Cairnes, Carl Menger, Lionel Robbins, Frank Knight, and many others were all *apriorists* of some sort or another. Economic theorems, these writers contended, were derived from "self-evident" axioms. Far from out of step, this is the way that economic theorizing was done by classical and neoclassical economists for more than one hundred years.

Since this time, however, economics has made several turns in its preferred approach to economic inquiry.[45] In opposition to Mises's methodological stance, in the 1950s the economics profession adopted "model and measure" as its mantra. With the later development of game theory and the introduction of the Folk Theorem the possibility of an infinite number of equilibria led to the emergence of a sort of formalistic historicism that used formal tools to describe particular-

---

44. Mises, *Human Action*, 40.
45. For a description of this movement see Peter J. Boettke, Christopher J. Coyne, and Peter T. Leeson, "Man as Machine: The Plight of 20th Century Economics," *Annals of the Society for the History of Economic Thought*, 43 (2003): 1–10.

istic economic phenomena. What both of these approaches have in common is an implicit rejection of the economic methodology employed by the classical economists as laid out and defended by Mises that inadvertently purges the peculiarly human element from economic science.

Because it began with the axiom of action, Mises's *apriorism* necessarily moved the human element to the forefront of economic analysis. The logical categories implied in the action axiom emphasized time, uncertainty, and change in process of a person's attempts to pursue his or her ends. Absent this *aprioristic* approach the importance of the real-world conditions that acting man or woman confronts are all but lost. In its place is substituted man/woman as machine, operating in a sterile environment characterized by ideal conditions that in no way reflect reality.

Recent demands for new empirical methods of research illustrate the bankruptcy of the non-*aprioristic* approach. Ironically it is Mises's radical *apriorism* that provides the answer to this burgeoning empirical problem. As Mises's approach implies, economic understanding increases by framing questions in terms of the particular but analyzing in terms of the logic of choice. Interpreting the particular by way of the universal yields the *analytical narrative*, which brings the real-world human chooser back to forefront of economic analysis.[46] The analytical narrative makes the *aprioristically* deduced pure logic of choice the handmaiden of institutionally focused ethnographic research. Borrowing from sociology and anthropology, economics may employ survey, interview, and participant observation techniques to glean new empirical knowledge from its subjects (the narrative) to be analyzed in light of *aprioristic* rational choice theory (the analytic), leading to analytically rigorous but institutionally rich examinations. It is this research methodology that emerges out of Mises's unique methodological approach to economic science, which offers the way out of the problems generated by the empiricist/positivist approach to economic questions.

---

46. The analytic narrative we propose here is rooted in the praxeological approach that places creative, uncertain human decision making at the center of its analysis. Although the analytic narrative advocated by R. Bates et al. in *Analytic Narratives* (Princeton, NJ: Princeton University Press, 1998) is similar in that it seeks to employ economic theory for the purpose of historical interpretation, theirs is rooted in a purely game-theoretic approach that substitutes a world of complete and perfect information in which agent choices are deterministic for one in which actors imperfectly seek changing goals under conditions of constant change.

Conclusion

Far from embarrassing, we have argued that Mises's methodological position was ahead of its time. His focus on the givenness of ends and the analysis of means to achieve these ends provides us with an alternative, prepositivistic notion of value-freedom. His clear statement on how the theory-ladenness of facts destroys any notion of unambiguous empirical test anticipated developments in postpositivist philosophy and yet does not slip into the epistemological abyss of postmodernism. Finally, his focus on the universal applicability of the science of human action (praxeology) paved the way for a unified social science grounded in methodological individualism.

Furthermore, Mises's work is not the armchair theorizing many have made it out to be. The entire purpose of the theoretical task is to enable better empirical investigation but these two tasks represent distinct epistemological moments (conception for theory, understanding for history). Mises was able to develop a system for analysis, which today is being discussed as the analytical narrative approach to political economy. It is this movement, we contend, that will save economics from its irrelevance by linking economic explanation back to the human actor—the alpha and omega of all of economic life. Mises's *Human Action* was a monumental achievement in technical economics, social philosophy, and public policy, but just as important is its contribution to the philosophy of the human sciences. Here Mises argued forcefully that the laws of economic science are deduced a priori and prove their relevance in the act of interpretation of historical phenomena. Without these a priori laws, we would be blind to the empirical world.

15

The Genius of Mises
and the Brilliance of Kirzner

What Mises taught us in his writings, in his lectures, in his
seminars, and in perhaps everything he said, was that economics
is crucially important. Economics is not an intellectual game.
Economics is deadly serious. The very future of mankind—
of civilization—depends, in Mises' view, upon widespread
understanding of, and respect for, the principles of economics.
—Israel Kirzner[1]

Introduction

THE NEOCLASSICAL MODEL of the pure market economy is
a frictionless world where the decentralized decisions of agents are coordinated
seamlessly through the price mechanism. The neoclassical model of market
failure and thus government interventionism, on the other hand, deals with the
complications of the real world (i.e., the frictions in the world) and demonstrates
how the price system cannot perfectly operate. In this view, government can
improve upon the failures of the market.

By contrast, the works of economists such as Armen Alchian, James Buchanan, Ronald Coase, Douglass North, Vernon Smith, and Elinor Ostrom
fully embrace the frictions that exist in the real world and attempt to show how
market forces work to adjust behavior and change practices to ameliorate the
imperfections in the world and promote the coordination of plans. The price
system is important precisely because we are imperfect actors in an imperfect
world of frictions, uncertainty, and human ignorance.

---

1. Israel M. Kirzner, "Lifetime Achievement Award Acceptance Speech" (Society for the
Development of Austrian Economics, Charleston, SC, November 19, 2006).

Ludwig von Mises and Israel Kirzner are two of the most prominent scholars who have attempted to gain a richer understanding of how the "invisible hand" operates in coordinating the vast array of economic exchanges that occur on a daily basis in the actual imperfect world. The invisible hand works precisely because of the imperfections in this vision of market theory and does not require any of the assumptions associated with the formal theory of general competitive equilibrium—neither large numbers, price taking, homogenous goods, nor perfect knowledge. As Ludwig von Mises wrote, "[w]hat distinguishes the Austrian School and will lend it immortal fame is precisely the fact that it created a theory of economic action and not of economic equilibrium or non-action."[2] Austrian economists, most notably Mises, Hayek, and Kirzner, have sought to demonstrate how human behavior guided by prices, as well as monetary profits and losses, and under a system of private property would adjust and cope with the world's imperfections. This methodology focuses on the institutional structure that creates a unique incentive-based framework that in turn influences the behavior of actors. This behavior includes the dissemination of information which then directly influences the decisions and actions of agents in coordinating their activities and hence in improving the overall efficiency of the economic system. It took some great minds to develop this analysis, and among them are Mises, Hayek, and Kirzner. For purposes of this chapter we focus our attention on the unique contributions of Mises and Kirzner.

Mises and the Market

Israel Kirzner often comments on the reaction he had upon hearing Mises explaining that the market is a process during his course of graduate studies at New York University. Kirzner describes the experience as intellectually jarring. Indeed, he understood what it meant to say "the market was a place," but what could it possibly mean to say, "the market is a process"? Mises meant that the market is not only a space where people may haggle over prices; it is also a process by which knowledge is generated, information comes to be known, and prices are determined throughout society. The Misesian emphasis over the

---

2. Ludwig von Mises, *Notes and Recollections* (South Holland, IL: Libertarian Press, 1978), 36.

notion of market as a process is what separates traditional market theory from the Austrian view. The market is central in the Austrian approach because it is a process.

Indeed, in the letters between Menger and Walras one can already trace the differences between an approach to the theory of price that focuses on price determination in a system of simultaneous equations on the one hand, and price formation through a process of ongoing bargaining and exchange on the other. But the leading representatives of the respective schools thought this was merely a difference in emphasis rather than a difference in substance. Hans Mayer identified in more depth the significant differences between what he called a "functionalist theory" and a "causal-genetic theory" of price.[3] The conscious application of the notion of market process analysis was juxtaposed with general equilibrium theory. While the other leading representatives of the Austrian school in Vienna at the time such as Machlup, Mayer, and Morgenstern clearly understood the importance of market process in economic analysis, it was Mises, Hayek, and later Kirzner who put forth a mature rendering of the Austrian market process analysis.

To understand the origin of market process analysis, one must go back to Mises's *The Theory of Money and Credit* (1912; repr., Indianapolis, IN: Liberty Press, 1980) in which he employed "period analysis" or the "step-by-step" methodology and sought, way ahead of his time, to integrate micro- and macroeconomic theory in developing an analysis of money and the widespread consequences of monetary mismanagement by political authorities. Mises's theory of the business cycle was intimately linked to the way he came to understand the market process. Mises, along with Hayek, worked on questions of business forecasting and what came to be known as the "Austrian theory of the trade cycle." Critical aspects of that theory were (1) a picture of the capital structure in an economy as consisting of heterogeneous capital good combinations that had to be maintained or reshuffled in more productive and advantageous combinations; (2) a vision of the production process as taking place over time, thus generating a need for a mechanism for the intertemporal coordination of

---

3. Hans Mayer, *Der Erkenntniswert der Funktionellen Priestheorien* [The cognitive value of functional theories of price], in *Classics in Austrian Economics: A Sampling in the History of a Tradition*, edited by Israel M. Kirzner, vol. II, *The Interwar Period* (1932; repr., London: Pickering & Chatto, 1994), 55–168.

production plans to meet consumer demands; and (3) the notion that increases in the money supply work through the economy not in an instantaneous adjustment of prices, but through relative price adjustments. Mises's work both defended the quantity theory of money against monetary cranks that sought to eliminate poverty by printing more money, and criticized the quantity theory as interpreted in mechanical interpretations which postulated instantaneous adjustments of the price system to changes in the quantity of money and therefore underestimated the negative consequences of the manipulation of money and credit by political authorities in an economy.

The link to the market process, while not explicit, was always present in this analysis. Entrepreneurs rely on price signals to guide them in their production projects so that they are allocating scarce capital resources in the most valuable direction and employing the least costly technologies. The capital structure does not automatically replenish itself but instead requires the careful calculations of economic actors to determine which production plans are the most profitable ones to pursue. If price signals are confusing, then decisions concerning the maintenance and allocation of capital will be mistaken from the point of view of economic value maximization. The monetary theory of the trade cycle developed by Mises and Hayek in the 1920s contrasted a vision of the entrepreneur-based economy with the more mechanistic understanding of a monetary economy associated with economists in the United States and the UK and the chaotic vision of economic life associated with the critics of capitalism.

Contemporaneously with the work on monetary theory and the trade cycle, Mises was embroiled in a debate over the economic feasibility of socialism. Mises's analysis of socialism is, like his monetary theory, based on the subjective theory of value as applied in the context of a capital-using economy. In fact, Mises went as far as to claim: "To understand the problem of economic calculation it was necessary to recognize the true nature of the exchange relations expressed in the prices of the market. The existence of this important problem could be revealed only by the methods of the modern subjective theory of value."[4] At the core of Mises's comprehensive critique of socialism lies his understanding of the market process. What makes socialism impossible is not only the perverse

---

4. Ludwig von Mises, *Socialism: An Economic and Sociological Analysis* (1922; repr., Indianapolis, IN: Liberty Fund, 1981), 186.

incentives of collective ownership and the cumbersomeness of bureaucracy; it is more importantly the inability to stimulate entrepreneurial innovation outside the context of a market economy and the lure of profit and the penalties of loss.

Indeed, the critical point Mises raised against the most coherent form of socialism was that collective ownership in the means of production would render rational economic calculation impossible. Without private property in the means of production, there would be no market for the means of production. Without a market for the means of production, there would be no market prices for the means of production. In the absence of market prices (reflecting the relative scarcities of capital goods), economic planners would not be able rationally to calculate the most economically efficient investment path. Without the ability to engage in rational economic calculation, production could not be rationally organized. No individual or group of individuals could discriminate between the numerous possibilities of methods of production to determine which ones are the most cost effective without recourse to calculations based on monetary prices. Monetary prices and profit and loss accounting are indispensable guides in the business of economic administration. In their absence, the human mind would be at a loss to decide between different processes of production. Socialism, in its attempt to overcome the anarchy of production, substitutes instead planned chaos. As Mises puts it:

> To suppose that a socialist community could substitute calculations in kind for calculations in terms of money is an illusion. In a community that does not practice exchange, calculation in kind can never cover more than consumption goods. They break down completely where goods of higher order are concerned. Once society abandons free pricing of production goods rational production becomes impossible. Every step that leads away from private ownership of the means of production and the use of money is a step away from rational economic activity.[5]

Mises's critique of socialism was greeted with resistance by such figures as Karl Polanyi, Fred Taylor, Oskar Lange, and Abba Lerner. The theoretical discussion among professional economists took place within the historical context of the 1920s and especially of the 1930s, when Western capitalist economies

---

5. Mises, *Socialism,* 102.

were embroiled in the Great Depression, while the socialist Soviet system of centralized economic planning was understood to have transformed a peasant country into an industrial economy in one generation. Supposedly capitalism was proved by the events of the 1930s to be not only unjust but also unstable and inefficient. Socialist central planning, on the other hand, provided the Soviet Union with the material base to fight the fascist threat that arose in Germany in the 1930s and 1940s.

All through the debate on the feasibility of socialism, Mises slowly developed a more mature understanding of the entrepreneurial market process. In *Socialism*, he argued that the price system as a whole serves a threefold function, which by definition socialism would have to do without. In a market economy, the current array of prices signals to decision makers the relative scarcities of the goods and services in question. If the price is relatively high, it can be inferred that the commodity in question is relatively scarce and thus must be economized in its use, whereas if the price is relatively low, it can be inferred that the commodity in question is relatively abundant and thus can be used more. The current array of prices aid decision makers in making decisions by providing *ex ante* knowledge of the situation. However, the price system also provides *ex post* knowledge to economic actors in the form of the constellation of prices that emerge in the next period and the profit and loss statements of businesses. If an actor can buy low and sell high, the market communicates that the previous decision was in the right direction, whereas if it is revealed that, based on that earlier knowledge, you bought high and now must sell low, an error in judgment is revealed that needs to be addressed. The very discrepancy between the *ex ante* expectations set by the array of prices at the moment of decision and the *ex post* realizations of profit and loss sets in motion the discovery of better ways to arrange economic activities. These discoveries are made either by the original parties to the transactions or by new parties who enter the fray and bid resources away from the earlier actors. It is through the price system and the constant adjustments of relative prices that economic coordination and continual learning occurs. The strong claims about the market system's ability to self-correct are predicated on the veracity of the price system to achieve coordination and learning.

With the rise of socialist planning in the world and the support it received from Western intellectuals, Mises decided to continue the fight against what he considered unorthodox and "bad" economics and started writing what would become his *magnum opus*, first published in 1940 in German and later published in English translation with significant modifications in 1949. In *Human Action: A Treatise on Economics* (1949; repr., Indianapolis, IN: Liberty Fund, 2010) Mises skillfully applied and developed the step-by-step methodology to the economics of time, uncertainty, economic calculations, the market economy, the process of price formation, interest, credit expansion, the trade cycle as well as many other topics. In this way, Mises expanded on the work of his Viennese teachers and colleagues in incorporating the dynamic element of the economic process into the analytical framework of modern economics. In *Human Action*, Mises develops further the idea of the market as a process and shows how market prices are generally "false," or nonequilibrium prices, yet are informationally and motivationally useful in guiding and coordinating economic activity through time. In this context, Mises stated that, "the essential fact is that it is the competition of profit-seeking entrepreneurs that does not tolerate the preservation of false prices of the factors of production. The activities of the entrepreneurs are the element that would bring about the unrealizable state of the evenly rotating economy if no further changes were to occur."[6]

Unlike what Walras had assumed, prices do not reflect all the knowledge available, and thus, discrepancies exist which create pockets of profit that entrepreneurs may discover. In other words, the communication system is not perfect; prices do not convey all the knowledge that Walras would like them to convey. However, it is precisely in this "imperfection" that lays the engine of the economic system. The imperfection of prices is what creates the ability of the system to communicate information concerning its own faulty communication properties.

Ultimately, the notion of market as a process in Mises's work rests on the idea of interconnectedness among human activities (i.e., "connexity" as Mises puts it). The connexity of the market can only be explained if one views the market as a process. The mechanism that creates the connexity of human activities is entrepreneurial monetary calculations. Its consequence is social cooperation under the division of labor upon which economic growth and development depends. This mechanism rests on the existence of private property, freedom of contract, and a medium of exchange. As money is present in all exchanges

6. Mises, *Human Action*, 337–38.

and thus links together the decisions of everyone by virtue of being a medium of exchange, entrepreneurs are able to discover opportunities that may require, for their exploitation, a large division of labor and knowledge. The simultaneous exploitation of numerous entrepreneurial discoveries creates a concatenation of affairs among the various economic actors because entrepreneurs bid resources away from their alternative uses. This bidding process (based on entrepreneurial monetary calculation) creates interconnectedness among human activities. Prices are not isolated elements in the marketplace; they result from the complex relationships that prevail at any moment in society, and upon which the material, scientific and technological advances of western civilization rests.

Kirzner and Entrepreneurial Discovery

Israel Kirzner has described his graduate education in economics at New York University as one of profound confusion and intellectual enlightenment. One night a week he learned standard price theory through close study of George Stigler's *Theory of Price* (Chicago: University of Chicago Press, 1946) and on another night of the week he learned about the market process from Ludwig von Mises and his *Human Action*. Both approaches were diametrically opposed to the macroeconomics of Keynesianism that was also taught at the time, but they also seem to oppose each other in a fundamental sense. It is against this background that Israel Kirzner developed his market process theory. In a series of books starting in 1960 and spanning more than three decades, Kirzner rigorously developed the modern Austrian theory of market process, specifically in the context of the role of the entrepreneur.

The brilliance of Kirzner rests in the way he opened the closed framework of traditional microeconomics by introducing the entrepreneurial element. In Walras's view, prices are parameters in the system that no agent can influence. Everyone is a price taker and prices convey sufficient information for every individual to make choices. Walras labored to solve the following problem. While prices are best seen as parametric from the perspective of each agent, they are seen as variables from the point of view of the system as a whole. In general equilibrium theory, prices are not under the influence of anyone in particular but are determined at the systemic level to clear markets. Prices are seen as conveying sufficient knowledge for agents to allocate resources to their most valued use, are incentives for action, and as such, they convey the necessary information for resources to be allocated efficiently.

This approach raises an immediate issue. If one adopts a parametric view of prices, it falls short of explaining how prices are determined at the systemwide level. The Walrasian dichotomy between prices as parameters for individuals and prices as variables at the systemwide level has propelled market theory into a corner. "How are market prices arrived at?" is the question that the Walrasian system of perfect competition cannot answer—except by stipulating the existence of a fictitious agent, the auctioneer. As Frank Hahn argued, this view has robbed economics of the ability to explain price changes and actual adjustments.[7] As Arrow put it:

> Even if we accept this entire story [that of general competitive equilibrium], there is still one element not individual [i.e., not chosen by individuals]: namely, the prices faced by firms and individuals. What individual has chosen prices? In the formal theory at least, no-one. They are determined on (not by) social institutions known as markets, which equate supply and demand. . . . The failure to give an individualistic explanation of price formation has proved to be surprisingly hard to cure.[8]

In this view of market theory, agents are passive in the sense that they do not originate change, they just respond like robots to the situation of the market and the incentives offered by parametric prices.

Ultimately, the parametric/incentive view of prices rests on a specific view of the economic problem and of knowledge. The Walrasian approach treated resources in the economy as fully known and given. Hayek in 1937 criticized this view by explaining unless one provides a theory of the acquisition of knowledge; one cannot explain the allocation of resources and the true role of prices. With Hayek, the economic problem becomes not only one of allocation of resources but one of acquisition and communication of knowledge, which is necessary for individuals to make the best allocative choices possible. Only by providing a solution to that problem can one offer a solution to the determination of prices.

---

7. Frank Hahn, *On the Notion of Equilibrium in Economics* (Cambridge: Cambridge University Press, 1973).

8. Kenneth Arrow, "Methodological Individualism and Social Knowledge," *The American Economic Review* 84, no. 2 (1994): 4.

Establishing the right economic problem led Hayek to focus on the nature of knowledge. The Walrasian approach treats knowledge as given, while the Hayekian view sees knowledge as dispersed and not available to all. If knowledge is idiosyncratic and tacit, then prices cannot be treated as parameters that convey all the existing information. Instead they are communicators of knowledge that individuals both determine and use as determinants in their choices.

Again, this is where Kirzner's brilliance lies: in providing a solution to the conundrum of price theory, i.e., the determination of prices. As Kirzner saw it, the problem of entrepreneurship as an analytical category stems from the insight that we cannot explain the existence of sheer novelty (and pure profit) referring to productive factors already in use. Kirzner presented the profession with the most daring solution, confronting head-on the problem of change and novelty by devising a theory that could account for the presence of pure profit in the market by focusing on the pure entrepreneurial element in human action. To that end, he distinguished optimizing behavior from entrepreneurial alertness. Isolating the two functions led him to posit the distinction between entrepreneurship and asset ownership. Kirzner also used the equilibrium construct as a foil against which he could study the role of the entrepreneurial function. For it is only against a background of optimizing agents (i.e., Robbinsian maximizers to use Kirzner's terminology) that one can illumine the role of the entrepreneur.

The essence of entrepreneurship in Kirzner's work also revolves around the fundamental idea that the discovery and exploitation of gains from trade does not take place automatically, but rather stems from purposeful human action. This departs from traditional microeconomics in which existing gains from trade are always known. Instead, Kirzner emphasizes that in order for these gains to be exploited, they first have to be noticed. The essence of the entrepreneurial function rests on this fundamental insight. In contrast with traditional microeconomics, Kirzner's view of the entrepreneurial function in the market process consists primarily in liberating human choice from its deterministic structure by introducing alertness. Alertness to unexploited gains from trade sets the market process in motion. Thus, it is also because of its relationship to market process that the notion of alertness is crucial.

A key foundation of Kirzner's market process theory is that the underlying variables, including tastes, technology, resource endowment, and the induced variables of profit and loss accounting, are in a lagged but determinant relationship. That is, given the dynamics of the economy, the underlying variables, at any one point in time, are not perfectly aligned. The market discovery process provides the mechanism through which the induced variables move in the same direction as the underlying variables. Overall, Kirzner's contribution to market process theory provides the missing link to the neoclassical theory. Given an institutional framework of private property, low barriers to entry, and frozen underlying variables, the process of entrepreneurship will lead to a pattern of production and exchange, which would guide the economy toward a state of equilibrium. The missing link in traditional price theory that Kirzner provided was an understanding of the disequilibrium foundations of the economy as well as the path from disequilibrium to a state of equilibrium (if and only if underlying variables are frozen).

When individuals determine prices, they act as entrepreneurs. This means that the marginal condition price theory has established that "price equals marginal cost" is not an assumption going into the theory. Rather it is a tendency of a competitive market process that results from individuals acting upon the discrepancies that may exist between their own knowledge and the knowledge available in the marketplace. The foresight of the entrepreneur is to discover the value of some knowledge that he or she possesses but which is not yet reflected in market prices.

What distinguishes Austrian economists is the elaborate understanding of the role of the entrepreneurial function and how it gives rise to the market process. The traditional understanding of the market is limited because it rests on a "closed" framework, which cannot account for novelty. Kirzner has drawn attention to the open-ended environment in which "relevant opportunities may exist without their having, at the outset of the analysis, already been recognized." As Kirzner explains, in an open-ended framework "there are no known limits to the possible. An economics that seeks to grapple with the real-world circumstance of open-endedness must transcend an analytical framework which cannot accommodate genuine surprise. Austrian economics has sought to accomplish this goal by focusing attention on the nature and function of pure entrepreneurial discovery."[9]

---

9. Israel M. Kirzner, foreword to *An Entrepreneurial Theory of the Firm,* by Frederic Sautet (London, Routledge, 2000), xiii.

The Refinement of the Market Process

The entrepreneurial role is one of a discoverer of information that was previously unknown. This discovery process rests on the capacity of entrepreneurs to notice information that is not presently conveyed by prices and to act upon it. Entrepreneurs act upon the knowledge they possess of the circumstances around which trades could take place. When an entrepreneur proposes a new good at a new price because he or she believes that enough people will be interested in a new product to make it worthwhile to produce it, she or he introduces new knowledge in the system, thereby reducing ignorance. The price system, in its inability to convey all information, creates the incentives to discover what is missing. The entrepreneurial role ultimately is one of discovering knowledge and thereby reducing ignorance.

Ignorance is always present. It is not, however, of the same nature in the open system as it is in the closed competitive equilibrium. In the former, ignorance is radical because it pertains to ignorance itself: individuals do not know what they do not know. This implies a world where "true uncertainty" exists, that is, where future events are truly unpredictable. It is because of this context of radical ignorance and true uncertainty that the Hayekian economic problem is real. Assuming the problem away, as competitive equilibrium does, reduces the economic problem to a mechanistic issue (i.e., which prices clear markets?), as opposed to an epistemic one (i.e., how can the system self-correct?).

In this context, the entrepreneurial function, this unique human characteristic, offers a response to the challenge of radical ignorance. The veil of ignorance is continually under attack because human imagination is always at work. It is important to emphasize that human imagination, the possibility of sheer creation of information, is the principal characteristic of the entrepreneurial function. However, in the social context, creativity is necessary but often not sufficient. What is also needed is a compass to determine, as Joseph Schumpeter emphasized, that invention (i.e., creativity) is also innovation (i.e., socially useful creativity). This compass is the profit and loss mechanism, which helps determine whether invention is socially useful and thus becomes innovation and is adopted by others. The two sides of the entrepreneurial coin are sheer creativity (of information) and discovery (of a knowledge gap in the social fabric through the price mechanism). These two aspects of entrepreneurship are the makeup of the market process (i.e., the constant discovery of socially relevant inventions). In this sense, the market process is a self-correcting system based on the discovery of hitherto ignored possibilities for trade. These possibilities for trade reflect at once the discovery of a social need that was not already expressed in the market (and thus was not transmitted by the price system) and the expression of human creativity.

Conclusion

The intellectual landscape of modern political economy has shifted considerably since the Classical period of the nineteenth century. In the twentieth century, economists sought to refine the universal principles of their discipline by expressing them in a more formal language with all the restrictive assumptions that needed to be employed to assure mathematical tractability. The entrepreneurial element of human action was a casualty of this mathematical revolution because it defies tractability. Both Mises and Kirzner at respective moments in the development of the discipline sought to reemphasize that the market is a process operating in an open-ended universe. One cannot explain the operation of the market and the adjustments of the price system without recourse to the entrepreneur.

For almost three-quarters of a century, economic discourse has embarked on a detour in which the role of the entrepreneur within the market economy is systemically ignored. Against this tide, Ludwig von Mises's genius provided an inspiring vision upon which Kirzner developed his theory of market process during the second half of the century. Kirzner understood well the implications of the idea that optimizing behavior cannot explain the market as a process. Without the introduction of ad hoc exogenous elements, economics is limited in its capacity to explain social change and novelty. This is not to say that the equilibrium construct is to be jettisoned; it occupies an important place in the toolbox of the economist, as it is only against equilibrium, seen as a foil, that one can understand change. Economics, however, focused so much on the absence of change that it became detrimental to what economists were trying to explain. In this sense Kirzner's brilliant research is fundamental, as it puts the notion of change—and entrepreneurial action in the face of the changing conditions—back at the center of economic theory and in particular our understanding of the market economy and the price system.

16

Hayek and Market Socialism
Science, Ideology, and Public Policy

Introduction

HAYEK'S RESEARCH PROGRAM is grounded in the teaching of Adam Smith and Carl Menger, who sought to understand social order not as the result of conscious design, but as the unintended consequences of individual human action. In addition to the emphasis on spontaneous order, Hayek learned from Menger that individual human action is guided by the subjective valuations of individuals and that the relevant valuation that individuals make is on the marginal unit of the good or service that is the object of deliberation. Throughout Hayek's career, at the center of his research efforts was the puzzle of how a social system can transform the individual subjective perceptions of some into useful information for others, so that they may coordinate their actions to produce an overall social order that yields benefits far greater than any individual in the system intended. In this regard, I do not believe it is an exaggeration to say that F.A. Hayek, more than any other economist in the twentieth century, pursued the Smithian research program in political economy and refined the "invisible-hand" style of reasoning that is the hallmark of the economic way of thinking.

Another major influence on Hayek was Wieser with his notion of opportunity cost reasoning and the question of the imputation of value. Wieser is usually credited with the idea that the cost of any economic decision is the next best alternative foregone in making that decision. In addition, Wieser—following Menger—saw the production process as unfolding through time where value flows up from lower-order goods to the higher-order goods used in producing them, and a stream of goods and services flows down from high-order goods to the lower-order goods we consume. The process of deriving the value of producer goods from the value of the resulting consumer goods is referred to as imputation. Hayek's early work in technical economics was precisely on this issue, and through studying this process of imputation he became sensitized to the misleading influence of equilibrium theorizing with regard to the complexity of this economic adjustment process through time.

Another major influence on Hayek's economics were Wicksell and the other Swedish economists of the late nineteenth and early twentieth centuries, who at the same time as the Austrians were focused on explaining the performance of the economic system through time and in this regard emphasized the role of individual expectations in realizing economic coordination.[1] *Ex ante* expectations guide individual decisions, and *ex post* realizations reveal the appropriateness of previous beliefs and lead to a realignment of behavior in response to the discrepancy between the *ex ante* and the *ex post*. Economic coordination is an intricate balancing act of resource scarcity, beliefs and expectations, and technological possibilities. Production plans must mesh with consumption demands. Within a capitalist economy, intertemporal coordination is guided by the interest rate, and thus if the interest rate mechanism is distorted, malcoordination will result and the economic system will underperform: production plans will not mesh with consumption demands and the economy will experience systemic waste and unemployment.

The final significant influence on Hayek, and the most significant I would argue, was Ludwig von Mises. The best way to understand Hayek is to see him as following up on the questions that Mises first posed about the economic system, clarifying those questions and providing more subtle answers. Mises's work on monetary theory and the trade cycle, the problems of socialism and interventionism, and the examination of alternative political and economic systems all served as the impetus for Hayek's research program. The relationship between Mises and Hayek is misunderstood by friend and foe as they had intertwined research programs, but separate professional fates.

---

1. See Peter J. Boettke and Christopher J. Coyne, "Swedish Influences, Austrian Advances: The Contributions of the Swedish and Austrian Schools to Market Process Theory," in *The Evolution of the Market Process: Austrian and Swedish Economics,* edited by M. Bellet, S. Gloria-Palermo, and A. Zouache (New York: Routledge, 2004), 20–31.

In Hayek's hands, the various propositions that were developed by Menger, Wieser, Wicksell and Mises were merged and led to a research program that emphasized three major points:

1. Economics must be conceived of as a science which studies coordination problems. It is the dovetailing of plans by economic actors that must result so that the complex social order can emerge as it unfolds through time. Incentives must be aligned between economic actors, and they must come to know not only what are the best opportunities currently available for mutually beneficial exchange, but continually discover new possibilities for mutual gain from exchange with others in the economic system.

2. Knowledge in a social system of exchange and production is dispersed among diverse and socially distant individuals and the ability of the system to achieve complex coordination is a function of its ability to mobilize this dispersed knowledge. The division of labor in society implies a division of knowledge, and the private property market economy is the best means available for mobilizing and using the dispersed knowledge in society to realize the complex coordination of economic plans that is the hallmark of advanced commercial society.

3. To be effective a market economy must operate within a framework of liberal institutions of governance that provide security of contract and stability of the legal framework. The rule of law is an essential component for economic progress, and the generality of law (as opposed to special privilege) provides the predictability required of economic activity to achieve an advanced state.

The common thread in Hayek's research program is how economic actors learn how to coordinate their actions with one another to realize their plans in the most effective manner possible. In other words, not only does the market system align the incentives of economic actors to allocate scarce resources efficiently, but it is also a learning system that prods economic actors to adjust their behavior to realize their plans in an ever-more efficient manner as they proceed through time.

Hayek's debate with the market socialists was an ideal setting for these ideas to be brought into sharp focus.

Hayek's Contribution to the Economics of Socialism

Hayek's starting point in the analysis of socialism is the acceptance of Mises's argument that rational economic calculation under socialism is impossible. However, the subsequent development of Hayek's writings is a consequence of his recognition that despite the fundamental correctness of Mises's argument, it was not going to deter attempts by (a) economists inspired by socialism to answer Mises in theory, and (b) those in political power who are inspired by socialism to realize socialism in policy practice. In theory, this led to Hayek's essays on knowledge and competition as a discovery procedure.[2] In the realm of practical policy, Hayek was led to emphasize the unintended undesirable consequences of pursuing socialism and interventionism.[3]

Hayek's argument, like Mises's, emphasized the evolution of the critique of socialism from incentives to information economizing, from the discovery of opportunities for mutual gain to the use of politics for predatory exploitation when the rule of law is weakened. To see the evolution of the argument against socialism, one has to put Hayek in the context of responding to the advocates of market socialism. Hayek sought to grant his opponents as favorable a position as possible so that even if under those favorable circumstances he could demonstrate that their position would fail, then his argument would have maximum persuasive power. In retrospect, it appears that this argumentative strategy has led some into misunderstanding his position on the multifaceted difficulties that socialism would face in practice.

The first level criticism of socialism is that private property in the means of production is a necessary condition for the coordination of economic activity. Private property provides economic actors with high-powered incentives to husband resources effectively. Without private property the incentives that economic actors face will not act to internalize the costs and benefits of decisions and will therefore lead to less prudent decisions. This argument can actually be dated back to Aristotle's critique of Plato. Hayek was certainly not ignorant of this argument. But his emphasis was not placed on this because advocates of socialism sought to sidestep the issue by postulating a change in the human

---

2. See F.A. Hayek, *Individualism and Economic Order* (1948; repr., Chicago: University of Chicago Press, 1996).

3. F.A. Hayek, *The Road to Serfdom* (Chicago: University of Chicago Press, 1944).

spirit due to collectivization. Actors under socialism would not need to have economic incentives to guide their behavior because their new nature would instead lead them to make the most judicious use of resources as possible for the good of society. Hayek could counter this argument in one of two ways: deny this transformation and thus have both sides talk past each other, or accept this assumption and then show that even under this assumption the means of collective ownership would not realize the ends of advanced material production. Hayek, as Mises did before him, chose this second path.

If economic incentives are not required for individuals to pursue the social good due to a change in human nature, then there still remains the question as to what exactly would be the correct actions required to achieve economic optimality and thus the social good. Here the argument moves beyond the incentive alignment question of coordination to the informational requirements of coordination. Once again private property plays a vital role because it is a precondition for exchange. The distinction between "mine" and "thine" permits the trading of goods and services and the establishment of exchange ratios. In an advanced economy these exchange ratios are expressed in monetary prices and they serve to economize on the amount of information that economic actors must process in making decisions. Relative prices economize on information and guide decision-making.

At these first two stages of the debate, the main advocates of socialism were noneconomists and Mises and Hayek were merely trying to communicate basic economic reasoning to individuals who portrayed an innocence of the subject. Both Mises and Hayek refused to battle over the ends of socialism and instead kept their argument to the claim that given the ends of socialism (advanced material production and enhanced social harmony) the means chosen (collective ownership of the means of production) would be ineffective in achieving that end due to the problems of incentive alignment and information processing. Without private property in the means of production, economic actors would not have the incentive to allocate scarce resources effectively nor would they be able to rely on relative monetary prices to guide their production plans even if we assumed they were rightly motivated to achieve the goals of socialism.

In the process of laying out this basic argument, Mises and Hayek would be led to make stunning discoveries of the crucial features of the price system and the market economy. Don Lavoie argued that one must read Mises's and Hayek's arguments as two sides of the same coin,[4] and I follow him in this regard and will not dehomogenize their different contributions to the analysis of socialism.[5] Mises emphasized how the ability to make rational economic calculations is a necessary condition for coordinating the complex division of labor that constitutes a modern market economy. Hayek emphasized the knowledge that goes into these economic calculations and how economic actors come to learn of, acquire, and use this knowledge. The current array of relative prices provide *ex ante* information to economic actors that aids them in the planning of their economic activity, and profit and loss accounting provides economic actors with the *ex post* information that provides the required feedback to economic actors. The very discrepancy between *ex ante* expectations and *ex post* realizations sets in motion an adjustment process by economic actors where they learn how to better arrange their affairs. The lure of pure profit and the penalty of loss serve to direct economic activities through time, ensuring a tendency toward exchange and allocative efficiency, as well as generating economic progress through innovation. The tool of profit and loss accounting rewards and penalizes economic actors so that the gains from mutual exchange are continually being recognized and pursued by participants in the market economy.

It is important to emphasize that private property provides the institutional prerequisite for monetary prices, and monetary prices are a necessary input into profit and loss accounting. In other words, private property is not only important for addressing the incentive issues that classical philosophy and economics stressed but is the institutional requirement which allows the

---

4. Don Lavoie, *Rivalry and Central Planning* (New York: Cambridge University Press, 1985).

5. There is a significant literature that emerged in the 1990s attempting to sort out the important differences between Mises and Hayek on the analysis of socialism and I would recommend the reader to consider carefully the arguments by Joseph Salerno ("Mises and Hayek Dehomogenized," *Review of Austrian Economics* 6, no. 2 (1993): 113–46) on this as I do believe he makes several valid points even if I ultimately push in a different direction. For my own position on the debate see my essay "Economic Calculation: The Austrian Contribution to Modern Political Economy," reprinted in my *Calculation and Coordination* (New York: Routledge, 2001), and also my introduction to the nine-volume reference work *Socialism and the Market Economy* (London: Routledge, 2000).

dispersed knowledge in society to be coordinated and an advanced division of labor to be realized.[6]

For private property rights to be effective in serving their function as the basis of prices and thus economic calculation they have to be recognized and respected or the economic system will become distorted. In an unhampered market economy, where private property is clearly defined and strictly enforced, the price system and the process of economic calculation will act to ensure economic efficiency and innovation. But the establishment of an unhampered market economy is a function of the political infrastructure within which private property rights are recognized and respected. Politics must seek to restrain the use of power and the predatory behavior of both public and private actors. Unless the political system is bound by strict limits, property rights will not be effective and the economic system will be hampered. Not only will economic coordination fail to materialize and thus arrangements will be less efficient than they could have been given the state of resource availability, technological possibilities, and consumer preferences, but the control of economic means will result in a loss of political freedom as well. Control of the economic means is not merely material control, but control over the means by which we pursue all our ends—even the lofty and spiritual ones.

Summing up, the argument made by Mises and Hayek can be said to progress from property rights to prices to profit and loss and finally to politics. And the consequences can be summed up with the terms incentive, information, innovation and infrastructure. Without the four Ps, the four Is will not emerge in a manner that would sustain an advanced economy. Secure private property rights provide the incentive to husband resources efficiently; a working price system will economize on the information that economic actors must use in arranging their affairs; accurate profit and loss accounting will teach economic actors about the appropriateness of their previous actions and direct them to innovate as they continually adjust their behavior to seek profits and avoid losses; and finally, a political system that wards off predation establishes a predictable infrastructure within which economic actors can realize the gains from exchange

---

6. Mises and Hayek, as we have seen, are both advocates of the private property market order and attempts to dehomogenize Mises and Hayek on the issue of private property and knowledge is mistaken.

and protect their freedom to choose. The commitment by Mises and Hayek to the liberal argument for limited government emerges as a consequence of their understanding of the operation of a functional market economy.

The LSE Contribution

The English-language debate on the economics of market socialism largely took place between scholars associated with the London School of Economics (LSE).[7] Of course, the debate was largely set off by Oskar Lange's response to Mises in 1936–1937, but it was published in an LSE journal and the impetus of much of the discussion was Abba Lerner. The LSE counter reaction to the Mises–Hayek critique was to argue that socialist policy and economic and political freedom were compatible. Durbin actually stated:

> We all wish to live in a community that is as rich as possible, in which consumers' preferences determine the relative output of goods that can be consumed by individuals, and in which there is freedom of discussion and political association and responsible government.[8]

He also added that, "We are socialist in our economics because we are liberals in our philosophy." Even Hayek's friend and comrade in the debate with the market socialists Lionel Robbins came to argue that:

> An individualist who recognizes the importance of public goods, and a collectivist who recognizes the desirability of the maximum of individual freedom in consumption will find many points of agreement in common. The biggest dividing line of our day is, not between those who

---

7. Coase (*The Firm, the Market and the Law* (Chicago: University of Chicago Press, 1988)) has explained how his own work on the transaction cost theory of the firm emerged from the discussions in this debate, and W.H. Hutt ("The Concept of Consumer Sovereignty," *Economic Journal* 50 (March 1940): 66–77) actually coined the term "consumer sovereignty" during this time as well and points to Collectivist Economic Planning as one of the sources of inspiration. So the debate is important not only for the assessment of economic systems, but also in forcing scholars to think creatively about the institutions of capitalism from a producer and consumer side.

8. E.F. Durbin, "Professor Hayek on Economic Planning and Political Liberty," *Economic Journal*, 55: 220 (December 1945): 357–70.

differ about organization as such, but between those who differ about the ends which organization has to serve.[9]

To Hayek the evolution of the argument in this direction must have seemed most puzzling and frustrating. In fact, I contend that the development of Hayek's research program over the next 40 years was not a consequence of him running away from economics, but of him running deeper underneath economic argumentation to understand the source of the misunderstanding by his former students and colleagues. Reflecting on his research program in an essay in 1964 Hayek stated the following:

> Though at one time a very pure and narrow economic theorist, I was led from technical economics into all kinds of questions usually regarded as philosophical. When I look back, it seems to have all begun, nearly thirty years ago, with an essay on "Economics and Knowledge" in which I examined what seemed to me some of the central difficulties of pure economic theory. Its main conclusion was that the task of economic theory was to explain how an overall order of economic activity was achieved which utilized a large amount of knowledge which was not concentrated in any one mind but existed only as separate knowledge of thousands or millions of different individuals. But it was still a long way from this to an adequate insight into the relations between the abstract rules which the individual follows in his actions, and the abstract overall order which is formed as the result of his responding, within the limits imposed upon him by those abstract rules, to the concrete particular circumstances which he encounters. It was only through a reexamination of the age-old concept of freedom under the law, the basic conception of traditional liberalism, and of the problems of the philosophy of the law which this raises, that I have reached what now seems to me to be a tolerably clear picture of the nature of the spontaneous order of which liberal economists have so long been talking.[10]

---

9. Lionel Robbins, *Economic Problems in Peace and War* (London: Macmillan, 1947).
10. F.A. Hayek, "Kinds of Rationalism," in *Studies in Philosophy, Politics and Economics* (1964; repr., Chicago: University of Chicago Press, 1967), 82–95.

Bruce Caldwell has argued that the development of Hayek's "Abuse of Reason Project" emerged as a consequence of this debate over market socialism.[11] The key idea being argued by Dickinson, Durbin, Lange, and Lerner was that a market socialist system could, through rational planning, eliminate the abuse of monopoly power and the irrational production of capitalism and yet ensure individual freedom by allowing a free market in consumer goods. The free market in consumer goods, it was reasoned, could also be used in aiding the trial-and-error process of coordinating production through planning because if the price of the consumer good is provided, then under conditions of equilibrium the price of the producer goods which are employed in the production of this consumer good can be derived as we learned with the theory of imputation discussed previously.

I cannot improve upon Caldwell's discussion of the particulars of Hayek's "Abuse of Reason Project," but I want to emphasize a slightly different interpretation, one that is not inconsistent with Caldwell, but that does stress Hayek's frustration with his LSE colleagues and how this frustration set him on a quest for answers in disciplines outside technical economics.

The intellectual exercise I wish to undertake is to compare Hayek's inaugural lecture at the LSE, "The Trend of Economic Thinking," with Lange's "On the Economic Theory of Socialism."[12] In 1933 Hayek had argued that:

1. Economics was born as a discipline out of the successive examination and refutation of Utopian schemes.

2. Liberal economists are as concerned with the welfare of the poor as the socialist but recognize the problems of interventionism and planning, and the power of the market to raise the living standards of the least advantaged in society. In fact, in 1933 Hayek wrote, "Recent additions to knowledge have made the probability of a solution of our difficulties by

11. Bruce Caldwell, *Hayek's Challenge: An Intellectual Biography of F.A. Hayek* (Chicago: University of Chicago Press, 2004).

12. F.A. Hayek, "The Trend of Economic Thinking," *Economica* (May 1933): 121–37, in F.A. Hayek, *The Collected Works of F.A. Hayek*, edited by edited by W.W. Bartley III, vol. 3 (1933; repr., Chicago: University of Chicago Press, 1991), 17–34; Oskar Lange, "On the Economic Theory of Socialism," in *On the Economic Theory of Socialism* (1936–1937; repr., Minneapolis: University of Minnesota Press, 1938), 55–129.

planning appear *less*, rather than more, likely." In making this reference Hayek is pointing to the contributions of *Collectivist Economic Planning* that he was editing, and the problem he is referring to is the Great Depression and the problems that the least advantaged in society had to face as a result.

3. It is only by denying economic laws, as the Historical School has done, that the policies of interventionism and socialism come to be adopted. A properly trained economist would be much more skeptical about the workability of such utopian schemes. The irony of the age, Hayek warns, is that our economic understanding has been vastly improved by developments in neoclassical economics, but there was a general public acceptance of historicism.

"Refusing to believe in general laws," Hayek argued, "the Historical School had the special attraction that its method was constitutionally unable to refute even the wildest of Utopias, and was, therefore, not likely to bring the disappointment associated with theoretical analysis."[13]

To someone like Hayek who held this position, imagine the sheer bewilderment he must have experienced when, within a few short years, he was confronted with the arguments of Keynes, Lange, and his students such as Lerner. His surprise would have been especially acute with Lange and Lerner because they used marginal analysis and neoclassical market theory to forge an argument for socialism.

I contend that this experience in the 1930s set Hayek off on his quest for understanding that led to his abandoning technical economics and branching into social philosophy and political economy.

Contrary to the model of market socialism, Hayek argued that his colleagues were missing out on the unintended consequences of their model. First, Hayek argued that a free market for consumer goods would not provide the implied value of the producer goods except for under conditions of equilibrium. In addressing this problem Hayek became suspicious of the preoccupation on equilibrium economics. Economists go astray when they assume what it is that they have to prove. Hayek stresses in this regard that the knowledge required to coordinate market activity emerges within, and only within, the competitive

---

13. Hayek, "Trend," 125, 22.

market process. Second, Hayek argued that the political consequences of pursuing planning will be unanticipated and undesirable from the point of view of the planners themselves. As he would write in *The Road to Serfdom*: "socialism can be put into practice only by methods which most socialists disapprove."[14] He was not challenging the intended liberalism of his market socialist opponents; he was arguing that there was an inconsistency between the goals they sought and the model they proposed for achieving those goals. The result was a tragic tale of best intentions paving the path to hell.

The "Abuse of Reason Project" would take the shape of both a critical examination of the methodology and methods that were becoming dominant in economics during the 1940s and 1950s and the ideological predispositions of the twentieth-century social science. In the realm of method and methodology, Hayek was critical of formalism and positivism. Formalism explained the preoccupation of economists with the equilibrium state of affairs. Positivism led to a demand for measurement in economics and this demand was met by the development of techniques to measure aggregate economic performance. The preoccupation with equilibrium masks the discovery procedures which constitute the entrepreneurial market economy and the aggregation techniques masks the underlying economic relationships that individuals enter into within the market process. In the realm of ideology, Hayek criticized the constructivist bias where scholars and policymakers believe that unless a social system is consciously designed it will be plagued by accident and irrationality. Constructivism, in short, is the exact opposite of the "invisible hand" style of reasoning one sees in Adam Smith and David Hume's analysis of civilization. Hayek picked up the modern defense of Smith and Hume, and the "Abuse of Reason Project" was where this defense took shape.[15]

The Relevance of Hayek Today

Today, Hayek's work has grown in stature and his ideas are being incorporated regularly in the modern development of economics and political economy. The gap between Samuelson and the Austrians was so wide in the 1940s that

---

14. Hayek, *Road to Serfdom*, 137.
15. Hayek would later state that his critique of constructivist rationalism was in the Humean spirit of "using reason to whittle down the claims of reason."

one did not even know how to engage the discussion between them, but by the 1990s the gap between microeconomists such as Paul Milgrom and John Roberts[16] and the Austrians had closed considerably, and the closing of the gap is in the direction of the sort of incentive alignment and information processing arguments that Austrians have been urging economists to take seriously since the 1930s and 1940s.

Hayek's influence can be seen in the realm of economic science, public policy analysis, and ideological commitment. In the realm of economic science, Hayek's influence can be seen in the cognitive direction of research that has been taken by Timur Kuran and Douglass North.[17] Hayek's influence can also be seen in the work of Mancur Olson and Andrei Shleifer et al. on institutional quality and the politics of predation.[18] Finally, the recognition of the importance of entrepreneurship to understanding both Smithian and Schumpeterian growth continues to spur economists to find ways to incorporate the elusive concept of entrepreneurship into the understanding of the competitive market process.[19] Some of this work is amenable to standard empirical work, but there has also been a growing recognition that work that emphasizes institutions and economic change must eschew cross-country data analysis and engage in detailed micro-data analysis of specific context. This can be accomplished through an analytic

---

16. Paul Milgrom and John Roberts, *Economics, Organization and Management* (Englewood Cliffs, NJ: Prentice Hall, 1992).

17. Timur Kuran, *Private Truths, Public Lies* (Cambridge, MA: Harvard University Press, 1995); Douglass North, *Understanding the Process of Economic Change* (Princeton, NJ: Princeton University Press, 2004).

18. Mancur Olson, *Power and Prosperity* (New York: Basic Books, 2000); Andrei Shleifer et al., "The New Comparative Economics," *Journal of Comparative Economics*, 31: 4 (December 2003), 595–619. For further analysis along the lines of institutional quality and sustainability, see Christopher J. Coyne, "The Institutional Prerequisites for Post-Conflict Reconstruction," *Review of Austrian Economics* 18, no. 3/4 (2005): 325–42; and Peter T. Leeson, "Endogenizing Fractionalization," *Journal of Institutional Economics* 1, no. 1 (2005): 75–98.

19. See W. Baumol, *The Free-Market Innovation Machine* (Princeton, NJ: Princeton University Press, 2002); Peter J. Boettke and Christopher J. Coyne, "Entrepreneurship and Development: Cause or Consequence?" *Advances in Austrian Economics* 6 (2003): 67–88; Christopher J. Coyne and Peter T. Leeson, "The Plight of Underdeveloped Countries," *Cato Journal* 24, no. 3 (2004): 235–49.

narrative approach,[20] ethnographic analysis of underground economies,[21] or micro-data surveys.[22] Empirical economics is going through a transformation just as drastic as theoretical economics and it is doing this in line with Hayek's focus on disaggregation and also in a manner consistent with the subjectivist notion of developing a political economy of everyday life that respects the meaning that individuals construct and place on their activities and the activities of others.

In the realm of public policy, arguments on institutions and institutional capacity are more prevalent today than ever.[23] The idea that we need simple rules for a complex world is not heretical.[24] In fact it is much more common than the idea that because of complexity we need detailed interventions.[25] It is now a common wisdom that rules outperform discretion in the realm of public policy. Policy analysis has moved to the level of the rules of the game that create the institutional environment within which economic activity takes place. This is seen most obviously in the public policy discussion on development economics and the emphasis on creating an institutional environment that cultivates an entrepreneurial environment where individuals are enabled to realize the mutual gains from trade. Cooperation is encouraged, and conflict minimized, due to the institutional environment that is adopted in any given society.[26]

In the realm of ideological commitment, a new generation of liberal scholars have emerged who have taken up Hayek's idea and run further with them than even Hayek dared to imagine. Kukathas, for example, argues that the toleration

---

20. See, e.g., R. Bates et al., *Analytic Narratives* (Princeton, NJ: Princeton University Press, 1998).

21. See, e.g., H. de Soto, *The Other Path* (New York: HarperCollins, 1989).

22. See, e.g., T. Frye, *Brokers and Bureaucrats* (Ann Arbor: University of Michigan Press, 2000).

23. See., e.g., F. Fukuyama, *State-Building: Governance and the World-Order in the 21st Century* (Ithaca, NY: Cornell University Press, 2004).

24. See R. Epstein, *Simple Rules for a Complex World* (Cambridge, MA: Harvard University Press, 1995).

25. The 2004 Nobel Prize to Kydland and Prescott for, in part, their work on rules versus discretion, can be seen as consistent with this basic Hayekian point.

26. See Elinor Ostrom et al., *Aid, Incentives and Sustainability: An Institutional Analysis of Development Cooperation*, Stockholm, Sweden: Swedish International Development Cooperation Agency, 2002.

of religious and ethnic minorities provided by liberal institutions must be pursued to its logical conclusion even in the world that we live in today.[27] Also, recent work on decentralized governance and law by Bruce Benson has developed Hayek's distinction between law and legislation in a consistent manner.[28] Finally, the work by scholars such as Barry Weingast on market-preserving federalism is another example of where the argument for decentralized governance and fiscal federalism that Hayek made is inspiring new theoretical presentation and empirical investigation.[29]

Conclusion

This short summary demonstrates just how much research Hayek's work has generated (and continues to generate) by scholars in economics and political economy that addresses the fundamental questions of social cooperation in a free society. Hayek's research program in economics and political economy contains many substantive points which have been demonstrated to be of continuing relevance in the further development of scientific economics, public policy analysis, and the ideological commitment to classical liberalism.

---

27. C. Kukathas, *The Liberal Archipelago: A Theory of Diversity and Freedom* (New York: Oxford University Press, 2003).

28. Bruce Benson, *The Enterprise of Law* (San Francisco: Pacific Research Institute for Public Policy, 1990).

29. Barry Weingast, "The Economic Role of Political Institutions," *Journal of Law, Economics and Organization* 11, no. 1 (1995): 1–31.

17

James M. Buchanan and the Rebirth of Political Economy

If not an economist, what am I? An outdated freak whose functional role in the general scheme of things has passed into history? Perhaps I should accept such an assessment, retire gracefully, and, with alcoholic breath, hoe my cabbages. Perhaps I could do so if the modern technicians had indeed produced better economic mousetraps. Instead of evidence of progress, however, I see a continuing erosion of the intellectual (and social) capital that was accumulated by political economy in its finest hours.   —James Buchanan[1]

Introduction

IT IS SOMEWHAT odd to consider anyone who has received the Nobel Prize to be an outsider. Outsider status is usually reserved for those who toil in obscurity. Buchanan attended the University of Chicago, taught at the University of Virginia, published articles in the *American Economic Review* and *Journal of Public Economy*, was named Distinguished Fellow of the American Economic Association, and received National Science Foundation as well as private foundation grants to develop public choice economics. His former students have taught at some of the finest institutions of higher learning (Cornell, Penn, Cal Tech, and the University of Virginia) and have held high public office (director of the Federal Trade Commission, director of the Office

---

1. James M. Buchanan, *What Should Economists Do?* (Indianapolis, IN: Liberty Press, 1979), 279.

of Management and Budget, and under secretary of the Treasury). Why should such a well-connected character be considered a dissenter?

Brave individuals who buck the intellectual trends of their time (usually at great professional cost) to pursue truth normally have not garnered so many rewards. But Buchanan's career, like some crucial aspects of his thought itself, is at tension with itself. True, he taught at the University of Virginia, but he left there because of internal university political troubles and has taught at lesser-known schools for the past 30 or so years.[2] The public choice revolution began at the University of Virginia in the 1960s; but it was at Virginia Tech in the 1970s that the revolution took hold and at George Mason University in the 1980s that victory was achieved on several theoretical fronts in public economics. Buchanan has spent a good part of his career as an insider who thought like an outsider, and as an outsider who possessed an insider's claim on the professional establishment. As he has argued, he never would have received the Nobel Prize if the committee consisted of *American* economists, for his work was by far appreciated more in Europe than at home in the U.S. research community.

Buchanan is not the only Nobel laureate to suffer this fate; Friedrich Hayek, Gunnar Myrdal, Herbert Simon, Ronald Coase, and Douglass North were all awarded the prize despite rejecting the conventional economic wisdom in terms of methodology, politics, and field of study. Buchanan, however, was special in one sense—he took great pride in his Southern heritage and the intellectual challenge he represented to the mainstream economic profession. As he himself put it:

> how many farm boys from Middle Tennessee, educated in tiny, poor, and rural public schools and at a struggling state-financed teachers college, have received the Nobel Prize? How many scholars who have worked almost exclusively at southern universities have done so, in any scientific discipline? How many of my economist peers who are laureates have eschewed the use of both formal mathematical techniques and the extended resort to empirical testing?[3]

---

2. See R. Cushman, "Rational Fears," *Lingua Franca* (November/December 1994): 42–54, for a discussion of the Virginia episode, the rise of rational choice political science, and the reaction it generated.

3. James M. Buchanan, *Better than Plowing* (Chicago: University of Chicago Press, 1992), 164.

Buchanan has made original contributions to methodology, social philosophy, and public policy economics, as well as the discipline of political science. I shall limit my discussion to three areas that define him as a major dissenter from the mainstream of professional opinion in economics. First, Buchanan burst the romantic vision of politics that dominated political science, and the economic treatment of market failure and public economics in general, during the 1950s to 1970s. Second, Buchanan challenged the formalism of modern economics with a restated, consistent subjectivism. Finally, Buchanan reintroduced economics to its sister discipline of moral philosophy and laid the foundation for a modern political economy.

Defining Dissent

The *Oxford English Dictionary* defines secular dissent as disagreement with a proposal or resolution—the opposite of consent. The meaning here is best understood within the context of political discourse. But, science is not politics. In politics, the goal is to reach consensus; in science the idea is to get at truth (however imperfectly we strive to attain that goal). Hence, the religious meaning of dissent might be more appropriate for economics.

The idea of modern economics as a secular religion has been explored both as satire and serious scholarship. Leijonhufvud exposes the rituals and the social structure of the economics profession in a satirical fashion to make the serious point that "Among the younger generations, it is now rare to find an individual with any conception of the history of Econ. Having lost their past, the Econ are without confidence in the present and without purpose and direction for the future."[4] On the other hand, Robert Nelson documents how economics became the theology of the modern age. Eliminating evil is no longer the divine prerogative; ensuring economic progress *is* because our modern secular religion teaches that "If all important material needs could be fully satisfied . . . the main cause of past wars, hatreds, and other banes of human history would be ended. There would be far less basis for envy, jealousy, and other sources of evil thoughts and actions."[5]

---

4. A. Leijonhufvud, "Life among the Econ," in *Information and Coordination* (New York: Oxford University Press, 1981), 359.
5. Robert H. Nelson, *Reaching for Heaven on Earth* (Lanham, MD: Rowman & Littlefield, 1991), 2.

If Leijonhufvud and Nelson are even partially correct, then perhaps looking at economics as a religious community within the institutions of higher education and protected by the social structure and norms of the profession would be a useful starting point from which to deal with the question of dissent. Within this religious community, how are nonconformists dealt with? Daniel Defoe's pamphlet *Shortest Way With The Dissenters* (an exercise in the literary hoax) recommended that dissenters either be put to death or exiled. The guardians of the consensus praised Defoe's analysis of the situation. Once it was revealed that the author himself was a dissenter, these guardians were so upset that their bigotry was exposed that Defoe was put in the pillory. While the high priests of modern economics do not champion such extreme measures, exile from the profession is not uncommon. Nonconformity within a certain range of questions is common in modern economics, but the range has a narrow width, as does the possible pool of answers. McCloskey has succinctly made this point:

> The typical, and narrow, American Department of Economics these days, ranges all the way from M to N. If one stands too close to such a range one can become convinced that it is "wide." But it does not stretch to Israel Kirzner or Barbara Bergmann or Jim Buchanan or Tom Weisskopf.[6]

A dissenter in economics is thus one who resists the dominant economic religion. They can do this by (1) eschewing mathematical modeling and econometric testing, and thus the basic *language* and *toolkit* of contemporary scientific economics; (2) articulating a philosophical case against modern economics; and/or (3) rejecting the professional strictures against normative theorizing and see policy relevance as a virtue. Any one of these positions would constitute a dissent from the current orthodoxy; holding all three is surely grounds for expulsion. It is all three, however, which characterize the work of James Buchanan.

The sociological question of why some ideas "stick" and other do not is particularly relevant for this discussion. An effective dissenter has to be Kuhn's "divergent thinker"[7]—one firmly rooted in the contemporary scientific tra-

---

6. Deirdre N. McCloskey, "Kelly Green Golf Shoes and the Intellectual Range from M to N," *Eastern Economic Journal* 21, no. 3 (Summer 1995): 414.

7. T.S. Kuhn, "The Essential Tension: Tradition and Innovation in Scientific Research," in *The Third University of Utah Research Conference on the Identification of Scientific Talent*, edited by C.W. Taylor (Salt Lake City: University of Utah Press), 162–74.

dition who has adopted a "convergent thinking" approach to science. Thus, the successful scientist displays the characteristics of a traditionalist and an iconoclast simultaneously.[8] This "essential tension" between convergent and divergent thinking is a striking characteristic of Buchanan, and it explains the paradox concerning his professional status. Because Buchanan was grounded in the conformity of neoclassicism, his dissent struck a chord in part of the profession and generated a paradigmatic shift in the way public economics was done.

An Overview of Buchanan's Contribution

Buchanan's personal biography can be found in his entertaining *Better than Plowing*. Born in rural Tennessee, educated at the local public school and then the local college, Middle Tennessee State Teacher's College (where he paid for his college fees and books by milking dairy cows), he then attended a year of graduate study in economics at the University of Tennessee (where he learned little economics, but much about life). He served in the navy during World War II, and then earned (with the aid of the GI subsidy) a PhD in economics from the University of Chicago. A libertarian socialist on his arrival at Chicago, Buchanan was "converted" to classical liberalism after six weeks of price theory with Frank Knight. Libertarian values remained, but Buchanan now understood that the market (not government) was the more consistent with those values. Also at Chicago, Buchanan discovered Knut Wicksell's principle of just taxation. The final intellectual influence was the Italian tradition of public finance that Buchanan was exposed to during a Fulbright Fellowship year. This tradition emphasized real as opposed to ideal politics.

From Knight, Buchanan got his theoretical framework and the idea that economics is not a science. From Wicksell, Buchanan learned that politics must be understood in an exchange framework. Efficiency in the public sector could be guaranteed only under a rule of unanimity for collective choices. From the Italians, Buchanan learned that public finance must postulate a theory of the state and that it would be best to reject utilitarianism and Hegelian

---

8. A change of heart in old age is not enough: that would just be attributed to softness of brain or sour grapes. No, the dissenter must be consistent from early on, yet couch the dissent in a manner that gets attention.

idealism in postulating such a theory. Once these three elements were brought together, the framework for Buchanan's contributions to public sector economics was set. All that remained was to work out the implications.[9]

Sandmo has argued that Buchanan's "main achievements have been to introduce his fellow economists to new ways of thinking about economic, in particular about the public sector and the interaction between economics and politics."[10] By recasting public finance in the light of this Knight/Wicksell/Italian connection, Buchanan was able to challenge the received wisdom of his day on several fronts.[11]

Buchanan challenged the accepted Keynesian doctrine on both methodological and analytical grounds.[12] The level of aggregation in Keynesian fiscal theory, for example, violated the political norms of democratic society, and fundamentally misconstrued the nature of the debt burden. Focusing on the aggregate unit, fiscal theorists were unable to address the problem of who pays for the creation of public goods and when the payments will be made. The prob-

---

9. On Buchanan's contributions to economics, see A. Atkinson, "James M. Buchanan's Contributions to Economics," *Scandinavian Journal of Economics* 89, no. 1 (1987): 5–15; Peter J. Boettke, "Virginia Political Economy: A View from Vienna," in *The Market Process: Essays in Contemporary Austrian Economics*, edited by Peter J. Boettke and David L. Prychitko (1987; repr., Aldershot, UK: Edward Elgar Publishing, 1994), 244–60; T. Romer, "On James Buchanan's Contributions to Public Economics," *Journal of Economic Perspectives* 2, no. 1 (Fall 1988): 165–79; and A. Sandmo, "Buchanan on Political Economy: A Review Article," *Journal of Economic Literature* 28, no. 1 (March 1990): 50–65. For an overview of the "new" political economy see D. Mueller, *Public Choice II* (New York: Cambridge University Press, 1989), and R. Inman, "Markets, Governments, and the 'New" Political Economy,'" in *The Handbook of Public Economics*, edited by A. Auerbach and M. Feldstein, vol. 2 (Amsterdam: North-Holland, 1987), 647–777. In *Beyond Politics: Markets, Welfare, and the Failure of Bureaucracy* (Boulder: Westview, 1994), W.C. Mitchell and R.T. Simmons provide a useful introduction to public choice.

10. Sandmo, "Buchanan on Political Economy," 62–63.

11. Buchanan is probably best known for his joint work with Tullock (*The Calculus of Consent* (Ann Arbor: University of Michigan Press, 1962), in Buchanan, *The Collected Works of James M. Buchanan,* vol. 3 (repr., Indianapolis, IN: Liberty Fund, 1999)), and Tullock's influence must be recognized in any assessment of Buchanan. The tension between Buchanan's philosophical perspective and Tullock's economistic one led to a very productive collaboration.

12. James M. Buchanan, *Public Principles of Public Debt* (Homewood, IL: Irwin, 1958).

lem was an elementary one—the principles of opportunity cost and economic decision making were forgotten.

The controversy over the burden of debt forced Buchanan to reexamine the conceptual foundations of economic science. This led to his slim volume *Cost and Choice*.[13] The opportunity cost logic of economics would lead to surprising results on a broad range of issues, from the burden of debt to issues concerning the military draft to the problem of externalities to the choice context of bureaucratic decision making. Compelling his fellow economists to reexamine the conceptual foundations of their discipline characterizes Buchanan's outsider status. The burden of debt debate, in other words, was typical of Buchanan's career; he was viewed as an outsider because he asked economists to pay attention to the most elementary principles of their discipline. By announcing that the modern technical Emperor has no clothes, Buchanan served an important intellectual function beyond his substantive contribution to the issue.[14]

During the 1970s, Buchanan's work became more philosophical. *The Limits of Liberty: Between Anarchy and Leviathan* (Chicago: University of Chicago Press, 1975) presents the contractarian perspective in political economy. This was followed by several collections of essays.[15] In the 1990s, Buchanan, in collaboration with Yoon, has addressed issues around increasing returns and the positive role of the work ethic.[16] Unlike other scholars working on the technical and policy implications of increasing returns, Buchanan focused on the effects of increasing returns on specific institutions and practices. His concern was

---

13. Buchanan, *Cost and Choice*, in Buchanan, *Collected Works*, vol. 6.

14. This contribution, of course, has not been consistently recognized by establishment economists who worship the god of formalism. But, Buchanan's methodological statements throughout his career have warned about the costs of formalism for economic understanding, and they provide inspiration to those working outside the current formalistic fashions that real progress can be made in economic thought by persistently pursuing the elementary principles of the discipline. It would seem that one formalistic principle, that of Occam's Razor, actually would side with the antiformalist.

15. James M. Buchanan, *Freedom in Constitutional Contract* (College Station: Texas A&M University Press, 1977); Buchanan, *Liberty, Market and State* (New York: New York University Press, 1986); Buchanan, *The Economics and Ethics of Constitutional Order* (Ann Arbor: University of Michigan Press, 1991).

16. James M. Buchanan and J.Y. Yoon, eds., *The Return of Increasing Returns* (Ann Arbor: University of Michigan Press, 1994).

to understand Adam Smith's argument about increasing returns from specialization, and how the institutional environment channels human inclinations
to "truck, barter and exchange" in order to realize the gains from increasing
returns.

There is a surprising unity in Buchanan's research program throughout his
career. The basic propositions which guide his work can be summarized neatly:[17]

- Economics is a "science," but it is a "philosophical" science, and the
  strictures against scientism offered by Knight and Friedrich Hayek
  should be heeded.
- Economics is about choice and processes of adjustment, not states of
  rest. Equilibrium models are only useful when we recognize their limits.
- Economics is about exchange, not about maximizing. Exchange and
  arbitrage should be the central focus of economic analysis.
- Economics is about individual actors, not collective entities. Only individuals choose.
- Economics is about a game played within rules.
- Economics cannot be studied properly outside of politics. The choices
  among different rules of the game cannot be ignored.
- The most important function of economics as a discipline is its didactic
  role in explaining the principle of spontaneous order.
- Economics is elementary.

From his early critique of social choice theory and welfare economics to his
most recent writings on constitutional design, Buchanan stresses these eight
points.

Finally, it is important to recognize the methodological schema that Buchanan employs to address questions in political economy and how this scheme
allows him to weave these eight propositions into a coherent framework for
social theory. Buchanan emphasizes that we must distinguish between pre-
and postconstitutional levels of analysis. Preconstitutional analysis concerns
the rules of the game, while postconstitutional analysis examines the strategies
players adopt within a set of defined rules. Political economy, properly understood, involves moving back and forth between these two levels. Successful

---

17. See Buchanan, *What Should Economists Do*, 280–82.

application of modern political economy to the world of public policy demands a *constitutional* perspective. In this regard, Buchanan introduces the vital distinction between "policy within politics" and systematic changes in the rules of the game. Lasting reform results not from policy changes within the existing rules but rather from changing the rules of governance. Thus, far from being a conservative intellectual, Buchanan is an intellectual radical seeking to get at the root cause of social and political ills.

The End of Romance

According to ancient legend, a Roman emperor was asked to judge a singing contest between two participants. After hearing the first contestant, the emperor gave the prize to the second on the assumption that the second could be no worse than the first. Of course, this assumption could have been wrong; the second singer might have been worse. The theory of market failure committed the same mistake as the emperor. Demonstrating that the market economy failed to live up to the ideals of general competitive equilibrium was one thing, but to gleefully assert that pubic action could costlessly correct the failure was quite another matter. Unfortunately, much analytical work proceeded in such a manner. Many scholars burst the bubble of this romantic vision of the political sector during the 1960s. But it was Buchanan and Gordon Tullock who deserve the credit for shifting scholarly focus.

Before public choice, economic theory frequently postulated an objective welfare function which "society" sought to maximize and assumed that political actors were motivated to pursue that objective welfare function. The Buchanan/Tullock critique pointed out: (1) that no objective welfare function exists, (2) that even if one existed societies do not choose (only individuals do), and (3) that individuals within the political sector, just as in the private sector, base their choices on their private assessment of cost and benefits.[18]

The major insights of modern political economy all flow from these three elementary propositions—the vote motive; the logic of dispersed costs and concentrated benefits; the shortsightedness bias in policy, and the constitutional

---

18. Sen ("Rationality and Social Choice," *American Economic Review* 85, no. 1 (March 1995): 1–24) has attempted to address Buchanan's critique of the social choice literature.

perspective in policy evaluation. Politics must be endogenous in any reasonable model of economic policymaking. But the intellectual spirit of the 1950s and early 1960s was one of zealous optimism about the nature of politics. Buchanan's warning of democratic folly, and the need for constitutional constraint, did not sit well with the intellectual idealist of the day. In the wake of the Vietnam War, and then Watergate, as well as the failed economics policies that emerged from both Democratic and Republican administrations, it is now difficult to imagine a noncynical view of politics. This is not an endorsement of apathy and malcontent with politicians. Nowhere in the Buchanan body of work is it suggested that politicians are any worse than the rest of us. Rather, his work simply stressed that politicians are just like the rest of us—neither sinners nor saints, but a bit of both.

Methodologically, Buchanan employed the assumption of economic man within politics not to describe the motivation of any particular political actor, but rather as a modeling strategy. As pointed out above, Buchanan learned from the Italians (and from Wicksell) that one must postulate a theory of the state. By postulating the revenue-maximizing leviathan, Buchanan was able to address the political rules of the game that would constrain the behavior of individuals within politics. In particular, if government officials are revenue-maximizing, then the question becomes what rules of the game are necessary to transform revenue-maximizing behavior into wealth-maximizing behavior? This is a question of constitutional design. In two books with Geoffrey Brennan, *The Power to Tax* (New York: Cambridge University Press, 1980) and *The Reason of Rules* (New York: Cambridge University Press, 1985), Buchanan employed the economic man assumption to establish rules that guard against "worst-case" scenarios in politics. Even if rulers were sinners, it would be important to design a constitution that would compel these sinners to act more like saints.

But to develop an idealized constitutional political structure (a vision of a workable utopia), one had to first deconstruct the idealist/romantic vision of politics, where unconstrained democracy is envisioned as a workable model of self-rule and to substitute a more realist vision of political processes. Buchanan (and Tullock) accomplished this with the aid of elementary economic reasoning, most notably the idea that only individuals choose, that in making their choices they weigh costs and benefits, and that the way individuals perceive costs and benefit depends on the institutional context within which they must choose. Simple concepts, applied consistently and persistently, often generate surprising results that must be repeatedly stressed.

Subjectivism and the Elemental Principles of Economics

Ironically, modern economists were reluctant to accept the "economic way of thinking," in particular, the central role of exchange and the notion of subjective tradeoffs. In his 1963 Presidential Address to the Southern Economic Association, Buchanan argued that economists should put the contribution of constrained maximization in perspective.[19] Resource allocation was *not* the central problem of economics. Economists should, Buchanan urged, concentrate on the human propensity to truck, barter, and exchange and on the institutional arrangements that emerge as a result of this propensity.

If this step is not taken, it is too easy for error to sneak into economic analysis and become embedded at the most fundamental level. The allocation definition of economics "makes it all too easy to slip across the bridge between personal and individual utility of decisions and 'social' aggregates."[20] Economists know that crossing the bridge is difficult, and Lionel Robbins was successful in keeping many from summing utilities in order to get across the bridge. But Robbins was only partially successful, for economists still thought that as long as they specified their social welfare function they could maximize to their own hearts' content. Buchanan pointed out that this intellectual exercise is illegitimate; economists *should not* engage in this activity.

The Buchanan critique of optimizing models is not about the introduction of value judgments via the social welfare function, nor is it a critique of formalization *per se*. Rather, the critique is that the subject matter of economics is lost in these exercises in applied mathematics, and that where the subject matter seems to creep back into the analysis it is mischaracterized. The mutual advantage that can be realized through exchange in specified institutional settings is the one important truth of political economy, Buchanan insists; modern economics has threatened our ability to understand this truth.

---

19. Buchanan, *What Should Economists Do,* 17–37.
20. Buchanan, *What Should Economists Do,* 22–23.

Consider, for example, Buchanan's critique of the model of perfect competition in the light of his plea for exchange *activity* to occupy the central place in economic theorizing. Perfectly competitive general equilibrium eliminates all social content from individual decision making. The individual confronts an array of externally determined variables, and the choice problem is transformed into a mechanical problem of computation. Within such a world there is only one equilibrium point, and so the model cannot capture the dynamics of competition or the trading behavior that would prod a system to equilibrium. Buchanan summarizes the point nicely:

> A market is not competitive by assumption or by construction. A market *becomes* competitive, and competitive rules *come to be* established as institutions emerge to place limits on individual behavior patterns. It is this *becoming* process, brought about by the continuous pressure of human behavior in exchange, that is the central part of our discipline, if we have one, not the dry rot of postulated perfection. A solution to a general-equilibrium set of equations is not predetermined by exogenously determined rules. A general solution, if there is one, *emerges* as a result of a whole network of evolving exchanges, bargains, trades, side payments, agreements, contracts which, finally at some point, ceases to renew itself. At each stage in this evolution toward solution there are *gains* to be made, there are exchanges possible, and this being true, the direction of movement is modified.
>
> It is for these reasons that the model of perfect competition is of such limited explanatory value except when changes in variables exogenous to the system are introduced. There is no place in the structure of the model for internal change, change that is brought about by men who continue to be haunted by the Smithean propensity. But surely the dynamic element in the economic system is precisely this continual evolution of the exchange process, as [Joseph] Schumpeter recognized in his treatment of entrepreneurial function.[21]

Subjectivist economics compels theorists to avoid the pitfalls of abstraction. It grounds economic analysis in the choices of individuals and demands

---

21. Buchanan, *What Should Economists Do*, 29–30 (emphasis in original).

that empirical analysis pay attention to the institutional context of choice and how agents perceive their institutional constraints. The mechanical model of allocational computation, and its corollary (the model of perfect competition), eliminates genuine choice from study just as the focus on aggregate data ignores the ideas, desires, beliefs, and cultural practices that motivate historical actors.

Buchanan's great contribution to subjectivist thought was to demonstrate how a consistently subjectivist position would lead to a different perspective on many issues. The contribution was to challenge the very notion of an objective social welfare function that was to be maximized. On a more concrete microeconomic analytical level, Buchanan was able to demonstrate how the burden of debt is passed on to future generations rather than consumed at the current moment in terms of real resources. In the burden of deft controversy, Buchanan criticized both the theory of functional finance and the traditional theory of public finance, which holds that the real cost of debt is incurred a the moment when the resources are employed.[22] The theory of functional finance was challenged on two grounds. First, it failed to postulate a model of political actors who would lack the incentive to run surpluses during good economic times. In bad times, of course, the incentive to run deficits is there, but why would a politician ever want to reduce expenditures and raise revenue during good times? The policy of functional finance, if pursued as designed, would reverse the logic of politics by concentrating costs and dispersing benefits during times of plenty; but this is incentive incompatible with electoral politics. Second, the Keynesian orthodoxy failed to take into account the generational transfer of the debt burden. Of course, this intergenerational transfer reinforced the political logic because the least informed and least organized interest group would be the as-yet born, and thus the constituency and politician can afford to ignore them.

---

22. Steven Pressman has pointed out to me that Abba Lerner's theory of functional finance argued the idea that governments had to balance their budgets on a cyclical basis. Instead, Lerner's idea was that governments could run deficits indefinitely as long as citizens were willing to lend the government money. This aspect of the doctrine did not become part of the Keynesian orthodoxy as reflected in the thought of Paul Samuelson, Robert Solow, James Tobin, and Lawrence Klein, who argued for cyclically balanced budgets. But implicit in the Buchanan critique is the idea that balancing the budget over the business cycle collapses into the Lerner position of indefinite deficits because of political behavior.

Buchanan's emphasis on the tight relationship between the act of choice and the notion of cost compelled him to criticize the traditional theory of public debt as well as the Keynesian theory of functional finance. During war, for example, it was typically argued that the opportunity cost of debt-financed public goods was the alternative use for which those resources would have otherwise been put. Steel was used to produce guns, not automobiles.

By introducing the distinction between choice-influencing and choice-influenced costs, Buchanan was able to show the fundamental error in traditional theory. It is true that resource use is shifted, but debt instruments entail obligations to service that debt. Buchanan argued that:

> In the decision-maker's subjective evaluation . . . costs are concentrated in the moment of choice and not in the later periods during which the actual outlays must be made. But the choice-influencing, subjective costs exist only because of the decision-makers recognition that it will be necessary to make future-period outlays.[23]

The choice-influenced costs of debt-financing (that is, the utility forgone as a result of the choice) are borne solely in the future.

Cost, Buchanan insisted, must be understood as the subjective assessment of trade-offs by individuals if it is going to have any meaning in a theory of decision making. A final example, which may drive the point home, is Buchanan's critique of Pigovian taxes as correctives. The Pigovian remedy was to bring marginal private costs (subjectively understood) into line with marginal social costs (objectively understood). The problem, Buchanan pointed out, was that the analyst had to specify the conditions under which objectively measurable costs could be ascertained by economic and policy actors. In general competitive equilibrium, measurable costs serve as a reasonable proxy for the subjectively held assessment of tradeoffs. But in general competitive equilibrium there are also no deviations between marginal private costs and marginal social costs. In other words, Buchanan (like Ronald Coase) pointed out that Pigovian tax remedies are either possible and redundant, or impossible to set because the

---

23. Buchanan, *Cost and Choice*, 60.

conditions presupposed for their establishment either eliminate their necessity or (if absent) preclude their enactment.[24]

The neoclassical project, where the subjective half of the 1870s revolution in value theory is emphasized as strongly as the marginalist half, leads to a different sort of economic science. In a broad-brush summary, it leads to a conception of economic science as a philosophical science and not as a technocratic one. Unlike other critics of modern economics (such as institutionalists or post-Keynesians), the subjectivist tradition retains a commitment to universality, has an emphasis on marginalism, and seeks to study how a systematic order emerges as the unintended consequence of individual choice. However, the subjectivist joins the institutionalist by highlighting the institutional context of choice, and the post-Keynesian by recognizing that the market order can break down and that theoretical problems result from treating time and ignorance seriously.

Subjectivism demands a major restructuring of economic theory. In addition to a renewed appreciation of the nature of choice, the context of choice comes to occupy a central stage within the subjectivist research program. There can be little doubt that Buchanan has been among the most important in resurrecting a broader notion of political economy; this conception is grounded in his appreciation of the subjective nature of choice and its implications for social order. In other words, subjectivism is the foundation of Buchanan's thought.

Economics, Social Philosophy, and Constitutional Political Economy

Positivism and formalism promised to lift economics from its immature past when ethical concerns and the ambiguities of philosophy and natural language clouded the thinking of its leading figures. Submission to empirical reality would compel those with a scientific mind to surrender ideological beliefs, and mathematical reasoning would eliminate the ability of theorists to slip in

---

24. Vaughn ("Does It Matter That Costs Are Subjective?" *Southern Economic Journal* 46: 1 (January 1980), 702–15) has pointed out the dilemma involved in this situation. To calculate the appropriate corrective tax, the policymaker must know the equilibrium price; yet the situation demanding correction implies a disequilibrium situation.

unwarranted assumptions. But these promises were false. Empirical reality is complex and must be viewed through a theoretical lens for us to make sense. In addition, mathematical reasoning might be precise but irrelevant. Mathematical modeling ensures *syntactic* clarity, but it does not guarantee *semantic* clarity. The model may be logically precise but lack meaning.

Both the empiricist and formalist aspiration were misapplied in the study of human beings. One cannot cast out of scientific court the very things (beliefs, desires, expectations) that motivate the subject of study without distorting the object of study. To put it another way, while eliminating anthropomorphism from the physical sciences was a noble cause, eliminating anthropomorphism from the study of humans eliminated the very thing that was supposed to be studied.

Along with figures such as Hayek, G.L.S. Shackle, Ludwig Lachmann, and Israel Kirzner, Buchanan fought persistently against the disappearance of the individual from economic analysis.[25] By insisting that economic processes always exist within a political/legal/social context, Buchanan begged economists to focus attention of the rule structure within which individual strategies would manifest themselves. Reform, he insisted, would not come from tinkering with individuals and their strategies, but only from changes in the rules of the game. By introducing the methodological schema of pre- and postconstitutional analysis, Buchanan was able to demonstrate the positive-scientific value of social philosophy for economics. He proposed both a positive analysis of normative issues and a recognition that political economists engage in normative analysis whether we want to admit it or not.

---

25. In the classroom, for example, one of the most challenging and interesting questions asked of students was to write the basic question: "Who is the individual in economics?" Buchanan's teaching method (at least by the time I had him as a formal instructor in the mid-1980s) was to assign no text, but to put on reserve about a dozen books that were to be read throughout the semester, and to grade students based on a series of short papers due about every two weeks throughout the semester. In one class I had with him, the writing assignments revolved around manipulating Adam Smith's deer-beaver model. Ironically, during that semester I also had the privilege of studying Great Books in Political Economy with Kenneth Boulding, who also spent most of the semester discussing Smith's basic model. I asked Boulding about this one afternoon, and he explained to me that Frank Knight (who taught both Buchanan and Boulding) spent his classes either discussing world religion or Adam Smith's deer-beaver model; so I should not fret, as I was simply being exposed to a long line of teaching methodology.

First, Buchanan proposed that preconstitutional analysis (the realm of social philosophy) could help economics understand two things: (1) the principle of voluntary exchange; and (2) the effects of strategies, given a set of rules, on the social and philosophical judgment of the rules themselves. Economists need to ask what rules of the game people would voluntarily agree to behind a veil of uncertainty and then examine how alternative rules would engender patterns of behavior and consequences for the economic game.[26] Going back and forth between the examination of pre- and postconstitutional choice constitutes the research program of modern political economy (and the integration of social and moral philosophy with economic science).

By introducing the theoretical construct of the veil of uncertainty, Buchanan was able to highlight the relevance of the Paretian norm for political economy. In the preconstitutional moment, no bargain concerning the rules of the game would be agreed to unless all parties expected to be made better off by adopting the rules in question. Since individuals were uncertain about where they would be situated in the postconstitutional environment, they would not agree to bargains that clearly valued one subgroup over any other. In this manner, the rights of the majority would surely be constrained by the interests of the minority. The concern here (following Wicksell) was with balancing the costs of decision externalities in politics with the costs of decision making. If a voting rule was such that a small minority could win, then that minority could impose costs on others and accrue benefits for themselves through the power of the state. To avoid this externality problem one could propose unanimity as the only rule, but unanimity entails increased costs associated with decision making. Conceptual unanimity emerged as the decision rule minimizing the total costs of political decision making, which again highlighted the relevance of the Paretian principle for understanding political agreement over the rules.

In the post constitutional environment, players of the political/economic game treat the rules as constraints and devise optimal strategies in response to them. Rules of the game that promise a "good" life but generate incentives leading to patterns of behavior not associated with the "good" life are, perhaps, rules in need of change. Buchanan has argued that classical political economy

---

26. The veil of uncertainty was introduced by Buchanan and Tullock in the *Calculus of Consent* before the veil of ignorance that John Rawls made famous.

discovered that as long as the state provided and maintained appropriate rules of the game, individuals could pursue their own interests and simultaneously enjoy the values of liberty, prosperity, and peace.[27] The classical liberal vision, however, was never implemented, and it failed to capture the imagination of intellectuals for more than a generation or two. Buchanan conjectures that this failure was due to the absence of a theory of justice in classical liberal political economy. Twentieth-century attempts to develop a model of social justice in order to correct this weakness have generated failed experiments in socialism and the social democratic welfare state. The failure of socialism and the welfare state can be directly attributed to the incentive incompatibility of the rules of these games with the strategies of the work ethic and personal responsibility, behavior associated with economic prosperity and social cooperation—or at least this is the type of argument that Buchanan's work would suggest. The veracity of this claim is not the issue here: rather I want to use it as an example of how Buchanan's work provides a positive analysis of how we choose among rules.

The Limits of Liberty contains Buchanan's most articulate statement of his political philosophic project. The subtitle of the book (*Between Anarchy and Leviathan*) neatly sums up Buchanan's research purpose. Frustrated with the failure of the classical liberal political philosophy to constrain the growth of government, some free market theorists (notably Murray Rothbard and David Friedman) suggested in the 1960s and 1970s that the market could provide endogenously the infrastructure that would govern its operation: anarcho-capitalism. In addition, Hayek's work was being interpreted myopically by classical liberal scholars throughout the 1970s and 1980s as a blanket indictment of rational constructivism.[28]

Buchanan shared the frustration of libertarians with the growth of the state in the twentieth century. A large part of the growth of the state had to do with the Romantic vision of politics that had captured the imagination of American liberals. In addition, from a technical perspective many arguments for government intervention were grounded in a poor understanding of economics and

---

27. Buchanan, *Economics and Ethics*.

28. I say myopically, because Hayek's thought was much more than just a warning against constructivism (but this is not the place to discuss Hayek's contributions in any detail). It is the myopic reading of Hayek's critique of rational constructivism that moves Buchanan into opposition with Hayek.

an even worse understanding of political processes. Much of the critique of the market was generated by those who failed to grasp the basic principles of spontaneous order analysis. Buchanan believed that rational analysis and the construction of the appropriate institutions of governance could emerge from the pens of economists and reform the system in a "desirable" direction.[29] Freedom was to be found in the constitutional contract, not in the absence of government (despite the philosophical attractiveness of anarchism) or in the submission to the forces of evolution. Anarchism promised devolution into Hobbesian war of all against all, and evolutionism promised nothing but the elevation of tradition to that of the sacred.

Buchanan put forth a modern argument for the state to establish governance structures, at the same time that he hoped to delineate the powers of the state. In this respect, Buchanan was pursuing the Madisonian project of empowering and then constraining government. In *The Limits of Liberty*, Buchanan distinguished between the "protective state" and the "productive state."[30] The protective state enforces the rights that emerged out of the preconstitutional moment. In this capacity, the state is external to contracting parties and does not attempt to "produce" anything other than contract enforcement. The productive state, on the other hand, produces collective goods. These two roles of the state are conceptually distinct, and failure to consistently distinguish these roles leads to confusion. The law, for example, is not an object of choice in the postconstitutional moment, whereas the supply and demand of public goods is subject to a process of collective choice.

With the development of the theory of the rent-seeking society, the productive state had to be further distinguished from what could be termed the redistributive state.[31] The productive state adds value by coordinating the plans of actors who are unable to do this through individual action. The redistributive state, however, simply transfers value from one party to another through

---

29. Though I should point out immediately that Buchanan never considered himself (or economics) as a savior. In fact, the economist as savior is to Buchanan the highest form of moral conceit. (See the quote from Knight in Buchanan, *Limits of Liberty*, in Buchanan, *Collected Works*, vol. 7, 209).

30. Buchanan, *Limits of Liberty*, 88–90.

31. See James M. Buchanan, R.D. Tollison, and G. Tullock, eds., *Towards a Theory of the Rent-Seeking Society* (College Station: Texas A&M University Press, 1980).

collective action. The logic of politics, unfortunately, biases the process of collective action in a manner which often transforms the productive state into the redistributive state, even against the best intentions of economic and political actors. This is one reason why Buchanan limits his reform proposals to the preconstitutional level; once the postconstitutional level is reached, changing the players will do little to effectuate lasting change. Reform is only possible, in Buchanan's system, at the level of the rules.

By focusing attention on the rules of political economy, Buchanan has opened up the discourse in economics to again deal with moral questions and the tradition of political philosophy.

Conclusion

As I have attempted to demonstrate, Buchanan dissented from mainstream economic thinking throughout his career. He was a non-Keynesian when Keynesianism was in vogue; he pursued a subjectivist research program when the majority of the profession lost sight of the subjectivist roots of the neoclassical revolution; he rejected the formal models of utility maximization and perfect competition when these models represented the toolkit of any respectable economist; and he reintroduced moral concerns into economics at a time when economists were content to worship at the shrine of scientism.

When Buchanan won the Nobel Prize in 1986, many rejoiced that an outsider could win the award. Buchanan himself interpreted this support (in the face of negative reaction form the popular press) as a penchant to root for the underdog. Surely, this sentiment underpinned the good wishes and hardy congratulations that Buchanan received. But the award represented more than that to many people. It represented a recognition that economics was too important to be left to the technicians and ideological eunuchs (two terms that Buchanan has employed to describe modern economists).[32] Over the past 50 years, economics has weeded out of scientific concern precisely those questions deserving serious scholarly attention. Buchanan pursued a research program more akin to his classical predecessors than to modern economists inspired by Paul Samuelson or Robert Lucas. For those of us who see economics as part of a broad interdisci-

---

32. Buchanan, *Liberty, Market,* 14.

plinary search for truth about man and the social organization of exchange and production, any nod in the direction of heterodox thinkers is interpreted as a sign that the economics profession may be regaining its "collective sanity."[33] Of course, our hopes are often dashed as soon as we discuss the prize with colleagues or graduate students who wonder where the lemma lies in the work of a Buchanan. But hope remains that economists will realize that our discipline possesses a cultural heritage and social capital that has been eroded by the blind quest for scientistic precision. In reviewing Samuelson's *Foundations* many years ago, Boulding wrote:

> Conventions of generality and mathematical elegance may be . . . barriers to the attainment and diffusion of knowledge. . . . It may well be that the slovenly and literary borderland between economics and sociology will be the most fruitful building ground during the years to come and that mathematical economics will remain too flawless in its perfection to be very fruitful.[34]

Boulding's words are even more telling today now that we have seen the fruits of the formalist revolution in economic theory and how it has cut economics off from the social theoretic discourse on the human condition. Buchanan was one of the few who, despite his deep commitment to the logic of economic argumentation, resisted the formalist revolution and strove to fit modern economics into the classical political economy project. One can disagree with this or that aspect of the project, but the scholarly enterprise demands our respect, admiration, and, most definitely, our emulation.

---

33. Please excuse the obvious violation of methodological individualism implied in this sentence.

34. Kenneth E. Boulding, "Samuelson's *Foundations*: The Role of Mathematics in Economics," *Journal of Political Economy* 56 (June 1948): 247, 199.

PART III

On the Practice of Economics

18

Where Did Economics Go Wrong?
Modern Economics as a Flight from Reality

ON MARCH 1, 1933, F.A. Hayek delivered his inaugural lecture at the London School of Economics and Political Science. Hayek, recently appointed to the Thomas Tooke Chair in Economic Science and Statistics at the LSE, sought to explain the trend in public opinion toward economic interventionism, embodied in the paradox that questions about economic matters were asked more frequently than questions related to any other academic discipline, even while the answers economists gave were largely disregarded by a skeptical public.

The cause of this paradox, according to Hayek, was twofold. First, the teachings of economics are counterintuitive (who would intuit that a law to raise wages might instead cause unemployment?). Second, these teachings expose as utopian many commonsensical solutions to concrete problems. "The existence of a body of reasoning which prevented people from following their first impulsive reactions, and which compelled them to balance indirect effects, which could be seen only by exercising the intellect, against intense feeling caused by the direct observation of concrete suffering, then as now, occasioned resentment."[1]

This resentment, Hayek argued, coupled with recent reexaminations of the analytical foundations of classical economics, had provided fertile ground for the German Historical school to rise to prominence among economists. The German school, along with American institutionalism, offered a method for the practical minded economist that did not possess the frustrating features of

---

1. F.A. Hayek, "The Trend of Economic Thinking," *Economica* (May 1933): 121–37, in *The Collected Works of F.A. Hayek, vol. 3: The Trend of Economic Thinking* (1933; repr., Chicago: University of Chicago Press, 1991), 21.

classical analytical economics. A body of thought that justified treating economic problems as unique—and their solutions as unbound by economic principles—was welcome relief for the would-be economic reformer.

The full effect of this trend, Hayek argued, was only being felt within the second generation of economists subject to its influence. The first generation, while rejecting the analytical method of classical economics, was nevertheless trained in it. Although they tried to shake off the rigorous logic of the classical school, economists trained in that way of thinking could not fully escape its influence. The second generation, however, not trained in the classical method, lacked the mental tools necessary to interpret economic phenomena in a theoretically coherent manner.

Hayek's argument can cut two ways, as I will try to demonstrate throughout this essay. On the one hand, Hayek was certainly right to suggest that the attempt to reject economic theory in the name of "realism" was inimical to satisfactory economics. We have no choice but to think in terms of models and simplifying assumptions. The world would be too complex to understand otherwise. But, on the other hand, the proposition that all thought is framed by theoretical concepts (whether consciously or unconsciously adopted) and, as a result, that all facts are theory-laden, does not license the adoption of any and every theory. Some theories are better than others. Hayek left this side of the argument unexamined. For his purposes, it was enough to contrast theory with historicism and maintain that theory is essential for proper economic analysis and public policy application.

Internal coherence is one way of adjudicating among theories, but so is correspondence to everyday life. Too much realism may kill analysis, but too little realism is unscientific. If theoretical coherence alone were all that mattered, then the only constraint on theoretical exercises would be the human imagination. Interesting puzzles would replace pragmatic solutions to problems encountered in the world—arguably, an accurate characterization of most contemporary economic theory. Economists must steer a course between (allegedly) pure description and the mere recording of events, on the one side, and self-indulgent mental gymnastics on the other. In 1933, Hayek addressed himself only to the problems associated with putatively unvarnished historical description.

The task of the economist, according to Hayek, was to construct from familiar elements, gleaned from our everyday experience in the world, a mental model aimed at reproducing the workings of the economic system. This task was misunderstood by economists of his day, he argued, because the self-organizing principles of the market economy were no longer understood. These principles were the great contributions of classical economics. But by the time neoclassical economists responded to the historicist challenge by developing marginal analysis, it was too late. The generation of economists now entrusted with designing public policy had lost an understanding of the basic properties of the market system. As a result, the trend in economic thinking was biased toward government planning of the economy. This trend was not only reflected in the growing interest in socialism but could also be detected in the reemergence of arguments for protectionism in international trade and for regulation of the domestic economy.

Where Hayek Went Wrong

Hayek's lecture is of interest to us today mainly for its early statement of themes that later came to dominate his research program. As Bruce Caldwell puts it, Hayek's lecture (although entitled "The Trend of Economic Thinking") "is probably best viewed as a suitable point of departure for explicating the trend of Hayek's thinking."[2] Hayek was prescient about the policy direction that would increasingly dominate economic thought, but he blamed the wrong forces for this trend. Historicism and institutionalism, along with Hayek's own Austrian school of economics, were to be completely displaced by formalism within the decade following Hayek's address. Interventionism and planning would be justified not on historicist grounds, but on the basis of the most advanced refinements of economic theory and technique that *neoclassical* economics—the very brand of economics Hayek tried to defend—had to offer.

The Austrians' theoretical arguments, however, soon came to be excluded from the canon of neoclassical "theory" by mathematical formalists, even while the empirical investigations of the American institutionalists and the German historicists were not considered "empirical" after the parallel development of

---

2. Bruce Caldwell, "Hayek's 'The Trend of Economic Thinking,'" *Review of Austrian Economics* 2 (1988): 178.

modern statistical techniques by econometricians.[3] The discipline of economics rejected both the Austrian and the historicist/institutionalist traditions of economic thought, yet reached nearly the same interventionist conclusions that the historical and institutionalist schools favored.

This was hardly the trend that Hayek detected in his inaugural address at the LSE. Nor was Hayek the only member of the Austrian school about to be blindsided by the direction of economics. Ludwig von Mises wrote in 1933 that there were no substantive differences between the various schools of modern neoclassical economics.[4] He viewed Austrian economics as squarely within the mainstream of neoclassical thought, the tradition identified by Hayek as yielding propositions that flew in the face of the simplistic intuitive appeal of government intervention and planning. For Mises, much as for Hayek, the enemies of modern economic science were Marxism, historicism, and institutionalism. Subtle differences in theory and the mode of its presentation among mainstream neoclassical economic theorists did not matter much, not when compared to this major division. Neoclassical economics—classical economics grounded in marginal utility theory—was scientific; other approaches were pseudoscientific.

Hayek's and Mises's myopia notwithstanding, among neoclassical economists the Austrians were indeed different. The Viennese economist Carl Menger and those following in his footsteps emphasized, in addition to subjectivism and marginal utility analysis, the role of knowledge and ignorance, time and uncertainty, and change and disequilibrium in understanding economic processes. Austrian and Swedish economists (and a few Americans and Britons, such as Frank Fetter and Philip Wicksteed) aside, neoclassical economists ignored these matters in their theorizing. But because Austrian economists agreed with the mainstream about the value of subjective utility and marginal analysis, they were viewed by the others, and more importantly by themselves, as indistinguishable from mainstream economists who overlooked market "imperfections" such as time and ignorance.[5]

---

3. Bruce Caldwell, "Austrians and Institutionalists: The Historical Origins of Their Shared Characteristics," *Research in the History of Economic Thought & Methodology 6*, 91–100.
4. Ludwig von Mises, *Epistemological Problems of Economics* (1933; repr., New York: New York University Press, 1981), 214.
5. Of course, the Austrians were involved in major debates of this era among mainstream

Hayek and Mises failed to see what was coming because the tension between neoclassical and Austrian economics only became acute during two economic debates that had not yet begun: one with John Maynard Keynes over macroeconomic theory and policy, and the other with Oskar Lange over the feasibility and desirability of socialism. Even the debate with Keynes was not, alone, enough to disturb the Austrians' vision of their school's "mainstream" status. In reality this debate revolved around fundamental issues in money and capital theory, but on the surface it was about more superficial questions of public policy. This was obscured, on both sides, by the fact that Hayek's brand of Continental capital and monetary theory was little understood and appreciated in England and America. John Hicks pointed out that while Hayek wrote in English, it was not English economics.[6] As a result, many of the analytical issues at stake were never adequately addressed.

Keynes, for example, never successfully responded to Hayek's critique of his *Treatise on Money*, in which Hayek questioned Keynes's tendency to treat real economic factors as aggregates, and criticized Keynes's failure to provide a theory of capital. The debate was a case study in mutual misunderstanding. Since Hayek shared the basically laissez-faire policy conclusions of many classical British economists, Keynes associated Hayek, incorrectly, with the British anti-interventionists' theoretical apparatus—which Hayek had (albeit unwittingly) jettisoned, at least in part. In this manner, Hayek was lumped by Keynes with the "classical" school that was to be overturned by *The General Theory of Employment, Interest and Money*. By the same token, according to the Austrians all that was needed to demonstrate the fundamental problems with Keynes was classical economics, for Keynes's *General Theory* was interpreted by Mises and Hayek as a return to the inflationist fallacies of the past (which even crude versions of the quantity theory of money had displaced) and to an economics of abundance, which denied that capital resources were scarce. But here the Austrians were

---

economists, notably the capital theory debate (with J. B. Clark) and the value and price theory debate (with Alfred Marshall).

These were, however, viewed as intramural analytical, not programmatic, debates. Marginalists were thought to be analytically united, despite differences over subsidiary assumptions or even broader issues of pre-analytical vision.

6. John Hicks, "The Hayek Story," in *Critical Essays in Monetary Theory* (Oxford: Clarendon Press, 1967), 203–215.

mistaken.[7] Certainly Keynes made fundamental errors in economic reasoning, but in many other respects, he had penetrated classical British economics deeply and had left it in tatters. Appeals to economic orthodoxy were not enough, either rhetorically or substantively, to forestall the rush to embrace Keynesian economics and policy.[8]

The Great Depression not only led to the embrace of Keynesian economics, it also lent new prestige to socialism. Capitalism, critics argued, was both unjust and chaotic. Business cycles were seen as manifestations of the inherent contradictions of capitalism. This message possessed a very practical appeal during the crisis, for obvious reasons.

Nothing in the popular version of this socialism would have shaken the self-image of Austrian economists as members of the economics mainstream. As early as the 1890s, Eugen von Boehm-Bawerk had used neoclassical economic theory to rebut Marx's understanding of the operation of capitalism. In 1920, Mises did the same thing for the idea of socialist economic planning, demonstrating that without private ownership in the means of production, socialist planners could not rationally calculate the alternative uses of scarce resources.[9] But in the 1930s, Oskar Lange used neoclassical equilibrium analysis to demonstrate that Mises's criticism was not valid—if one assumed that perfect knowledge was available to the planners. For in that case, they could calculate the alternative use of resources just as the competitive market supposedly does, through a process of trial and error. Socialist planners would draw on knowledge of supply and demand conditions in the same manner that economic agents within a market economy were pictured as doing in the neoclassical model of

---

7. Henry Hazlitt's critique of the Keynesian system, presented in *The Failure of the "New Economics": An Analysis of the Keynesian Fallacies* (Princeton, NJ: Van Nostrand, 1959), argues that many of the fallacies within Keynesianism are the consequence of misunderstanding orthodox doctrine. See also Henry Hazlitt, ed., *The Critics of Keynesian Economics* (Princeton, NJ: Van Nostrand, 1960).

8. See Robert Skidelsky, *John Maynard Keynes: The Economist as Savior, 1920–1937* (New York: Penguin, 1992), for an intellectual biography of Keynes during the time of the writing of *The General Theory*.

9. Ludwig von Mises, "Economic Calculation in the Socialist Commonwealth," in *Collectivist Economic Planning*, edited by F.A. Hayek (1920; repr., London: Routledge, 1935); and Mises, *Socialism: An Economic and Sociological Analysis* (1922; repr., Indianapolis, IN: Liberty Fund, 1981).

the perfectly competitive economy in equilibrium. If this model was theoretically coherent, then Lange's model of market socialism was equally coherent.

Lange's defense of socialism on neoclassical grounds took the Austrians by surprise, as did its acceptance by mainstream economists. Such established figures as Frank Knight and Joseph Schumpeter concurred with Lange's assessment of the analytical issue, and younger economists, such as Abba Lerner, began to develop Lange's argument further. In response, both Mises and Hayek started to articulate more clearly and precisely what differentiated Austrian economics from the neoclassical orthodoxy. But by this time they were already too far outside of the mainstream to command its attention any longer. Mises and Hayek came increasingly to be viewed as politically motivated pundits of the right, not as serious economists. By 1950 at the latest, the Austrian school of economics was forced underground—to the extent that, by now, it is questionable whether it should be considered part of the discipline of economics any more. By midcentury Hayek's prediction had come true: interventionism, even socialism, came to dominate economics. But the source of this trend was not antitheoretical historicism. It was neoclassical theory itself.

The Formalist Revolution

In the eyes of professional economists, Austrian economics was soundly defeated by both Keynesianism and neoclassical socialism. Whereas Keynesianism challenged the macroeconomic stability of capitalism, neoclassical socialism challenged its microeconomic efficiency. Lange and Lerner's argument could be interpreted as demonstrating that ideal market socialism could perform as well as ideal capitalism. A stronger interpretation, however, was that in the face of allegedly widespread monopoly power in real-world capitalism, real-world market socialism would be even *more* efficient.

What made the neoclassical mainstream receptive to these ideas was its failure to take seriously such factors as the use of (and imperfections in) economic knowledge, the presence of ignorance and uncertainty, the passage of time, and changes in economic conditions. All of this was assumed away in mainstream equilibrium models. Meanwhile, Austrians continued to uphold the counterintuitive policy conclusions of earlier economic theory because, if one *did* take these factors seriously, new forms of interventionism premised upon perfect knowledge in a timeless, changeless equilibrium seemed utterly fantastic, hence irrelevant.

Austrians, for example, argued that monetary inflation worked its way through the economic system by means of a ragged process of relative price adjustment. Thus, the nominally unimportant effect of inflation on money prices could have very real effects on the underlying distribution of resources: relative price signals could become distorted, misleading investors. The injection of money into one sector of the economy could create the illusion of increased real demand there, leading to unneeded new investment. Moreover, investment required resources that, far from being an undifferentiated aggregate, "capital," were both heterogeneous and specific to certain projects. The capital needed to build a house is different from that needed to build a car. Distortions in investment caused by monetary disturbances in the price system could therefore have severe consequences. Blinded by its maintenance of a stable supply of "capital," the government could overstimulate the supply of, for instance, houses at the expense of what consumers actually wanted, such as cars. Mainstream neoclassical economics, however, overlooked these problems either by rejecting the quantity theory of money altogether as Keynesians did, or else by accepting the Monetarists' crudely mechanical version of it, which took evenly proportionate adjustments in the general price level to be the main consequence of increases in the money supply. The theoretical and methodological work of Mises and Hayek, which emphasized processes of adjustment to real-world changes in the "data" that the mainstream saw as given and unproblematic, appeared anachronistic to economists whose attention was focused on an imaginary state of equilibrium, whether perfect or imperfect (i.e., marred by unemployment).

In 1947, the gap between the Austrians and the mainstream of neoclassical economics was widened by the publication of Paul Samuelson's *Foundations of Economic Analysis*.[10] Samuelson pioneered a synthesis of neoclassical and Keynes-

---

10. Paul A. Samuelson, *Foundations of Economic Analysis* (Cambridge, MA: Harvard University Press, 1947). Samuelson's hold over economists can be explained on two levels. First, economists suffer from physics envy; Samuelson's mathematization of economics promised to complete the transformation of economics into social physics that was started by Leon Walras. Second, Samuelson was not only smart, but strategic. Shortly after his *Foundations* became the major textbook in graduate education, Samuelson's *Economics* became the leading undergraduate text. Samuelson influenced students on their way in and on their way out. Within a decade, Samuelson became

ian economics, as well as endorsing the Lange-Lerner argument for market socialism.[11]

Samuelson also furthered the neoclassical case against the free market in the 1950s, with his development of the theory of market failure. Previously, the model of a perfectly competitive market was primarily used in thought experiments designed to be contrasted with real-world market institutions. Such counterfactual thought experiments illuminated the positive function of those institutions.[12] In a world of complete information, for example, neither firms nor profits would logically exist. Therefore, the contrast of this imaginary world against the real world of firms and profits showed that such institutions may have some functional significance in coping with *im*perfect and *in*complete information.

This counterfactual use of the theory of perfect competition was reversed by the formalist revolution in economics.[13] The departures of reality from the

---

synonymous with economics, and his hold over the style—if no longer the substance—of economic reasoning has not waned since.

11. See Samuelson, *Foundations*, 203–53, where he discusses welfare economics and the implications of the competitive model. Also see Samuelson, *Economics* (New York: McGraw-Hill, 1961), 678–89 and 818–36, for his undergraduate textbook's treatment of the issues related to socialist planning.

12. See, e.g., Frank H. Knight, *Risk, Uncertainty and Profit* (1921; repr., Chicago: University of Chicago Press, 1971).

13. One of the best examples of this reversal is to consider the interpretive difference between Samuelson and Hayek on the implications of the equilibrium pricing theories of Vilfredo Pareto (*Manual of Political Economy* (1909; repr., New York: Augustus M. Kelley, 1971) and Barone ("The Ministry of Production in the Collectivist State," in Hayek, *Collectivist Economic Planning*, 245–90) for collectivist planning. Hayek included a translation of Barone's essay in his *Collectivist Economic Planning* precisely because he thought it was clear that Barone demonstrated the practical inability of the collectivist planning system to replicate what is achieved in the competitive market economy. Similarly, Pareto is explicit that the collectivist planner would confront an insurmountable task even in a simple economy, whereas the capitalist system solves the problem of economic calculation every day through the impersonal market process. Both Barone and Pareto, however, demonstrated that in order to achieve economic efficiency in production, collectivism would have to solve the same set of equations as competitive capitalism. In other words, there was a formal similarity in the economic problem in both capitalism and socialism. The recognition of this formal similarity was preliminary to the analysis of the problems that collectivist planning would confront, not their solution. Yet since Samuelson contended that Mises's critique of socialism was refuted in advance by

model of perfect competition were now thought to highlight interventions in the market economy that would be necessary to approximate equilibrium. Competitive equilibrium and the maximizing behavior that would ideally produce it represented the hard core of the research program of economists from 1950 on. As this happened, economics as a discipline was transformed.[14]

The central role the model came to play was independent of whether it was employed by the minority who thought the market economy approximated the model, or the majority who thought that capitalism deviated significantly enough from the model that a great deal of government intervention was justified. In both cases, formalism led to utopianism. Either (in the minority view) reality was idealized, so that it approximated the model, or (in the majority view) reality became a dystopia, devoid of dynamic adjustment properties, and utopian properties were inadvertently attributed to interventions designed to make reality match the model. Absent from both types of formalism was recognition of any possibility other than all or nothing. Either the real world exemplified static equilibrium, or it could not approach that state without a push from the state. The intermediate possibilities represented by real-world institutions of adjustment to disequilibrium became invisible because the model contained only equilibrium.

Competitive equilibrium required (1) perfect information, (2) large numbers of buyers and sellers, and (3) costless mobility of resources. Under this set of restrictions, the logic of the model determined (4) that each market participant would treat prices as given and (5) that prices would equal the marginal costs of production. As a result, firms would produce at minimum average cost and earn zero economic profits. In the 1950s and 1960s, mainstream theory produced two fundamental welfare theorems that followed from proofs of the (mathematical) existence and stability of this competitive equilibrium. The first welfare theorem

---

the work of Barone and Pareto, he contended that the collectivist planning system could simply replicate the trial-and-error process explicated by Barone and Pareto. The fact that both Barone and Pareto explicitly denied that such a replication was possible in practice is brushed aside by Samuelson.

14. Besides Samuelson, the most important figures in this transformation of economics were Kenneth Arrow, Gerald Debreu, and Frank Hahn. It is no coincidence that each of these individuals made major contributions to market failure theory in addition to their development of the model of general competitive equilibrium.

stated that an economy in competitive general equilibrium was Pareto-efficient. The second theorem stated that any desired Pareto-efficient economy could be achieved through the decentralized market mechanism. Together, these two welfare theorems prove that *if* the appropriate conditions hold, the market mechanism yields the best possible economy.

That, however, is a big *if*. Without perfect futures markets, for example, intertemporal allocations could not be assumed to be optimal. Unless the strict conditions required for general competitive equilibrium were met, the economic theorist could not with any confidence make pronouncements about the efficiency of market allocations. In fact, he or she could be confident that the market would yield suboptimal results that demanded corrective government action.

The new role played by competitive equilibrium was fostered by Samuelson's methodological innovations. Samuelson sought to rewrite economics into the language of mathematics so as to eliminate the vague assumptions that underlay debates among "literary economists" of previous generations. Restating economics in the axiomatic language of mathematics, Samuelson argued, would force economists to make explicit assumptions that they had previously held implicitly. But the techniques of mathematics available to Samuelson required well-behaved and linear functions; otherwise, results would be indeterminate and the promised precision would not be achieved. In order to fit economic behavior into mathematical language, the real world had to be drained of its complexity. The problem situation of economic actors had to be simplified drastically so as to yield the precise formulations Samuelson sought.

Samuelson's research program eliminated the conscious component from the economic choices facing individuals in a world of uncertainty. Choice was reduced to a simple determinate exercise within a given ends-means framework, something an automaton could master. The task of discovering not only appropriate means, but also which ends to pursue, was left out of the equation. Moreover, it was forgotten that market institutions and practices arise in large part precisely *because* of deviations from the perfect-market model. Just as the friction between the soles of our shoes and the sidewalk enables us to walk, the imperfections of the real world give rise to the essential institutions and practices that make economic life possible. The complexity of both institutions and individuals is impossible to model precisely, so it was pushed aside by simplifying assumptions.

The huge gap between the older view preserved in Austrian economics and the new use of equilibrium models can be illustrated by considering the reception of Ronald Coase's work on transaction costs. Viewed as a practitioner of counterfactual thought experiments, what Coase was focusing on (in both his 1937 paper on the theory of the firm and his 1960 paper on the problem of social costs) was the origin of actual market and legal institutions as mechanisms for coping with real-world positive transaction costs.[15] Without transaction costs, Coase argued in 1937, there would be no need for firms. Transactions in spot markets would be all that would be necessary to coordinate production. In addition, without transaction costs, Coase argued in 1960, there would be no need for property law. Voluntary negotiations between economic actors would resolve all conflicts over property rights. The actual existence of firms and the law can be seen, therefore, as evidence of the ubiquity and intractability of transaction costs.

Coase's project, however, has been largely misunderstood by formalist neoclassical economics. Instead of highlighting the functional significance of real-world institutions in a world of positive transaction costs, Coase's work has been interpreted as describing the welfare implications of a zero-transaction-cost world. The "Coase Theorem" has been taken to hold that in a world of zero transaction costs, the initial distribution of property rights does not matter; for as long as individuals are free to transact, resources will be channeled toward their most highly valued use.[16]

---

15. See Ronald Coase, *The Firm, the Market and the Law* (Chicago: University of Chicago Press, 1988).

16. In perhaps the best intellectual biography of Coase to date, Steven Medema (*Ronald H. Coase* (New York: St. Martin's Press, 1994)) argues that Coase was concerned with examining the consequences of alternative legal arrangements on economic performance rather than in using economic techniques to examine the law. This difference in emphasis explains Coase's lack of interest in Posnerian law and economics, a movement more concerned with the use of economic techniques to examine the efficiency of various legal arrangements. Coase not only suggested an alternative comparative institutional program of research, but thoroughly questioned the logical coherence of mainstream neoclassical economics. Part of the equilibrium exercise that Coase engaged in was to show that pursuing the logic of maximizing within an environment of zero transaction costs led to conclusions different from those suggested by Pigovian welfare economics.

Coase's theoretical insights into the role of institutions of property and contract, however, were not all that was buried by the formalist revolution. Historical work on the complex web of institutions that undergird capitalist dynamics produced by the earlier generation of neoclassical scholars, such as Knut Wicksell, Frank Knight, and Jacob Viner, as well as Mises and Hayek, was swept aside in the rush toward formal theorizing. The real problem with the trend in economic thinking in the 1930s and 1940s was neither the critique of theory carried on by historicism and institutionalism nor the war against classical liberalism launched by Keynesians and socialists. The antitheoretical stance of historicism and institutionalism was self-defeating, and Keynesianism and socialism would rise and fall with the tides of politics. The real problem for economics was that the medium was becoming the message, as the strictures of formalism denied scientific status to *realistic theory*.

Ideas that defied the techniques of formal analysis came to be considered unworthy of serious consideration. Even when an idea was thought to be interesting, if it could not be translated into an appropriate model, there was not much that could be done with it.[17] The substance of economics was displaced by mathematical technique, and fundamental economic knowledge was set

---

If transaction costs were zero, then economic actors would negotiate away the conflict; if transaction costs (including informational costs) were positive, then how would authorities know what the right level of tax or subsidy should be to correct the situation? Coase's research program entailed both a critique of prevailing practice and a positive alternative program that is now emerging in the New Institutional Economics, of which Coase is still the leading representative.

17. Paul Krugman (*Development, Geography, and Economic Theory* (Cambridge, MA: MIT Press, 1995)) admits that the development theory of Albert O. Hirschman and Gunnar Myrdal was essentially correct in its emphasis on strategic complementarity in investment and in using coordination failures to explain why some countries are rich while others remain poor. But these ideas were ignored by economists in the 1950s and 1960s because they were not properly modeled—which Krugman defends, because only a properly modeled idea deserves serious attention by the profession. Avinash Dixit (*The Making of Economic Policy: A Transaction-Cost Politics Perspective* (Cambridge, MA: MIT Press, 1996)) makes a similar argument with respect to the economic theory of politics. It is this attitude among the second and third generation of economists after Samuelson that has come to dominate mainstream economics.

back—despite the obvious progress made in the precision with which economists could say what was left to say.[18]

The first casualty of the formalist revolution was the historically and institutionally rich tradition of economics still evident in the 1930s. Case studies of particular industries, for example, had been common. After the development of econometrics, however, the case study approach was discarded in favor of large-sample data analysis. The second casualty of the formalist revolution was what might be called "the economist's way of thinking," the defining characteristic of the discipline in both its classical and early neoclassical renditions. The best of the earlier economics combined an appreciation for the particularities of institutional context with theory grounded in the generalities of choice under conditions of scarcity. Individuals always face trade-offs, in this view, but the manner in which they weight their choices is contingent upon the particular context of choice.

Samuelson drained economic theory of institutional context, and the econometric approach to empirical economics eliminated historical detail. Parsimony won out over thoroughness. Economics moved at this time from one side of the cultural divide (the liberal arts) to the other side (the sciences)—or at least that was the self-image of economists, who equated science more with precision than accuracy. The physicist does not allow the impossibility of making accurate predictions in many real-world contexts (such as meteorology) interfere with the pursuit of precise formal laws that govern them. By myopically pursuing only the formal aspects of the discipline, economics was reduced to its present state, in which we continually know more and more about less and less.[19]

---

18. I have addressed this evolution in economic thought in Peter J. Boettke, "What Is Wrong with Neoclassical Economics (And What Is Still Wrong with Austrian Economics)," in *Beyond Neoclassical Economics*, edited by Fred Foldvary (Aldershot, UK: Edward Elgar Publishing, 1996), Cf. Robert Heilbroner and William Milberg, *The Crisis of Vision in Modern Economic Thought* (New York: Cambridge University Press, 1995).

19. Nothing I have said in this paragraph is original to me: See Albert O. Hirschman, "Against Parsimony: Three Easy Ways of Complicating Some Categories of Economic Discourse," in *Rival Views of Market Society* (Cambridge, MA: Harvard University Press, 22–40) and Amartya Sen, *On Ethics and Economics* (Oxford: Blackwell, 1987). Hirschman has proposed that we complicate economic discourse by recognizing the incredible complexity of human nature, while Sen suggests that we recapture moral philosophy in economic discourse.

Equilibrium: Description of Reality, Normative Critique, or Ideal Type?

In light of the formalist revolution in economic theory, we can usefully distinguish the older use of the equilibrium model as an *ideal type* from its use by free market Chicago-school economists as a description of reality, as well as its use by interventionist neo-Keynesians as a critical standard with which reality could be indicted when it failed to measure up.[20] In the latter two uses of equilibrium, it constitutes a static ideal, and the question is whether reality does or does not match it. In the ideal-type use, by contrast, the question is how departures from the ideal type—denied by the Chicago school and equated with market "failure" by neo-Keynesians—may constitute forms of incomplete success. An ideal type is intended neither to describe reality nor to indict it. It is instead a theoretical construct intended to illuminate certain things that *might* occur in reality; empirical investigation determines whether these phenomena are actually present and how they came to be there.[21] In this view, disequilibrium

---

20. Various scholars often blend the different uses. Frank Knight, for example, used equilibrium as an ideal type in his classic *Risk, Uncertainty and Profit*, but in *The Ethics of Competition* (1935; repr., New York: Augustus M. Kelley, 1951) he used it as a critical normative standard. Alfred Marshall is remembered as the pioneer of partial equilibrium analysis (which assumes an overall equilibrium in the economy, but focuses on a particular market), often assumed to be the hallmark of the Chicago-school approach, but we can also read Marshall as an ideal type theorist when he states that equilibrium analysis is preliminary to an "advanced study" that would be more evolutionary in nature (*Principles of Economics* (Philadelphia: Porcupine Press, 1920), 269). Nevertheless, even in these cases one can easily distinguish between the various deployments of the equilibrium construct.

21. See Jeffrey Friedman, "Economic Approaches to Politics," *Critical Review* 9, no. 1–2 (1995): 1–24, for this version of Weber's methodology of ideal types. Cf. Max Weber, *Economy and Society: An Outline of Interpretive Sociology*, edited by Guenther Roth and Claus Wittich, vol. 1 (1956; repr., Berkeley: University of California Press, 1978), 9–12. Fritz Machlup, *Methodology of Economics and Other Social Sciences* (New York: Academic Press, 1978), 207–301, discusses the ideal-type methodology as applied to economics in general. Cf. Weber, *Economy and Society*, 10, on "the 'imaginary experiment' which consists in thinking away certain elements of a chain of motivation and working out the course of action which would then probably ensue, thus arriving at a causal judgment." Mises (*Human Action: A Treatise on Economics* (1949; repr., Indianapolis, IN: Liberty Fund, 2010), 236–37) describes this approach as "the method of imaginary construction." Cf. Hayek, *Pure Theory of Capital*, 1941, (Chicago Il: University of Chicago, 1941), 14–28.

is not necessarily a market failure; something less than perfection may yet be better than any attainable alternative.

Deployed as an ideal type, equilibrium analysis allowed economists to describe what the world would be like in the absence of imperfections such as uncertainty and change. The descriptive value of the model lay precisely in its departure from observed reality, for this underscored the function of real-world institutions in dealing with *imperfect* knowledge, uncertainty, and so forth. Equilibrium was used as an ideal type by such Austrian economists as Mises and Hayek; early Chicago-school theorists, such as Frank Knight; LSE theorists, such as Coase; and Swedish-school theorists, such as Knut Wicksell. By contrast, economic formalism was, at first, virtually defined by the use of equilibrium as a standard for criticizing reality that, on the one hand, ignored its dynamic elements and, on the other, assumed that static perfection must (somehow) be attainable. Samuelson, Kenneth Arrow, Frank Hahn, and, more recently, Joseph Stiglitz are the major theorists who have employed equilibrium models in this manner.

Almost simultaneously with the emergence of equilibrium as an *indictment* of reality, University of Chicago economists such as Milton Friedman, George Stigler, Gary Becker, and Robert Lucas began to use it as a *description* of reality. In their view, real markets come breathtakingly close to approximating the efficiency properties of general competitive equilibrium. And even if a real-world market deviates from the ideal, the predictions of the model approximate behavior in the real world better than alternative models do. Real-world markets, in other words, act "as if" they were in competitive equilibrium. In fact, Becker and Lucas treat the existence of equilibrium as an explicit core *assumption* of their analysis of economic phenomena. By collapsing the gap between the model and reality, the Chicago school in its purest form does away with the need for intervention of the sort advocated by Samuelson et al. Hence the current reputation of laissez-faire as a wildly unrealistic economist's dogma. In comparison with the implausible assumptions of Chicago-school laissez-faire, government regulation has come to be seen not as a utopian outgrowth of crude, "intuitive" economic thought, but as a form of hardheaded realism.

From the perspective of those who see equilibrium as an ideal type, both its empirical idealization and its use as an indictment of a static reality appear deficient. The Chicago school's use of equilibrium to describe reality conflates the mental and empirical worlds. And while those who use equilibrium to indict reality recognize that the world is not perfect, their ignorance of the ways imperfect institutions do produce a semblance of economic order gives them an unduly pessimistic view of the market and an unrealistically optimistic tendency to rely on legal fiat to bring reality up to par. *In both cases, the heuristic value of equilibrium is sacrificed.* By ignoring the dynamics of disequilibrium, both traditions obscure the possibility that real-world market institutions may have coordinative properties even in the presence of dispersed knowledge, pervasive ignorance, the irreversibility of time, and changing conditions.[22] While the descriptive use of equilibrium readily leads to an endorsement of market transactions, it does so on an unrealistic basis. The proof is that the Chicago school lacks a theory explaining how markets achieve whatever degree of success they do; all the important work, as critics never tire of pointing out, is done by the model's assumptions. Similarly, the use of equilibrium as an indictment of reality fails to allow that existing imperfections may, in a dynamic world, be a source of motivation and learning that leads to the correction of market errors.

Both predictive and normative uses of equilibrium portray markets as essentially static. This constitutes an unwitting rejection of the heart of Hayek's contribution, despite the lip service often paid by formalist economists to his seminal essays on "Economics and Knowledge" (1937) and "The Use of Knowledge in Society" (1945).[23]

"Information" as a Bridge to Reality

The central concern of economics, Hayek suggested, is to explain "how the spontaneous interaction of a number of people, each possessing only bits of knowledge, brings about a state of affairs in which prices correspond to

---

22. Those inclined toward the descriptive use of equilibrium basically deny that these seemingly complex problems exist in the world. Philosophically, the argument relates back to the ancient assertion that change is an illusion. On the other hand, those who use equilibrium as an indictment of reality view the existence of a problem as, by *definition,* evidence that the ideal solution of competitive equilibrium is obtainable somehow. If the market does not attain perfection, then the state *must* be capable of it.
23. The relevant papers by Hayek are collected in F.A. Hayek, *Individualism and Economic Order* (1948; repr., Chicago: University Press of Chicago, 1996).

costs, etc., and which could be brought about by deliberate direction only by somebody who possessed the combined knowledge of all those individuals." Economic theory, in other words, should explain observed reality. The empirical observation that prices do *tend to* correspond to costs is the starting point of economic science. But formal neoclassical theory, instead of discerning how diffuse information is processed and used by imperfect economic actors, falls "back on the assumption that everybody knows everything" and so evades "any real solution of the problem."[24]

Hayek went further, arguing that the kind of knowledge that is dispersed among market participants is "knowledge of the kind which by its nature cannot enter into statistics."[25] The content of market prices is not the sort of information that can be treated as a commodity. It is not, therefore, the *costliness* of information that is essential to Hayek's story, but rather its *dispersal*. Its dispersal makes economic knowledge inaccessible except under special, institutionally fragile circumstances. The relevant economic knowledge, as Hayek put, is "the knowledge of the particular circumstances of time and place."[26] It can only be used and discovered in particular institutional contexts—contexts that are abstracted away in the timeless, placeless formalism of equilibrium modeling; hence the irrelevance of contemporary economics for comparing the effects of alternative real-world institutional arrangements on actual economic performance.[27]

The fundamental purpose of economic analysis, once Hayek's view of economic knowledge is accepted, is to determine how a dynamic system of production uses dispersed knowledge of time and place in a manner that aligns production plans with consumption demands. The money-price system, within an institutional environment of well-defined and enforced private property

---

24. F.A. Hayek, "Economics and Knowledge," in *Individualism and Economic Order*, 50–51.

25. F.A. Hayek, "The Use of Knowledge in Society," in *Individualism and Economic Order*, 83.

26. Hayek, "Use of Knowledge," 80.

27. In "Economics and Knowledge," Hayek argues that the pure logic of choice is a necessary, though not sufficient, component of an explanation of systematic economic coordination. An understanding of economic coordination requires an empirical understanding of *learning*. Hayek's research program for economics would have shifted it from the determination of optimal resource use under given conditions to the exploration of the impact of alternative institutional environments on learning.

rights, serves this aligning function in at least three ways. First, *ex ante*, prices transmit knowledge about the relative scarcities of goods to various market participants so they may adjust their behavior accordingly. If the price of a good goes up, this informs economic actors that the good has become relatively more scarce and that they should economize on its use. For this reason, participants in the market have an incentive to include the knowledge contained in prices in their actions *over time*. Second, the price system serves the *ex post* function of revealing the ultimate profitability or unprofitability of economic actions. Prescient entrepreneurship (in the broad sense of the term) is rewarded with profits; errors are penalized by losses. Market prices, therefore, not only motivate future decisions by conveying information about changing market conditions but also help market participants evaluate the appropriateness of past market decisions and correct erroneous ones.

Seen in this light, the market process is a matter of *dynamic adjustment*. What is it adjustment *to*? It is, in effect, adjustment to the gaps between a static equilibrium of universal satisfaction and the many departures from this model that are present in the real world. Each of these gaps between the counterfactual and the factual represent a profit opportunity. Price *information* is also *motivation* for profitable real-world adjustment, over time, to the profit opportunities of a particular place.[28]

---

28. Picking up a theme first raised by Oskar Morgenstern, Hayek emphasized that perfect foresight was a defining characteristic of equilibrium but not a precondition that must be present for equilibrium to be obtained. Logically, in fact, what Morgenstern had demonstrated was that if economic agents possessed perfect foresight, then a determinate equilibrium solution would evade them. As Joan Robinson also emphasized, the only way to achieve an equilibrium would be to already *be* in equilibrium—no process toward equilibrium could be articulated on the basis of a theory of perfect foresight. The implication for Hayek of this theoretical conundrum was that economists should focus attention not on the state of equilibrium, but on dynamic adjustment and learning through time. "A theory which starts out by assuming that adjustments have proceeded to the point where no further changes are required," Hayek stated, "is without relevance to our problems. What we need is a theory which helps us to explain the interrelations between the actions of different members of the community during the period (which is the only period of practical importance) *before* the material structure of productive equipment has been brought to a state which will make an unchanging, self-repeating process possible" (Hayek, *Pure Theory of Capital*, 16–17).

Formal equilibrium theory contains only a distorted, static image of these aspects of the price system. As they came to recognize this deficiency in mainstream neoclassical economics, Hayek and others in the Austrian tradition sought to explain how the price system works in real-world *disequilibrium*.[29] The Austrian critique of the standard model is that it has no place for the multifaceted role that disequilibrium prices serve within the market process.

The very idea of an economic theory of the market *process* stands in contrast to the static nature of equilibrium analysis. Since only an array of *disequilibrium* prices sets in motion the competitive process characterizing real-world markets, the formalist orthodoxy, by its very nature, must ignore this process. As Mises wrote:

> The activities of the entrepreneur or of any other actor on the economic scene are not guided by considerations of any such thing as equilibrium prices and the evenly rotating economy. The entrepreneurs take into account anticipated future prices, not final prices or equilibrium prices. They discover discrepancies between the height of the prices of the complementary factors of production and the anticipated future prices of the products, and they are intent upon taking advantage of such discrepancies.[30]

Prices serve as the basis of economic calculation only in the context of a process of competition brought into being by what formalism assumes away: disequilibrium. Real-world market prices do not perfectly contain all of the relevant information required for competitive equilibrium; if such information were known already, there would be no need for economic activity in the first place. Under disequilibrium conditions, however, the active bidding up of prices when demand exceeds supply, and their bidding down when supply ex-

---

29. Israel M. Kirzner, "Entrepreneurial Discovery and the Competitive Market Process: An Austrian Approach," *Journal of Economic Literature* 35 (March 1997), 60–85, is an examination of how the theory of entrepreneurial learning fits into this research program and contrasts with standard price theory. Franklin Fisher, *Disequilibrium Foundations of Equilibrium Economics* (New York: Cambridge University Press, 1983), is a discussion by a leading equilibrium theorist of the necessity of disequilibrium foundations for equilibrium economics. A theory of convergence to equilibrium, according to Fisher, has to be developed, not assumed.

30. Mises, *Human Action*, 329.

ceeds demand, generates the incentives and information necessary to coordinate economic decisions. The discrepancy between the current array of prices and the anticipated future array of prices provides the incentive for entrepreneurs to discover hitherto unknown opportunities for economic profit. Of course, in this process of perceiving the future, entrepreneurs may (and do) make errors, but these errors can, by creating further discovery opportunities, generate further activity aimed at allocating or reallocating resources in a more effective manner to obtain the ends sought after. "The market process," Israel Kirzner writes, "emerges as the necessary implication of the circumstances that people act, and that in their actions they err, discover their errors, and tend to revise their actions in a direction likely to be less erroneous than before."[31] While the assumption of perfect knowledge was essential for modeling the state of competitive equilibrium, it precluded an examination of the path by which adjustment toward equilibrium could be achieved. If the system were not already in equilibrium, one could not explain how it would get there. Omniscience logically results in nonaction. A profit opportunity that is known to all can be realized by none. Thus, if it is to be realistic, the model's assumptions have to be relaxed, but then it becomes overly complex and loses its formal elegance.

This dilemma has dogged a significant strand within the mainstream of economic thought that, since about 1960, has tried to take up Hayek's challenge and examine the informational aspect of markets. This research program is of vital importance in evaluating the current state of economics not only because it is the rising orthodoxy at the moment, but because it attempts to grapple with the main feature of reality that, in the Austrian view, is obscured by economic formalism. But because the new economics of information is itself formalist in its use of equilibrium models, it has been fated to oscillate between utopianism about the informational properties of real markets and utopianism about the alternatives.

Classical economics had focused exclusively upon the incentive to purchase more or less of a particular good that prices provided. The new economists of information recognize that prices serve a communicative function as well. They see that prices transmit vital knowledge about (for instance) relative scarcities,

---

31. Israel M. Kirzner, *Perception, Opportunity and Profit* (Chicago: University of Chicago Press, 1979), 30.

enabling economic participants to coordinate their decisions. Chicago's George Stigler is usually credited with being the first economist to develop an informational model consistent with standard neoclassical price theory. Stigler argued that individuals will optimally search for the information necessary to accomplish their goals in the market, but unlike Hayek, he assumed that they would do so in an optimal manner by comparing the marginal cost of information with the marginal benefit of continuing to search for it.[32] In other words, Stigler joined the informational content of markets with the assumption that equilibrium models should be seen as describing actual behavior. In Stigler's view, there was economic ignorance in the real world, but it was the optimal level of ignorance. The attempt to eliminate the remaining ignorance would entail searches for information that were more costly than the benefits they could produce.

Following Stigler, economists such as Armen Alchian and Jack Hirshleifer developed information-search models in which various aspects of the economic system such as advertising, middlemen, unemployment, queues, and rationing take on a new meaning and functional significance.[33] At the same time, economists who treated equilibrium as a critical norm rather than a reality, such as Kenneth Arrow, Leonid Hurwicz, and Roy Radner, also sought to develop models that accounted for informational imperfections.[34] Where Stigler's approach extended the assumption of maximizing behavior to the information-search process, predicting that markets would see various practices emerge to economize on the search process and generate an optimal flow of information, the Arrow/Hurwicz/Radner approach argued that in the face of incomplete information, maximizing agents would be unable to coordinate their behavior with others in an optimal manner unless an appropriate mechanism could be

---

32. George Stigler, "The Economics of Information," *Journal of Political Economy*, 69: 3 (June 1961), 213–25.

33. On the theory of search, in contrast to the Austrian view of the market process, see Jack High, *Maximizing, Action, and Market Adjustment: An Inquiry into the Theory of Economic Organization* (Munich: Philosophia Verlag, 1990), 28–36, 83–124.

34. This line of literature explored information/communication and motivational questions associated with the structure of incentives. The main conclusion was that decentralization was less important than incentives. But the version of decentralization explored in these models was far different from Hayek's hypothesis about the use of knowledge in society, even though Hayek was supposed to be the starting point of this literature.

designed anterior to the market.[35] The first approach presupposed the efficiency of market allocations, the second their inefficiency and the prevalence of market failure. Neither approach adequately dealt with disequilibrium or the multi-informational components of market processes that help economic actors adjust to and learn from disequilibrium.

Among contemporary economists, Joseph Stiglitz and Sanford Grossman have elaborated the second approach more systematically than anyone else. Their research on the informational role of prices has led to a fundamental recasting of many basic questions in orthodox economic theory.[36] Grossman and Stiglitz understand Hayek to be arguing that prices are "sufficient statistics" for economic coordination, and they conclude that this argument is flawed. In situations where private information is important, they contend, market prices will be informationally inefficient, for the market will not provide the appropriate incentives for information acquisition; thus, the case for economic decentralization is not as theoretically strong as Hayek suggests.

Grossman and Stiglitz's reasoning, however, begs the question against Hayek by starting from the unrealistic assumption of rational expectations equilibrium. Given this assumption, they maintain, prices will reveal information so efficiently that no one could gain from the revelation of privately held information.[37] Individual agents can simply look at prices and obtain free what would be costly

---

35. Information economics led economists to investigate agency costs, informational asymmetries, strategic interaction, and organizational design. These are all important problems, but the models developed to explore them arguably fail to capture how real-world adjustment processes deal with them.

36. For overviews of this work in information-theoretic research in economics see Joseph Stiglitz, *Whither Socialism?* (Cambridge, MA: MIT Press, 1994) and Sanford Grossman, *The Informational Role of Prices* (Cambridge, MA: MIT Press, 1989). A textbook-style treatment of information-theoretic economics in general can be found in Donald Campbell, *Incentives: Motivation and the Economics of Information* (New York: Cambridge University Press, 1995). An Austrian critique of the Stiglitz-Grossman program can be found in Esteban Thomsen, *Prices and Knowledge: A Market-Process Perspective* (New York: Routledge, 1992). For critical discussion of Stiglitz, *Whither Socialism?* see Peter J. Boettke, review of *Whither Socialism?* by Joseph Stiglitz, *Journal of Economic Literature* (March 1996); and David L. Prychitko, review of *Whither Socialism?* by Joseph Stiglitz, *Cato Journal* 16 (Fall 1996).

37. By the mid-1970s the strong assumption of rational expectations had become common in all models.

to acquire privately. This free-riding leads to an underproduction of information by the market. Prices, as a result, will necessarily fail to reflect all the available information. Grossman states the supposed paradox as follows:

> In an economy with complete markets, the price system does act in such a way that individuals, observing only prices, and acting in self-interest, generate allocations which are efficient. However, such economies need not be stable because prices are revealing so much information that incentives for the collection of information are removed. The price system can be maintained only when it is noisy enough so that traders who collect information can hide that information from other traders.[38]

This paradox does challenge Stigler's model of information searching, as well as the traditional welfare theorems of general competitive equilibrium when they are viewed as describing the decentralized price system. But long before Grossman and Stiglitz, Hayek recognized that the first and second welfare theorems provided neither an accurate description of how actual market processes coordinate economic plans, nor of how the institutional environment of the decentralized market generates desirable consequences. Hayek suggested that economists redirect their research program to emphasize the use of dispersed knowledge and the impact of alternative institutional arrangements on learning. Hayek's theoretical criticisms of standard welfare economics, though, are largely obscured by Grossman and Stiglitz's analysis because it translates Hayek's view of dispersed knowledge into the language of modern formal information theory. This leaves out questions of the *context* and the *tacit dimension* of knowledge.

The economic problem, Hayek emphatically stated, was *not* that posed by standard welfare economics, namely the allocation of scarce resources among competing ends.[39] This way of stating the problem—which leads the neoclas-

---

38. Sanford Grossman, "On the Efficiency of Competitive Stock Markets Where Traders Have Diverse Information," *Journal of Finance*, 31: 2 (May 1976): 585.

39. James M. Buchanan also forcefully argues that economists should concentrate their efforts on exchange relationships and the various institutional arrangements that result from these relationships, rather than equilibrium states, placing Buchanan alongside Mises and Hayek and earlier thinkers such as Richard Whateley ("What Should Economists Do?" in *What Should Economists Do?* (1964; repr., Indianapolis: Liberty Press, 1979), 17–37). Also see Israel M. Kirzner, *Competition and Entrepreneurship* (Chicago: University of Chicago Press, 1973), 212–42.

sical mainstream to regard general equilibrium as a solution—"habitually disregards" essential elements of the phenomena under investigation, according to Hayek, by ignoring "the unavoidable imperfection of man's knowledge and the consequent need for a process by which knowledge is constantly communicated and acquired." Equilibrium theorizing is not to be rejected, according to Hayek, but its real purpose must be constantly kept in mind. Formal modeling can be a very good servant, but a poor master; unless we remember that the situation the model describes has little direct relevance for the solution of practical problems, it can lead to mistaken judgment. Hayek constantly reiterated that the equilibrium model "does not deal with the social process at all and that it is no more than a useful preliminary for the study of the main problem."[40]

The essence of the coordinative property of the price system lies not in its ability to convey perfectly correct information about resource scarcity and technological possibilities, but in "its ability to communicate information concerning its own faulty information-communication properties."[41] Disequilibrium relative prices, imperfect as they are, nevertheless provide some guidance in error correction and avoidance. This dynamic process of error detection and correction is absent from formal models of economic "information" premised on static equilibrium.

The informational role of prices goes to the heart not only of Hayek's challenge to economic orthodoxy, but of the particular issue that led Hayek to launch this challenge: the debate over socialism.[42]

---

40. Hayek, "Use of Knowledge," 78, 91.

41. Israel M. Kirzner, "Prices, the Communication of Knowledge, and the Discovery Process," in *The Political Economy of Freedom: Essays in Honor of F.A. Hayek,* edited by Kurt Leube and Albert Zlabinger (Munich: Philosophia Verlag), 196.

42. There has been some debate over the relative importance of Mises's calculation argument and Hayek's knowledge problem. But they seem to me to be two sides of the same coin. Calculation without knowledge is oxymoronic, and knowledge without the ability to do economic calculation is unimportant. Private property and monetary calculation are the means by which the knowledge problem can be solved in complex economies. That is the argument Mises's and Hayek's critiques of socialism shared, despite their differences of emphasis. As Mises points out in liberalism, the "decisive objection that economics raises against the possibility of a socialist society [is that] it must forgo the intellectual division of labor that consists in the cooperation of all entrepreneurs, landowners, and workers as producers and consumers in the formation of market prices" (*Liberalism* (1927; repr., Irvington-on-Hudson, NY: Foundation for Economic Education,

Socialism Revisited

Mises began the debate by pointing out that unlike socialism, capitalism could rely on the information and incentives of the private property order that are manifested in the practice of "economic calculation" based on market prices. Eventually the debate led Hayek to realize that the neoclassical mainstream, as embodied in the socialist economists, was treating economic knowledge as given—not in need of discovery by entrepreneurs. This error is revived by the new information economics, in the sense that it does not recognize the possibility of genuine ignorance. Both the laissez-faire Stigler and the interventionist Stiglitz (and others) treat knowledge "as if" it exists on a bookshelf, so that the only question is whether it is in one's interest to pull it off the shelf or communicate it accurately to others. Searching for existing, already discovered information is important, but it is not the activity captured in economic calculation. Since Grossman and Stiglitz confuse the "informational" role of prices discussed by Hayek with the pregiven information assumed by static equilibrium models, they misconstrue the socialist calculation debate as pitting capitalism, in which prices allocate resources based upon an imperfect arbitrage process, against socialism, in which the allocation of resources is performed by central administrators but will be imperfect because of the cost of monitoring them.

Once Grossman and Stiglitz questioned the informational efficiency of the price system, then some alternative theoretical framework for assessing economic systems was required. Raaj Sah and Stiglitz went on to develop an alternative framework for comparing economic systems, continuing the program laid out by Grossman and Stiglitz for examining the comparative costs of different systems of economic coordination.[43] "Informational" questions continue to be at the center of the research agenda, although the focus of comparative assessment is not limited to the informational efficiency of monetary prices.[44]

1985), 75). See Peter J. Boettke, "Economic Calculation: The Austrian Contribution to Political Economy" (1998) for further discussion.

43. Raaj K. Sah and Joseph Stiglitz, "Human Fallibility and Economic Organization," *American Economic Review* 75 (May 1985), 292–97; Sah and Stiglitz, "The Architecture of Economic Systems," *American Economic Review* 76 (September 1986), 716–27.

44. The informational content of a multitude of market practices, not just monetary prices, is recognized by Hayek and others in the Austrian tradition, such as Fritz Machlup. Stiglitz's attempt to remedy the unrealistic nature of descriptive equilibrium by pay-

Armed with their putatively realistic—yet, in fact, static—understanding of economic information, Sah and Stiglitz propose that economists turn to the "quality of decision making" within different organizational structures as the standard of comparison. "How individuals are arranged together affects the nature of the errors made by the economic system," they write.[45] In addressing this issue, Sah and Stiglitz begin by postulating that in a market system, if one entrepreneur fails to pursue a profitable opportunity, it is likely that some other entrepreneur will remedy this failure. In a planned economy, though, the decision by the planning board not to pursue a production project rules out its adoption by anyone else. What impact, then, do market and planned economies have on the ability to choose good over bad production projects?

Suppose we have an urn filled with ping-pong balls, each ball corresponding to a production project. In polyarchical economies (markets) we would expect more of both good and bad projects to be chosen. Hierarchical (planned) economies, on the other hand, will choose fewer good projects, but also fewer bad ones. Therefore, according to Sah and Stiglitz, "the incidence of Type I error is relatively higher in a hierarchy, whereas the incidence of Type II error is relatively higher in a polyarchy."[46] Type I error means the rejection of a project that should have been accepted, while Type II error is the acceptance of a project that should have been rejected.

While this exercise is theoretically interesting, it does little to explain the way economic systems actually work. In the real world, Type I and Type II errors are linked and omnipresent. Rejecting a project that should have been accepted allows someone to use the resources freed up by this rejection to pursue a project that should have been rejected. The question, then, is what systemic mechanisms can detect errors of both kinds and provide information and incentives to correct them.[47] "An appraisal of the efficiency of the market process," as Kirzner puts it, "involves an appraisal of the way the market process disseminates [the] missing links of information necessary for the discovery of superior opportunities for the

---

ing attention to information is doomed to failure because information is dynamic, yet formalism renders it inherently static.

45. Sah and Stiglitz, "Architecture," 716.
46. Sah and Stiglitz, "Architecture," 719.
47. See Peter J. Boettke, *Why Perestroika Failed: The Politics and Economics of Socialist Transformation* (New York: Routledge, 1993), 135–38.

allocation of resources."[48] In making such an appraisal, production projects cannot be treated as essentially known and given; they must be discovered by real-world entrepreneurs operating in specific institutional contexts. The Sah-Stiglitz framework brushes aside any context in which innovation and the discovery of economic information affect economic performance. By viewing economic projects as items in a metaphorical urn, they treat economic information as if it were on the shelf already, such that the only question is how to give people sufficient incentives to get them to pull it off the shelf and use it. This is to ignore the fundamental question raised by Mises and Hayek: how information gets onto the shelf in the first place.

Hayek's insight—supposedly the starting-point of Stiglitz's concern with information[49]—is that the market process allows us to exploit, utilize, and discover knowledge that had hitherto been *unknown* to market participants. Entrepreneurs do not choose the optimal production project from an array of known projects; they must *discover* opportunities for profitable ventures. They must be alert to as-yet overlooked opportunities and exercise good judgment in pursuing them. As Don Lavoie puts it, "the key point of the calculation argument is that the required knowledge of objective production possibilities would be unavailable without the competitive market process."[50]

The Sah-Stiglitz framework, by ignoring both the necessary ignorance of economic actors and the corresponding problem of knowledge discovery, directs attention away from the questions real-world comparative-systems analysis must ask. The problem is not the establishment of the optimal conditions of competitive equilibrium, but rather the detection of errors—deviations, as it were, from equilibrium. To find such an error is to produce economic information that is useful in a world that does *not* approximate equilibrium; to use this information to make a profit is to move that world a little closer to the normative ideal. A comparison of capitalism and socialism that ignores their systemic ability (or inability) to engage in such error detection and correction is but another exercise in the use of equilibrium to indict reality while ignoring its positive dimension.

48. Israel M. Kirzner, *Market Theory and the Price System* (Princeton, NJ: Van Nostrand, 1963), 301–02.

49. See Stiglitz, *Whither Socialism?*, 6, 24–26.

50. Don Lavoie, *Rivalry and Central Planning* (New York: Cambridge University Press, 1985), 102.

Similar difficulties afflict the work of Pranab Bardhan and John Roemer, who argue that the revolutions of 1989 have unjustly discredited the socialist model.[51] The system that failed in 1989, they point out, was characterized by public ownership of the means of production; noncompetitive, undemocratic politics; and central command over resource allocation. Bardhan and Roemer offer instead a model of socialism that jettisons central commands and non-competitive and undemocratic politics, but public ownership remains intact. They interpret public ownership broadly to mean that the political process is in charge of distributing the profits of firms in order to achieve an egalitarian distribution of the economy's surplus. They claim that while a competitive market economy is necessary to achieve the efficient allocation of resources, private ownership is not a prerequisite for competitive markets.

In Bardhan and Roemer's view, unbridled capitalism generates negative externalities, not the least of which are political. The high degree of ownership concentration under capitalism perversely affects the political process through the influence of the wealthy, they allege. Thus, the efficiency gains of capitalism are offset by the subversion of democracy. Separating economics from politics, and vice versa, is essential to the establishment of a socially harmonious and just system.

The traditional problem with public ownership was the inability to separate political from economic criteria in resource-allocation decisions. Bardhan and Roemer try to avoid this problem by giving firms, not government, the power to allocate resources. But in order to prevent the unequal distribution of wealth, Bardhan and Roemer postulate a model of competition between firms in which property nonetheless remains collectively owned. The real issue, they argue, is competitiveness, not property ownership. The market must be constrained by egalitarian ownership: democracy in distribution, but competition in provision. Concretely, this means the distribution of equal entitlements to firms' profits in the form of shares that can be traded openly, but not cashed in. Shares can only be traded for other shares, not for money. Such a market, according to Bardhan and Roemer, would provide the necessary signals that a capitalist market provides, yet would prevent the concentration of capital.

---

51. Pranab Bardhan and John Roemer, "Market Socialism: A Case for Rejuvenation," *Journal of Economic Perspectives* 6, no. 3 (1992): 101–16.

To Bardhan and Roemer, the key question their model must answer is how to motivate the managers of public firms to act efficiently. They contend that modern research in industrial organization has demonstrated that the owner-entrepreneur model is no longer applicable to capitalist economies. The modern corporation can, however, be disciplined through the capital market and the managerial labor market, so Bardhan and Roemer proceed to replicate them through incentives schemes that tie a manager's reputation and salary to performance and to the distribution of unsellable shares in their firms. Monitoring has been achieved on the economic front, and political control over the distribution of wealth has been maintained.

The perspective undergirding this model is the Stiglitzian program for recasting economic theory along "informational" lines. If one desires a society of change and mobility, then one should choose capitalism. But if stability and security are desired, then one should opt for socialism. Once incomplete and imperfect information are introduced, Chicago-school defenders of the market system cannot sustain descriptive claims of the Pareto efficiency of the real world. Thus, Stiglitz's use of rational-expectations equilibrium assumptions to achieve a more realistic understanding of capitalism than is usual among rational-expectations theorists leads, paradoxically, to the conclusion that capitalism deviates from the model in a way that justifies state action—socialism—as a remedy.[52]

One might well prefer even more realism, however—if one is willing to return to the days when accuracy was more important than mathematical virtuosity. While Stiglitz, Grossman, and Sah admirably introduce realistic elements into the equilibrium framework, that framework remains primary, preventing them from addressing the central issues of the socialist calculation debate. Human fallibility is introduced, but our capacity to adapt to changing conditions and to learn from false starts and ill-fated projects is not. Human imperfection is introduced into the analysis, but only to be condemned by contrast with the equilibrium ideal. Still missing from the analysis is an examination of how imperfect human beings attempt to cope in a real world of

---

52. Stiglitz does demonstrate the sensitivity of general equilibrium results to initial assumptions. Even rational expectations models do not yield Chicago-type efficiency conclusions once slight changes in the initial assumptions are made as (half-hearted) concessions to realism.

ignorance and uncertainty. As a result, we get the bifurcation of the world into a private sector that obeys rational-expectations postulates while being unable to do anything to cope with the slightest departure from general equilibrium, and a public sector that, being the creation of the normative equilibrium theorists' imagination, is able to rectify the resulting problems "as if by an invisible hand." As in the earlier neo-Keynesian synthesis of Paul Samuelson, the gap between norm and reality is closed by the omniscient state.

In Mises and Hayek's analysis, on the other hand, the complex web of institutions and habits that come into existence because of disequilibrium are the object of study. According to Mises and Hayek, legally secured property rights aid social learning in an imperfect real world by encouraging investment, motivating responsible decision making, allowing economic experimentation aimed at error correction, and providing the basis for economic calculation by expanding the context within which price and profit/loss signals can reasonably guide resource use. Formal models of competitive equilibrium, such as Lange's model of socialism, were not able to deal with such institutional questions; formal models modified to be superficially realistic, such as Stiglitz's new economics, are equally inadequate.[53]

In the Austrian argument the concrete context within which decisions are made conveys vital information. It is not just that information is costly to obtain, but that it is *different information* if it is stimulated by a context of rivalrous, private property exchange. The knowledge actors rely on to make decisions is not universal and abstract, as it must be if it is to be replicated through either bureaucratic planning or political deliberation.

Moreover, in Bardhan and Roemer's model there is no realism, even of a superficial sort, concerning the workings of democracy. In the real world of mass democracies, principal/agent problems[54] are just as real as those facing

---

53. Lange, for example, accused Mises of "institutionalism" for suggesting that the ability to engage in rational economic calculation was related to a specific institutional context, namely private property in the means of production. See Oskar Lange, "On the Economic Theory of Socialism," in *On the Economic Theory of Socialism*, edited by Benjamin Lippincott (1939; repr., New York: Augustus M. Kelley, 1970). Stiglitz, *Whither Socialism?*, 174–75, also doubts the importance of private property in influencing economic performance.

54. Cf. the "state theory" discussed in Peter B. Evans, Dietrich Rueschmeyer, and Theda Skocpol, eds. *Bringing the State Back In* (New York: Cambridge University Press, 1985).

modern corporations, not to mention problems of preference falsification[55] and pervasive ignorance.[56] Bardhan and Roemer equate political failure with the inequality of influence brought about by the power of money. (This equation is more assumed than proved.) Absent inequalities of wealth, they imagine that effective interest groups could not be formed, so the democratic process would enact the "will of the people." This leaves unexamined the question of the quality of democratic decision making even in the absence of interest groups, and it ignores the possibility that such factors as ideology, personal influence, identity politics, xenophobia, and differential ignorance[57] can be the source of unequal power as easily as money can.

From Political to Economic Utopianism and Back Again

Samuelson's synthesis created a rather strange mix of general equilibrium microeconomics with Keynesian macroeconomics. As Robert Lucas repeatedly pointed out in the early 1970s, graduate students were taught one thing during their Monday/Wednesday microeconomic theory courses, and another thing on Tuesdays and Thursdays in their macroeconomic theory courses. The link between microeconomics and macroeconomics was supposed to be found in the labor market. But if the labor market was in competitive equilibrium, this implied that the full-employment output level had been achieved, i.e., that there was no macroeconomic problem.

The circle was squared in Samuelson's neo-Keynesian model by means of "wage stickiness" and the "money illusion." Unemployment, according to classical economists, was due to wage rigidity caused by labor union or government restrictions on wage adjustments. When there were no such rigidities, then wage cuts could serve to clear the labor market, and widespread, persistent

55. Timur Kuran, *Private Truths, Public Lies* (Cambridge, MA: Harvard University Press, 1995).

56. See, e.g., Philip E. Converse, "The Nature of Belief Systems in Mass Publics," in *Ideology and Discontent*, edited by David E. Apter (New York: Free Press, 1964), 206–61; see Friedman, "Public Opinion and Democracy."

57. See, e.g., W. Russell Neuman, *The Paradox of Mass Politics: Knowledge and Opinion in the American Electorate* (Cambridge, MA: Harvard University Press, 1986); John Zaller, *The Nature and Origins of Mass Opinion* (Cambridge: Cambridge University Press, 1992).

unemployment could not occur. Keynesian economics, however, raised the possibility that unemployment could emerge endogenously in free markets because, first, discoordination between savings and investments in the capital market could produce an effective demand failure that would reinforce pessimistic expectations;[58] and, second, because of workers' psychological resistance to nominal pay cuts, and their inability to distinguish nominal from real wages. The second of these problems has, like neoclassical socialism, been taken up by both descriptive and normative equilibrium theorists; indeed, the attack on this aspect of Keynesianism was central in the rise of the Chicago school—and, in turn, to its current displacement by the New Keynesianism.

In the Keynesian system as modeled by Samuelson, workers care about their relative nominal wage rather than their real wage. In bad times, then, workers will resist downward adjustments in relative nominal wages that might bring the labor market into equilibrium. This "stickiness" in wage adjustment makes the emergence of an unemployment equilibrium possible.[59] Only the tools of monetary and fiscal policy can shift the economy away from such a condition and toward full employment. Workers will be less aggressive in resisting the gradual and indirect downward adjustment of their real wages through inflation than they will in resisting direct downward adjustments of their nominal wages by their employers. Public policy prescriptions guided by Samuelson's neo-Keynesian synthesis, then, were predicated on the ability of the government to intervene so as to avoid the excesses of boom and bust and promote economic growth. The interventionist consensus came to be embodied in the idea that there existed a stable tradeoff between inflation and unemployment and that it was the job of policymakers to negotiate this tradeoff.

---

58. See John Maynard Keynes, *The General Theory of Employment, Interest, and Money* (1936; repr., New York: Harcourt, Brace & Jovanovich, 1964), 245–71.

59. Equilibrium here is defined in its classical sense: a state of affairs where there are no endogenous forces that will change the existing state of affairs. Defining the equilibrium state was fundamental to the Keynesian project. As Franklin Fisher writes: "The central question which Keynes sought to answer in *The General Theory of Employment, Interest and Money* was that of whether (and how) an economy could get stuck at an underemployment equilibrium. To show this, it is not enough to show that such an equilibrium exists, we must also show that it has at least local stability properties so that an economy that gets close enough to such a point will not escape from it without an exogenous change in circumstances" (Fisher, *Disequilibrium Foundations,* 9).

The major difficulty with this model was that it relied on an assumption of worker irrationality that was every bit as implausible as the hyperrationalistic assumptions with which the Chicago school would soon replace it.

Samuelson's assumption that workers were systematically and repeatedly fooled by the money illusion was less a real synthesis of equilibrium modeling with Keynesian economics than an ad hoc, a priori amendment to the neoclassical microeconomic model of rationally self-interested behavior. As such, it was vulnerable from two directions: either from an institutionalist attempt to preserve its ad hoc, "empirical" elements at the expense of neoclassical theory (post-Keynesianism),[60] or from a hyperformalist attempt to purify the synthesis by purging it of its Keynesian contaminants. The second route, needless to say, is the one that had the most appeal to a discipline now wedded to formal technique. This explains the astonishing success the Chicago school's "New Classical" economics would have in the 1970s in altering the policy agenda of a discipline that had been resolutely interventionist since the Great Depression.

The first shot in the Chicago counterrevolution was Milton Friedman's analysis of adaptive expectations. Next, the neo-Keynesian synthesis was thoroughly discredited by the development of rational expectations theory.[61] Samuelson's reconciliation of the microeconomic ideal type with involuntary unemployment was repudiated, along with Keynesian prescriptions, in favor of the view that there could be no involuntary unemployment, hence that government action was unnecessary. The result was a doctrinaire derivation of the laissez-faire conclusions that had been overturned by the formalist revolution; economics was now cleansed of Keynesian impurities that had been introduced in the interest of realism. Equilibrium theory was now used not to indict the market economy but to insist that it was perpetually in a state of rest. Pressed by the Chicago school for a coherent—formalistic—theory of how reality deviated from equilibrium theory, the neo-Keynesian synthesis imploded.

---

60. See Paul Davidson, "The Economics of Ignorance or Ignorance of Economics?" *Critical Review* 3, no. 3–4 (1989): 467–87; and David L. Prychitko, "After Davidson, Who Needs the Austrians? Reply to Davidson," *Critical Review* 7, no. 2–3 (1993): 371–80.
61. Friedman's theory of adaptive expectations was actually his last in a long line of criticisms of the Keynesian analytical and public policy system. His work on consumption theory had questioned the behavioral premise of the Keynesian theory of consumption, his work on the quantity theory of money challenged Keynesian monetary theory, and his work on rules versus discretion raised doubt about Keynesian fine-tuning.

Since formalist economics could not model the real-world processes of capitalist adjustment to disequilibrium, economists now had to choose between an irrational world of disequilibrium (original Keynesianism), a rational but unrealistic world of equilibrium (New Classical economics), and an untenable mixture of the two (neo-Keynesianism). Neo-Keynesian economists, committed to formalism, had tried to fit Keynes's speculations about the failure of capitalist economies to maintain full employment into the program of general equilibrium theory. By the 1950s, their model had come to represent the intellectual standard of argument to which all economists who wanted to receive a serious professional hearing had to adhere. But Keynes's economics raised questions that were outside the scope of the model.[62]

The Chicago school resolved the tension between neo-Keynesian theory and reality by insisting that reality must approximate (equilibrium) theory. But since the Chicago school was as committed to formalist methods as the neo-Keynesians were, it could provide no more of a theoretical explanation of how real-world market economies could approximate full-employment equilibrium than Samuelson could plausibly explain how an unemployment equilibrium came into being. Perfect markets were a presumption, not a conclusion of New Classical economics, just as rigid unemployment was a presumption of neo-Keynesianism.

The techniques of rational expectations and the development of New Classical economics came to dominate economic thinking in the 1970s and 1980s.[63]

---

62. Keynes's theory of the failure of modern capitalism relied on cultural and psychological factors as much as economic ones. The emergence of the much-vaunted "casino" character of the stock market was, according to Keynes, a result of a change in the culture (and the population pool) of trading. In the nineteenth century, more civilized and cultured traders guarded against wide swings due to animal spirits. In the twentieth century, however, old habits evaporated and with them breaks against the wild tides of optimism and pessimism. The interventionist policies Keynes advocated to correct for market breakdown were predicated on the assumption that those in government would be in a better position to assess the efficiency of capital investment (especially in the long term) than those trapped in the hustle and bustle of current market behavior.

63. For a collection of the main papers see Robert E. Lucas and Thomas Sargent, eds., *Rational Expectations and Econometric Practice,* 2 vols. (Minneapolis: University of Minnesota Press, 1981). Also see Brian Snowdon, Howard Vane, and Peter Wynarczyk, *A Modern Guide to Macroeconomics: An Introduction to Competing Schools of Thought* (Aldershot, UK: Edward Elgar 1994), 188–218; and Kevin Hoover, "New Classical Economics,"

The assumption of perfect knowledge allowed the New Classicists to interpret all actual ignorance as optimal. Involuntary unemployment could not exist in this model because once search costs were included the labor market was forever in equilibrium. Disequilibrium was considered incompatible with economic theory.[64] If someone was unemployed, it must be because he or she preferred to continue the search for a new job rather than accept work at the prevailing wage.

New Classical economists also sought to place the theory of the business cycle on firm equilibrium foundations.[65] Robert Lucas's theory of the business cycle presumed that noise in price signals prevented economic actors from distinguishing between changes in relative prices caused by market conditions and changes in the general price level caused by inflation. Increases in the money supply that translated into a change in the general price level should have no effect on the level of output, but if a change in the general price level were misinterpreted by economic actors as a change in relative prices, then the level

---

in *The Elgar Companion to Austrian Economics,* edited by Peter J. Boettke (Aldershot, UK: Edward Elgar Publishing, 1994), 576–81.

64. See, for example, Lucas's interview in Arjo Klamer, *Conversations with Economists* (New York: Rowman & Littlefield, 1984). This dismissal of disequilibrium theory aborted not only the development of traditional Keynesian analysis, but also the work of Clower and Leijonhufvud, post-Keynesian analysis of the sort done by Paul Davidson, as well as Austrian economics. Fisher has characterized Lucas's position "always-clearing markets." When one takes this position, equilibrium analysis does not need any justification. Movements of actual market prices are to be analyzed as a sequence of temporary equilibria. Price offers are instantly adjusted to the short-run equilibrium point. See Fisher, *Disequilibrium Foundations,* 5–6.

65. When Lucas first articulated an equilibrium theory of the business cycle he would often cite Hayek (a recent Nobel Laureate at the time) as a precursor of his approach. Hayek did, in fact, insist that Keynesians had committed an error by not developing an equilibrium theory of the business cycle. But what Hayek meant was that one cannot offer an explanation of unemployment unless one begins in a state of full employment and explains why the unemployment resulted in the first place. In the system articulated by Keynes and his early followers, full employment was denied at the start of analysis— one began with unemployment (idle resources). Hayek used the equilibrium state of full employment only as a preliminary to the real analysis, which was to explain how unemployment may emerge. Hayek's position, then, was in direct opposition to both Keynes and Lucas. Keynes assumes what needs to be explained, and Lucas treats equilibrium not only as the beginning, but also the end, of his analysis.

of output could be distorted by the confusion. In this, the simplest version of Lucas's story, distortions must be caused by unanticipated changes in the money supply. The Chicago school's later "real"—as opposed to monetary—business cycle theory emphasized exogenous factors such as technological change and random shocks to explain fluctuations in the aggregate level of output.

The New Classical economics demanded too much. Economic agents were modeled to continually and optimally update their knowledge about the state of the world. In addition, economic agents were assumed to share the monetarist understanding of the effect of monetary policy on the price level. These assumptions gave economic actors the ability to checkmate policymakers. Systematic, rational government intervention was therefore useless. Only unanticipated government policy could affect the aggregate level of output. Despite the flawless precision of this model, it produced a view of the world that was obviously contrary to reality. It is not controversial to insist that real involuntary unemployment, for example, existed during the 1930s. Yet the Keynesian explanation of how this phenomenon occurred assumed economic agents without adaptive qualities.[66] Constrained by the methodological demands of formalism, economists had no way to explain imperfect adaptation to changing economic conditions, so they opted to explain away such imperfections rather than accept them, à la neo-Keynesianism, as brute facts.

The perfect-market assumption and the extreme policy implications of New Classical economics led, in reaction, to the development of the New Keynesian economics and a resurrection of the analytical importance of involuntary unemployment.[67] The New Keynesians sought to provide rational-choice

---

66. One of the problems with the Keynesian system was the lack of symmetry in the motives and behavior attributed to economic agents, as opposed to the economist-experts who would fine-tune the economy. Economic agents were assumed to be irrational and self-interested, whereas government policymakers were presumed to be completely rational and public spirited. Like all ideal types, this one *might* be found to represent reality in a given time and place; but this needs to be proved, not assumed. Otherwise the theorist can simply predetermine policy conclusions by manipulating assumptions.

67. See Robert Gordon, "What Is New-Keynesian Economics?" *Journal of Economic Literature* 28: 3 (September 1990), 1115–71; and Lawrence Summers, *Understanding Unemployment* (Cambridge, MA: MIT Press, 1990).

microeconomic foundations for wage and price stickiness.[68] The first New Keynesian models emphasized nominal rigidities in the price system. In contrast to the New Classical model, which assumed that prices were perfectly flexible, the New Keynesians emphasized that prices are often quite inflexible for a variety of reasons. Real-world labor markets, New Keynesians contended, are often characterized by inflexibility due to the prevalence of long-term contracts, so even if agents have rational expectations, nominal rigidities prevent perfect adjustment and create the need for Keynesian interventionist policies.

However, the early New Keynesian models were criticized by New Classical theorists for lacking a rational-choice foundation for the long-term labor contracts to which they attributed market rigidity. Why would profit-maximizing firms repeatedly lock themselves into long-term contracts that would prove suboptimal at some later date? The next generation of New Keynesian models emphasized real rigidities in market adjustment, while retaining the behavioral assumption of rational expectations (or near rationality) throughout the structure of the model. In a world of imperfect information and imperfect market structure, New Keynesian economists such as Stiglitz were able to demonstrate that a nonmarket-clearing equilibrium could emerge.[69] Thus, real rigidities

---

68. For a collection of the main papers in New Keynesian thought, see Gregory Mankiw and David Romer, eds., *New Keynesian Economics*, 2 vols. (Cambridge, MA: MIT Press, 1991). Also see Snowdon, Vane, and Wynarczyk, *Modern Guide*, 286–330; and Sean Keenan, "New Keynesian Economics," in *The Elgar Companion to Austrian Economics*, edited by Peter J. Boettke (Aldershot, UK: Edward Elgar Publishing, 1994), 582–87. One of the crucial differences between New Classical and New Keynesian models can be found in the assumption of *price taking* behavior within the New Classical models and *price making* monopolistic behavior within the New Keynesian models.

69. As Samuelson emerged as the central figure in the formalist revolution, Stiglitz is emerging as the central figure in contemporary economics. Not only does Stiglitz's work, like Samuelson's, dominate the graduate curriculum, but he has published an introductory-level textbook, *Economics* (New York: Norton, 1993) summarizing the extent of his vast contributions to economics for a new generation of students. Just as Samuelsonianism defined economics from the 1950s through the 1970s, Stiglitzian economics is likely to dominate economic thinking and education from now until well into the twenty-first century. Stiglitz's influence has also been more direct, as he has served as the chief economist in the President's Council of Economic Advisors and the World Bank. Many Stiglitz-inspired arguments have been deployed in policy debates over intervention in the healthcare industry (adverse selection), banking (adverse selection and moral hazard), and antitrust (imperfect competition).

were capable of generating involuntary unemployment in long-run equilibrium. Furthermore, New Keynesian models were immune from the criticisms leveled against Keynes and the neo-Keynesians for assuming persistent worker irrationality and misperception of the price level. The New Keynesian models are populated by maximizing agents who suffer no informational disequilibrium yet who experience involuntary unemployment. This was an intuitively pleasing development because, as Robert Gordon points out, it is evident that unemployed workers and firms are unhappy about their condition. "Workers and firms do not act as if they were making a voluntary choice to cut production and hours worked."[70] Paul Krugman writes that

> the new Keynesian idea serves a critically important purpose. During the 1970s conservative macroeconomics had Keynesianism on the run with its assertion that it was a logically flawed theory—that it could not be right. The new Keynesian theory showed, on the contrary, that the idea that recessions represent a market failure that can be corrected by government action can indeed be right. This is useful, because in reality Keynesianism is basically right, so it's nice to have a theory that lets us admit it.[71]

New Keynesianism is able to achieve this result by means of the efficiency wage theorem. If workers' productivity depends on their wages, it may be rational for employers to offer a wage rate that exceeds the market-clearing level.[72] They may refuse to lower wages to the market-clearing level, fearful that the productivity of their existing workforce will fall. A higher-than-market-clearing wage

---

The effect of Stiglitz's influence is to make economics even more presumptively interventionist than Samuelson preferred. Samuelson treated market failure as the exception to the general rule of efficient markets. But the Greenwald-Stiglitz theorem posits market failure as the norm, establishing "that government could *potentially* almost always improve upon the market's resource allocation." And the Sappington-Stiglitz theorem "establishes that an *ideal* government could do better running an enterprise itself than it could through privatization" (Stiglitz, *Whither Socialism?*, 179).

70. As quoted in Snowdon, Vane, and Wynarczyk, *Modern Guide*, 288.

71. Krugman, *Peddling Prosperity*, 215.

72. In other words, the causation implied in the marginal productivity theory of wages is reversed in the efficiency wage theorem. Rather than workers being paid according to their marginal productivity, they are productive according to what they are paid.

may therefore be rational, since workers, realizing that the wage is significantly higher than wages they could obtain by working elsewhere, will work harder, shirk less, quit less often, and be loyal and diligent.[73] The downside of the higher-than-equilibrium wage, however, is that both unemployed workers and firms face difficulties in bidding down the price of labor.[74] Too-high wages, and thus involuntary unemployment, are structurally embedded in capitalism.

This model is, however, as formalistic as its neo-Keynesian and New Classical predecessors. The New Keynesians raise many interesting questions about market frictions, but since the model of general competitive equilibrium remains the benchmark, the efficiency wage simply replaces the money illusion as an ad hoc, empirically ungrounded dogma purporting to explain why, in an otherwise perfect world that approximates the equilibrium model, inconveniences such as unemployment seem to occur. To be sure, New Keynesianism is an improvement upon the New Classical assumption of the instantaneous adjustment of all markets, including the one for labor; the New Keynesians at least take notice of the existence of involuntary unemployment. But their explanation of this phenomenon is inconsistent with even the most cursory examination of the way real-world firms tend to set wages. Everyday experience suggests that high wages are often *caused by*, rather than the cause of, talents that are in great demand; and that when demand for a worker's talents slackens, his or her wages are cut. Such observations reopen the door to explanations of involuntary unemployment in which some exogenous factor renders labor unable to accept wage cuts in order to avoid unemployment, since if there is systemic unemployment, something must be disrupting the market's profit-and-loss error-correction mechanism. At this point economics will have parted

---

73. Potential employees are assumed to know more about their work skills and personal qualities than employers. Since the costs of hiring and firing are not trivial, firms are concerned about hiring people they will have to eventually let go because of low productivity. In this situation, the New Keynesian model suggests that applicants who offer to work for less than the efficiency wage will send a signal that they are low-productivity workers. This is a version of adverse selection.

74. Unemployed workers are seen as unable to bid wages down for a variety of reasons that have been summarized as the advantages of insiders (incumbent workers) over outsiders (unemployed workers). The cost of replacing insiders with outsiders is often quite high, including fitting the outsiders into the insiders' work environment if the insiders perceive the threat of wage cuts from the outsiders.

decisively with New Keynesianism, since the latter view *presupposes* that the market contains endogenous sources of mass unemployment.[75]

It is entirely possible, of course, that in some firms, industries, or even entire economies, the New Keynesian story will turn out to hold good. But surely the burden is on the spinners of this tale to demonstrate how often it is anything more than speculation; and they have no more discharged this obligation than their New Classical opponents have demonstrated the existence of perfect markets. Instead, the New Keynesians appear to be satisfied with having put rational-choice foundations under Keynes's conviction that market adjustments alone *cannot* solve unemployment. Like rational-expectations theorists who developed elaborate "proofs" of how the (neo-)Keynesian picture *could not* be true, the New Keynesians start with the assumption that it (or something very much like it) must be true, and then try to explain how this "reality," as Krugman puts it, might have come to be. In the end, then, the New Keynesians are as ideological as the Chicago school. In the hands of both, economics is reduced to a game in which preconceived notions about the goodness or badness of markets are decked out in spectacular theory. In neither case do economists fulfill the fundamental scientific responsibility of testing the veracity of their explanations.

To make such a serious charge against the two dominant schools of contemporary economics, however, is to do little more than notice the logical implication of their use of the equilibrium model as either a representation of reality or an indictment of it. And this brings us back to the marginalization of the old style of neoclassical economics that took place shortly after Hayek's speech of 1933. It was, after all, an ideological impulse—the desire of left-wing economists to justify Keynesian interventionism and socialism—that led to the initial triumph of formalism. These economists needed no persuading that the market had little capacity for self-correction and adjustment to disequilibrium; thus, they treated the state as a *deus ex machina* that could close the gap between theory and reality. The Chicago school's reaction against this view was equally ideological, for all its scientism; but here the *deus ex machina* was the market itself. Even while Hayek was seen as ideological because of his inability to make his

---

75. Cf. Don Bellante, "Sticky Wages, Efficiency Wages, and Market Processes," *Review of Austrian Economics* 8 (1994), 21–33.

case in the language of "scientific" formalism, the introduction of this language actually had the effect of licensing any ideological predisposition that *could* be translated into its terminology.

Both the Chicago school's utopian view of reality and its opponents' dystopian view were given life by the assumption that equilibrium was necessarily intended to be a description of the market. The Chicago school simply affirmed this intention by praising the "magic of the market." The Keynesians, neo-Keynesians, and New Keynesians also affirmed the intention, but they denied that the resulting description was accurate. They were led, in consequence, to view the model as an ideal that is attainable only by government action; they replaced the magic of the market with the magic of the state. Neither the Keynesians nor the Chicagoans explain how imperfection can be *institutionally* remedied, rather than circumvented by either market or political actors with heroic capacities.

What both schools overlooked was the fact that equilibrium is a static construction that could not possibly represent a dynamic world of time, ignorance, and uncertainty; but that the divergence between ideal and reality can highlight the ways reality may have institutionalized error-correcting properties that can, in fact, be seen as propelling the world in a direction reminiscent of general equilibrium. But like any ideal type, equilibrium is a postulate *that is not necessarily affected in the real world.*[76] The main task of any science is to investigate the degree of correspondence between various ideal types and empirical reality; but this means that science is primarily a matter of experimentation or, in social science, historical research—not model-building but model-testing (i.e., testing of the applicability of intelligible models to given situations). Still, the "falsification" of an ideal type in a given instance does not require that it be discarded as useless. It may aid the scientist in constructing ever more realistic models of the circumstances of that particular time and place. This procedure

---

76. In this paragraph I follow Jeffrey Friedman, "Introduction: Economic Approaches to Politics," in *The Rational Choice Controversy: Economic Models of Politics Reconsidered*, edited by Jeffrey Friedman (New Haven, CT: Yale University Press, 1996), 16ff, which elaborates a Weberian, particularistic methodology; but I disagree with ibid., 9, which blames preformalist economics for assuming, rather than investigating, the correspondence of its ideal types with reality.

once allowed economics to be something quite different from an exercise in the provision of rationales for predetermined conclusions.

What Went Wrong

I do not claim that economists who followed the ideal-type procedure, such as Hayek, were immune from ideology themselves. But in principle, treating models as ideal types allows one, or one's colleagues, to root out one's ideological prejudices by subjecting one's models to the empirical test of applicability as well as the philosophical test of intelligibility.

This view of ideal-typical science is itself, of course, an ideal type; it will apply more to some scientists or disciplines in some eras, and less to others. Unfortunately, since 1933 the trend of Western economic thinking has been to turn this ideal type—and this ideal—into nothing but a pious hope. Despite economists' official adherence to Milton Friedman's methodological positivism, the testing of theories against reality has become less and less central to their activity; instead, the generation of formal models has become an end in itself.[77] This was virtually inevitable, since the tenets of formalism require that economic argument must be placed in a certain language if it is to be considered scientifically legitimate.[78]

As a result, none of the main centers of economic education convey a *theoretical* understanding of *real-world* market institutions. That is not viewed as their educational purpose. Deirdre N. McCloskey has pointed out that "economics in American universities has become a mathematical game. The science has been drained out of economics, replaced by a Nintendo game of assumptions with as much practical payoff as chess or lotto."[79] Instead of producing economists who seek to understand the working properties of economic forces

---

77. Cf. Friedman, "Introduction," 12–13; Thomas Mayer, *Truth versus Precision in Economics* (Aldershot, UK: Edward Elgar, 1993).

78. After the 1940s, as Robert Solow puts it, "judicious discussion is no longer the way serious economics is carried out" (1997, 42). Model-building has become the standard intellectual exercise.

79. Deirdre N. McCloskey, "The Arrogance of Economic Theorists," *Swiss Review of World Affairs* (October 1991): 12.

in real historical time, "the graduate schools in economics have been producing scientific illiterates." These are sharp criticisms, but they are more or less on target. Arjo Klamer and David Colander's study, *The Making of an Economist* (Boulder, CO: Westview, 1990) details how the formalist revolution substituted mathematical skill for sensitivity to historical and institutional details, and how students have responded predictably to the internal reward system set up by formalist economics.

The devolution of thought that Hayek perceived at the time he wrote "The Trend of Economic Thinking" provides a useful point of comparison with the present situation. Just as Hayek saw the real danger as residing in the second generation of antitheoretical economists, the first generation of formalists, having been taught by older economists, still possessed a sense of historical and institutional realism that was absent in the next and subsequent generations. Equilibrium models still had to meet some standard of realism, even if these standards no longer had official methodological legitimacy. Thereafter, however, it was the model, and not the world, that became the dominant source of intellectual excitement. Technique has trumped substance ever since.

As a result of this natural progression of the formalist revolution, a new form of theoretical relativism has emerged. Hayek saw historicism as providing a relativistic challenge to the analytical claims of classical and neoclassical economics, especially when applied to public policy. Arguments for laissez-faire were rejected by historicists on the grounds that they were based either on faulty assumptions about human nature, or on analysis that may have been true for one period of history but was irrelevant in another period. But this apparently fact-based, scientific approach did not actually provide empirical evidence that, say, the "laws" of supply and demand were "repealed" in certain historical epochs. To do this, historicism would have had to explain what motivated observed economic relationships in the absence of such "laws." But, for the most part, no such alternative explanations were forthcoming. Instead, historicists typically pointed to some phenomenon that seemed on the surface to contradict economic "laws," and then reached the sweeping conclusion that in the face of such phenomena, one should abandon theorizing about them in favor of data collection and policy adhocery. This naïve empiricism had the effect of substituting confused, sub rosa theorizing for the careful, refutable theorizing embodied in classical economics and canonized in Weber's method of ideal types. In the guise of repudiating the classical economic assumption that instrumentally rational behavior is an ideal type that is *universally* instantiated in the real world, historicism proposed an equally a priori, unscientific theoretical scheme—a scheme of historically determined motivational pluralism unfounded on any rigorous investigation of behavioral evidence—but one that could not even be debated intelligently, since the theoretical claims about a given era were implicit and incoherent.

The formalist revolution generated a similar disregard for empirically meaningful and rigorous theorizing. Ideal-type theorizing had been designed to establish whether real-world *processes* might explain the movement of disequilibrium phenomena toward an ever-elusive hypothetical equilibrium. But to render the equilibrium model in mathematical terms, formalists had to view it as a static condition against which disequilibria could only be compared timelessly—or banished as an illusion.

Different formal models generate different conclusions, and since each model is, in principle, equally unable to explain real-world disequilibria, there is no way to choose between them in any absolute sense. Economic arguments against interventionism based on New Classical assumptions could just as easily be false as arguments for intervention based on New Keynesian assumptions could be true. All we have is a succession of logically consistent and very elegant models that say little or nothing about the world—except that anything is possible.

What is true of contemporary macroeconomics is also true for microeconomics. Consider the situation in industrial organization. As Franklin Fisher pointed out in a review essay on the *Handbook of Industrial Organization*, the main organizing principle of modern industrial organization is that there are no organizing principles.[80] Modern theory simply demonstrates that anything can happen, given different assumptions. All of the models are admittedly unrealistic and do not illuminate real situations in the economy. This is viewed as a pragmatic weakness, but not a "theoretical" weakness, since theory has been divorced from reality. The unrealistic simplicity of the models is designed to allow theorists to do complicated mathematics, not to allow testing against reality. Conversely, the empirical analysis that does occur is rarely informed by theory. And any policy preference can be backed up in some vague way by one model or another.

---

80. Franklin Fisher, "Organizing Industrial Organization: Reflections on the *Handbook of Industrial Organization*," *Brookings Papers: Microeconomics* 1991 (1991): 201–40.

Ironically, the interventionism this allows is a product of the methodology of the arch-laissez-faire Chicago school. Samuelson was responsible for transforming economic theory into a branch of applied mathematics, but Milton Friedman must share some of the responsibility for transforming the psychology of economists by means of his seminal *Essays on Positive Economics* (Chicago: University of Chicago Press, 1953)—one of the staples of graduate economic education over the last four decades, along with Samuelson's bible of technical economics.

Friedman argued that an assumption's realism mattered little as long as it could produce positive predictions. Part of what went wrong with economics, it might be argued, is that this testing is the exception rather than the rule.[81] But the problem goes deeper. Even in the wake of formalism, theorists had been constrained by a historical and institutional sensitivity that prevented them from introducing blatantly false assumptions.[82] Friedman himself, for example, had attacked Abba Lerner's *The Economics of Control* (London: Macmillan, 1944) for failing to address many of the institutional questions that would arise from using the price system in the absence of private property ownership. *The Economics of Control* was economics in a vacuum, according to Friedman, and was not "combined with a realistic appraisal of the administrative problems of economic institutions or of their social and political implications."[83] But just such an appraisal is undermined by Friedman's methodology. All Lerner had done (like Lange before him), after all, was replicate for socialism the unrealistic model assumed to be legitimate for capitalism—the model of perfectly competitive general equilibrium—that Friedman had placed at the foundation of the Chicago school's understanding of economic *reality*. Change a few assumptions here and there, and it follows that general equilibrium socialism can achieve the same efficiency properties as general equilibrium capitalism. Since real-world capitalism deviates considerably from competitive equilibrium (and is more likely to correspond to monopolistic rather than competitive equilibrium), real-world socialism built on the Lange-Lerner model would outperform capitalism. Yet in his role as comparative systems economist rather than methodologist,

---

81. See, e.g., Alexander Rosenberg, *Economics—Mathematical Politics or Science of Diminishing Returns?* (Chicago: University of Chicago Press, 1992).
82. Unless, of course, the purpose of the introduction of such assumptions was to engage in a counterfactual mental experiment.
83. Friedman, *Essays,* 319.

Friedman implies that only a serious case of confusing mental constructs with empirical reality could result in this judgment.

By the same token, Friedman's famous advocacy of economic laissez-faire, unlike that of such later Chicagoans as Gary Becker, is in most cases unconnected to the general equilibrium model. Rather, Friedman's policy outlook is deeply shaped by Hayek's analysis of the informational difficulties of government planning and Hayek's understanding of spontaneous order, combined with James Buchanan's work in public choice theory and constitutional political economy.[84] Later economists, however, took Friedman's methodology more seriously than he himself seems to have done. His pragmatic concerns were swept away in favor of elegant formal modeling. The economic world is no longer an object of study; the formal model of an abstract economy is what is of concern to economic scientists.[85] Thus, Gary Becker defines the economic approach as the relentless and unflinching use of the postulates of maximizing behavior, market equilibrium, and stable preferences.[86] His efficiency claims about the market are predicated on the assumption that these postulates are descriptively accurate, even though they are propositions in comparative statics while the real world is evidently dynamic.

Faced with the kind of criticisms of this view that have been raised by Arrow, Stiglitz, and other market-failure theorists, Chicago economists typically respond by insisting that the real world is in equilibrium *when all the appropriate costs are included in the analysis.* In other words, the market-failure theorists have made an illegitimate comparison between an ideal state and the imperfect world. Demsetz's attack on the "nirvana fallacy" is an example of this style of Chicago response to suggested market failures. Demsetz argues that Arrow's market failure theory results from an illegitimate chain of reasoning that begins with a deduced discrepancy between the ideal situation and the real situation,

---

84. See, e.g., Milton Friedman, *Free to Choose* (New York: Harcourt, Brace & Jovanovich, 1980).

85. In the new interventionism, one set of assumptions (optimal search, perfect competition, etc.) is replaced by another (asymmetric information, imperfect competition, etc.) and the logical results are derived. The model, not the economy, is the subject under investigation.

86. Gary Becker, *The Economic Approach to Human Behavior* (Chicago: University of Chicago Press, 1976), 5.

which is then transformed into a demand for perfection by the use of an unexamined alternative arrangement. This call for perfection by incantation is guilty of the fallacy of the free lunch, i.e., the belief that the alternative arrangement could be established costlessly.[87]

This response, while making an important analytical point about comparative institutional analysis, nevertheless contains a bias in favor of the status quo that Demsetz fails to justify. He implies that whatever exists must be efficient; otherwise, change for the better would have already occurred. But if the economy were as efficient as Demsetz assumes, many of the phenomena Chicago economists study—including money, firms, and law—would not exist.[88] Such institutions enable economic processes in the real world to achieve whatever degree of self-correction and economic coordination the formal model of competitive equilibrium was supposed to capture in the first place; yet these institutions come into being only to the extent that equilibrium is not a description of reality, but an ideal type that does *not* describe reality.

The New Classical economics that emerged in the 1970s and 1980s displayed the same complacency about the status quo, dismissing involuntary unemployment as theoretically incoherent and empirically void. For involuntary unemployment to be a myth, the New Classical economists posited economic actors who adjusted their behavior so quickly (for all practical purposes, instantly) that equilibrium would be achieved at all points. Compared to this, the New Keynesian efficiency-wage theorem appears the model of sober realism.[89]

---

87. Harold Demsetz, "Information and Efficiency," *Journal of Law and Economics* (March 1969), 1–22.

88. This, for example, is why Coase is to be contrasted with Stigler or Becker or Posner. The starting point of Coase's analysis was that in general equilibrium the phenomena he sought to illuminate would be absent. The causes of the phenomena must therefore be found in deviations from equilibrium—in Coase's case, positive transaction costs. In Mises's *Human Action*, this method of contrast is employed throughout to illustrate the functional significance of various market insititutions in a nonequilibrium world of change. By exploring the logic of a world free of change, one can by way of contrast explore the world of change, which would be too complex to examine directly without the help of this mental tool.

89. The same can be said of the direction in which research on market socialism is going. At the moment these models are not as well worked-out as the New Keynesian models. But in the work of Roemer the key issue is one of mechanism design and determining the appropriate monitoring/contractual relationship to align incentives. In short, Roemer is

New Keynesianism interventionism is nourished by leaks in the supposedly watertight equilibrium theory of the Chicago school. But the arguments for the new interventionism are simply variations on the bad habits that gave rise to the Chicago school. Imperfect market theory, like perfect market theory, is addressed to a model, not to the world the model is supposed to illuminate.

• • •

Alan Coddington has pointed out that "instead of asking how reason can be applied to the knowledge that men can or do have of their economic circumstances," modern economic theory "asks how reason can be applied to circumstances which are perfectly known." The troublesome problems of "what can be known, and how it can come to be known—problems of ignorance, uncertainty, risk, deception, delusion, perception, conjecture, adaptation and learning—are then tackled as a complication and refinement on the theory."[90] Modern theorists' static conception of reason is in direct conflict with the passage of real time.[91] The postulates of rational choice theory can only generate formal proofs if the future (with its novelty, uncertainty, and ignorance) is excluded. Modeling that excludes this component of reality not just for counterfactual purposes, but as part of realistic attempts to describe or condemn the market, are bound to be insufficient.[92]

---

trying to use the rational choice equilibrium framework to solve the problems associated with market socialism. As New Keynesian models increasingly question the efficiency of financial and labor markets under capitalism, the need for Roemerian solutions appears to grow, just as in the 1930s and 1940s the socialist models had a parasitic relationship to Keynesianism.

90. Alan Coddington, "Creaking Semaphore and Beyond: A Consideration of Shackle's 'Epistemics and Economics,'" *British Journal of the Philosophy of Science* 26 (1975): 151.

91. Gerald P. O'Driscoll and Mario J. Rizzo, *The Economics of Time and Ignorance* (New York: Basil Blackwell, 1985), 52–70.

92. A great deal of contemporary economics refines traditional theory by incorporating more realistic situations, such as increasing returns, multiple equilibria, and findings from experimental economics. In a recent survey of modern economic theory, David Kreps contends that these developments (especially experimental economics) have the potential of making economics relevant to reality ("Economics—The Current Position," *Daedalus* (Winter 1997), 59–85). But, like market failure theory, the point of much of this work is to demonstrate how real-world behavior deviates from the standard equilibrium model. The standard model remains the point of reference, so the passage of time, the generation of new knowledge, and changing conditions have yet to be incorporated.

This is not, as I have tried to demonstrate throughout this chapter, simply a methodological complaint. It has a host of serious implications. The temporal structure of production, for example, with its employment of heterogeneous components to form the various combinations that make up the unique capital structure of a given economy, are excluded from modern analysis. As a result, the way market signals constantly reorganize capital combinations remains invisible to the modern economist. Nor is the impact of monetary price adjustments on the pattern of exchange and production fully incorporated into economic theory: either prices are assumed to represent the underlying information perfectly (competitive equilibrium), or they are assumed to reflect that information so imperfectly that they constitute market failure. In both instances, the informational content of the price system is misrepresented. As should be obvious, this has profound implications for understanding various economic systems and paths of economic development.

The precision of equilibrium modeling is gained at the expense of correspondence with the imprecise world the model was once supposed to help us understand. Paradoxically, the careful expression of imprecise concepts and processes in natural language supplies us with a more accurate picture of the economic world than the most rigorous mathematical modeling. Careful thought requires coherence; relevant thought requires correspondence to reality. Good economics requires both coherence and correspondence.

The often-stated argument that mathematical modeling eliminates ambiguity in thought by forcing theorists to state assumptions explicitly is based on a conflation of the concepts of *syntactic* and *semantic* clarity. Mathematical reasoning ensures that modeling is disciplined by syntactic clarity, but semantic ambiguity is the result.[93] The abandonment of mathematical reasoning using equilibrium models would herald a return to semantically rigorous standards of argument about the economic world "out there."

The twentieth century's oscillation between perfect market theory and market failure theory, both of which take as the terms of debate the formal model of general competitive equilibrium, will inevitably be won by theorists of market failure. It is obvious that the economic world is not perfectly competitive (or

---

93. Coddington, "Creaking Semaphore," 159.

even near that state of affairs). Hence the triumph of the interventionism that Hayek forecast—not because economic theory has been rejected, but because it has been misconceived. While Stiglitz and other contemporary market failure theorists intend to rebut Hayek's analysis of the benefits of the private property, competitive price system, in reality their response to Hayek constitutes a non sequitur.[94] Since Hayek's argument did not depend on the achievement of static equilibrium, the deviations of real markets from the model do not constitute re- buttals to him: indeed, deviations from the model were Hayek's starting point.

To address Hayek's argument seriously, economists would have to drop the false precision of equilibrium models and engage in careful reasoning about imprecise phenomena, such as the passage of time, the limits of our knowledge, the uncertainty of the future, and the discovery of opportunities.[95] Perhaps Hayek's argument cannot be sustained when confronted in this manner, but this we will not know until seven decades' worth of disastrous formalization is abandoned and the realities of economic life are re-engaged.

---

94. See, for example, Stiglitz, *Whither Socialism?*, 24–26 and 269–77. Also see John Roemer's 1995 essay review of Stiglitz's book, which he refers to as "An Anti-Hayekian Manifesto," *New Left Review* (May/June 1995), 112–29.

95. As Karen Vaughn concludes in her book on the migration of the Austrian school to America, "It seems indisputable that scientific understanding would be much improved if at some point in the future we could genuinely and intelligently say, along with Mil- ton Friedman, there is no such thing as Austrian economics, only good economics and bad economics. But this time we would mean that good economics was an economics not only of preferences and constraints, but also an economics of time and ignorance" (*Austrian Economics in America* (New York: Cambridge University Press, 1994), 178).

19

Man as Machine

Introduction

THE GREAT AUSTRIAN economist Ludwig von Mises tried
to capture the differences between the natural and human sciences with the
following quip: "You throw a rock in water, it sinks; throw a stick in water, it
floats; but throw a man into water, and he must *decide* to sink or swim." Mises
was not denying the scientific nature of economics with this tale of human
volition. Rather, he was attempting to get across to his audience the essential
defining character of the human sciences—we study man with his purposes
and plans. As Fritz Machlup once put it, economics is like the physical sciences
to the extent that matter can talk.[1]

Unfortunately, economics in the twentieth century proceeded as though
it didn't matter that the central focus of the subject was human actors. Wasn't it
true that the physical sciences progressed when purposes and plans were stricken
from the analysis? Lightening was not due to the anger of the gods but was a
result of physical properties. The purging of anthropomorphism was appropriate in the physical sciences. But the purging of man from the human sciences
results in the abolition of its subject matter. The human element is eliminated
and replaced with a utility machine. Economics developed a theory of the machine economy but lost sight of the human economy.

The machine economy has two features that added to its attractiveness to
scholars suffering from an inferiority complex in relation to the natural sciences.

---

1. Fritz Machlup, *Methodology of Economics and Other Social Sciences* (New York: Academic Press, 1978).

It permitted explicit modeling in a way that human volition denies, and it encouraged calibrated measurement of aggregate effects. Model and measure were the hallmarks of science and machine economics enabled economists to pursue modeling and measuring without reservation. Of course, some economists resisted these steps—perhaps none as vociferously as the Austrian economists Mises and Hayek.[2] But the critics were, for the most part, silenced. In this chapter, we highlight the path that economic theory took in the twentieth century as a result of purging human nature from itself and then suggest ways to bring humans back to the center of economic analysis.

The movement in economic thinking is composed of four competing visions. Furthermore, only one of these visions is compatible with an understanding of economics that both recognizes the universal nature of economic truths and makes humanity the alpha and the omega of economic thinking. This vision, our first, belongs to the predominantly verbal economic analysis of Adam Smith, new institutional economics, and the Austrian tradition, which emphasizes the centrality of acting man in its study and maintains the universal nature of economic propositions. The second vision is that of historicism and old institutionalism. Here, while the mode of expression is verbal and the place of human actors prominent, it is believed that economic truths revealed through study are merely *particular* truths, wholly specific to time and place. The third vision belongs to the neoclassicism of twentieth-century economics. The human element is virtually purged from the analysis and in its place *homo economicus*, the cyborglike optimizer, is substituted. Because an acting person is conspicuously absent from this vision and the understanding about what constitutes economic truth shifts from understanding humans to generating predictive power, the mode of exposition is purely a formal one of mathematical modeling and statistical testing. Though the individual may be missing, because of the perceived belief in a unique equilibrium, determinism makes possible economic laws universal in nature. Finally, the fourth vision presents a sort of hybrid between the previous two strands of thought. In the wake of the folk theorem and notion of multiple equilibria, the vision maintains the formal analysis of our third vision

---

2. While the old institutionalists rejected the modeling strategy, they embraced the importance of measurement.

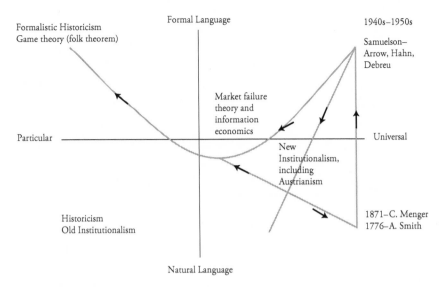

Formalistic Historicism
Game theory (folk theorem)

Formal Language

1940s–1950s

Samuelson–
Arrow, Hahn,
Debreu

Market failure
theory and
information
economics

Particular

Universal

New
Institutionalism,
including
Austrianism

Historicism
Old Institutionalism

1871–C. Menger
1776–A. Smith

Natural Language

Figure 19.1. Trends in Economic Thinking

but discards the notion that economic truths are necessarily universal truths. In this vision, as in the third, robotic reaction dominates the analysis and the human actor is relegated to the sidelines. The four visions outlined above and their relationship to one another are presented above in Figure 19.1.

The Primacy of Man

For Smith and his contemporaries, the human actor was at the center of economic study. This is partly the result of their concern with what they understood to be the moral relevance of exchange activities, which they viewed as inextricably linked to an understanding of market behavior. Nonetheless, this emphasis on the individual as the ultimate subject matter of economics was borne out of an appreciation that all economic activity is ultimately the activity of fallible, creative, and choosing actors. For economists of Smith's age, economic truth was to be found in exploring the motivations and outcomes, both intended and unintended, of human action. Owing to this emphasis of the uniquely human element of economics, economic truths, Smith and his cohorts believed, were necessarily universal in nature. Some nations were rich while others were poor not because of unique geography, relative abundance of resources, or serendipity of historical time, but because some nations pursued policies of easy taxes, a fair administration of justice, and a private property order conducive to wealth while others did not.[3] In the eyes of someone like Smith, this was as true for England as it was for Africa. Furthermore, the mode of expressing these truths was a verbal one. Although the technologies of modern mathematical and statistical modeling were largely unavailable to economists of the eighteenth and nineteenth centuries, from the writings of Smith we can infer that this "constraint" was really no constraint at all. His focus on the dynamic nature of man and market activities was in his mind both best expressed and understood in plain language. Thus, it is not at all apparent that, had the formal tools available to economists today been available to Smith and his contemporaries, that they would have actually employed them.[4]

The nineteenth century in economic thought saw the rise of historicism, particularly as manifested in the economics of the German Historical school. Although these economists like Sombart or Schmoller put the human element at the center of economic study and consequently employed verbal methods of analysis, for them the notion of universal economic truths were chimerical. The "economic laws" effective in Germany in the nineteenth century were precisely that—truths that were specific to the people of the nineteenth-century Germany. Old institutional economics later emerged with a similar approach to the study of economics. Man was central to the analysis but the universality of economic truths was not.

---

3. As Smith wrote in the 1755 manuscript which summarized his research and eventually resulted in *An Inquiry into the Nature and Causes of the Wealth Of Nations*: "Little else is requisite to carry a state to the highest degree of opulence from the lowest barbarism, but peace, easy taxes, and a tolerable administration of justice; all the rest being brought by the natrual course of things" (1776; repr., Chicago: University of Chicago Presss, 1976), xl). Also see Stewart's discussion of the "Life and Writings of Adam Smith" written in 1793 and reprinted in Smith's *Essays on Philosophical Subjects* ("Account of the Life and Writings of Adam Smith, L.L.D," in *Essays on Philosophical Subjects*, edited by W.P.D. Wrightman (1793; repr., Oxford: Oxford University Press, 1980), 269–351).
4. Thus, we are suggesting that the Arrow/Debreu model, rather than formalizing the "invisible hand," has actually inhibitied our understanding of it.

Contra historicism, economics in the tradition of the Austrian school such as Carl Menger, Ludwig von Mises, and F.A. Hayek emphasize the primacy of man in the vein of Adam Smith.[5] As Menger argued, "man with his needs and his command of the means to satisfy them, is himself the point at which human economic life both begins and ends."[6] The economist, qua the human being, is the subject of his own study. In this sense the human sciences possess an advantage over the physical sciences. Because of this unique position, the human sciences are able to know the ultimate causes of phenomena—the human as the chooser.[7] This enables the sciences of human action to pursue the logic of cause and effect. As Hayek stated: "We thus always supplement what we actually see of another person's action by projecting into that person a system of classification of objects which we know, not from observing other people, but because it is in terms of these classes that we think ourselves."[8] For the Austrians, precisely what makes economics different from other sciences is that it deals with purposeful actors. The importance of time, uncertainty, and learning are all emphasized, as these are the conditions necessary for human choice, and with which real world man must constantly cope. To ignore these issues or move them to the background of economic analysis is to purge the peculiarly human element that economics must concern itself with. The world confronts humans with unceasing change. There is nothing static or neat about a person's attempts to realize his or her ends. While comparative statics may provide a useful model for explaining some observed behavior, as its root, static analysis ignored the dynamic processes that are inextricably linked to man's attempted to better his position. The recognition of the importance of processes as characterizing the economic world of real human actors further highlights the centrality of conscious, purposive agents in the Austrian framework. In a world of dynamic change, something must be driving the movements—an

---

5. Carl Menger, *Principles of Economics* (1871; repr., New York: New York University Press, 1981); Ludwig von Mises, *Human Action: A Treatise on Economics* (1949; repr., Indianapolis, IN: Liberty Fund, 2010); F.A. Hayek, *Individualism and Economic Order* (1948; repr., Chicago: University of Chicago Press, 1907).

6. Menger, *Principles*, 108.

7. See Mises (*Human Action*, 17–18) where he discusses human action as the ultimate given.

8. Hayek, *Individualism*, 63.

understanding of the market as a process requires a creator of change. This generator of change is the creative imagination of the entrepreneur, who in the attempt to earn profits and avoid losses drives the market process. Thus at the foundation of the Austrian approach is the entrepreneurial element in human action.[9] As Mises points out, "This function is not the particular features of a particular special group or class of men; it is inherent in every action and burdens ever actor. . . . The term entrepreneur . . . means: acting man exclusively seen from the aspect of the uncertainty inherent in every action."[10]

Economic decision makers do not simply react to given data and allocate their scarce means to realize given ends. The entrepreneurial element in human action entails the discovery of new data and information; discovering anew each day not only the appropriate means, but the ends that are to be pursued.[11] Moreover, the ability to spot changes in information is not limited to a selective group of agents—all agents possess the capacity to do so. Entrepreneurial discoveries are realizations of *ex post* errors made by market participants which either caused them to be, *ex ante*, over- or underpessimistic in their expectations. The existence of error provides scope for profit opportunities that actors can realize if they move in a direction less erroneous than before.

The Austrian appreciation of the primacy of the human in economic analysis does not dampen the universality of economic truths. However, given the complexity of the human predicament, natural language is far better suited than formalism for conveying these truths. Although the particular ends sought and means employed vary among people, places and time, purposeful behavior in the most general sense is itself an omnipresent feature of the world. Thus, although the applicability of particular laws of economics derived from the starting point of human action will vary from place to place, their truth-value is universal. The universality of purposeful human behavior begets the universality of the

---

9. According to Kirzner: "[T]he competitive market process is essentially entrepreneurial. . . . The entrepreneurial eleemnt in the economic behavior of market participants consists . . . in their alertness to previously unnoticed changes in circumstances which may make it possible to get far more in exchange for whatever they have to offer than was hitherto possible." (*Competition and Entrepreneurship* (Chicago: University of Chicago Press, 1978), 15–16).

10. Mises, *Human Action*, 252–53.

11. Kirzner, *Competition*, 30–87.

economic truths that explain this behavior. Economics can explain the tendencies and direction of change, even if it cannot explicitly model or measure the statistical significance of change.

Pursuing the Human Element: The Rise of Neoclassicism[12]

As the twentieth century progressed, the idea that economics should strive for quantitative laws and predictive capacity gained hold. This was partly a result of an increasing number of mathematical and statistical tools that appeared to make this possible. And certainly as the sophistication of computing technology grew and its cost fell, more economists made use of these tools in their analyses. The idea took hold in economic thinking that economic truth could best be discovered via the quantitative approach of the natural sciences. To be sure, with the aid of mathematics, the natural sciences had succeeded in progressing at a rate much faster than its sister social sciences. Thus it is not altogether impossible to understand why many in the economics profession looked to the method and approach of the hard sciences as a guide.

Neoclassical economists took the opportunity to increasingly introduce formalistic tools from the natural sciences to economics. On a theoretical front, the crowning achievement of this effort was the development of general equilibrium theory, formalized by Arrow, Hahn, and Debreu. These economists and their cohorts articulated the mathematical conditions under which a deterministic

---

12. The term "neoclassicism" is necessarily vague and encompassing. While recognizing the significant variants within the neoclassical tradition, our criticism is directed at the formalistic strain of neoclassical economics. It is our contention that the term "neoclassicism" has become obscured in the latter part of the twentieth century. Originally, neoclassicicism entailed universal propositions about the world derived using marginal analysis. In the second half of the twentieth century, the scope of neoclassical economics transformed from elaborating universal propositions about the world to formal analysis with particular implications. For example, is it reasonable to place both Josh Stiglitz and Robert Lucas in the neoclassical camp? The drastic differences between the two highlights the obfuscation of what neoclassicism entails. Also see Fisher's critical essay of modern industrial organization ("Organizing Industrial Organization: Reflections on the *Handbook of Industrial Organization*," *Brookings Papers: Microeconomics* 1991 (1991): 201–40). Fisher argues that the main organizing principle of modern industrial organization is that there are no organizing principles. Modern theory simply demonstrates that anything can happen, given different assumptions.

equilibrium for the entire economy would hold. By solving a complex system of simultaneous equations, they were able to describe a general equilibrium. In the wake of this achievement, the well-known first and second theorems of welfare economics were also forged. This in turn led economists like Samuelson and others to create the notion of a social welfare function and with it the field of modern welfare economics. Neoclassical economists made no bones about the universality of general equilibrium, the first and second welfare theorems, or the implications of the burgeoning field of welfare economics. For the most part, these "economic truths" were mathematical ones—thus the question of their universality was really no question at all. Economic laws derived this way have as much universality as the mathematical truths that compose them.

Much of this "scientific progress" in neoclassical economics, however, came at a price. More specifically, the human element became less and less central to the neoclassical conception of economic activity. In the general equilibrium framework, for instance, where there are an infinite number of agents, all of whom are price takers, who changes the price to enable the market to clear? The answer of neoclassical economists is the fictional "Walrasian auctioneer." But this answer misses the crux of our simple question; the "Walrasian auctioneer" is fictional. He or she certainly has no counterpart in the real world of acting people, so how does general equilibrium analysis enable us to better understand the real world of real people? In the real world, market participants, actively pursuing their interests, make price offers and refusals, the interaction of which ultimately generates the market-clearing price. This process takes place in time and is highly imperfect. Where though do time and imperfection play a role in general equilibrium analysis?

Similarly, in the general equilibrium world, the fictional "Walrasian auctioneer" does not permit any false trading, but this is clearly not the case in the real world. The real world is populated by ignorant actors who face uncertainty and make mistakes. This feature of markets made possible by human actors is critical to understanding the actual market process but remains absent in the general equilibrium analysis. It is as though precisely the features that make an individual human are assumed away or swept under the rug by employing the fictional "Walrasian auctioneer." In the timeless world of general equilibrium there can be no process, no "how we get from here to here" but rather just "here" and "there." To make the human element central to economic analysis, however, means to explore. Simply describing actors' start states and the end states that would result, were they able to achieve their ends, ignores precisely the process of movement that economics need to explain.

A key element of the neoclassical research effort described previously is the examination of comparative statics as a means to understanding the welfare and efficiency properties of economic outcomes under varying conditions. This endeavor, however, largely ignored the role of the human actor in economic analysis. The Samuelson-Bergon social welfare function, which was to represent the aggregate preferences of all members of society, dealt with individuals in such an abstract way as to virtually purge them completely from the analysis. Rather than understanding human preferences as the constantly changing, immeasurable, and creative products of choice and decision making, neoclassical welfare economics treated them as the homogeneous, static outcomes of deterministic assumptions. In a sense, the neoclassical notion of welfare economics divorced economics from man. In light of Arrow's impossibility theorem, it became unclear in what way the construction of a social welfare function was even meaningful, but this did not prevent many neoclassical economists from continuing to employ them as valid and significant means of analyzing the welfare properties of differing static states. In the end, while neoclassical economics succeeded in making economics look like physics, it is questionable to what extent it developed our understanding of market processes and fallible human behavior that characterize the real world.[13] Without a doubt, formalism added technical sophistication to the field, but these advances did not come without a cost in terms of the human element's centrality to economic study.

Ultimately, this technique-driven modeling type of economics also ran into a problem with its twin sister—statistical measurement. What is the empirical relevance of the model? Anomalies accumulated and models' irrelevance to the real world was highlighted by both friends and foes alike. Something had to change. However, what has changed is not the "model and measure" mentality, but rather the tools of the modeling.

---

13. Alexander Rosenburg (*Economics—Mathematical Politics or Science of Diminishing Returns?* (Chicago: University of Chicago Press, 1992)) argues that economics can either be interesting mathematics or an empirically progressive science but not both.

From Bad to Worse: Formalistic Historicism

The most recent trend in mainstream economics is grounded in increasing influence of game theory. John von Neumann and John Nash, key players in the development of game theory, were both trained mathematicians. Another key contributor was von Neumann's co-author, Oskar Morgenstern. Morgenstern, who can be placed within the Austrian tradition, attempted to emphasize the importance of imperfect foresight and the role of market process. However, in the end, Morgenstern's insights were discarded and the game theoretical structure was built around static assumptions such as homogenous beliefs and preferences and perfect foresight of the players involved.[14] In short, Morgenstern's questions were discarded as the central emphasis and focus was instead placed on the technical aspects.[15]

Although game theory was first met with great interest and enthusiasm, this quickly dwindled as many in the profession had difficulty extending the framework beyond the two player games von Neumann and Morgenstern had focused on. Rizvi contends that game theory truly took hold in the economics profession when it realized that there were major difficulties with the general equilibrium framework.[16] Among these difficulties was the inability of general equilibrium theory to account for imperfect competition. Simply put, game theory allowed theorists to analyze many scenarios where general equilibrium theory had little to add. In line with the criticism of neoclassical economics, perhaps the most substantial criticism of game theory is that it distorts the nature of the economic actor. Simplifying assumptions are made in order to model various scenarios which otherwise would be too complex. In many

---

14. Phillip Mirowski, *Machine Dreams: Economics Becomes a Cyborg Science* (New York: Cambridge University Press, 2002).

15. Game theory focuses on three important facts of human action and social cooperation: strategic interactions, bargaining and negotiation, and framing—how the rules of the game influence the way players play the game. The major weakness of game theory from the standpoint of Austrian economics is the common knowledge assumption (see Nicolai Foss, "Austrian Economics and Game Theory: A Stocktaking and an Evaluation," *Review of Austrian Economics* 13 (2000): 41–58).

16. S. Abu Turab Rizvi, "Game Theory to the Rescue," *Contributions to Political Economy* 13 (1994): 1–28.

cases, for instance, it is assumed that players know more than they actually do (or could). In such instances, these models are as unrealistic as the neoclassical models that assume that economic actors possess perfect knowledge. In evolutionary game theory, strict rules are set up which players must follow as if they were automatons devoid of unique characteristics and traits—i.e. preferences, tastes, imperfect foresight, etc. Further, these foundational rules assume away the entrepreneurial aspect of human action. In cases where perfect knowledge is assumed, there is simply nothing new for actors to learn. And, in cases where players' actions are severely restricted via the rules of the game, their ability to be alert to new opportunities is extremely limited.

In connection with this analysis, we must also address the issue of equilibrium in game theory. While general equilibrium theory focuses on one final static equilibrium, the folk theorem tells us that there can be multiple equilibria in many game theoretic situations. As mentioned previously, both neoclassical and game theorists have failed to consider the market process with emphasis on learning and discovery to solve the coordination problem set forth by Hayek.[17] Simply put, how do agents, with imperfect knowledge and foresight, coordinate their activities with others? Too often, this critical question is swept aside via the assumptions of the model. Further, assuming that individuals are able to coordinate their activities, it is far from clear that they would be able to obtain an equilibrium given the constant introduction of new knowledge and information. Given this realization, it is clear that many game theoretic models describe a fixed moment in time with a given stock of knowledge. Finally, the question of universality must be addressed. In many cases, game theorists model some scenario which shows the achievement of one of the multiple potential equilibria as dictated by the folk theorem. They then claim that the equilibrium achieved is not universal. That is, the equilibrium achieved is one of an infinite number of possible equilibria that happened to hold at the particular time and place being analyzed, but which does not necessarily hold in all the cases with similar circumstances.

We find ourselves in the undesirable situation where the defining characteristic of economic analysis is no longer the universal propositions that are produced through a variety of languages (natural and formal), but instead where

---

17. Hayek, *Individualism*, 33–57.

any particular proposition can be proven using one language (formal). We term this intellectual position *formalistic historicism.*

The Austrian arguments against historicism are no longer strictly relevant, and the Austrian arguments against formalism, while relevant, misunderstood how much the ground has shifted since the 1950s. In the previous period, the universal propositions claimed by economists from Smith to Menger were represented in a formal model only under highly restrictive assumptions. Under these restrictive assumptions, a unique price and quantity vector could be found which would clear the market. But these restrictive assumptions were significantly divorced from reality. Problems of asymmetric information, imperfect market structure, externalities, and public goods lead to suboptimal allocation and use of scarce resources. The theory of market failure thus developed in response. But there was always a problem of the ad hoc nature of the introduction of these deviations from the ideal.

New Institutional Economics (law and economics, public choice, New Economic History, etc.) developed in reaction to this ad-hocery. The result was the development of the theory of government failure and comparative institutional analysis. But these developments were made in largely natural language and many of the formalist establishment did not accept these results. Theorists were confronted with a choice: either return to the institutionally rich world of natural language or push into the realm of formalism and permits particularism.

The majority of economists in the mid-1980s were willing to take the analysis into this formalistic historicism (a position that would have been absurd in the 1950s). Concepts such as multiple equilibria and path dependency emerged as unifying themes in economic analysis. Despite a certain liberation this brought, it didn't bring us any closer to the study of man.

Where Do We Go from Here?

There are many problems with formalistic historicism, but it has also sown the seeds of its own correction. Since theories can be developed to prove anything, empirical work is relied upon more and more to adjudicate between theories. This is most evident in the work on growth theory, but it permeates all fields in contemporary research. This demand for empirical work has coincided with an increasing acceptance of alternative forms of evidence. In-depth case studies, comparative historical analysis, interviews, and surveys are accepted as evidence alongside large-scale econometric models.

It is our contention that this opening up of the nature of acceptable empirical work represents a great opportunity for Austrians to bring the human actor back into the analysis. The Old Historical school thought that anthropological and narrative historical evidence demonstrated the particularities of the individual. Ironically, it is our argument that by exposing formalistic historicism to evidence from anthropology and history, we regain the universal nature of the human sciences. If there was nothing universal about the human condition, then what could we learn from studying others? Other people would remain beyond our capacity to understand. On the other hand, if all individuals were identical, then what could we learn from studying others? Nothing, because there would not be anything unique to their circumstances; economic understanding would increase by framing questions in terms of the particular but analyzing terms of the logic of choice. Interpreting the particular by way of the universal yields the *analytical narrative*.[18] The analytical narrative entails the application of Austrian economics as a tool of interpretation of ethnographic data. This approach emphasizes the open-endedness of choice as opposed to the close-endedness required by formalistic interpretations of rational choice. The analytical narrative, if conducted in the way we suggest, brings us back to the lower right-hand quadrant in Figure 19.1. The person as chooser returns with both human character and particular circumstances.

The entrepreneurial element in human action operated on our knowledge of particular time and place to realize the gains from mutually beneficial interaction. In the analysis of the market process championed by Mises and Hayek, the entrepreneur is the prime mover. This entrepreneur is caught between alluring hopes and haunting fears as he or she attempts to recognize the hitherto unrecognized or to improve on the delivery of the recognized opportunities for exchange. The market process emerges out of the previously existing imperfections on the market. Today's inefficiency represents tomorrow's profit opportunity for the entrepreneur who is able to fix the imperfection in a way

---

18. For the most well known rendering of the analytical narrative, see R. Bates, A. Greif, M. Levi, J.-L. Rosenthal, and B.R. Weingast, *Analytic Narratives* (Princeton, NJ: Princeton University Press, 1998).

that allows individuals to realize gains from exchange that had previously gone unexploited.

Converting either the individual or the economy into a machine necessarily eliminates the messiness of entrepreneurial discovery and adjustment from the process. It is also the case that the machine imagery pushed institutional contingencies out of economics. But Austrian analysis, by insisting on the central human element in economic life and the institutional context within which human beings act, maintains a position within the economics discipline that is analytically rigorous (logic of choice) and institutionally rich (narrative history).

Conclusion

The intellectual landscape of modern political economy has shifted considerably since the beginning of the twentieth century. We have argued that the discipline began the century in a position where economists thought they had discovered universal laws which they could express in the prose of natural language. Their opponents denied this, but they did so by arguing that economic theory was not universal. By midcentury, the discippline moved to a position where economists thought they had refined the universal principles by expressing them in the nonambigious language of mathematics. However, to convey economic propositions in such terms, restrictive assumptions had to be employed to assure mathematical tractability. The entrepreneurial element of human action was a casualty of the mathematical revolution in economics because it defies tractability. Unfortunately for economic science, we cannot explain the operation of the market and the adjustements of the price systyem without recourse to the entrepreneur.

Instead of recognizing this, economic discourse embarked on a detour which resulted in a form of formalistic historicism dominating economics by the last decade of the twentieth century. We enter the new century with hope that the universal logic of economic science and their contingencies of human volition and historical conditions can coexist under the intellectual umbrella of the sciences of human actors. This is the inspiring vision that Ludwig von Mises provided in 1949. More than fifty years later, Mises's pioneering work provided the foundation for a science of economics that is at once humansitic in its methods and humanitarian in its concerns.

20

The Limits of Economic Expertise

WHAT ROLE IS there for government in promoting the economic well-being of citizens within its national boundaries? This question has vexed social philosophers for centuries. If we assume that political authority derives its legitimacy in part from the satisfaction it affords its subjects, then it follows that a "good" government will adopt policies that will enhance the economic well-being of its citizens. What exactly those policies are has been one of the main subjects of controversy in economics since its founding. Some have contended that the role of government is to be at best a referee, whereas other economists have argued the government must actively participate in the economic game.

We identify two theoretical tensions that exist in this debate. First, from Adam Smith onward a large part of the teachings of economics has stressed the mutually beneficial aspects of trade. But for the gains from exchange to be had, the economist postulates some level of coercion to ensure the provision of the basic framework of property and contract. Without the government providing the legal infrastructure, mutual gains from exchange will go unrealized. To fund government provision of this framework and to empower government to enforce this framework, the presumption toward voluntarism must be suspended. How precisely to negotiate this divide is something that economics and political economy wrestles with to this day.

Second, there is an interesting relationship between the epistemic outlook of economics and the disposition of the economist that plays itself out in the history of development economics. To simplify two continuums down to their poles, we can see the discipline of economics as moving between "epistemic modesty" and "epistemic hubris" in the way it understands its own claims to

Table 20.1. The Status of Economics and the Role of the Economist

	Economist as Student	Economist as Savior
Economics has epistemic modesty.	Happy cautionary prophet	Frustrated engineer
Economics has epistemic hubris.	Frustrated cautionary prophet	Practicing engineer

scientific knowledge (particularly in the sense of prediction and control), and we can envision economists as approaching their work as either "students of society" or "saviors of society." The interaction between the dominant culture of the discipline and the disposition of the economist is portrayed in Table 20.1.

We broadly categorize the results in terms of "cautionary prophets" or "engineers." We use "prophet" in the sense of a person who offers predictive warnings ("if you do *x*, *y* will happen") rather than someone who is divinely inspired or the like. By using the adjective "cautionary," we are suggesting that the economist as prophet is largely in the business of cautioning us about the limits of what we can and cannot do. The economist as prophet is more likely to utter "Thou Cannot" than "Thou Shalt Not." This sort of economist has a default, though not inviolable, respect for the workings and value of institutions that have survived the process of social evolution. This puts him or her in the position of cautioning those who would remake or ignore the lasting results of those historical processes.

Over the last 150 years, the economist as engineer, by contrast, has moved through two distinct, though related, worldviews with respect to historically emergent institutions. During the late nineteenth century, a period characterized by "frustration," the engineering-oriented economist was interested in the role of institutions but concerned with designing new social institutions to replace those seen as responsible for the problems of the day. The spirit of science and engineering, which had been apparently so successful in taming nature, would be used to rein in the forces of the social world so that they would serve the cause of human betterment by being the results of human reason rather than blind evolution. By the middle of the twentieth century, with the failures of wholesale institutional redesign more obvious, the economist as engineer was more likely to ignore historically emergent institutions, focusing instead on the problems of optimal resource and income allocation as explored in what amounted to an institutional vacuum. What unites the engineers of the two centuries, and makes grouping them together intellectually coherent, is their rejection of the cautionary prophet's default respect for historically successful social institutions. The older ones rejected it because they thought they could do better; the more recent ones simply ignore the issue.

In this chapter, we explore how these interrelationships between economists as prophets or engineers and economics as epistemically modest or hubristic play out in the debates over the state's role in promoting economic development. Clearly the state plays a role, but does it do so by establishing the framework within which economic transactions occur or by serving as a corrective to the failure of voluntary action to promote development? That is, how modest or self-confident is economics about what economists can directly contribute to economic development? Douglass North has written that it is important in these discussions to remember that, no matter how predatory and exploitive the state may in fact be, the state is necessary for economic development.[1] Adam Smith provided a classic statement of this when he argued in the notebooks that eventually led to the *Wealth of Nations* that "little else is requisite to carry a state to the highest degree of opulence from the lowest barbarism, but peace, easy taxes and a tolerable administration of justice; all the rest being brought about by the natural course of things."[2] This is a call for limited government, but still an effectively organized government capable of defining property rights and enforcing contracts. On the other hand, the mercantilist writers before Smith and the German protectionist economists as well as the Keynesian economists after Smith argued vigorously that the state cannot remain on the sidelines and referee the economic game. The state is in a unique position to serve as a corrective to social ills and thus plays a definite and active role in promoting the wealth of a nation. Intertwined in the history of these debates over the state's role in political economy are questions of the nature of economic expertise, the epistemic assumptions of economics, and the disposition of the economist.

---

1. Douglass North, *Structure and Change in Economic History* (New York: Norton, 1981), 24.
2. Adam Smith, *An Inquiry into the Nature and Causes of the Wealth of Nations,* edited by Edwin Cannan (1776; repr., Chicago: University of Chicago Press, 1976), xliii.

From Moral Philosophy to Science and Back Again?

Before we focus more precisely on the history of development economics, we need a broad, if brief, overview of economics' self-understanding of its own epistemic standpoint. Restricting ourselves to the last 350 years or so, we can see an oscillation between epistemic modesty and epistemic hubris about the scientific status of economics and its implications for economic policy. In Smith we find repeated cautions about the limits of the expertise of the moral philosopher, particularly in light of what the state can do with respect to economic policy and the differences between the knowledge of the economist and the knowledge of the economic actor. Jeffrey Young distinguishes between two forms of knowledge present in Smith—"contextual" and "system."[3] The former refers to the knowledge actors use, based on their experiences, to make their day-to-day decisions of "ordinary life." The latter, by contrast, is what the philosopher produces and, in so doing, "reveals what is hidden to agents in ordinary life." Young's distinction is also seen in Smith's famous "chessboard" passage from *The Theory of Moral Sentiments,* where he distinguishes between the "principle of motion" of individual actors and the systemic rules laid down by the legislature.[4] Of particular importance in that passage is Smith's discussion of the "arrogance" of those who would seek to arrange actors as if they were pieces on a chessboard. The whole notion of the "invisible hand," particularly as Smith understood it to be linked with the divine, is yet another example of his call for philosophical humility before greater social forces.

During the early nineteenth century, economics remained largely under the sway of relatively modest views of its own position among the sciences. In the decades to follow, two developments began to push at the prevailing methodological self-conception. The first, to be explored in more detail later, was an emphasis on the importance of the "folk" knowledge of the actor and an increased skepticism about the knowledge of the expert. This argument was linked with the historical school and some of the protectionist thinkers in Germany and the United States. They attacked the then current orthodoxy

---

3. Jeffrey Young, "Unintended Order and Intervention: Adam Smith's Theory of the Role of the State" *History of Political Economy 37*; 2005; ed. Steven Medema; 91–119.
4. Adam Smith, *The Theory of Moral Sentiments* (1759; repr., Indianapolis, IN: Liberty Fund, 1982), 234.

from one side, arguing that it was, in some sense of the term, "too" scientific because it paid insufficient attention to: (1) how enough attention to how natural laws of human development functioned and (2) how best to facilitate those processes. At the same time, some of these thinkers also argued that economics was *unscientific* for not paying enough attention to how natural laws of human development functioned and how best to facilitate those processes.

The second development was the rise of socialist thought, particularly Marxism, which began to criticize classical orthodoxy for, in some sense of the term, not being scientific enough. Marx's laws of history represented, in his view, a more scientific approach to understanding the developmental path of industrial economies than did the classical worldview. Although Marxism suggested humility in the face of these larger historical laws, the culmination of that historical process would be a world where humans used their knowledge of social forces to make history rather than be subject to it. The Marxian future where production would be directed "in accordance with a settled plan" would be a social order rationally constructed according to our knowledge of the laws of production.[5] Engels captured this nicely by analogizing capitalism to lightning and socialism to electricity under human control.[6] Just as a scientific understanding of nature had enabled us to take powerful natural forces and subject them to human control, so could a scientific understanding of the social world, led perhaps by economics, enable us to use rationality to control the forces of production.

Despite their attempts to change the basic outlook of the discipline, both the historicists and the Marxists remained part of heterodoxy. Nonetheless, they, especially the Marxists, did have their effects. At the same time, the disposition of many coming to study economics was changing as well. Given the events surrounding the Industrial Revolution, including factory conditions and changes in the distribution of wealth and income, more people came to economics predisposed to be saviors rather than students.[7] Combined with the Progressive

---

5. Karl Marx, *Capital* (New York: Modern Library Edition, 1906), 92.

6. Frederick Engels, *Socialism: Utopian and Scientific* (1892; repr., New York: International Publishers, 1972), 68–70.

7. The Social Gospel movement of the nineteenth century, discussed by Bradley Bateman in *History of Political Economy* 37 (2005) "Bringing In The State? The Life and Times of Laissez Faire in 19th Century United States" *History of Political Economy 37*, 2005 ed. Steven Medema, 175–99, is a good example of the rise of the savior disposition among those with an interest in economic issues.

movement in the United States and similar movements elsewhere in the world, this move toward the savior approach put increasing pressure on the discipline of economics to shift its self-understanding.

Into the late nineteenth and early twentieth centuries, economics continued to borrow from the natural sciences with increasing frequency. As Philip Mirowski's work demonstrates, the importation of natural science concepts profoundly affected the development of neoclassical economics.[8] The marriage of the language of equilibrium, energy, and "forces" to the rise of positivist philosophy in the early twentieth century began to increase the level of intellectual self-confidence among economists. With a philosophical outlook that emphasized prediction and control and a set of theoretical tools that emphasized modeling and empirical testing, neoclassical economics looked increasingly like an extension of engineering. The belief in the real-world applicability of general equilibrium models reached its peak in the 1930s and 1940s in the literature on planning and market socialism. The growing interaction between economists, game theorists, and the military-industrial complex further cemented the view of economic problems as static, allocative, quasi-engineering problems. Books like Abba Lerner's *The Economics of Control* (London: Macmillan, 1944) were examples of this vision of economics at work.

For the young person approaching economics with the savior disposition, the newfound scientific self-confidence of economics presented a perfect match. Economics became an opportunity to put one's desire to save the world to work by becoming a practicing social engineer. For those less inclined to be the savior, the state of the discipline became a source of frustration. Although the "student" is always inclined to play the role of cautionary prophet, that role is largely reduced to irrelevance when the dominant discourse of the discipline is closer to that of the engineer. During the middle of the twentieth century, economics was too busy imagining what it could do and had little time for those who kept warning that those tasks could not be done. Many heterodox economists of the period, mostly those skeptical of significant state intervention, but even some Marxists as well, found themselves in the role of the frustrated cautionary prophet, believing that the scientific self-confidence was really intellectual

---

8. Philip Mirowski, *More Heat than Light: Economics as Social Physics, Physics as Nature's Economics* (Cambridge: Cambridge University Press, 1989).

hubris. In the face of the triumph of science, views akin to those of the moral philosophers of 150 years earlier were seen as mere metaphysics.

In the last 30 years, however, the discipline has shifted somewhat. For various reasons, including the real-world failures of policies based on the engineering approach, economics has swung away from the most extreme sorts of hubris found earlier in the twentieth century. Advances in philosophy and our understanding of the human mind have challenged the stronger claims of positivism and rationalism and led to renewed appreciation for the role of social institutions in guiding fallible humans of bounded or limited rationality through a complex and uncertain world. The increased emphasis on the rhetoric of economics and the history of the discipline, and not just the history of ideas, have all helped rein in the unrealistic ambitions of the early twentieth century. One interesting twist is that the engineering mentality remains in form but not function in the increasing complexity of mathematical economics. The result is that those who come to the discipline as saviors find themselves frustrated by the arid policyless world of supposedly "pure" economics yet also perhaps frustrated by the swing back toward epistemic modesty. In addition, the student is heartened, perhaps, by the newfound modesty, as he or she sees the role of cautionary prophet as somewhat more available. However, the institutional structures of the discipline continue to disproportionately reward those with the engineering skills, even if they do not perform the engineering functions. The result is frustration of one sort or another for all but those who see beauty inherent in the tools.

In the rest of this chapter, we overlay this story on the history of the state's role in development economics to explain the twists and turns this discipline has taken in trying to account for why some nations are rich and others are not.

The Modest Economist and the Limited State

The history of the state's role in economic thought begins with the earliest contributors to modern economic thought. The liberal moral philosophers of the eighteenth century, particularly those associated with the Scottish Enlightenment, saw a clear connection between the development of trade and commerce and the development of the various measures of "civilization." In their view, the extension of trade was the result of limiting the state's role in attempting to be the direct source of economic development and of restricting that role to providing the institutional infrastructure that facilitates trade. In turn, this view of the state implied a much more modest role for the economist/moral philosopher in contributing to the wealth of nations.

The civilizing effect of trade could be seen at three levels. First, the spread of trade created incentives for individuals to interact through persuasion via mutual benefit, rather than through zero- or negative-sum games of force or deception. In doing so, trade engendered peaceful relations among individuals by creating interdependencies through the division of labor and exchange. Second, trade promoted orderly and prosperous societies through the invisible hand/spontaneous ordering processes of the market. Not only did it create more civilized relationships among individuals, it created more civilized social orders. Finally, trade promoted more civilized relationships among nations through the extension of the Ricardian law to international trade: nations that kept barriers to international trade low developed cooperative and interdependent relationships with other nations, reducing the net benefits, and thus the frequency, of armed conflict. This section explores each of these arguments in turn.

Adam Smith recognized early in the *Wealth of Nations* that market economies had civilizing effects on individuals in several ways. The transition from older forms of economic organization to markets entailed a movement from societies that were frequently coordinated by face-to-face interaction to ones that required new processes of social coordination that could work among anonymous actors. As Smith put it in the well-known passage near the start of the *Wealth of Nations,*

> In civilized society [man] stands at all times in need of the co-operation and assistance of great multitudes, while his whole life is scarce sufficient to gain the friendship of a few persons.[9]

Smith argues that we could try to gain this cooperation by appealing to the benevolence of others with beneficent acts, but that is unlikely to work where their motive for cooperation is not some personal connection but only self-love. Our beneficence leads to the reward of self-approbation from the impartial spectator, but not to the concrete sorts of cooperation and pecuniary benefits that economic processes depend on. Thus, says Smith, we must find a way to

---

9. Smith, *Wealth of Nations,* 18.

appeal to others' self-love, and the famous passage about the butcher, baker, and brewer follows in turn.

In addition to the ways in which Smith and others argued that commerce demonstrated that direct action by the state was not necessary for encouraging cooperative behavior among individuals, it was also clear that such action was not necessary for the generation of broader notions of social order. The invisible hand of the Scottish Enlightenment helps explain how a nation's internal trade could generate orderly, but unplanned, institutions and outcomes. The thrust of the Smithian system was that the "system of natural liberty" would generate the wealth of nations, and not the state's intentional attempts to create national wealth. However one reads the metaphor of the invisible hand, its very invisibility invokes processes other than the very visible activities of the state in generating economic development.

This increase in commerce, which was mainly focused on the towns, had other salutary effects on the broader social order. As Smith argues in the chapter "How the Commerce of the Towns Contributed to the Improvement of the Country," there were three ways that town-based commerce generated beneficial unintended consequences for the country areas. The first two were more narrowly economic, but the third, which he attributes to Hume, was the one he thought was most important:

> Commerce and manufactures gradually introduced order and good government, and with them, the liberty and security of individuals, among the inhabitants of the country, who had before lived almost in a continual state of war with their neighbors, and of servile dependency upon their superiors.[10]

This argument is a nice condensation of the views of the Scots with respect to the necessary and unnecessary roles of the state. Smith argues here that it is commerce, which clearly in some sense precedes the state, that generates the "demand" for political reform and good government and the spread of civilization to the countryside. Trade is, for Smith, a natural human proclivity but one that generates the best consequences when property and liberty are secure. An

---

10. Smith, *Wealth of Nations*, 433.

increased volume of trade leads to greater benefits from the state being both limited and well respected.

The third way in which the state's forbearance was believed to generate civilizing effects was through international trade. The idea that specialization and the division of labor led to salutary effects within the nation was clear in Smith's mind. His linking that division of labor to the "extent of the market" provided a principle by which the ongoing evolution and growth of economies could be rendered intelligible. Both Jean-Baptiste Say and David Ricardo extended that insight in important ways, with Say's law explaining how production was the source of demand and Ricardo using the concept of comparative advantage to extend the Smithian insight to trade among nations. Commerce could generate the very same interdependencies among nations as it did among individuals. In the case of nations, these interdependencies would lead to a reduction in the level of conflict among them.

For the early political economists, the state's role was largely limited to the protection of person and property, as they argued that unhampered trade would generate the beneficial effects that some believed required an activist state. The state's job was to provide the legal-political infrastructure that made commerce possible. Like the gardener who cultivates an environment in which plants can thrive, the state was seen, largely, as providing the institutions that individuals required to benefit from the gains from trade. Smith, it could be argued, saw himself as explaining the economic and social forces that were actually at work in the social world of his time, and, in identifying them, he offered a vision of humility for the ability of humans to consciously manipulate those economic processes. The institutional infrastructure was the key to the wealth of nations, as it would direct our passions into channels that generated public benefits, if only unintentionally.

For Smith and his contemporaries, the claims of economics were modest ones. It made no claim to being able to remake the world; it could only offer some general advice about what needed to be done, but it could say a great deal about what not to do. The student would find this a congenial atmosphere and would happily play the role of cautionary prophet. It is worth noting that from the early years of the Enlightenment and well into the nineteenth century, the role of cautionary prophet was more radical than conservative, given that Smith's

work was an attempt to bring reason to the study of society.[11] The cutting edge
of knowledge was, in fact, the ability to talk about how reason demonstrated,
in Hume's words, the limits to reason. We are often accustomed to seeing the
cautionary prophet as a "conservative" voice, but in the context of Smith's time
it was quite the opposite. Not surprisingly, this modest role for economics and
the economist did not sit well with those who approached economics as saviors.
They would have their turn in the next stage of development economics.

Protectionism and National Identity:
The Savior as Frustrated Engineer

The argument for unhampered trade, particularly among nations, put forward by Smith and others was in response to earlier arguments that we now
broadly categorize under the name "mercantilism." There remains much debate as to whether the mercantilism of the pre-Smithian period can be understood as a coherent theoretical system. In his overview of mercantilist thought,
Lars Magnusson argues that although there was no cohesive doctrine or set of
policy proposals, what the various pre-Smithian British mercantilist thinkers
"mainly shared was a preoccupation with the question of how a nation could
become rich and thus also achieve greater national power and glory."[12] For most
mercantilists, doing so required that the state manage trade, especially with the
goal of generating a favorable balance of trade. The response from the classical
economists, as we have shown, was to argue that national wealth was better
understood in terms of how goods and services were best delivered to the population, and that markets and trade were the best means to that end.

At much the same time as these promarket arguments were being developed
in Great Britain and in areas of the Continent, another school of mercantilist

---

11. A good example of just such a radical cautionary prophet was Richard Cobden in
nineteenth-century England. Largely in agreement with Smithian arguments, Cobden
was particularly effective in advocating the epistemically modest vision of economics
and in actually affecting policy concerning free trade as a result. He was both committed to free trade and clearly radical.

12. Lars Magnusson, "Mercantilism," in *The Blackwell Companion to the History of Economic Thought*, edited by Warren J. Samuels, Jeff E. Biddle, and John B. Davis (Malden,
MA: Blackwell, 2003), 46–60.

thought was emerging in the United States and in Germany.[13] Like the earlier mercantilists, these thinkers did not always form a coherent school of thought. However, the most full-fledged statement of the general thrust of their ideas came from the German Friedrich List in his *Nationale System der Politischen Ökonomie* in 1841. List's ideas, and those of similar thinkers in the United States (e.g., Alexander Hamilton and Henry Carey), are often categorized as "national economics," as they, like their British predecessors, were focused on the development of the nation's wealth and power. List's work is also sometimes linked to the German historical school, as his central idea was that the economic theory and policy that was appropriate to a particular country depended on that country's stage of development. By making economic theory historically dependent, List fits with the German historicists, and by arguing that free trade was sometimes not the best policy option, List followed in the tradition of the pre-Smithian mercantilists.

At the time List was writing, the highly decentralized nature of the multiple political entities that comprised Germany led to a number of tariffs among them that limited intranational trading. Combined with very low to nonexistent import tariffs, the various German states were lucrative markets for foreign sellers, especially the British. With foreign goods making up a relatively large part of the economy, the various German states wanted some way to rebuild their national industries and national identities. List's work landed nicely into this historical environment. As we argue later, much of List's work, and the circumstances that produced its reception, foreshadows similar ideas and historical contexts in the emergence of approaches to economic development in the twentieth century, as Magnusson notes as well.[14]

List argued that economic development was best understood as a series of stages of maturation, from "barbaric" to "pastoral" to "agricultural" to "agricultural-manufacturing" to "agricultural-manufacturing-commercial." Specifically, List claimed nations could pass from the first to third stage making use of free trade, but that some form of protectionism was necessary to

---

13. See Stephen Meardon, "How TRIPs Got Legs: Copyright, Trade Policy, and the Role of Government in 19th Century American Economic Thought" *History of Political Economy 37,* 2005 ed. Steven Medema, 145–74 for more on the U.S. economists William Cullen Bryant and Henry C. Carey.

14. Magnusson, "Mercantilism," 58–59.

reach the final stage when, once again, free trade was most desirable. The central theoretical premise was that the very unevenness of world economic development precluded free trade from being desirable in all circumstances. When one country moved to the later developmental stages, its ability to export cheaper manufactured goods to countries in earlier stages would preclude the development of their own manufacturing industries, preventing the less-developed country from moving to the higher stages of development. The implication is that nations should adopt protectionist strategies, in particular what today would be called "infant industry" protections, to make sure that internal industries have sufficient time to develop without the competition from cheaper imports.

The nationalist aspect of List's approach demands some further attention. Like others in the early nineteenth century (e.g., Thomas Carlyle, as David Levy demonstrates[15]), List objected to the "cosmopolitanism" of the classical economists. Where the focus for some critics was on the implication that free trade would overthrow long-standing hierarchies of race or gender, for List the concern was with the cross-national application of economic theory and its focus on the individual rather than the nation. As his stages-of-development approach indicates, one at the very least had to recognize that different theories might apply to different countries. In addition, List was concerned with the effects of free trade on the nation as a whole. For example, if such trade meant that industries or people were displaced, it should be seen as harmful. He also claimed that nations should attempt to husband "productive power" rather than wealth itself. In an interesting turn on the older mercantilist tradition, he saw the real national goal as not the collection of money but the increase of the productive powers of industry. And unlike the charge sometimes leveled at the older mercantilists, he understood that productive power was not the same as wealth and explicitly preferred the power to the wealth.

One element that List brought to his version of the mercantilist view is that nationalism and national identity were part of what was at stake in economic development. Writing in Germany of the early to mid-nineteenth century, List naturally would see nation building as central to his theoretical stance. Much of the concern with the infant-industry argument is that free trade makes the

---

15. David M. Levy, *How the Dismal Science Got Its Name: Classical Economics and the Ur-Text of Racial Politics* (Ann Arbor: University of Michigan Press, 2002).

development of a nation's economy dependent on forces that it cannot control. When world prices and free trade guide the direction of economic development, nations cannot control whether and how their own productive powers evolve, thus they cannot determine their own national identity and destiny. In some ways, this is a precursor of Marxian arguments about the hidden nature of capitalist laws and the need to take control over what has previously controlled us. In the twentieth century, the building of national identity and these elements of Marxism would come together in the economic development policies of the postcolonial world.

Three aspects of List's framework are noteworthy for the broader story we are telling. The first is that this view assumes that industrialization is central to economic development. List was explicit in believing that rapid and early industrialization was desirable even if it meant that the nation was worse off temporarily. As we show later, this claim was at the center of debates in the emergence of both the Soviet model in the 1920s and postwar development economics. The second aspect is that it focuses on the nation as the unit of analysis. By starting with the stage of development that the nation is in and asking what is necessary for enhancing the nation's industrial strength, List's approach can avoid asking whether the policies it recommends actually work to the benefit of most or many individuals. Where it does ask that question, it answers it by putting the interests of the "nation" over those of the individual. Finally, List's approach is a clear precursor of the "import substitution" policies that dominated much of development economics in the mid-twentieth century.

The views associated with List and the historical school redefined the role that economists, or those knowledgeable about economics, might play with respect to the broader society. Economists disposed to be saviors could make a claim to understanding the "real" processes at work and staking a further claim to having sufficient knowledge to design policies that would produce both better economic outcomes and other goals, such as enhanced national identity. Though not as comprehensively as would be seen in the twentieth century, List and the historicists gave the savior some scope to become an engineer. Rather than humility in the face of social processes that could be understood but not controlled, this critique of the Smithian paradigm suggested that economists should have confidence that they could be key contributors to the activist work of the state. Later in the nineteenth century, this confidence would reach a higher plateau in the role played by members of the later German historical school, as the so-called Socialists of the Chair. Seeing themselves as the intellectual defenders of those in power, they came even closer to the engineer than the cautionary prophet.

The relationship between policy and the economist's role can be cumulative—that is, changes in the dominant perception of policy can alter economists' perceptions of their own roles in society. We do not suggest that narrow self-interest in access to power explains the changes in ideas; rather, it is more likely the other way around: changes in beliefs about "how the world works" will change economists' self-perceptions. In addition, once that self-perception begins to change, and economists both see themselves and are treated as saviors, it can in turn affect how they attempt to understand the world. If the savior can become an engineer and appear to have success in doing so, more potential saviors will be attracted to economics. As the saviors become engineers, they will look for ways of understanding the world that play to the strengths of the savior-cum-engineer. They will see the world in engineering terms. There is, perhaps, a kind of lock-in here where self-perceptions, actual access to power, and the human capital of economists are mutually reinforcing in ways that make alternative visions appear to have very high transition costs.

Nonetheless, by the mid-nineteenth century, the saviors of the List/historical school remained frustrated engineers, as the dominant self-understanding of the discipline stayed largely in the same camp as Smith's time. Put somewhat differently, being the savior at this time required that one be heterodox, and thus it meant frustration in terms of influencing both the discipline and policy. Only when the discipline changed in ways that enabled the "savior-cum-engineer" to be part of orthodoxy would that frustration end.

The Rise of the Engineers in the Twentieth Century

Despite the potential for such an intellectual lock-in, the late nineteenth century and early twentieth century saw both the rise of the savior and the continued strength of the student. With respect to the latter, Max Weber emerged as one of the leading social scientists in the world. Of his many scholarly contributions, the one his name is most identified with is his claim about the protestant work ethic and capitalist development. In *The Protestant Ethic and the Spirit of Capitalism*, Weber sought to explain how religious beliefs affect economic organization and performance. Whether one agrees with him or not, one must agree with the importance of the way Weber addressed the question of the wealth and poverty of nations. Too often in the history of political economy, thinkers sought to explain the differences between nations by reference to natural resource endowment. But Weber sought to blend an analysis of material resources with noneconomic factors to address why industrial capitalism appeared in the West, specifically northwestern Europe, and not in China, even though, only a few centuries earlier, China was by far richer and more technologically advanced than Europe. Weber did not provide the monocausal answer to that question that his critics often accuse him of.[16] Protestantism is only one of the differentiating characteristics in his explanation. Protestantism provided the ethical or moral justification for practices conducive to economic development, but it was not the source of development.[17] In his *General Economic History*, Weber contrasted the legal structure of Chinese society, which was not conducive to the development of capitalism, with the Western legal structure, which was conducive to capitalist development.[18] Chinese law, according to Weber, was based on spiritual and magical practices, whereas the Western legal tradition was inherited and evolved out of the formal legal rules of Judaism and Roman law. The Western legal tradition relied on a logical mode of juristic reasoning, instead of discretionary, ritualistic, religious, or magical considerations found in the Chinese legal system.

The main reason that the legal system mattered for economic development is that it enabled the calculative capabilities of individuals to be used in making decisions about enterprise activities. Because the legal system possessed some certainty in its rules, individuals could engage in rational calculation about the consequences of decisions. Another major factor in Weber's analysis is a fixed tax system, rather than an arbitrary one, and the reason that this fiscal arrangement is vital to economic growth is the same as that for legal certainty; it encourages a longer-term horizon among decision makers, and it provides an incentive for responsible decision makers. We return to this explanation in

---

16. Max Weber, *The Protestant Ethic and the Spirit of Capitalism* (1904–1905; repr., New York: Scribners, 1958).

17. For an overview of Weber's project for the social sciences, see Richard Swedberg, *Max Weber and the Idea of Economic Sociology* (Princeton, NJ: Princeton University Press, 1998).

18. Max Weber, *General Economic History* (1927; repr., New Brunswick, NJ: Transaction, 1995).

the section on the institutional revolution in development economics. But first we explore the consequences for economic theory and policy from not following in the Weberian path of focusing on the comparative historical political economy of development. From the time of Adam Smith to Max Weber it was common practice to distinguish between the capitalist civilized world and the noncapitalist barbaric world. The idea of an advanced civilized world that was not capitalistic in orientation was simply a contradiction. Weber's focus on institutions harkened back to the Smithian vision, and Weber's recognition of the power of economic calculation under decentralized decision making suggested a Smithian humility in the economist's own role in second-guessing the products of undesigned social processes.

The Smith-Weber distinctions among countries would fade for a variety of reasons with the rise of the engineering mentality in the twentieth century. Questions about how the institutional infrastructure of a society was or was not conducive to growth were replaced with those about the appropriate policy mix to be implemented by government to achieve economic development. As we show, this, not surprisingly, changed the role played by economists in the process. Poor countries had to catch up to the rich countries, and the process of capital accumulation and capitalist development that occurred in the West was simply too slow. The advantage of backwardness was that concerted effort by the state could speed economic development.[19] Three developments in twentieth-century thought and history undermined the earlier emphasis on the institutional infrastructure of society and how that affected economic performance:

1. Formalism and positivism in economics
2. The Bolshevik Revolution and the rise of socialism
3. The Keynesian Revolution in macroeconomics and the rise of international public policy institutions grounded in that revolution

Each of these three shifted attention away from the appropriate *institutional* structure of good governance to the necessary *activities* that government must undertake—a move from designing rules to direct action. This in turn facilitated

---

19. See A. Gerschenkron, *Economic Backwardness in Historical Perspective* (Cambridge, MA: Harvard University Press, 1962).

the emerging shift from cautionary prophet to engineer and the corresponding attraction of the savior to economics.

Formalism directed economists' attention away from how the institutional structure of society directed actors to behave in directions more or less conducive to economic development. Instead, optimization against given constraints, the classic technique of the engineer, became the focus of intellectual attention. Positivism also contributed in the shift away from institutions by delegitimizing the study of ideology as an important component in social theory. Political, legal, and economic institutions are sustained through ideological systems of thought. Out of fear of ideological campaigns such as fascism, positivism sought to eliminate all nontestable propositions from economic science.

The combination of the formalistic preoccupation with equilibrium properties and the positivistic disregard for ideas meant that the sorts of questions that dominated the discussion of the wealth and poverty of nations from Smith to Weber were pushed aside in the field of political economy. In fact, political economy was pushed aside in favor of the idea of scientific economics. The natural tendency of neoclassical development economics was to ignore political, legal, and economic institutions and instead search for empirical measures of development. The question of the institutional infrastructure of development was considered to be unscientific. Measurement equaled science, whereas discussions of property rights, rule of law, constitutional constraints, and legitimating belief systems were dismissed as prescientific musings by worldly philosophers. The triumph of the engineer was at hand.

The Keynesian mindset and analytical toolkit were suited to fill the void once the classical and Weberian treatment of the wealth and poverty of nations was pushed aside. First, Keynesian theory reinforced the general post–Great Depression intellectual climate of opinion that capitalism was inherently unstable. Aggregate demand failure periodically results from the chaotic and irrational decisions of investors. Free market competition could not be relied on to self-correct for the systemic consequences of the errors committed by private actors. Laissez-faire was dead as a legitimating ideology. Second, the aggregate techniques developed in the Keynesian revolution provided economists with a way to measure economic development. Economic development became synonymous with measured growth in per capita income. Obviously the equating of economic development with the emerging neoclassical theory of economic growth had profound consequences for the theoretical foundations of economic development. Third, as the Keynesian hegemony emerged after World War II, various international institutions were formed to carry out public policy grounded in the Keynesian vision and analysis of the government's role in economic development.

The effect of these philosophical and methodological changes on the economist's role was profound with respect to the practice of economics. With the claim to scientific status at their fingertips, economists could move from cautionary prophets to engineers because they now had the tools of objective science to guide policy in ways that did not appear to invoke ideology. Moreover, with the philosophical shifts reflected by positivism and formalism, the engineer not only had the tools but the philosophical blessing to pursue his craft. The shift in focus from the institutional framework to the levers of policy, combined with the rise of formalist and scientistic modes of thought, fed powerfully into the state's own interest in having such policy tools at *its* fingertips. For obvious reasons, the state's interests are conservative here, in that it does not wish to challenge the prevailing set of institutions and would prefer to work within that set to affect policy. This coincidence of interests made for another powerful form of intellectual lock-in that reinforced the role of economist as savior, though this time disguised, through the language of science and objectivity, as a "mere" student.

Although we turn to the Soviet case in the next section, it is important to mention here how that experience influenced thought precisely at the moment of positivist and Keynesian ascendancy. The perceived success of Soviet planning in modernizing a peasant society into an industrial and military power demonstrated that an alternative to the capitalist path to modernity was indeed viable and that the savior as engineer was a model to emulate. Even if the Soviet case was marred by political tyranny in the 1920s and 1930s, surely a more democratic society could accomplish the same societal transformation without the abuse of human rights.

The promise of Soviet planning in terms of economic development was first accepted in the 1920s and 1930s prior to full knowledge of the political repression of the purges and collectivization. At the time the Western democracies were trapped in the crisis of the Great Depression, and the Soviet system seemed to avoid that problem through rational central planning of the economy. The

Soviet system promised to be more economically efficient and more socially just. After knowledge of the political purges and the death toll of collectivization became common, the argument switched from one of Soviet promise to one of merging socialist planning with the democratic institutions of the West. Soviet political institutions lost intellectual legitimacy, but Soviet economic policies continued to hold sway over the hearts and minds of economic reformers. These reformers would occupy the key policy positions throughout the Western democracies and international agencies entrusted with world economic development after World War II.

By the war's end, the distinction between the capitalist and noncapitalist world had given way to a distinction between first world (capitalist-developed), second world (socialist-developed), and third world (under-developed) countries. An intellectual and geopolitical battle began between the first world and second world countries to export policy advice to third world countries on how to pursue the path to modernity. The intellectual and historical evidence demonstrates that policy advice provided to the underdeveloped world by the capitalist nations as well as the socialist ones was almost identical and reflected the intellectual transformation of the political economy of development economics that we have just outlined, in addition to giving economists a starring role as saviors of the third world as "practicing engineers." Both first world and second world economists jettisoned the older focus on the institutional infrastructure in society and emphasized a proactive role of government (and its economists) in engineering the path of economic development.

The Soviet Model and the Collapse of Development Planning

When the Bolsheviks rose to power in 1917, Lenin and his colleagues sought to construct a communist economy. Paul Roberts and Peter Boettke provide evidence of the ideological motivation of the policies of comprehensive centralized planning that were followed between 1917 and 1921.[20] However, those

---

20. Paul Craig Roberts, *Alienation and the Soviet Economy: The Collapse of the Socialist Era* (Albuquerque: University of New Mexico Press, 1971); Peter J. Boettke, *The Political Economy of Soviet Socialism: The Formative Years, 1918–1928* (Boston, MA: Kluwer, 1990).

policies met with a refractory reality that forced the Bolshevik regime to change course with the New Economic Policy (1921–1928). The ideological tension that existed over the NEP led to a major intellectual debate among the Bolshevik ruling elite on the nature of socialism and the path of development. The quality of the economic debate was sophisticated as far as politicized discussions of economic policy permit. Nikolai Bukharin argued for a market-based policy that served socialist goals by permitting accumulation and retaining planning control over the "commanding heights" so that peasant Russia would be transformed under a balanced growth policy into an industrialized society, at which time full-blown socialism would once again be pursued to its logical end of the eradication of the market mechanism. Lev Shanin argued that Soviet Russia had a comparative advantage in agricultural production and thus Russia should pursue a policy of agricultural exportation and capital importation (unbalanced growth policy) to industrialize the economy to prepare for full-blown socialism. Evgeny Preobrazhensky, in contrast to both Bukharin and Shanin, never retreated from the communist policies adopted during 1917–1921. The first act of any socialist state, Preobrazhensky argued, was to nationalize industry, and the path from capitalism to socialism will be planned and follow a rational strategy.

On an academic level these alternative positions were developed in the Soviet journal, the *Planned Economy*.[21] Alec Nove suggests that it was in these pages that "development economics could be said to have been born."[22] Nove makes an interesting point in intellectual history. The emphasis in postwar development economics on "growth" and "long-range" planning of an economy follows directly from Soviet discussions in the 1920s. Evsey Domar has remarked that his study of the debates in the *Planned Economy* was "a valuable source of ideas" in the development of the Harrod-Domar model of economic growth.[23]

---

21. A comprehensive discussion of the Soviet industrialization debate can be found in Alexander Erlich's *Soviet Industrialization Debate, 1924–1928* (Cambridge, MA: Harvard University Press, 1960). Erlich, however, tends to reconstruct the arguments from the debate in terms that are understood in the neoclassical synthesis. Boettke (*Political Economy*, 147–91) provides an interpretation of these debates that attempts to put them within the context of the ideological debates inside the Bolshevik leadership.

22. Alec Nove, *An Economic History of the USSR* (Baltimore, MD: Penguin, 1969), 129.

23. Evsey Domar, *Essays in the Theory of Economic Growth* (New York: Oxford University Press, 1957), 10.

However, Domar's reconstruction of the Soviet debates minimizes the intellectual influence of Karl Marx and plays up the anticipation of Keynesian ideas. Although the Keynesian interpretation possesses some appeal because of the shared engineering mentality, it does not do justice to the Marxian background of the arguments in the Soviet industrialization debate. For the purposes of this chapter, however, we are not concerned with getting the interpretation of the Soviet debate right. Instead, our focus is on simply pointing out the link between the debate and the subsequent development of postwar development economics.

The belief that emerged out of the Soviet experience and the rise of Keynesianism was that development economics was synonymous with macroeconomic growth, and the public policy implications were that government could design, control, and engineer economic growth through various crucial interventions. Underdevelopment was a consequence of weak investment, lack of technology, and shortfalls in the stock of human capital. Government policies were to serve as correctives to the failures of market-driven development and as an engine of economic growth and development in their own right. A fixation on industrialization as the path and measure of development was central to the development planning process, and this was oftentimes complemented by the adoption of import-substitution policies that saw protectionism as a means to the end of statistically measured growth.

As we have shown, this line of thought was hardly original in its broad contours, which recall the nationalism and protectionism of List and other nineteenth-century thinkers. The difference this time was the additional support garnered from the misinterpretation of the Soviet experience and the theoretical framework of Keynesianism that had begun to dominate economic thought and economists' abilities to ground their roles as saviors in the language of science and the tools of engineering. One reason for the confidence of economists was that the arguments for development planning made during the twentieth century grew out of the then-mainstream of economic thinking, in contrast to the heterodoxy of their predecessors a century before. As a result, these ideas had a practical influence on real-world economies that the economic nationalism of List and others never really achieved. The changes in the methodological and philosophical winds in the early twentieth century made the later versions of economic nationalism into orthodoxy and turned frustrated engineers into practicing ones.

One of the more fascinating puzzles of the mid-twentieth century is the disjunction between generally accepted beliefs about the success of the industrialization of the Soviet economy and the reality of its effects on the lives of the citizenry. After Stalin consolidated his power, he moved to rapidly industrialize the Soviet economy, believing that it was the path to both the growth needed to implement socialism and the power needed to counterbalance the West. The 5-year planning model involved transfers of wealth from agriculture to industry via the forced collectivization of the former and state planning of the latter. By many of the accepted measures, this attempt was successful. Reported growth rates in per capita GDP and other macroeconomic variables, as well as the buildup of military resources, pushed the Soviet Union into the ranks of a world power. The strategy of forced industrialization appeared to be the path to economic development and political influence.

In retrospect, many of the beliefs about the strength of the Soviet economy turned out to be illusory. This illusion came in three forms. First, the data produced by the Soviets themselves were systematically overstated, both intentionally for propaganda purposes and through mismeasurement and miscommunication. Second, the estimates made by CIA economists also systematically overstated the health of the Soviet economy: "In 1986, for example, the CIA estimated that Soviet per capita GNP was about 49 percent of that in the United States. The revised estimate now puts that figure at about 25 percent."[24]

The third source of illusion was perhaps the most important. Whatever the truth of the macroeconomic variables, day-to-day life for the Soviet citizenry did not match the picture they painted. The reality of breadlines, backward and dysfunctional technology, inadequate medical care, and dangerous employment conditions was more like that of a third world country than a developed world power. Various measures of well-being demonstrated the ways in which the Soviet citizenry lagged behind the West to a degree that far exceeded the differences in conventional measures of economic success. Comparative data on consumer items such as passenger cars and telephones show the Soviet economies, and Soviet-style economies of Eastern Europe, as lagging significantly behind those of the West. Per capita food consumption and a variety of health

---

24. Peter J. Boettke, ed. Introduction to *The Collapse of Development Planning* (New York: New York University Press, 1994), 7.

indicators, including infant mortality, show similar trends.[25] The measured industrial output did not translate into better opportunities and outcomes for most economic actors, and the investments in military equipment did not translate into effective military power, as the failure of Soviet technology in the first Gulf War demonstrated. The emergence of economic doctrines that saw C, I, and G, or their sum as measures of economic development precluded analysts from asking important questions about the *composition* of those variables or whether they translated into meaningful gains in living standards for those affected by them. The doctrines also were both the cause and the effect of the savior-cum-engineer approach to economics.

The problem with the equation of statistical aggregates that measure "growth" with the more general notion of "development" is that, paraphrasing a remark of Friedrich Hayek's in a different but not unrelated context, the aggregates "conceal the most fundamental mechanisms of change."[26] In the Smithian tradition, economic development was seen as the progressive extension of the division of labor (and the extent of the market), along with the emergence of institutional arrangements that would both facilitate that evolution and respond to the new practices and structures that it produced. For example, the focus on aggregates made it difficult to see how investment expenditures were or were not producing a structure of capital that was sustainable and that could actually produce consumer goods that added to well-being, not to mention whether the existing political and economic institutions were capable of generating a sustainable capital structure. The generation of such a structure was emphatically not an engineering problem of maximizing K against constraints, as Hayek attempted to argue in that same response to Keynes.

In addition, in many places in the developing world, the aggregates concealed the fact that many of the resources counted in official GDP figures were actually diverted to the more narrow well-being of the political class. The classic picture of the gleaming third world capital surrounded by extreme poverty symbolizes that concern. The understanding of development that pervaded the twentieth

---

25. Peter J. Boettke, *Why Perestroika Failed: The Politics and Economics of Socialist Transformation* (New York: Routledge, 1993), 35–36.
26. F.A. Hayek, "Reflections on the Pure Theory of Money of Mr. J.M. Keynes," in Hayek, *The Collected Works of F. A. Hayek*, edited by Bruce Caldwell, vol. 9 (1931; repr., Chicago: University of Chicago Press, 1995), 128.

century could easily be blind to those differentials and their underpinnings in the particular political and economic institutions in these countries. These concerns were especially noteworthy with respect to the role of aid from the West. Even where aid made up a very small portion of GDP, it was often a substantial portion of government revenues, which in turn frequently benefited government officials rather than those in need of assistance.[27] All of this emphasis on measurement and aggregates distracted attention from the institutional concerns of the Smithian vision.

The data on the effects of development planning in the non-Soviet world bear out these concerns. In India, over 40 years of development planning leading up to the early 1990s had left India's per capita income at around $300, with approximately 40 percent of the population living below the poverty line. Because population grew significantly over that period, the lack of growth meant an increase in the absolute number of Indians below the poverty line during the peak decades of development planning.[28] The story in Africa was similar, with the continent's annual GNP growth rate from 1965 to 1986 averaging 0.9 percent. Put against rising population, this meant a decline in per capita GNP of about 14.6 percent for sub-Saharan Africa. In addition, food production per person "fell by 7 percent in the 1960s, 15 percent in the 1970s, and continued to deteriorate in the 1980s."[29] As George Ayittey also notes, the grandiose plans of African governments were expected to be paid for by "huge surpluses in the rural sector."[30] This is a good example of the borrowing of the failed Soviet model by postcolonial planners.

A story that remains untold in the evolution of theories of economic development is the role of Western universities as the intellectual conduit from the Soviet model and early Keynesian models to development planning in the third world. Many of the postcolonial leaders, as well as the civil servants who

27. David Osterfeld, *Prosperity versus Planning: How Government Stifles Economic Growth* (New York: Oxford University Press, 1992), 150–51.
28. Shyam Kamath, "The Failure of Development Planning in India," in *The Collapse of Development Planning*, edited by Peter J. Boettke (New York: New York University Press, 1994), 91.
29. George Ayittey, "The Failure of Development Planning in Africa," in *The Collapse of Development Planning*, edited by Peter J. Boettke (New York: New York University Press, 1994), 155.
30. Ayittey, "Failure," 162.

staffed the planning bureaucracy, were educated in Western universities during the 1950s and 1960s when Keynesianism and the related growth models were the mainstream of economic thinking. Some postcolonial leaders were also trained in the Marxist tradition, which was also reasonably alive and well in the universities, but even those who pursued advanced degrees in economics at top-flight universities came away with a set of beliefs about what produced development which included doctrines that would later be shown to be, at the very least, inadequate and, more often, destructive. It was through these institutions that the economist as savior moved from the first world to the third world. Where Western doctrines were translated into guidance for development in the South and East, the economist, with the engineering tools of science at hand, was easily seen as the savior. The ways in which many students from the third world of that era, and still today, imagine themselves using their Western educations to return home and solve the problems of their native lands reflect this marriage of activist government and the economist as savior-cum-engineer. The intellectual environment and economics' self-understanding enabled these engineers to practice their trade on their home countries. The Western universities continue to be an intellectual conduit for policymaking in the third world, but as economic thought has evolved on these questions, Western-trained economists are now more critical of planning-based approaches and have turned more attention to the institutional environment.

A Return to Humility?

At the close of the twentieth century, a coincidence of three empirical facts of political economy worldwide forced economists and public policymakers to rethink the underlying engineering vision of economic policy. The three empirical facts were (1) the breakdown of the Keynesian consensus on macroeconomic policy, (2) the collapse of state communism in Eastern and Central Europe, and (3) the frustration with foreign-aid programs in less-developed countries.[31] At

---

31. See, respectively, James M. Buchanan and Richard Wagner, *Democracy in Deficit: The Political Legacy of Lord Keynes*, in Buchanan, *The Collected Works of James M. Buchanan*, vol. 8 (1977; repr., Indianapolis, IN: Liberty Fund, 2000); Boettke, *Why Perestroika*; William Easterly, *The Elusive Quest for Growth: Economists' Adventures and Misadventures in the Tropics* (Cambridge, MA: MIT Press, 2001).

the same time that these facts came to be increasingly recognized by scholars, policymakers, and the public, economic scholarship had undergone a transformation. While new Keynesian economics, information economics, and game theory came to be part of the toolkit of modern economics, so did rational expectations theory and new classical macroeconomics, the Chicago school of law and economics, the Chicago new learning in industrial organization, the Washington and UCLA schools of property rights economics, Schumpeterian evolutionary economics, the market process of economics of the Austrians as well as neo-Marshallian industrial organization, and public choice theory of political economy. Many of these scholarly developments in economics eventually would go under the banner of new institutionalism in economics, political science, and sociology.

One could argue that the breakdown of Keynesianism led to a reemergence of laissez-faire policy in economic debates, and the transition experience in the wake of the collapse of communism led to the focus on the vital role of institutions. Unlike the nineteenth-century critics of laissez-faire, whose focus on institutions was an attempt to redesign them through the use of reason, the recent resurgence of interest in institutions reflects a return to the cautious respect of an earlier era. To some, a defense of laissez-faire and an emphasis on institutions would be at odds, given the belief that the institutionless approach of much of twentieth-century economics was also a defense of laissez-faire. But there is no conflict between laissez-faire policy prescriptions and an analytical emphasis on institutions, as demonstrated by the work of classical economists such as David Hume and Adam Smith as well as more modern economists such as F.A. Hayek and James Buchanan. It is not the laissez-faire tradition that ignored institutions, rather it was the engineering vision of economics that first thought it could transcend evolved institutions, then later saw institutions as irrelevant to a framework of optimization and equilibrium. Both engineering approaches effectively ruled out as "unscientific" serious discussion of the role of historically evolved institutions, and neither approach was one that unambiguously supported laissez-faire.[32]

---

32. In *Development, Geography, and Economic Theory* (Cambridge, MA: MIT Press, 1995), Paul Krugman argued that the resistance of mainstream economists to discuss ideas that defy immediate formalization often leads them to ignore ideas which in the end prove to be the most fundamental to solving the pressing problems of economic policy. Krugman

Only the very sterile engineering version of economics could ignore the crucial role of institutions or could imagine that the transition problem or the economics of underdevelopment could be boiled down to a prescription for getting the prices right. Of course, allowing prices to float freely to clear markets and guide producers and consumers in orienting their behavior to one another is necessary but not sufficient for development, as the ability to get the prices right is a function of the effective operation of a complex array of institutions such as those associated with the definition and enforcement of private property rights.[33]

Overviews of the role of institutions in economic development can be found in Ostrom et al. and Ahrens.[34] Although this work stresses our need to overcome the market-government dichotomy that reflected the ideological battle from the classical to neoclassical period, there should be no mistaking that the government's role in economic development has been severely restricted in comparison with the postwar policy consensus of government as a corrective to

---

uses the fields of both economic development and economic geography as examples to show how the obsession with formalization led to their decline as fields of research in the economics profession. The story of the rise and fall and rise again of development economics is a complicated one. But the fact, as Krugman points out, that the field defied formalization even by its top practitioners in a discipline where formalization was the sign of scientific advance played a significant role. It is important to note that in Krugman's analysis the reason for the difficulty in formalization was not related to the issues we have discussed, but instead technical—the difficulty of squaring economies of scale with models of perfect competition. In fact, what Krugman argues in these lectures is that a new class of models that have challenged the competitive market structure model is now able to absorb in a rigorous way the ideas of economies of scale and economic geography. Ideas that defied formalization can now be taken off the shelf, dusted off, and incorporated into contemporary thinking in economics and public policy.

33. See the interesting note by Raghuram Rajan in "Assume Anarchy? Why an Orthodox Economic Model Might Not Be the Best Guide for Policy," *Finance & Development* 41, no. 3 (2004): 56–57. Rajan's argument is straightforward. The complete market model assumes that the institutional framework necessary for its operation is in place, whereas in the former socialist countries and in the less-developed world it is precisely the absence of this framework that must be addressed if a successful transition to a more peaceful and prosperous social order is to be achieved.

34. Elinor Ostrom et al., *Aid, Incentives and Sustainability: An Institutional Analysis of Development Cooperation* (Stockholm: Swedish International Development Cooperation Agency, 2002); J. Ahrens, *Governance and Economic Development: A Comparative Institutional Approach* (Cheltenham, UK: Edward Elgar Publishing, 2002).

the social ills that result from market failures.[35] The quality of the institutions of governance (both the private and public devices in operation in a society for warding off predation) determine the capacity of a society to realize the gains from specialization and exchange and stimulate the long-term investment behavior that leads to wealth creation. As Mancur Olson summarizes the point:

> Though low-income societies obtain most of the gains from trade from self-enforcing trades, they do not realize many of the largest gains from specialization and trade. They do not have the institutions that enforce contracts impartially, and so they lose most of the gains from those transactions (like those in the capital market) that require impartial third-party enforcement. They do not have the institutions that make property rights secure over the long run, so they lose the gains from capital-intensive production. Production and trade in these societies is further handicapped by misguided economic policies and by private and public predation. The intricate social cooperation that emerges when there is a sophisticated array of markets requires far better institutions and economic policies than most countries have.[36]

The most drastic change in modern economic thought is in fact the emphasis now placed on the study of the institutions (rules of the game and their enforcement) required to realize the intricate social cooperation of an advanced market economy. This requires not just economic and financial institutions but also political, legal, and social institutions that serve to align incentives and use and communicate information effectively so that millions of individuals can coordinate their affairs. Without the effective operation of these institutions that afford complex coordination, individuals will not generate the material standards of living that are prerequisites for human flourishing.

---

35. As we have stressed, the classical economists did not subscribe to this dichotomy either, so while people characterize their position as representative of this dichotomy, this is actually a false depiction. However, the neoclassical synthesis did speak in terms of this dichotomy and in particular by stressing market failure and government correctives to questions of insufficient aggregate demand, unemployment equilibrium, capital market instability, and underdevelopment.

36. Mancur Olson, "Big Bills Left on the Sidewalk: Why Some Nations Are Rich, and Others Poor," *Journal of Economic Perspectives* 10, no. 2 (1996): 22.

The dilemma of underdevelopment is that while there are many different ways for individuals to live their lives, there are few ways that they can live prosperously. For generalized societal prosperity to be realized, an alignment of cultural norms, formal legal rules, and economic organizations must occur. Absent this alignment of informal and formal rules and organizations, generalized prosperity will go unrealized.

Whether the state plays a positive role in this alignment is unimportant for our present purpose. What matters for the metadiscussion of the vision of the state in economic development is that under this configuration the state is not an active player entrusted to correct social ills, and economists are not engineers putting that vision into practice under the guise of science. That vision of the state is consistent with another era of economic thinking and policy. Rather than a focus on the state's role in correcting market failures, the focus is now on the governing capacity of an array of private and public institutions that are entrusted to ward off predation by either private opportunists or public exploiters. Overcoming poverty is not a consequence of the state closing an investment gap or fixing human capital shortfalls in a society, let alone population control through contraceptive education.

The state's role has indeed withered away and with it, perhaps, will wither the role of the economist. Vernon Smith has characterized the visionary implications of the new thinking in economics that emerges from both experimental research and the analytical focus on institutions as a transformation from "constructivist rationality" to "ecological rationality."[37] In the field of development economics, this is a move from the government directly orchestrating economic activity to providing the fertile conditions for bottom-up development. This represents a swing back toward the more humble self-understanding of what economics can contribute, in that the role of the economic policymaker moves from engineering economic development to cultivating economic development. As a result, the savior moves back to the frustrated engineer, and more room opens up for the student to play the role of cautionary prophet and have that role respected. Furthermore, the fact that the move back toward humility can be defended on the basis of better scientific knowledge about the workings of

---

37. Vernon Smith, "Constructivist and Ecological Rationality in Economics," *American Economic Review* 93, no. 3 (2003): 465–508.

the human brain[38] gives, ironically, the cautionary prophet newfound scientific legitimacy and makes the savior-cum-engineer seem somewhat unscientific.[39]

With the swing back toward humility in the discipline, the economist as student is perhaps in the ascendance, and the debate over the economic role of the state in economic development has come full circle. We are back again to Smith's admonition that "little else is requisite to carry a state to the highest degree of opulence from the lowest barbarism, but peace, easy taxes and a tolerable administration of justice; all the rest being brought about by the natural course of things." An emphasis on how actors make choices in alternative institutional contexts also pushes the economist away from being the savior-cum-engineer and back toward being the student-cum-cautionary prophet: humble in the face of processes that economists did not design and cannot control.

---

38. See, e.g., F.A. Hayek, *The Sensory Order* (Chicago: University of Chicago Press, 1952).
39. This view is consistent with the argument Bruce Caldwell (*Hayek's Challenge: An Intellectual Biography of F.A. Hayek* (Chicago: University of Chicago Press, 2004)) makes about Hayek's contribution. Hayek's work on the philosophy of mind provided a scientifically based critique of scientism.

21

High Priests and Lowly Philosophers

Do not pry into things too hard for you
Or investigate what is beyond your each.
Many have been led astray by their theorizing,
And evil imaginings have impaired their judgments.
Stubbornness will come to a bad end,
And he who flirts with danger will lose his life.
When calamity befalls the arrogant, there is no cure;
Wickedness is too deeply rooted in them.

—Ecclesiastes 3:21, 24–26, 28

Introduction

IN HIS BOOK, *Reaching for Heaven on Earth*,[1] Robert Nelson established that modern economics had indeed taken on a theological significance that was denied from other social sciences and policy-relevant disciplines. This claim is worthy of serious attention, but Nelson's route to this conclusion is interesting in its own right. In writing about the role of economists in government, Nelson argued that economists do not limit their advice to technical expertise. Instead, they use their positions as economic advisors to strongly advocate particular programs. In short, they do not just discuss the means-ends efficiency of a proposed policy independent of their own value assessment of that policy but rather infuse their economic advice-giving with their own values. The economic way of thinking is a powerful tool for organizing and

---

1. Robert H. Nelson, *Reaching for Heaven on Earth* (Lanham, MD: Rowman & Littlefield, 1991).

interpreting events and may well be value-neutral; but economists as advisors are definitely not value-neutral.

This conclusion led Nelson to ponder why it is then that economists are given a privileged position in the policy arena. Why are other disciplines that also provide a useful framework for thinking about important problems not afforded the same public hearing on issues of public policy? Nelson reasoned that since the economic way of thinking provides a way for us to understand and legitimate our modern world, perhaps economics has become the modern theology that has replaced traditional theology as the set of doctrines that give meaning to our social reality and hope to our endeavors for improving our lives. At least that is what Nelson sought to explore in *Reaching for Heaven on Earth*, and to amazing effect. Since economic progress was seen as the solution to social ills, the discipline of economics is awarded a special status as the harbinger of progress and its practitioners are transformed from lowly philosophers, who only study the world, to high priests of social control, who are responsible for ushering in an age of unlimited progress and prosperity.[2]

In *Economics as Religion*,[3] Robert Nelson develops this line of argument even further and explores the theological underpinnings of such economic luminaries as Frank Knight and Paul Samuelson. The history of twentieth-century economics, in fact, could be read as how it came to be that Knight's Calvinistic economics was rejected in favor of Samuelson's secular religion of

---

2. Nelson's work should not be read as an indictment of economics in the least. All that he is attempting to show is that economists do not practice a form of value-free analysis, and, in fact, cannot practice value-freedom when they offer policy guidance. Moreover, rather than a flippant critique of economics, Nelson actually engaged in historical research to demonstrate that many of the founders of political economy and economics had deep theological commitments. They used the intellectual constructs from their theology to construct their economics, and they spoke of the discipline of economics itself and its policy advice in messianic terms. For a discussion of the relationship between value-neutral economics and value-relevant political economy, see Peter J. Boettke, "Is Economics a Moral Science?" *Journal of Markets & Morality* 1, no. 2 (1998): 212–19 (arguing that economists can provide value-relevant knowledge grounded in value-neutral analysis); Peter Boettke, "Why Are There No Austrian Socialists? Ideology, Science and the Austrian School," *Journal of the History of Economic Thought* 17 (1995): 35–56.

3. Robert H. Nelson, *Economics as Religion: From Samuelson to Chicago and Beyond* (University Park: Penn State University Press, 2002).

scientific management.[4] In fact, Nelson[5] demonstrates how Samuelson's claims to scientific value-freedom are merely rhetorical flourish. Instead, Samuelson's ideas are the logical outgrowth of the intellectual movement of American Progressivism in which government, in seeking to create the Kingdom of God on earth, must act as a corrective to social ills, such as unemployment, and plan the social order. Guided by the teachings of scientific management, the practice of public administration promised not just efficiency in public affairs but to be morally uplifting as well. Thus, the liberal state would be transformed by science to become the administrative state with the goal of eradicating social ills. Samuelson, according to Nelson, must be seen as providing the "scientific blessing for the American welfare and regulatory state."[6]

Building on Nelson's analysis, we contend that the transformation of economics from a discipline that studies the economy to one that is entrusted with its control has threatened the very "soul" of economics. The false pretense of scientific management led economists to promise to accomplish tasks that they cannot legitimately achieve. False theory combined with bad philosophy generated scientific claims that must now be rejected. But this does not mean that economics as a way of thinking about the world and organizing its facts must be rejected. Quite to the contrary, the teachings of economics are necessary for understanding the complexities of social reality. Perhaps its two most important public roles are (1) to explain how within a specific set of institutional arrangements the power of self-interest can spontaneously generate patterns of social order that simultaneously achieve individual autonomy, generalized prosperity, and social peace; and (2) through means-ends analysis, to provide parameters

---

4. Despite his severe criticism of religion, Knight could not escape his background in Christian thought. For Knight, as in earlier Christian theology, private property and the market economy exist because of original sin. Prior to the fall of man neither would be necessary and thus in an ideal world they would not exist either. But in the imperfect world we live in, property and markets serve to counter the natural proclivity of fallen man to strive for power and advantage over other men. Property and markets may be an imperfect solution, but they are better than the alternatives. See Nelson, *Economics,* 136–137.

5. Nelson, *Economics,* 37–48.

6. Nelson, *Economics,* 263.

on people's utopian notions of economic policy.[7] The first captures the didactic role of the economist in teaching the nuances of Adam Smith's "invisible hand" and the second captures the contribution that economics as a technical discipline can offer to public policy discourse. When economists move beyond these roles and instead try to employ economics as the primary tool for social control, they run afoul and distort the teachings of the discipline.

We provide three cases in which the scientistic pretensions of economists got the better of them in the twentieth century: Keynesian demand management, the practice of cost-benefit analysis by regulators and lawyers, and the debate over market socialism. If our argument is right the role of the economist should move from high priest back to lowly philosopher. In taking this "demotion," economists may find it harder to justify their employment, but the discipline and those who practice it will also regain their "soul" as they reject the false god of scientism and its pretensions of social engineering.

Keynesian Demand Management

There has always been a subculture in the discipline of political economy that argued that the practitioner of political economy could be entrusted to devise schemes of social control that would outperform the "accidental" outcomes of laissez-faire. Thomas Malthus and J.B. Say exchanged words in the early nineteenth century over whether or not a market economy would generate "gluts" or whether the market is a self-regulating mechanism that would tend toward equilibrium when aggregate supply and aggregate demand are equated.[8] The majority of economists sided with Say and maintained that this self-regulating

---

7. See James M. Buchanan, "Economics as a Public Science," in Buchanan, *The Collected Works of James M. Buchanan,* vol. 12 (1996; repr., Indianapolis, IN: Liberty Fund, 2000). Buchanan argues that the task of economics as a public science is to provide an understanding of the workings of an organized economy to citizens and the consequences of alternative interventions into that working economy so that these citizens can be informed participants in the democratic process. In Buchanan's way of thinking, economists must differentiate between the analysis of what is, what could be, and what ought to be in performing their task of providing citizens with the information required to make intelligent democratic decisions.
8. The letters from J.B. Say to Malthus were collected and published in 1821: Jean Baptiste Say, *Letters to Mr. Malthus* (1821, repr., New York: Augustus M. Kelley, 1967).

aspect of a market economy was one of the most powerful principles taught by the discipline of economics. Nevertheless, the debate over self-regulation did not cease. Karl Marx's writings on the inherent tendency of the capitalist system to lead to monopoly on the one hand, and suffer periodic crises on the other, were direct challenges to the vulgar teachings of political economy that taught self-regulation.

By the late nineteenth century, laissez-faire was increasingly under attack as both a scientific and public policy doctrine. J.S. Mill may have given theoretical presumption to the laissez-faire principle, but the exceptions to that principle that he articulated, which called for direct government action, were vast.[9] Political careers were built on the claim that monopoly power needed to be reined in and that business fluctuations had to be controlled through public policy. In the United States, antitrust legislation was introduced along with the establishment of the institutions of public administration to oversee the implementation and enforcement of this legislation. The banking system was also transformed in an effort to eliminate "panics."

By the beginning of the twentieth century, the dominant school of economic thinking in the United States was critical of the unrealistic political economy of classical economics. This school advocated an institutional economics that denied any universal laws of economics and demanded a more activist government to regulate and control the economy and promote efficiency and social justice. Of course, there were pockets of defenders of classical political economy, and even more practitioners of the new science of neoclassical economics; but the Progressive era marshaled in the intellectual domination of the institutional school of economic thought. This domination was not limited to the teachings of economics, but permeated law schools and the budding discipline of public administration.

When the Great Crash of 1929 turned into the Great Depression of the 1930s, the remaining voices for laissez-faire were silenced. Economists who had held the classical position were either ignored or they changed their song to be more in tune with the times. Government had to do something to address social ills. Of course, some economic research argued that the Great Depression was caused

---

9. John Stuart Mill, *Principles of Political Economy* (1848; repr., New York, NY: Augustus M. Kelley, 1976), 941–79.

by government policy failures—a credit expansion of the 1920s generated a boom-bust cycle, and government interventions in the 1930s (most notably trade restrictions) hampered the ability of the market adjustment process to work to eliminate the crisis; but this message was ignored. Instead, the message that resonated with policymakers, the public, and a new generation of economists was that laissez-faire capitalism was prone to monopoly and business cycles as revealed in the "Robber Baron" age, the fraud perpetrated on consumers by poor products, the exploitation of workers in factories, and the indignity of unemployment as experienced in the 1930s. It was the job of the economists to address these social ills with the tools of the discipline and the expertise of public administration.

Keynesian economics filled this demand perfectly. John Maynard Keynes' work, *The General Theory of Employment, Interest, and Money*,[10] provided a critique of the classical model of self-regulation of markets, a diagnosis of why the economies of Great Britain and the United States had entered a depression, and policy advice on how to alleviate the problems of unemployment and instability. For the sake of this discussion, what matters most are the general ideas behind this promise; Keynes argued that investment was unstable because it was based on the volatile expectations of investors and their moods of optimism and pessimism.

In addition, Keynes argued that the introduction of money into an economic system repudiated the classical law of markets that maintained self-regulation. Prices were not linked to the supply and demand for money any more than investment was determined by the interest rate in the modern economy, according to Keynes. The introduction of expectations into economic analysis ruptures the old relationships that were established in classical economics. For example, during a recession, because of expectations that the economy is caught in a liquidity trap, attempts to get out of that trap through a monetary policy stimulus will be ineffective. If investment is not rational, but instead based on "animal spirits," then private markets cannot be relied upon to assess the marginal efficiency of capital allocations among competing projects. Finally, in the

---

10. John M. Keynes, *The General Theory of Employment, Interest, and Money* (1936; Repr., New York: Harcourt, Brace & Jovanovich, 1964).

economy so described by Keynes, resources can remain idle and not be reemployed in alternative uses. The automatic adjustments that classical economics assumed do not come into operation because the economy can get stuck in an unemployment equilibrium. By definition, equilibrium is a point where no one in the system has any incentive or inclination to move from his or her current position. To move out of that equilibrium, a force outside the system must be introduced. Keynes forcefully argued that government was the entity that could most effectively affect social change.

As Roger Garrison has argued, Keynesian economics is the income-expenditure Keynesianism of basic textbook economics.[11] This simple model served as the basic tool for understanding Keynesian public policy for a generation of economists, and it was a staple of Samuelson's presentation in his *Economics*.[12] In fact, the Keynesian shift from analytical perspective to social philosophy is embodied in Samuelson's classic textbook. In the 1948 edition, for example, Samuelson does not introduce basic supply and demand until page 447[13] precisely because of the notion that microeconomic principles only become effective after one has ensured that the macroeconomic system is in balance. Left to its own devices, the capitalist system will suffer from aggregate demand failure and results in an unemployment equilibrium. It is the economist's task to engineer this full employment equilibrium, at which point the self-regulating tendencies of a market economy may be relied upon in situations in which externalities are absent, production and exchange is limited to private goods (and not public goods), and the market structure is deemed competitive.

For our story, the significant point to recognize is how Keynes's *General Theory* and later Samuelson's *Economics* reverse the presumption of Mill's *Principles*. With Mill, the presumption was still with laissez-faire and the exceptions he enumerated justify the interventions of government into the economy. But by the time we get to Keynes and then Samuelson, the presumption is that government must intervene at all times to maintain economic civilization and that only in certain circumstances could the laissez-faire principle be relied

11. Roger Garrison, *Time and Money: The Macroeconomics of Capital Structure* (New York: Routledge, 2000).

12. Paul A. Samuelson, *Economics,* 1st ed. (New York: McGraw-Hill, 1948), 225–79.

13. Samuelson, *Economics,* 447.

upon.[14] In addition, it is important to realize the changing role of economists that this shift in presumption requires. At the time of Mill, the economist could still take the stance of student of society, but by the time we get to Keynes and Samuelson the economist's task is to assume the role of society's savior using the scientific tools of the craft to maintain societal balance and right social wrongs.[15] "Where the complex economic conditions of life necessitate social coordination and planning," Samuelson wrote, "there can sensible men of good will be expected to invoke the authority and creative activity of government."[16]

---

14. To put a fine point on this, Samuelson wrote:

> No longer is modern man able to believe "that government governs best which governs least." In a frontier society, when a man moved farther west as soon as he could hear the bark of his neighbor's dog, there was some validity to the view "let every man paddle his own canoe." But today, in our vast interdependent society, the waters are too crowded to make unadulterated "rugged individualism" tolerable. (*Economics*, 152)

Samuelson, in the next paragraph, admits that this system of "rugged individualism" led to rapid material progress, but he quickly adds that it also resulted in business cycles, the wasteful exhaustion of resources, income inequality, political corruption by moneyed interests, and the substitution of "self-regulating competition in favor of all-consuming monopoly." *Id.*

15. For an examination of the economist and the economic role of the state, see Peter Boettke and Steve Horwitz, "The Limits of Economic Expertise," Annual supplement, *History of Political Economy* 37 (2005): 10–39. Though different terms are employed in this article, the basic idea is that there are only two stable intellectual equilibria: (1) economist as student and state as referee of the economic game and (2) economist as savior and state as active player in the economic game. The classical argument preached humility to economists and sought to constrain the abuse of power by the state and its agents; the modern argument preached activism and the need for agents of the state to use the power of the government to actively intervene on behalf of the people. The classical argument warned of the perversity of unintended consequences in government interventions, whereas the modern argument warned of the perversity of voluntary choice due to monopoly, externalities, public goods, and macroeconomic instability. The classical argument tended to push us to the student/referee equilibrium, while the modern argument tended to push us to the savior/player equilibrium. The puzzle for a contemporary of political economy that finds the humility argument of the classics persuasive is whether an argument that satisfies the modern mind can be made that leads to the student/referee equilibrium. This intellectual puzzle is separate from the material self-interest puzzle of how one would get economists to give up on an argument that privileges them in the public policy discourse.

16. Samuelson, *Economics*, 153.

Ludwig von Mises and F.A. Hayek were two of the strongest critics of this Keynesian transformation of the discipline of economics. Mises tended to stress the logical fallacies committed by Keynesian economics,[17] whereas Hayek tended to stress the heroic assumptions made on behalf of economists put in the position of engineering social change through macroeconomic modeling.[18] For the income-expenditure model to work, the economist-engineer must know the aggregate level of current consumption, investment, and public spending, as well as what the full employment level of output would be. He or she must also know the precise manner in which the multiplier effect will work to translate an increase in government expenditures into an increase in aggregate demand to achieve that full employment level of output. Each step of the analysis presupposes that the detailed knowledge of economic life is readily available to the macroeconomist and that each policy step advocated will result in the precise effect on economic activity that is intended to achieve economic balance at full employment levels. In short, the model assumes what it has to prove.

Moreover, macroeconomic theories tended to mask the real economic data that human actors use in forming their economic plans. Macroeconomic public policy is both mistaken and arrogant. Hayek argued that the "pretense of knowledge" evident in macroeconomic modeling resulted not in the solution of social ills, such as unemployment, but instead in a pattern of resource employment that cannot be maintained. As Hayek stated:

> What this policy has produced is not so much a level of employment that could not have been brought about in other ways, as a distribution of employment which cannot be indefinitely maintained and which after some time can be maintained only by a rate of inflation which would rapidly lead to a disorganization of all economic activity.[19]

The collapse of the Keynesian hegemony in the 1970s reflected the intellectual victory of Hayek's critique of Keynes. Most economists, however, have not followed Hayek's plea for humility and the attempt to understand economic

---

17. Ludwig von Mises, *Human Action: A Treatise on Economics* (1949; repr., Indianapolis, IN: Liberty Fund, 2010), 710–803.
18. F.A. Hayek, *New Studies in Philosophy, Politics, Economics and the History of Ideas* (Chicago: University of Chicago Press, 1978), 98–100.
19. Hayek, *New Studies*, 29.

life in aggregate terms continues. The resurrection of Keynesian economics in the hands of Joseph Stiglitz[20] and Paul Krugman[21] requires the same heroic assumptions about the power of economists to fine-tune the world with the levers of economic policy that was evident in the Keynes/Samuelson era, despite subtle shifts in the theoretical argument. As Robert Nelson indicated, Stiglitz has pointed out that the theoretical underpinnings of Samuelson's economics contained fundamental misconceptions that are now well understood.[22] But Samuelson's work established the scientific status of economics in American society and provided many economists with government jobs in which they could use their scientific authority to influence public policy.

Even though Stiglitz understands the faulty foundations of Samuelsonian economics, he does not suggest that the revolution of information economics that he led, or the institutional economics associated with Coase and North, or the public choice revolution led by Buchanan and Tullock, should lead to a questioning of the position of economists in society that Samuelson's work established. If anything, Stiglitz believes that his contribution to modern economics has justified the role of the economists in society as redefined by Keynes and Samuelson even more so than in their own writings. The faith in the saving power of public administration guided by economic models does not die easily.

Cost-Benefit Analysis

The new economics as embodied in Samuelson, was predicated on the following three propositions:

1. The laissez-faire presumption has been reversed by the economics of Keynes and the development of economics since Keynes.
2. Modern economics has provided the analytical toolkit for economists to assume the role of scientist cum social engineer.
3. The analytical toolkit of modern economics is aided by new statistical measuring techniques that guarantee that abstract mathematical economic models can be accurately calibrated, generate clear predictions,

---

20. Joseph Stiglitz, *Globalization and Its Discontents* (New York: Norton, 2002).
21. Paul Krugman, *The Return of Depression Economics* (New York: Norton, 1999).
22. See Nelson, *Economics*, at 261.

be cleanly tested against the data, and thus provide the basis for successful economic policy initiatives.

In order for these propositions to work, we must assume that objective data exists and can be collected and analyzed in an economical manner. Obviously the development of computing power in the twentieth century had a major influence on the manner in which economics is done, but that is not the side of the story we want to emphasize. The point we want to highlight is more subtle; economists have to assume that certain data exist for them to manipulate, which we contend does not in fact exist.[23] In the case this section analyzes, the data assumed is the objectivity of costs and benefits.

Cost-benefit analysis permeates the field of public economics. It is not only the cornerstone of analyses of externalities, but also analyses of taxation, regulation, and alternative legal arrangements. The modern field of law and economics, for example, would be unrecognizable if cost-benefit analysis were rejected.

Conceptually, the economic way of thinking has no problem with the logic of cost-benefit analysis. The problem is when one tries to operationalize the analysis by assuming that costs and benefits are quantifiable entities that can

---

23. This is true for macroeconomics as well as the microeconomic questions we are going to address in this section. Gross domestic product, for example, attempts to measure the value produced in an economy in a given year by adding up the final good prices. There are sophisticated attempts made to avoid double counting, etc., but the entire enterprise faces an even more daunting problem. In order for the addition of these final good prices to have any meaning, the analyst must assume they are in fact the equilibrium prices that reflect the full opportunity cost of production for each good. But that would be true only if the conditions of general competitive equilibrium held true. First, the conditions of general competitive equilibrium are highly restrictive and one could argue that they are never approximated in the real world. Second, if the conditions of general competitive equilibrium were said to hold true, then the sort of policy designs advocated by the Keynesian macroeconomist would be redundant, as the ideal equilibrium allocation of scarce resources would already be obtained. In short, by definition, the sort of idle resource argument of Keynesians presupposes the absence of general competitive equilibrium. If that is the case then the price data would not be able to be added in any meaningful sense to provide the basis for public policy decisions. To get meaningful data, the Keynesian economist has to assume the existence of data, which, if it did exist, would mean that Keynesian policy solutions are unnecessary. The fact that in the face of such a logical conundrum the Keynesian ascendancy occurred almost unchallenged demonstrates Nelson's point about the victory of faith over reason in modern political economy, and how once ideas and interests align how difficult it is to overturn a belief system.

be measured and compared. In standard Pigouvian welfare economics, deviations from the ideal allocation of resources result because of external economies. Private marginal benefits/marginal costs deviate from the social marginal benefits/marginal costs. A positive externality is said to lead to an undersupply of the good or service in question because the private marginal benefits from producing the good or service are less than the social marginal benefits it would produce. A negative externality generates the opposite problem. Undesirable goods and services are supplied beyond their ideal level because the private marginal costs of producing the good or service is less than the social marginal costs the good or service generates. In the standard drill, in the case of positive externalities, the government should subsidize the production of the good and service so as to bring the private and social costs into alignment; whereas in the case of negative externalities, the government should tax the activity so as to again bring about the alignment of private and social costs. Conceptually, the logic of this approach is unassailable; but as a tool for public policy, it is about as misguided as one could get and it has done tremendous damage to the way that economic discourses of public policy issues are conducted.[24] Ronald Coase[25] and James Buchanan[26] pointed out the fundamental problems with Pigouvian welfare economics long ago. Their work was revolutionary, but the most radical implications of their work were ignored in subsequent years as the culture of economics became deeply committed to the analysis and measurement of data. Science, after all, is measurement, as everyone likes to say. And if you cannot

---

24. The economic policy "think tank" world is divided into promarket and antimarket forces and the dialogue between them is one of warring cost-benefit analyses. The promarket groups show that the costs of this or that intervention will exceed the benefits and this is usually communicated by the cost to the average family of four. The antimarket forces, not to be outdone, respond by providing "evidence" that an unhampered market economy will generate costs to average citizens well in excess of the benefits generated in the market. This is the way the discourse proceeds, but neither of them actually has the data to make the argument they want to make, so they make assumptions and guess. At best, what we get is ideological commitments wrapped in numbers and disguised in the trappings of science. At worst, all we get is the manipulations by vested interests to achieve their political goals at the expense of others.

25. Ronald Coase, "The Problem of Social Cost," *Journal of Law & Economics* 3, no. 1 (1960): 1–44.

26. James M. Buchanan, *Cost and Choice*, in Buchanan, *Collected Works*, vol. 6.

measure, measure anyway rather than threaten the scientific stature of a discipline. So despite the profound insights of Coase and Buchanan, cost-benefit analysis is far from being abandoned by practitioners of political economy—many of whom actually profess allegiance to Coase and Buchanan.

The Coase/Buchanan critique of Pigou can be summarized in the following manner. Either Pigouvian solutions are redundant because private actors would negotiate away the conflicts (in the case of zero transaction costs), or the Pigouvian solution is nonoperational (in the case of positive transaction costs, including information costs). If private actors are unable to glean the costs and benefits and bring them into alignment, then how are government officials to do so? Rather than measure that which we cannot reasonably assume we can measure, both Coase and Buchanan advocate an opportunity cost approach to public economics. The comparative institutional analysis that such an approach leads to would, as Coase put it, "start our analysis with a situation approximating that which actually exists, to examine the effects of a proposed policy change and to attempt to decide whether the new situation would be, in total, better or worse than the original one."[27]

The blackboard economics of Pigou, caught as it is in the logical contradiction of being either redundant or nonoperational, remains hard to abandon.[28] William Baumol, for example, vehemently resisted the implications of Coase and Buchanan and argued that the Pigouvian tradition was "impeccable" even while admitting that "all in all, we are left with little reason for confidence in the applicability of the Pigouvian approach, literally interpreted. We do not know how to calculate the required taxes and subsidies and we do not know how to approximate them by trial and error."[29] Baumol's intellectual dance led Coase to pen one of the most stinging indictments of modern economics when, after summing up Baumol's position that the logic of the Pigouvian approach was "impeccable" if by "impeccable" one meant that "if its taxation proposals were carried out, which they cannot be, the allocation of resources would be

---

27. Coase, "Problem," at 23.

28. See Ronald Coase, *The Firm, the Market and the Law* (Chicago: University of Chicago Press, 1988), 157–85 (elaborating further on the contradiction of Pigouvian welfare economics).

29. William J. Baumol, "On Taxation and the Control of Externalities," *American Economic Review* 62 (1972): 307, 318.

optimal."[30] Coase added: "This I have never denied. My point was simply that such tax proposals are the stuff that dreams are made of. In my youth it was said that what was too silly to be said may be sung. In modern economics it may be put into mathematics."[31]

The Debate over Market Socialism

The debate over market socialism in the first half of the twentieth century provides another stark example in which economists let pretensions of scientism get the better of them. In the years leading up to 1920, Friedrich von Wieser, Joseph Schumpeter, Leon Walras, Vilfredo Pareto, Enrico Barone, Fredrick Taylor, and Frank Knight all pointed out that if socialism was to rationalize production, it would have to succeed in satisfying the same formal requirements that capitalism was said to achieve under conditions of equilibrium.[32] In other words, if rationalization implied the most efficient use of resources, which is the meaning it would have to have, then socialist rationalization would need to satisfy the optimality conditions that are described using marginalist principles.

The Polish economist, Oskar Lange, rose to this challenge in 1936–1937 with a proposal for market socialism that not only satisfied the formal requirements of capitalism in general equilibrium but was argued to actually perform better than the market economy by wiping out monopoly and business cycles believed to plague real-world capitalism.[33] In deploying the formal similarity argument, Lange provided the following blueprint. First, allow a market for consumer goods and labor allocation. Second, put the productive sector into state hands but provide strict guidelines for production to firms. Namely, inform managers that they must price their output equal to marginal costs and produce that level of output that minimizes average costs. Adjustments can be made on a trial-

---

30. Coase, *The Firm*, 185.

31. Coase, *The Firm*, 185.

32. See, e.g., Peter J. Boettke, ed., *Socialism and the Market: The Socialist Calculation Debate Revisited*, vol. 4 (London: Routledge, 2000) (containing papers on this "formal similarity" argument and the subsequent attempts to develop a marginalist economics of socialism).

33. Oskar Lange, "On the Economic Theory of Socialism." In *On the Economic Theory of Socialism* (1936–1937, Repr., Minneapolis: University of Minnesota Press, 1938).

and-error basis, using inventory as the signal. The production guidelines will ensure that the full opportunity cost of production will be taken into account and that all least-cost technologies will be employed. In short, these production guidelines will assure productive efficiency is achieved even in a setting of state ownership of the means of production.

Lange went even further in his argument for socialism. Not only is socialism, by mimicking the efficiency conditions of capitalism, able to theoretically achieve the same level of efficient production as the market, but it would actually outperform capitalism by purging society of monopoly and business cycles that plague real-world capitalism. In the hands of Lange, neoclassical theory was to become a powerful tool of social control.

Hayek's response to Lange's model for market socialism was multipronged and attacked its informational assumptions rooted in the neoclassical model of general equilibrium.[34] First, Hayek argued that the models of market socialism proposed by Lange and others reflected a preoccupation with equilibrium. These models possessed no ability to discuss the necessary adaptations to changing conditions required in real economic life. The imputation of value to capital goods from consumer goods represented a classic case in point. Joseph Schumpeter had argued that once consumer goods were valued in the market (as they would be in Lange's model), a market for producer goods was unnecessary because we could impute the value of corresponding capital goods *ipso facto*.[35]

This "solution" was of course accurate in the model of general equilibrium in which there is a prereconciliation of plans (i.e., no false trades). Hayek's concern, however, was not with the model, but with how imputation actually takes place within the market process so that production plans come to be coordinated with consumer demands. This is not a trivial procedure and requires various market signals to guide entrepreneurs in their decision processes on the use of capital-good combinations in production projects. In a fundamental sense, Hayek was arguing that market socialism could not answer this problem by assuming it away. Of course, if we focus our analytical attention on the properties of a world in which all plans have already been fully coordinated (general

---

34. Hayek, *Individualism and Economic Order* (1948, Repr., Chicago: University of Chicago Press, 1996, 33–56, 77–91, 181–208).

35. Joseph Schumpeter, *Capitalism, Socialism, and Democracy* (New York: Harper Perennial, 2008, 167–231).

competitive equilibrium), then the process by which that coordination came about in the first place will not be highlighted.

This was Hayek's central point. Absent certain institutions and practices, the process that brings about the coordination of plans (including the imputation of value from consumer goods to producer goods) would not take place. Some alternative process would have to be relied upon for decision making concerning resources, and that process would by necessity be one that could not rely on the guides of private property incentives, relative price signals, and profit/loss accounting since the socialist project had explicitly abolished them. In other words, the ipso facto proposition of competitive equilibrium was irrelevant for the world outside of that state of equilibrium. The fact that leading neoclassical economists (like Knight and Schumpeter) had not recognized this elementary point demonstrated the havoc that a scientistic preoccupation with the state of equilibrium, as opposed to the process that tends to bring about equilibrium, can have on economics.

In Hayek's view, the problem with concentrating on a state of affairs as opposed to the process was not limited to assuming that which must be argued, but in directing attention away from how changing circumstances require adaptations on the part of participants. As we noted previously, equilibrium, by definition, is a state of affairs in which no agent within the system has any incentive to change. If all the data were frozen, then indeed the logic of the situation would lead individuals to a state of rest in which all plans were coordinated and resources were used in the most efficient manner currently known. The Lange conditions would hold—prices would be set to marginal cost (and thus the full opportunity cost of production would be reflected in the price) and production would be at the minimum point on the firm's average cost curve (and thus the least-cost technologies would be employed). But what, Hayek asked, do these conditions tell us about a world where the data are not frozen? What happens when tastes and technologies change?

Effective allocation of resources requires that there is a correspondence between the underlying conditions of tastes, technology, and resource endowments, and the induced variables of prices and profit-and-loss accounting. In perfect competition, the underlying variables and the induced variables are in perfect alignment and thus there are no coordination problems. Traditions in economic scholarship that reject the self-regulation proposition tend to deny that there is any correspondence between the underlying conditions and the induced variables on the market.

Hayek, in contrast to both of these alternatives, sought to explain the lagged relationship between the underlying and the induced. Economics for him is a discipline of tendency and direction, not a science of exact determination. Changes in the underlying conditions set in motion accommodating adjustments that are reflected in the induced variables on the market. The induced variables lag behind but are continually pulled toward the underlying conditions.

Hayek argued that perfect knowledge is a defining characteristic of equilibrium but cannot be an assumption within the process of equilibration. The question instead is how do individuals come to learn the information that is necessary for them to coordinate their plans with others? In "Economics and Knowledge" and "The Use of Knowledge in Society,"[36] Hayek develops the argument that how economic agents come to learn represents the crucial empirical element of economics and that price signals represent the key institutional guidepost for learning within the market process. Traditional neoclassical theory taught that prices were incentive devices, which they indeed are. But Hayek pointed out that prices also serve an informational role, which is overlooked by modern economists preoccupied with models of equilibrium.

Hayek emphasized different aspects of the argument developed in these two classic articles over his career and came to place particular emphasis on the contextual nature of knowledge that is utilized within the market process. Knowledge, he pointed out, does not exist disembodied from the context of its discovery and use. Economic participants base their actions on concrete knowledge within a particular time and place. This local knowledge that market participants utilize in orienting their actions is simply not abstract and objective and thus is incapable of being used by planners outside of that context to plan the large-scale organization of society.

---

36. F.A. Hayek, "Economics and Knowledge," in *Individualism and Economic Order* (1937; 1948; repr., Chicago: University Press of Chicago, 1980); Hayek, "The Use of Knowledge in Society," in *Individualism and Economic Order* (1944; repr., Chicago: University of Chicago Press, 1948), 33–56 and 77–91.

Hayek's reasoning for why planning cannot work is not limited to the problem that the information required to coordinate the plans of a multitude of individuals is too vast to organize effectively. The knowledge utilized within the market by entrepreneurs does not exist outside that local context and thus cannot even be organized in principle. It is not that planners would face a complex computational task; it is that they face an impossible task because the knowledge required is not accessible to them no matter what technological developments may come along to ease the computational task.

Market socialism requires a shift in the discipline of economics from understanding the workings of the economy to attempting to plan the economy. The scientific tools of neoclassical economics—most notably, general equilibrium—mislead socialists' proponents to believe they can effectively plan. Economists are no longer students of economy but become active players—engineers who plan economic activity. Of course, as both history and Hayek's work demonstrated, the position required by socialism is unsustainable in the long run. Hayek theoretically devastated the socialist program with the arguments discussed above. Most powerfully of all, however, the dramatic collapse of the Soviet Union at the beginning of the last decade revealed to the world the disaster brought by economic hubris on the part of those who believed they could centrally direct economic life.

Conclusion

Robert Nelson's *Economics as a Religion* is not only a fascinating read but also a profound work on the social role that economics has come to serve in modern times. As he writes:

The most vital religion of the modern age has been economic progress. If economists have had a modest impact in actually generating this progress, or even understanding the actual mechanisms by which it has occurred, they have had a large role in giving it social legitimacy. They have been the modern priesthood of the religion of progress, interpreting its forms, refining its messages, and assuring the faithful that progress would continue.[37]

---

37. Nelson, *Economics*, 329.

He goes on to state that we economists "like other priestly classes of history, live a secure and protected existence, often in the groves of the academy."[38]

Nelson limits his analysis mainly to the positive description of how economic growth has become the modern religion and economists its priestly guardians. We jump off from his profound analysis to look at the darker side of this transformation of our discipline. Using basic economic reasoning, we would expect a protected priestly class to respond rationally to the incentives and abuse of their privileged position and attempt to erect barriers to competitors. As economists, we ourselves are committed to the idea that economics as a discipline is vital to understanding the forces that shape our world. But we also believe that the priesthood status of our fellow economists has done severe damage to our discipline and in the long run will delegitimize the teachings that economics offers.[39]

We have focused on three areas in which economists in the twentieth century sought to justify an expanded role for economists as social engineers. In each instance, we have postulated that the argument given by economists was unjustified. Economics as a discipline would be better served by humility in the face of social complexity, rather than attempting to stretch the discipline beyond what it is capable of achieving. Our argument is simple: if we demand of a discipline something that it is incapable of doing, then intellectual resources will be wasted in the attempt to provide the unobtainable. Both type 1 and type 2 errors will be made in intellectual decision making as projects will be pursued that should have been rejected, and worthy projects will be foregone.

Can the situation of economics be reversed? We do not know. We know that if we argue that the situation is hopeless; we would in essence be admitting that the situation is ideal, as Frank Knight believed. On the other hand, we also recognize that change requires a bold intellectual entrepreneur to seize the opportunity and reorient the discipline. The reorientation we are calling for, however, is one that would reduce the prestige and power of the economists in modern society. Entrepreneurial action is usually not set in motion when the reward for the innovation is a reduction in relative status. On the other hand, we have argued that if economists give up their privileged position in society, they

---

38. Nelson, *Economics*, 332.

39. And this delegitimization will have huge negative consequences for society by clouding the understanding of the principle of spontaneous order and the means/ends analysis that places parameters on utopian aspirations by political entrepreneurs.

might regain their "soul." Perhaps the profit opportunity waiting to be seized by the economist-cum-intellectual entrepreneur is the long-term legitimacy of the discipline of political economy. In order to seize this legitimacy, the economist must forego the false promises of a pseudoscientific enterprise of modern economics with its belief in efficient public administration guided by the techniques of model and measure that have characterized economics since Samuelson. Such an economist might face the wrath of his fellow economists in his own age. But one can hope that such an economist, by preaching the wisdom of humility, will be honored to be working in the tradition of political economy's intellectual giants, such as Smith, Hume, Mises, Hayek, and Buchanan. It is only by rejecting his high priest status and embracing his position as a lowly philosopher that the economist has an opportunity to save economics from damnation due to arrogance. "For every one who exalts himself will be humbled, but the one who humbles himself will be exalted."[40]

---

40. Luke 14:11.

PART IV

Conclusion

22

A Few Critical Paragraphs That Should Shape What We Teach, and Why We Teach, Economics

Smith, Mises, and Hayek

THE TEACHING OF economics, I have tried to stress throughout this volume, is not a trivial endeavor. The subject is illuminating and the stakes are high; if we fail in our task as economic educators, then we fail in our job as economists. There is no way around this conclusion. Economics is not merely a game to be played by clever professionals, but a discipline that touches upon the most pressing practical issues at any historical juncture. The wealth and poverty of nations is at stake; the length and quality of life turns on the economic conditions individuals find themselves living within.

The discipline of economics illuminates all walks of human life, and as such it is an ambitious science. It explains the doings of man, whether in the marketplace, the voting booth, the church, the family, or any other human capacity. The economic way of thinking is not just one window on the world; it is *the only window* that deals with man as a human actor. This may sound arrogant to the casual reader, but economics also teaches humility. As F.A. Hayek put it, "The curious task of economics is to demonstrate to men how little they really know about what they imagine they can design."[1]

The mainline of economic teaching from Adam Smith to F.A. Hayek taught not only what economics can tell us but more importantly what it *cannot* tell us. There are real limits to economic analysis, and efforts at economic control. The main reasons economics got off track in the twentieth century are because of a failure to recognize those limits and a confusing of the policy sciences with the engineering sciences. Based on the knowledge of the physical sciences, the

---

1. F.A. Hayek, *The Fatal Conceit: The Errors of Socialism* (Chicago: the University of Chicago Press, 1991), 76.

engineering sciences created technological solutions unimaginable to previous generations. My grandparents entered this world when most travel was conducted by horse and buggy, they departed from this earth in a world which had not only experienced transatlantic flight but had placed a man on the moon. Since their passing, the Internet has developed and transformed not only the way we communicate, but also the way we shop, the way we learn, and the way we form social bonds. These amazing technological advances tend to reinforce the idea that through our reason men can conquer any and all problems they face through science. But even in this case of technological innovation, we tend to forget something vital to the story of progress. Technological knowledge was transformed into useful knowledge through the ordinary business of commerce. Without the guiding role of property, prices and profit/loss accounting, the gains from innovation would not be realized. The reason for this is simple—without the guiding signals and incentives of the price system, economic actors cannot sort out from the array of technologically feasible projects those that are most economical to pursue. And absent that economic knowledge, technological ventures will be plagued by a systemic waste of resources.

However, there is an even more subtle point to make than the necessity of commerce to guide technological innovation. Commercial life did not emerge through design, but instead out of the human proclivity to truck, barter, and exchange with one another. Specialization in production and exchange existed well before economists came up with those terms to help explain that behavior. Economists, in other words, did not invent the economy but rather came to their study with the economy already operating and were tasked with the role of providing philosophic understanding of already existing practice. This is radically different than the civil engineer who designs the bridge to ease travel between Manhattan and Brooklyn. The demand by politicians and the public that economics be more like engineering is perhaps the greatest corrupting force on the science.

But if we accept the judgment that economics cannot play the role of social engineering, we need not be content with economics being purely philosophical. Economics and political economy are capable of generating significant empirical information. The discipline can inform us about how alternative institutional frameworks will impact our ability to realize the gains from trade and innovation. If the institutional framework impedes trade and innovation, then those gains will go unrealized; if the institutional framework encourages those aspects of an economy, then those gains will be realized. I often tell students that humankind has demonstrated two natural propensities—to truck, barter, and exchange (as Adam Smith taught); and to rape, pillage, and plunder (as Thomas Hobbes taught us)—and which propensity is pursued is a function of the institutional framework within which individuals find themselves living and interacting. The life experience can be a virtuous cycle of wealth creation and healthier and wealthier lives, or it can be a nasty and brutish hell on earth. So while economics cannot give us exact point predictions, it can, as a science, inform us of tendencies and directions of change as well as the wealth-creating or wealth-destroying capacity of the political economic system.

The mainline of economics explained the operation of the economy not by making heroic assumptions about the cognitive capability of individuals, nor did it describe politics by reference to benevolent despots. Instead, the political economy of Adam Smith to F.A. Hayek takes humans as they are and seeks to find the institutional framework that both constrains bad people so they do least harm when in positions of power and uses the ordinary motivations of humans and their limited cognitive capabilities to realize social coopera-tion under the division of labor. The mainline economists found that in the private property market economy and a constitutionally limited government, such constraining individuals' aggressive ambitions on the use of power and individuals' unique knowledge of time and place could be marshaled to realize a peaceful and prosperous social order.

What economics and political economy had to guard against was human hubris. Hubris can come in two forms: a hubris that one is of a higher moral character, and a hubris that one is of a higher intellectual caliber than one's fellow citizens. It is this hubris that Hayek called *The Fatal Conceit*.

The intellectual culture in which Adam Smith wrote was sympathetic to such a critique of hubris. Consider the following passage from *The Wealth of Nations*:

What is the species of domestic industry which his capital can employ, and of which the produce is likely to be of the greatest value, every indi-vidual, it is evident, can, in his local situation, judge much better than any statesman or lawgiver can do for him. The statesman who should attempt to direct private people in what manner they ought to employ their capitals would not only load himself with a most unnecessary attention, but assume an authority which could safely be trusted, not only to no single person, but to no council or senate whatever, and which would nowhere be so dangerous as in the hands of a man who had folly and presumption enough to fancy himself fit to exercise it.[2]

The "man of system"—as Smith termed this hubris in *The Theory of Moral Sentiments*—was the object of ridicule.[3] Only he would be "wise in his own conceit" or in possession of the "folly and presumption" to believe he should lord over other men in their affairs of commerce.

By the time that John Maynard Keynes wrote *The General Theory of Employment, Interest, and Money*,[4] something had radically changed in the intellectual culture. Now rather than an object of ridicule, the man of systems was in demand to fix the problems of the vagaries of commercial life and the problems of modern industrial society with unemployment and business fluctuations. Economics since that time has been derailed educationally and as a tool for public policy. It became the handmaiden of the man of systems and not the reason to doubt the wisdom of that conceit of men. We have *The Economics of Control* and not the *Common Sense of Political Economy*.[5]

Economists are tasked with speaking truth to power, not catering to power. The discipline, from Smith to Hayek, has taught us about the need to limit power to curb the predatory capabilities of mankind. And when we don't heed its teachings, we don't overturn the basic results that Adam Smith, J.B. Say, and F.A. Hayek arrived at about the power of the market to create wealth and of politics to destroy it. The twentieth-century experiment with communism reinforces this basic lesson of mainline economics. As Ludwig von Mises put it:

---

2. Adam Smith, *An Inquiry into the Nature and Causes of the Wealth of Nations* (1776; repr., Chicago: University of Chicago Press, 1976), 478.

3. Adam Smith, *The Theory of Moral Sentiments* (1759; repr., Indianapolis, IN: Liberty Fund, 1982), 233.

4. John Maynard Keynes, *The General Theory of Employment, Interest, and Money* (1936; repr., New York: Harcourt, Brace & Jovanovich, 1964).

5. Abba Lerner, *The Economics of Control* (London: Macmillan, 1944); Philip H. Wicksteed, *The Common Sense of Political Economy: Including a Study of the Human Basis of Economic Law* (London: Macmillan, 1910).

The body of economic knowledge is an essential element in the structure of human civilization; it is the foundation upon which modern industrialism and all the moral, intellectual, technological, and therapeutical achievements of the last centuries have been built. It rests with men whether they will make the proper use of the rich treasure with which this knowledge provides them or whether they will leave it unused. But if they fail to take the best advantage of it and disregard its teachings and warnings, they will not annul economics; they will stamp out society and the human race.[6]

The business we are engaged in as practitioners and teachers of economics is a serious one. We must push out the frontiers of knowledge in our research and be able to communicate to our students, to policymakers, and to the general public the fundamental truths of mainline economics. We don't just need logically valid economic models and sophisticated statistical techniques. Instead we need logically sound economic reasoning and a grasp of human history. We have to understand man as a fallible yet capable chooser, who lives within an institutional framework that is historically contingent.

As I have tried to argue in this book, economics is both an illuminating and entertaining discipline and a discipline that tackles the most important questions of our age where questions of life and death hang in the balance. It is our professional responsibility to teach our students the sheer fun of using the economic way of thinking to make sense of the world and the stakes involved when the knowledge from the science of economics is denied for reasons of political expediency.

The mainline of economic teaching provides us with core truths that hold across time and place. Readers of this book will hopefully see these collected essays not as a catechism of settled doctrine, but instead as an enticing invitation to the science of human action and its most developed branch, economics. We need to attract to the study of humans the best and brightest of each generation; they need to find the study of economics intellectually exciting and worthy of their attention. They also have to be immune to the intellectual tendency to think of themselves as fit for the task of planning the system or

---

6. Ludwig von Mises, *Human Action: A Treatise on Economics* (1949; repr., Indianapolis, IN: Liberty Fund, 2010), 885.

optimally tinkering with the system. It is a fine intellectual balancing act to steer a course away from what Hayek called "rational constructivism," toward what Vernon Smith calls "ecological rationality." The fate of the discipline of economics will turn on the ability of those of us in the mainline of economics to provide an enticing enough invitation to each generation; and the fate of humanity will turn on the ability of those within the mainline of economics to beat back economic ignorance, special interest politics, and the hubristic ambitions of the man of systems.

Truth in economics, as in all scientific endeavors, ultimately matters much more that popularity and power. And the task of teaching that truth in economics to generations of students is a worthy and honorable vocation. In fact, it is a calling that demands our most careful attention and dedication to the craft of scholarship and teaching. The best economists read widely and deeply, think hard, speak directly, and write clearly. This is a serious business for serious people, but it also happens to be an amazing intellectual adventure into the "doings of man" in all their given variety and diversity, and across time and place. It is my sincere hope that the various explorations in economic principles of the mainline of economic science, and the examples of the master teachers who taught these principles to me, effectively communicates my enthusiasm for the disciplines of economics and political economy, and more importantly can serve as an invitation to my readers to join the great economic conversation.

Bibliography

Adaman, F., and Pat Devine. 1996. "The Economic Calculation Debate: Lessons for Socialists." *Cambridge Journal of Economics* 20(5): 523–37.

Ahrens, J. 2002. *Governance and Economic Development: A Comparative Institutional Approach.* Cheltenham, UK: Edward Elgar Publishing.

Albert, H., 1984. *"Modell-Denken und historische Wirklichkeit."* In *Ökonomisches Denken und soziale Ordnung,* edited by H. Albert, 39–61. Tübingen: J.C.B. Mohr.

Aligica, P. Dragos, and Peter J. Boettke. 2009. *Challenging Institutional Analysis and Development: The Bloomington School.* New York: Routledge.

Anderson, Gary, and Peter J. Boettke. 1993. "Perestroika and Public Choice: The Economics of Autocratic Succession in a Rent-Seeking Society." *Public Choice* 75(2): 101–18.

———. 1997. "Soviet Venality: A Rent-Seeking Model of the Communist State." *Public Choice* 93(1–2): 37–53.

Arrow, Kenneth. 1994. "Methodological Individualism and Social Knowledge." *The American Economic Review* 84(2): 1–9.

Atkinson, A. 1987. "James M. Buchanan's Contributions to Economics." *Scandinavian Journal of Economics* 89(1): 5–15.

Ayittey, George. 1994. "The Failure of Development Planning in Africa." In *The Collapse of Development Planning,* edited by Peter J. Boettke. New York: New York University Press: 146–81.

Bardhan, Pranab, and John Roemer. 1992. "Market Socialism: A Case for Rejuvenation." *Journal of Economic Perspectives* 6(3): 101–16.

———, eds. 1993. *Market Socialism: The Current Debate.* New York: Oxford University Press.

Barone, Enrico. 1908. "The Ministry of Production in the Collectivist State." In *Collectivist Economic Planning,* edited by F.A. Hayek. Repr., London: Routledge, 1935, 245–90.

Barzel, Yoram. 1989. *Economic Analysis of Property Rights.* New York: Cambridge University Press.

Bastiat, Frederic. 1964. "A Petition" in *Economic Sophisms,* Irvington-On-Hudson: Foundation For Economic Education.

Bateman, Bradley. 2005. "Bringing In The State? The Life and Times of Laissez-Faire in the 19th century United States." *History of Political Economy,* 37 ed. Steve Medema, 175–99.

Bates, R., A. Greif, M. Levi, J.-L. Rosenthal, and B.R. Weingast. 1998. *Analytic Narratives.* Princeton, NJ: Princeton University Press.

Baumol, William J. 1972. "On Taxation and the Control of Externalities." *American Economic Review* 62, 307–22.

———. 2002. *The Free-Market Innovation Machine.* Princeton, NJ: Princeton University Press.

Becker, Gary. 1976. *The Economic Approach to Human Behavior.* Chicago: University of Chicago Press.

Bellante, Don. 1994. "Sticky Wages, Efficiency Wages, and Market Processes." *Review of Austrian Economics* 8, 21–33.

Benson, Bruce. 1990. *The Enterprise of Law.* San Francisco: Pacific Research Institute for Public Policy.

Berger, Peter. 1963. *Invitation to Sociology.* New York: Doubleday.

Berliner, Joseph. 1957. *Factory and Manager in the USSR.* Cambridge, MA: Harvard University Press.

Boehm-Bawerk, E. 1884–1921. *Capital and Interest,* 3 vols. Repr., South Holland, IL: Libertarian Press, 1949.

———. 1891. "The Historical versus the Deductive Method in Political Economy." *Annals of the American Academy of Political Science* 1. In *Classics in Austrian Economics,* edited by Israel M. Kirzner, 109–29. Repr., London: Pickering & Chatto, 1994.

Boettke, Peter J. 1987. "Virginia Political Economy: A View from Vienna." In Boettke and Prychitko, *The Market Process: Essays in Contemporary Austrian Economics,* 244–60.

———. 1989. "Evolution and Economics: Austrians and Institutionalists." *Research in the History of Economic Thought & Methodology* 6, 73–89.

———. 1990. *The Political Economy of Soviet Socialism: The Formative Years, 1918–1928.* Boston, MA: Kluwer.

———. 1992. "Analysis and Vision in Economic Discourse." *Journal of the History of Economic Thought* 14 (Spring), 84–95.

———. 1993. *Why Perestroika Failed: The Politics and Economics of Socialist Transformation.* New York: Routledge.

———, ed. 1994. *The Collapse of Development Planning.* New York: New York University Press.

———, ed. 1994. *The Elgar Companion to Austrian Economics.* Aldershot, UK: Edward Elgar Publishing.

———, ed. 1994. Introduction to *The Collapse of Development Planning.* New York: New York University Press.

———. 1994. "The Political Infrastructure in Economic Development." In Boettke, *Calculation and Coordination,* 234–47.

———. 1995. "Hayek's *The Road to Serfdom* Revisited: Government Failure in the Argument against Socialism." *Eastern Economic Journal* 25 (Winter), 7–26.

———. 1995. "Why Are There No Austrian Socialists? Ideology, Science and the Austrian School." *Journal of the History of Economic Thought* 17 (Spring): 35–56.

———. 1996. Review of *Whither Socialism?* by Joseph Stiglitz. *Journal of Economic Literature* 34(1) (March): 189–91.

———. 1996. "What Is Wrong with Neoclassical Economics (And What Is Still Wrong with Austrian Economics)." In *Beyond Neoclassical Economics,* edited by Fred Foldvary. Aldershot, UK: Edward Elgar Publishing, 22–40.

———. 1997. "Where Did Economics Go Wrong: Modern Economics as a Flight from Reality." *Critical Review* 11(1): 11–64.

———. 1998. "Economic Calculation: The Austrian Contribution to Political Economy." *Advances in Austrian Economics* 5: 131–58.

———. 1998. "Is Economics a Moral Science?" *Journal of Markets & Morality* 1(2): 212–19.

———. 1998. "Ludwig von Mises." In *The Handbook of Economic Methodology,* edited by J. Davis, D. Wade Hands, and U. Maki. Cheltenham, UK: Edward Elgar Publishing, 534–40.

———. 1999. "Which Enlightenment, Whose Liberalism: F.A. Hayek's Research Program for Understanding the Liberal Society." In *The Legacy of F.A. Hayek: Politics, Philosophy, Economics,* edited by Peter J. Boettke, vol. 1, xi–lv. Cheltenham, UK: Edward Elgar Publishing.

———. 2000. *The Intellectual Legacy of F.A. Hayek,* 3 vols. Aldershot, UK: Edward Elgar Publishing.

———, ed. 2000. *Socialism and the Market: The Socialist Calculation Debate Revisited,* 9 vols. London: Routledge.

_____. 2001. *Calculation and Coordination: Essays on Socialism and Transitional Political Economy.* New York: Routledge.

_____. 2001. "Why Culture Matters: Economics, Politics, and the Imprint of History." In Boettke, *Calculation and Coordination,* 248–65.

_____. 2002. "Relevance as a Virtue in Economics." *Quarterly Journal of Austrian Economics* 5(4): 31–36.

_____. 2008. "The Austrian School of Economics." In *A Concise Encyclopedia of Economics,* edited by David Henderson. http://www.econlib.org/library/Enc/Austrian SchoolofEconomics.html.

_____. 2009. "Institutional Transition and the Problem of Credible Commitment." *Annual Proceedings of the Wealth & Well-Being of Nations* 1: 41–51.

_____. 2009. Review of Eric Jones's *Cultures Merging. Economic Development & Culture Change,* 57(January): 434–37.

_____, ed. 2010. *The Handbook of Contemporary Austrian Economics,* Cheltenham, UK: Edward Elgar Publishing.

Boettke, Peter J., and Christopher J. Coyne. 2003. "Entrepreneurship and Development: Cause or Consequence?" *Advances in Austrian Economics* 6: 67–88.

_____. 2004. "Swedish Influences, Austrian Advances: The Contributions of the Swedish and Austrian Schools to Market Process Theory." In *The Evolution of the Market Process: Austrian and Swedish Economics,* edited by M. Bellet, S. Gloria-Palermo, and A. Zouache, 20–31. New York: Routledge.

_____. 2006. "The Role of the Economist in Economic Development." *Quarterly Journal of Austrian Economics* 19(2): 47–68.

_____. 2009. "Best Case, Worse Case, and the Golden Mean in Political Economy." *Review of Austrian Economics* 22(2): 123–25.

Boettke, Peter J., Christopher J. Coyne, and Peter T. Leeson. 2003. "Man as Machine: The Plight of 20th Century Economics." *Annals of the Society for the History of Economic Thought* 43: 1–10.

_____. 2006. "High Priests and Lowly Philosophers: The Battle for the Soul of Economics." *Case Western Reserve Law Review* 56(3): 551–68.

_____. 2008. "Institutional Stickiness and the New Development Economics." *American Journal of Economics & Sociology* 67(2): 331–58.

Boettke, Peter J., and Steven Horwitz. 2005. "The Limits of Economic Expertise." Annual supplement, *History of Political Economy* 37: 10–39.

Boettke, Peter J., and Peter T. Leeson. 2003. "The Austrian School of Economics, 1950–2000." In *The Blackwell Companion to the History of Economic Thought,* edited by Warren J. Samuels, Jeff E. Biddle, and John B. Davis. Oxford: Basil Blackwell Publishers, 445–53.

———. 2004. "Liberalism, Socialism and Robust Political Economy." *Journal of Markets & Morality* 7(1): 99–111.

———. 2006. *The Legacy of Ludwig von Mises: Theory and History,* 2 vols. Aldershot, UK: Edward Elgar Publishing.

Boettke, Peter J., and David L. Prychitko, eds. 1994. *The Market Process: Essays in Contemporary Austrian Economics.* Aldershot, UK: Edward Elgar Publishing.

———. 1996. "Mr. Boulding and the Austrians." In *Joseph Schumpeter, Historian of Economics,* edited by L. Moss, 250–59. New York: Routledge.

———. 1998. *Market Process Theories,* 2 vols. Aldershot, UK: Edward Elgar Publishing.

Boettke, Peter J., and Karen I. Vaughn. 2002. "Knight and the Austrians on Capital and the Problems of Socialism." *History of Political Economy* 34(1), 155–76.

Boulding, Kenneth E. 1936. "Time and Investment." *Economica* 10 (May): 196–220.

———. 1941. *Economic Analysis.* New York: Harper & Brothers.

———. 1948. "Samuelson's *Foundations*: The Role of Mathematics in Economics." *Journal of Political Economy* 56 (June): 187–99.

———. 1950. *A Reconstruction of Economics.* New York: John Wiley & Sons.

———. 1956. *The Image.* Ann Arbor: University of Michigan Press.

———. 1958. *The Skills of the Economist.* Cleveland: Howard Allen.

———. 1962. *Conflict and Defense.* New York: Harper & Row.

———. 1966. *The Impact of the Social Sciences.* New Brunswick, NJ: Rutgers University Press.

———. 1970. *Economics as a Science.* New York: McGraw-Hill.

———. 1971. "After Samuelson, Who Needs Adam Smith?" *History of Political Economy* 3 (Fall): 225–37.

———. 1971. "Introduction." In *Collected Papers,* vol. 1. Boulder: Colorado Associated University Press, vii–xi.

———. 1973. "The Misallocation of Intellectual Resources in Economics." In *Collected Papers,* vol. 3. Boulder: Colorado Associated University Press, 535–52.

———. 1978. *Ecodynamics.* New York: Sage.

———. 1981. *Evolutionary Economics.* New York: Sage.

———. 1985. "My Life Philosophy." *The American Economist* 29 (Fall): 5–14.

———. 1985. "Systems Research and the Hierarchy of World Systems." *Systems Research* 2: 7–11.

———. 1990. *Three Faces of Power.* New York: Sage.

Brennan, Geoffrey, and James M. Buchanan. 1980. *The Power to Tax*. New York: Cambridge University Press.

———. 1985. "The Reason of Rules." In Buchanan, *Collected Works*, vol. 10. Indianapolis, IN: Liberty Fund, Inc.

Buchanan, James M. 1954. "Social Choice, Democracy and Free Markets." In Buchanan, *Collected Works*, vol. 1, 89–102. Indianapolis, IN: Liberty Fund, Inc.

———. 1958. *Public Principles of Public Debt*. Homewood, IL: Irwin.

———. 1959. "Positive Economics, Welfare Economics, and Political Economy." In Buchanan, *Collected Works*, vol. 1, 191–209.

———. 1960. *Fiscal Theory and Political Economy*. Chapel Hill: University of North Carolina Press.

———. 1962. "What Should Economists Do?" In Buchanan, *Collected Works*, vol. 1, 28–42.

———. 1967. "Politics and Science." In Buchanan, *Collected Works*, vol. 1. 230–43.

———. 1969. *Cost and Choice*. In Buchanan, *Collected Works*, vol. 6.

———. 1972. "Politics, Property and the Law." *Journal of Law & Economics*. In *Freedom in Constitutional Contract*, 94–109. Repr., College Station: Texas A&M University Press, 1979.

———. 1975. *The Limits of Liberty: Between Anarchy and Leviathan*. In Buchanan, *Collected Works*, vol. 7.

———. 1977. *Freedom in Constitutional Contract*. College Station: Texas A&M University Press.

———. 1977. "Law and the Invisible Hand." In Buchanan, *Collected Works*, vol. 17.

———. 1979. "Politics without Romance." In Buchanan, *Collected Works*, vol. 1, 45–59.

———. 1979. *What Should Economists Do?* Indianapolis, IN: Liberty Press.

———. 1982. "Order Defined in the Process of Its Emergence." In Buchanan, *Collected Works*, vol. 1, 244–45.

———. 1983. "Political Economy: 1957–1982." In Buchanan, *Collected Works*, vol. 19, 38–49.

———. 1986. "Better than Plowing." In Buchanan, *Collected Works*, vol. 1, 11–27.

———. 1986. "Cultural Evolution and Institutional Reform." In Buchanan, *Collected Works*, vol. 18, 311–23.

———. 1986. *Liberty, Market and State*. New York: New York University Press.

———. 1986. "The Potential for Tyranny in Politics as Science." In Buchanan, *Collected Works*, vol. 17, 153–70.

———. 1991. *The Economics and Ethics of Constitutional Order*. Ann Arbor: University of Michigan Press.

————. 1992. *Better than Plowing.* Chicago: University of Chicago Press.

————. 1993. "Asymmetrical Reciprocity in Market Exchange." In Buchanan, *Collected Works,* vol. 12, 409–25.

————. 1996. "Economics as a Public Science." In Buchanan, *Collected Works,* vol. 12, 44–51.

————. 1999–2001. *The Collected Works of James M. Buchanan,* 20 vols. Indianapolis, IN: Liberty Fund.

————. 2001. "The Qualities of a Natural Economist." In Buchanan, *Collected Works: Ideas, Persons, and Events,* vol. 19, 95–107.

Buchanan, James M., and G. F. Thirlby, eds. 1973. *L.S.E. Essays on Cost.* London: London School of Economics.

Buchanan, James M., R.D. Tollison, and G. Tullock, eds. 1980. *Towards a Theory of the Rent-Seeking Society.* College Station: Texas A&M University Press.

Buchanan, James M., and Gordon Tullock. 1962. *The Calculus of Consent.* In Buchanan, *Collected Works,* vol. 3.

Buchanan, James M., and V. Vanberg. 1991. "The Market as a Creative Process." In Buchanan, *Collected Works,* vol. 18, 289–310.

Buchanan, James M., and Richard Wagner. 1977. *Democracy in Deficit: The Political Legacy of Lord Keynes.* In *Collected Works,* vol. 8.

Buchanan, James M., and J.Y. Yoon, eds. 1994. *The Return of Increasing Returns.* Ann Arbor: University of Michigan Press.

Caldwell, Bruce. 1984. "Praxeology and Its Critics: An Appraisal." *History of Political Economy*: 363–79.

————. 1988. "Hayek's 'The Trend of Economic Thinking." *Review of Austrian Economics* 2, 175–78.

————. 1989. "Austrians and Institutionalists: The Historical Origins of Their Shared Characteristics." *Research in the History of Economic Thought & Methodology 6,* 91–100.

————. 1997. "Hayek and Socialism." *Journal of Economic Literature* 35(4): 1856–90.

————. 2004. *Hayek's Challenge: An Intellectual Biography of F.A. Hayek.* Chicago: University of Chicago Press.

Campbell, Donald. 1995. *Incentives: Motivation and the Economics of Information.* New York: Cambridge University Press.

Chafuen, Alejandro A. 2003. *Faith and Liberty: The Economic Thought of the Late Scholastics.* Lanham, Md.: Lexington Books, 2003.

Cheung, S. 1973. "The Fable of the Bees: An Economic Investigation." *Journal of Law & Economics* 16(1): 11–33.

Coase, Ronald. 1959. "The Federal Communications Commission." *Journal of Law & Economics* 2(1) 1–40.

———. 1960. "The Problem of Social Cost." *Journal of Law & Economics* 3(1): 1–44.

———. 1988. *The Firm, the Market and the Law.* Chicago: University of Chicago Press.

Coddington, Alan. 1975. "Creaking Semaphore and Beyond: A Consideration of Shackle's 'Epistemics and Economics.'" *British Journal of the Philosophy of Science* 26, 151–63.

Collins, Randall. 1998. *The Sociology of Philosophies: A Global Theory of Intellectual Change.* Cambridge, MA: Belknap Press of Harvard University Press.

Converse, Philip E. 1964. "The Nature of Belief Systems in Mass Publics." In *Ideology and Discontent,* edited by David E. Apter. New York: Free Press, 206–61.

Cottrell, Allin, and W. Paul Cockshot. 1993. "Calculation, Complexity and Planning." *Review of Political Economy* 5(1): 73–112.

Cowen, Tyler. 2007. *Discover Your Inner Economist: Use Incentives to Fall in Love, Survive Your Next Meeting, and Motivate Your Dentist.* Boston, MA: Dutton Adult.

Cowen, Tyler, and R. Fink. 1985. "Inconsistent Equilibrium Constructs: Mises and Rothbard on the Evenly Rotating Economy." *American Economic Review* 75: 866–69.

Coyne, Christopher J. 2005. "The Institutional Prerequisites for Post-Conflict Reconstruction." *Review of Austrian Economics* 18(3/4): 325–42.

———. 2007. *After War: The Political Economy of Exporting Democracy.* Stanford, CA: Stanford Economics & Finance.

Coyne, Christopher J., and Peter T. Leeson. 2004. "The Plight of Underdeveloped Countries," *Cato Journal* 24(3): 235–49.

Cushman, R. 1994. "Rational Fears." *Lingua Franca* (November/December): 42–54.

Davidson, Paul. 1989. "The Economics of Ignorance or Ignorance of Economics?" *Critical Review* 3(3–4): 467–87.

De Roover, Raymond. 1976. *Business, Banking, and Economic Thought in Late Medieval and Early Modern Europe.* Chicago: University of Chicago Press.

De Soto, H. 1989. *The Other Path.* New York: HarperCollins.

Demsetz, Harold. 1969. "Information and Efficiency." *Journal of Law & Economics* (March), 1–22.

Dixit, Avinash. 1996. *The Making of Economic Policy: A Transaction-Cost Politics Perspective.* Cambridge, MA: MIT Press.

Domar, Evsey. 1957. *Essays in the Theory of Economic Growth.* New York: Oxford University Press.

Durbin, E.F. 1945. "Professor Hayek on Economic Planning and Political Liberty." *Economic Journal* 55 (December): 357–70.

Easterly, William. 2001. *The Elusive Quest for Growth: Economists' Adventures and Misadventures in the Tropics*. Cambridge, MA: MIT Press.

Ehrlich, Alexander. 1960. *The Soviet Industrialization Debate, 1924–1928*. Cambridge, MA: Harvard University Press.

Elster, Jon. 2009. *Alexis de Tocqueville: The First Social Scientist*. New York: Cambridge University Press.

Engels, Frederick. 1892. *Socialism: Utopian and Scientific*. Repr., New York: International Publishers, 1972.

Epstein, R. 1995. *Simple Rules for a Complex World*. Cambridge, MA: Harvard University Press.

Euken, W. 1940. *The Foundations of Economics*. Repr., Chicago: University of Chicago Press, 1951.

Evans, Peter B., Dietrich Rueschmeyer, and Theda Skocpol, eds. 1985. *Bringing the State Back In*. New York: Cambridge University Press.

Fisher, Franklin. 1983. *Disequilibrium Foundations of Equilibrium Economics*. New York: Cambridge University Press.

———. 1991. "Organizing Industrial Organization: Reflections on the *Handbook of Industrial Organization*." *Brookings Papers: Microeconomics* 1991: 201–40.

Fleischacker, Samuel. 2004. *On Adam Smith's* Wealth of Nations. Princeton, NJ: Princeton University Press.

Foss, Nicolai. 2000. "Austrian Economics and Game Theory: A Stocktaking and an Evaluation." *Review of Austrian Economics* 13: 41–58.

Friedman, Jeffrey. 1995. "Economic Approaches to Politics." *Critical Review* 9(1–2): 1–24.

———. 1996. "Introduction: Economic Approaches to Politics." In *The Rational Choice Controversy: Economic Models of Politics Reconsidered,* edited by Jeffrey Friedman. New Haven, CT: Yale University Press, 1–24.

———. 1996. "Public Opinion and Democracy." *Critical Review* 10(1): i–xii.

Friedman, Milton. 1947. "Lerner's Economics of Control." *Journal of Political Economy* 55(5): 405–16.

———. 1953. *Essays in Positive Economics*. Chicago: University of Chicago Press.

———. 1962. *Capitalism and Freedom*. Chicago: University of Chicago Press.

Friedman, Milton, and Rose Friedman. 1980. *Free to Choose*. New York: Harcourt, Brace & Jovanovich.

Frye, T. 2000. *Brokers and Bureaucrats*. Ann Arbor: University of Michigan Press.

Fukuyama, F. 2004. *State-Building: Governance and the World-Order in the 21st Century*. Ithaca, NY: Cornell University Press.

Garrison, Roger. 1984. "Time and Money." *Journal of Macroeconomics* 6(2) (Spring), 197–213.

———. *Time and Money: The Macroeconomics of Capital Structure*. New York: Routledge.

Gerschenkron, A. 1962. *Economic Backwardness in Historical Perspective*. Cambridge, MA: Harvard University Press.

Goethe, Johann Wolfgang von. 1995. *Scientific Studies,* vol. 12. Translated by Douglas Miller. Princeton, NJ: Princeton University Press.

Gordon, Robert. 1990. "What Is New-Keynesian Economics?" *Journal of Economic Literature* 28(3) (September), 1151–71.

Granick, David. 1954. *Management and the Industrial Firm in the USSR*. Repr., Westport, CT: Greenwood Press, 1980.

Greaves, P. 1974. *Mises Made Easier: A Glossary for Ludwig von Mises's* Human Action. New York: Free-Market Books.

Gregory, Paul. 2003. *The Political Economy of Stalinism*. New York: Cambridge University Press.

Grice-Hutchinson, Marjorie. 1952. *The School of Salamanca: Readings in Spanish Monetary Theory, 1544–1605*. Oxford University Press.

———. 1978. *Early Economic Thought in Spain 1177–1740*. London: Allen & Unwin.

Grossman, Gregory. 1977. "The 'Second Economy' of the USSR." In *The Soviet Economy,* edited by Morris Bornstein. Repr., Boulder, CO: Westview, 1981.

Grossman, Sanford. 1976. "On the Efficiency of Competitive Stock Markets Where Traders Have Diverse Information." *Journal of Finance* 31 (May), 573–85.

———. 1989. *The Informational Role of Prices*. Cambridge, MA: MIT Press.

Grossman, Sanford, and Joseph Stiglitz. 1976. "Information and Competitive Price Systems." *American Economic Review* 66 (May), 246–53.

———. 1980. "On the Impossibility of Informationally Efficient Markets." *American Economic Review* 70 (June), 393–408.

Hahn, Frank. 1973. *On the Notion of Equilibrium in Economics*. Cambridge: Cambridge University Press.

Hamilton, Alexander. 1787. *The Federalist Papers #1*. http://thomas.loc.gov/home/histdox/fed_01.html.

Hayek, F.A. 1931. "Reflections on the Pure Theory of Money of Mr. J.M. Keynes."

In Hayek, *Collected Works*, vol 9. Repr., Chicago: University of Chicago Press, 1995, 121–46.

———. 1933. "The Trend of Economic Thinking." *Economica* (May): 121–37. In Hayek, *Collected Works*, vol. 3, 17–34.

———, ed. 1935. *Collectivist Economic Planning*. London: Routledge.

———. 1937. "Economics and Knowledge." In Hayek, *Individualism and Economic Order*, 33–56.

———. 1941. *The Pure Theory of Capital*. Chicago: University of Chicago Press.

———. 1943. "The Facts of the Social Sciences." In Hayek, *Individualism and Economic Order*, 57–76.

———. 1944. *The Road to Serfdom*. Chicago: University of Chicago Press.

———. 1945. "The Use of Knowledge in Society." In Hayek, *Individualism and Economic Order*, 77–91.

———. 1946. "Individualism: True and False." In Hayek, *Individualism and Economic Order*, 1–32.

———. 1948. *Individualism and Economic Order*. Repr., Chicago: University of Chicago Press, 1996.

———. 1952. *The Counter-Revolution of Science*. Repr., Indianapolis, IN: Liberty Fund, 1979.

———. 1952. *The Sensory Order*. Chicago: University of Chicago Press.

———. 1960. *The Constitution of Liberty*. Chicago: University of Chicago Press.

———. 1964. "Kinds of Rationalism." In *Studies in Philosophy, Politics and Economics*. Repr., Chicago: University of Chicago Press, 1967, 82–95.

———. 1967. "The Results of Human Action but Not of Human Design." In *Studies in Philosophy, Politics and Economics*. Chicago: University of Chicago Press, 96–105.

———. 1973. *Law, Legislation and Liberty*, 3 vols. Chicago: University of Chicago Press.

———. 1978. *New Studies in Philosophy, Politics, Economics and the History of Ideas*. Chicago: University of Chicago Press.

———. 1991. *The Fatal Conceit: The Errors of Socialism*. In Hayek, *Collected Works*, vol. 1. Chicago: University of Chicago Press.

———. 1988–2010. *The Collected Works of F.A. Hayek,* edited by Bruce Campbell, 19 vols. Chicago: University of Chicago Press.

Hazlitt, Henry. 1946. *Economics in One Lesson*. New York: Harper & Brothers.

———. 1959. *The Failure of the "New Economics."* Princeton, NJ: Van Nostrand.

———, ed. 1960. *The Critics of Keynesian Economics*. Princeton, NJ: Van Nostrand.

Heilbroner, Robert, and William Milberg. 1995. *The Crisis of Vision in Modern Economic Thought*. New York: Cambridge University Press.

Heyne, Paul, Peter J. Boettke, and David L. Prychitko. 2010. *The Economic Way of Thinking*, 12th ed. Upper Saddle River, NJ: Prentice Hall.

Hicks, John. 1967. "The Hayek Story." In *Critical Essays in Monetary Theory*. Oxford: Clarendon Press, 203–15.

High, Jack. 1990. *Maximizing, Action, and Market Adjustment: An Inquiry into the Theory of Economic Organization*. Munich: Philosophia Verlag.

Hirschman, Albert O. 1977. *The Passions and the Interests*. Princeton, NJ: Princeton University Press.

———. 1986. "Against Parsimony: Three Easy Ways of Complicating Some Categories of Economic Discourse." In *Rival Views of Market Society*. Cambridge, MA: Harvard University Press, 142–60.

Hoover, Kevin. 1994. "New Classical Economics." In *The Elgar Companion to Austrian Economics,* edited by Peter J. Boettke. Aldershot, UK: Edward Elgar Publishing, 576–81.

Horwitz, Steven. 1996. "Money, Money Prices and the Socialist Calculation Debate." *Advances in Austrian Economics* 3: 59–77.

———. 2000. *Microfoundations and Macroeconomics: An Austrian Perspective*. New York: Routledge.

Hume, David. 1758. *Essays Moral, Political, and Literary*. Repr., Indianapolis, IN: Liberty Fund, 1985.

Hutchison, T.W. 1938. *The Significance and Basic Postulates of Economic Theory*. Repr., New York: Augustus M. Kelley, 1965.

Hutt, W.H. 1936. *Economists and the Public*. Repr., New Brunswick, NJ: Transaction Publishers, 1990.

———. 1940. "The Concept of Consumer Sovereignty." *Economic Journal* 50 (March): 66–77.

Ickes, B., and Clifford Gaddy. 1998. "Russia's Virtual Economy." *Foreign Affairs* 77(5) (Fall), 53–67.

Inman, R. 1987. "Markets, Governments, and the 'New' Political Economy." In *The Handbook of Public Economics*, edited by A. Auerbach and M. Feldstein, vol. 2, 647–777. Amsterdam: North-Holland.

Jones, Eric. 2006. *Cultures Merging*. Princeton, NJ: Princeton University Press.

Kamath, Shyam. 1994. "The Failure of Development Planning in India." In *The Collapse of Development Planning*, edited by Peter J. Boettke. New York: New York University Press, 90–145.

Kant, Immanuel. 1958. *The Critique of Pure Reason*. Translated by N.K. Smith. New York: St. Martin's Press.

Kaufmann, Felix. 1944. *The Methodology of the Social Sciences*. London: Oxford University Press.

Keenan, Sean. 1994. "New Keynesian Economics." In *The Elgar Companion to Austrian Economics,* edited by Peter J. Boettke. Aldershot, UK: Edward Elgar Publishing, 582–87.

Keynes, John Maynard. 1936. *The General Theory of Employment, Interest, and Money*. Repr., New York: Harcourt, Brace & Jovanovich, 1964.

Keynes, John N. 1891. *The Scope and Method of Political Economy*. Cambridge, MA: C. J. Clay, M.A. & Sons, at the University Press.

Kirzner, Israel M. 1960. *The Economic Point of View*. Princeton, NJ: Van Nostrand.

———. 1963. *Market Theory and the Price System*. Princeton, NJ: Van Nostrand.

———. 1978. *Competition and Entrepreneurship*. Chicago: University of Chicago Press.

———. 1979. *Perception, Opportunity and Profit*. Chicago: University of Chicago Press.

———. 1984. "Economic Planning and the Knowledge Problem." *Cato Journal 4* (Fall), 407–25.

———. 1987. "The Economic Calculation Debate: Lessons for Austrians." *Review of Austrian Economics* 2, 1–18.

———. 1992a. *The Meaning of Market Process: Essays in the Development of Modern Austrian Economics*. New York: Routledge.

———. 1992b. "Prices, the Communication of Knowledge, and the Discovery Process." In *The Meaning of the Market Process: Essays in the Development of Modern Austrian Econmoics*. London: Routledge, 130–51.

———. 1997. "Entrepreneurial Discovery and the Competitive Market Process: An Austrian Approach." *Journal of Economic Literature* 35 (March), 60–85.

———. 2000. Foreword to *An Entrepreneurial Theory of the Firm,* by Frederic Sautet. London, Routledge, xiii–xiv.

———. 2001. *Ludwig von Mises*. Wilmington, NC: ISI Books.

———. 2006. "Lifetime Achievement Award Acceptance Speech." Society for the Development of Austrian Economics, Charleston, SC, November, 19, 2006.

———. 2009. *The Economic Point of View,* edited by Peter J. Boettke and Frederic Sautet. Indianapolis, IN: Liberty Fund, Inc.

Klamer, Arjo. 1984. *Conversations with Economists*. New York: Rowman & Littlefield.

Klamer, Arjo, and David Colander. 1990. *The Making of an Economist*. Boulder, CO: Westview.

Klein, Dan, ed. 1999. *What Do Economists Contribute?* New York: New York University Press.

———. 2001. *A Plea to Economists Who Favour Liberty: Assist the Everyman.* London: Institute for Economic Affairs.

Klein, Peter. 1996. "Economic Calculation and the Limits of Organization." *Review of Austrian Economics* 9(2): 3–28.

Knight, Frank H. 1921. *Risk, Uncertainty and Profit.* Repr., Chicago: University of Chicago Press, 1971.

———. 1935. *The Ethics of Competition.* Repr., New York: Augustus M. Kelley, 1951.

———. 1940. "What Is Truth in Economics?" *Journal of Political Economy* 48: 1–32.

———. 1951. "The Role of Principles in Economics and Politics." *American Economic Review* 41(1): 1–29. In *Selected Essays of Frank H. Knight,* edited by Ross Emmett, vol. 2, 361–91. Repr., Chicago: University of Chicago Press, 1999.

———. 1960. *Intelligence and Democratic Action.* Cambridge, MA: Harvard.

Koppl, Roger. 2002. *Big Players and the Economic Theory of Expectations.* New York: Palgrave Macmillan.

Kornai, Janos. 1992. *The Political Economy of Communism.* Princeton, NJ: Princeton University Press.

Kreps, David. 1997. "Economics—The Current Position." *Daedalus* (Winter), 59–85.

Krugman, Paul. 1994. *The Age of Diminished Expectations: U.S. Economic Policy in the 1990s.* Cambridge, MA: MIT Press.

———. 1994. *Peddling Prosperity.* New York: Norton.

———. 1995. *Development, Geography, and Economic Theory.* Cambridge, MA: MIT Press.

———. 1999. *The Return of Depression Economics.* New York: Norton.

Kuhn, T.S. 1959. "The Essential Tension: Tradition and Innovation in Scientific Research." In *The Third University of Utah Research Conference on the Identification of Scientific Talent,* edited by C.W. Taylor, 162–74. Salt Lake City: University of Utah Press.

Kukathas, C. 2003. *The Liberal Archipelago: A Theory of Diversity and Freedom.* New York: Oxford University Press.

Kuran, Timur. 1995. *Private Truths, Public Lies.* Cambridge, MA: Harvard University Press.

Lange, Oskar. 1936–1937. "On the Economic Theory of Socialism." In *On the Economic Theory of Socialism.* Repr., Minneapolis: University of Minnesota Press, 1938, 55–129.

Lavoie, Don. 1985. *National Economic Planning: What Is Left?* Cambridge: Ballinger.

_____. 1985. *Rivalry and Central Planning.* New York: Cambridge University Press.

Leeson, Peter T. 2005. "Endogenizing Fractionalization." *Journal of Institutional Economics* 1(1): 75–98.

_____. 2007. "Trading with Bandits." *Journal of Law & Economics* 50(2): 303–21.

_____. 2009. "The Laws of Lawlessness." *Journal of Legal Studies* 38(2): 471–503.

_____. 2009. *The Invisible Hook: The Hidden Economics of Pirates.* Princeton, NJ: Princeton University Press.

Leijonhufvud, A. 1981. "Life among the Econ." In *Information and Coordination*, 347–59. New York: Oxford University Press.

Lerner, Abba. 1944. *The Economics of Control.* London: Macmillan.

Levy, David M. 1990. "The Bias in Centrally Planned Prices." *Public Choice* 67: 213–26, 213–16.

_____. 2002. *How the Dismal Science Got Its Name: Classical Economics and the Ur-Text of Racial Politics.* Ann Arbor: University of Michigan Press.

Lewin, Peter. 1999. *Capital in Disequilibrium: The Role of Capital in a Changing World.* New York: Routledge.

Lewis, Michael. 2003. *Moneyball: The Art of Winning an Unfair Game.* New York: Norton.

Lucas, Robert E. 1972. "Expectations and the Neutrality of Money." *Journal of Economic Theory* 4: 103–24.

Lucas, Robert E., and Thomas Sargent, eds. 1981. *Rational Expectations and Econometric Practice,* 2 vols. Minneapolis: University of Minnesota Press.

Machlup, Fritz. 1978. *Methodology of Economics and Other Social Sciences.* New York: Academic Press.

Magnusson, Lars. 2003. "Mercantilism." In *The Blackwell Companion to the History of Economic Thought*, edited by Warren J. Samuels, Jeff E. Biddle, and John B. Davis. Malden, MA: Blackwell, 46–60.

Mahovec, Frank. 1995. *Perfect Competition and the Transformation of Economics.* New York: Routledge.

Mankiw, Gregory, and David Romer, eds. 1991. *New Keynesian Economics*, 2 vols. Cambridge, MA: MIT Press.

Marget, Arthur. 1938–1942. *The Theory of Prices*, 2 vols. Repr., New York: Augustus M. Kelley, 1966.

Marshall, Alfred. 1920. *Principles of Economics.* Philadelphia: Porcupine Press.

_____. 1961. *Principles of Economics*, 9th ed. New York: Macmillan.

Marx, Karl. 1906. *Capital.* New York: Modern Library Edition.

Mayer, Hans. 1932. *Der Erkenntniswert der Funktionellen Priestheorien* [The cognitive value of functional theories of price]. In *Classics in Austrian Economics: A Sampling in the History of a Tradition,* edited by Israel M. Kirzner, vol. II, *The Interwar Period.* Repr., London: Pickering & Chatto, 1994, 55–168.

Mayer, Thomas. 1993. *Truth versus Precision in Economics.* Aldershot, UK: Edward Elgar Publishing.

———. 2009. *Invitation to Economics.* New York: Wiley.

McCloskey, Deirdre N. 1987. *The Writing of Economics.* New York: Macmillan.

———. 1991. "The Arrogance of Economic Theorists." *Swiss Review of World Affairs* (October).

———. 1995. "Kelly Green Golf Shoes and the Intellectual Range from M to N." *Eastern Economic Journal* 21(3) (Summer): 411–14.

———. 1996. *The Vices of Economists, The Virtues of the Bourgeoisie.* Amsterdam: Amsterdam University Press.

———. 2006. *The Bourgeois Virtues: Ethics for an Age of Commerce.* Chicago: University of Chicago Press.

———. 2010. *Bourgeois Dignity: Why Economics Cannot Explain the Modern World.* Chicago: University of Chicago Press.

McGinnis, M., ed. 1999. *Polycentricity and Local Public Economies: Readings from the Workshop in Political Theory and Policy Analysis.* Ann Arbor: University of Michigan Press.

———, ed. 1999. *Polycentric Governance and Development: Readings from the Workshop in Political Theory and Policy Analysis.* Ann Arbor: University of Michigan Press.

———, ed. 2000. *Polycentric Games and Institutions: Readings from the Workshop in Political Theory and Policy Analysis.* Ann Arbor: University of Michigan Press.

McKenzie, R., and Gordon Tullock. 1989. *The New World of Economics.* Homewood, IL: Irwin.

Meardon, Stephen. 2005. "How TIRPs Got Legs: Copyright, Trade Policy, and the Role of Government in 19th Century American Economic Thought," *History of Political Economy,* 37 (Suppl 1): 145–74.

Medema, Steven G. 1994. *Ronald H. Coase.* New York: St. Martin's Press.

———. 2009. *The Hesitant Hand.* Princeton, NJ: Princeton University Press.

Menger, Carl. 1871. *Principles of Economics.* Repr., New York: New York University Press, 1981.

Milgrom, Paul, and John Roberts. 1992. *Economics, Organization and Management.* Englewood Cliffs, NJ: Prentice Hall.

Mill, John Stuart. 1848. *Principles of Political Economy.* Repr., New York, NY: Augustus M. Kelley, 1976.

Mirowski, Philip. 1989. *More Heat than Light: Economics as Social Physics, Physics as Nature's Economics.* Cambridge: Cambridge University Press.

————. 2002. *Machine Dreams: Economics Becomes a Cyborg Science.* New York: Cambridge University Press.

Mises, Ludwig von. 1912. *The Theory of Money and Credit.* Repr., Indianapolis, IN: Liberty Press, 1980.

————. 1920. *Economic Calculation in the Socialist Commonwealth.* Repr., Auburn, AL: Ludwig von Mises Institute, 1990.

————. 1922. *Socialism: An Economic and Sociological Analysis.* Repr., Indianapolis, IN: Liberty Fund, 1981.

————. 1927. *Liberalism.* Repr., Irvington-on-Hudson, NY: Foundation for Economic Education, 1985.

————. 1933. *Epistemological Problems of Economics.* Repr., New York: New York University Press, 1981.

————. 1944. *Omnipotent Government.* New Haven, CT: Yale University Press.

————. 1949. *Human Action: A Treatise on Economics.* Repr., Indianapolis, IN: Liberty Fund, 2010.

————. 1957. *Theory and History.* New Haven, CT: Yale University Press.

————. 1978. *Notes and Recollections.* South Holland, IL: Libertarian Press.

————. 1978. *The Ultimate Foundation of Economic Science.* Kansas City, KS: Sheed & McMeel.

Mitchell, W.C., and R.T. Simmons. 1994. *Beyond Politics: Markets, Welfare, and the Failure of Bureaucracy.* Boulder: Westview.

Mokyr, Joel. 2010. *The Enlightened Economy: An Economic History of Britain 1700–1850.* New Haven, CT: Yale University Press.

Moss, Laurence S., ed. 1993. *Economic Thought in Spain.* Aldershot, England: Edward Elgar, 1993.

Mueller, D. 1989. *Public Choice II.* New York: Cambridge University Press.

Murrell, Peter. 1983. "Did the Theory of Market Socialism Answer the Challenge of Ludwig von Mises? A Reinterpretation of the Socialist Controversy." *History of Political Economy* 15(1): 92–105.

Nelson, Robert H. 1991. *Reaching for Heaven on Earth.* Lanham, MD: Rowman & Littlefield.

———. 2002. *Economics as Religion: From Samuelson to Chicago and Beyond.* University Park: Penn State University Press.

Neuman, W. Russell. 1986. *The Paradox of Mass Politics: Knowledge and Opinion in the American Electorate.* Cambridge, MA: Harvard University Press.

North, Douglass. 1981. *Structure and Change in Economic History.* New York: Norton.

———. 2004. *Understanding the Process of Economic Change.* Princeton, NJ: Princeton University Press.

Nove, Alec. 1969. *An Economic History of the USSR.* Baltimore, MD: Penguin.

Nozick, Robert. 1974. *Anarchy, State and Utopia.* New York: Basic Books.

Nutter, G. Warren. 1962. *The Growth of Industrial Production in the Soviet Economy.* Princeton, NJ: Princeton University Press.

O'Driscoll, Gerald P., and Mario J. Rizzo. 1985. *The Economics of Time and Ignorance.* New York: Basil Blackwell.

Olson, Mancur. 1996. "Big Bills Left on the Sidewalk: Why Some Nations Are Rich, and Others Poor." *Journal of Economic Perspectives* 10(2): 3–24.

———. 2000. *Power and Prosperity.* New York: Basic Books.

Osterfeld, David. 1992. *Prosperity versus Planning: How Government Stifles Economic Growth.* New York: Oxford University Press.

Ostrom, Elinor. 1990. *Governing the Commons: The Evolution of Institutions for Collective Action.* New York: Cambridge University Press.

———. 1998. "A Behavioral Approach to the Rational Choice Theory of Collective Action" (presidential address, American Political Science Association 1997). *American Political Science Review* 92(1), 1–22. In *Polycentric Games and Institutions: Readings from the Workshop in Political Theory and Policy Analysis,* edited by M. McGinnis. Repr., Ann Arbor: University of Michigan Press, 2000.

———. 2005. *Understanding Institutional Diversity.* Princeton, NJ: Princeton University Press.

Ostrom, Elinor, C. Gibson, S. Shivakumar, and K. Andersson. 2002. *Aid, Incentives, and Sustainability: An Institutional Analysis of Development Cooperation.* Stockholm: Swedish International Development Cooperation Agency.

Ostrom, Vincent. 1973. *The Intellectual Crisis in American Public Administration.* Tuscaloosa, AL: University of Alabama Press.

———. 1997. *The Meaning of Democracy and the Vulnerability of Democracies.* Ann Arbor: University of Michigan Press.

Pareto, Vilfredo. 1909. *Manual of Political Economy.* Repr., New York: Augustus M. Kelley, 1971.

Poteete, A., M. Janssen, and Elinor Ostrom. 2010. *Working Together: Collective Action, the Commons, and Multiple Methods in Practice*. Princeton, NJ: Princeton University Press.

Powell, Benjamin. 2006. "In Reply to Sweatshop Sophistries." *Human Rights Quarterly* 28(4): 1031–42.

Prychitko, David L. 1993. "After Davidson, Who Needs the Austrians? Reply to Davidson." *Critical Review* 7(2–3): 371–80.

———. 1996. Review of *Whither Socialism?* by Joseph Stiglitz. *Cato Journal* 16 (Fall), 280–89.

Rajan, Raghuram. 2004. "Assume Anarchy? Why an Orthodox Economic Model Might Not Be the Best Guide for Policy." *Finance & Development* 41(3): 56–57.

Rizvi, S. Abu Turab. 1994. "Game Theory to the Rescue." *Contributions to Political Economy* 13: 1–28.

Rizzo, Mario. 2005. "The Problem with Moral Dirigisme: A New Argument Against Moralistic Legislation." *NYU Journal of Law & Liberty* 1(2): 790–844.

Robbins, Lionel. 1932. *Essay on the Nature and Significance of Economic Science*. London: Macmillan.

———. 1947. *Economic Problems in Peace and War*. London: Macmillan.

Roberts, Paul Craig. 1971. *Alienation and the Soviet Economy: The Collapse of the Socialist Era*, New York: Holmes & Meier.

———. 2002. "My Time with Soviet Economics." *The Independent Review* 7(2): 259–64.

Rodrik, Dani. 2007. *One Economics, Many Recipes: Globalization, Institutions, and Economic Growth*. Princeton, NJ: Princeton University Press.

Roemer, John. 1994. *A Future for Socialism*. Cambridge, Mass.: Harvard University Press.

———. 1995. "An Anti-Hayekian Manifesto." *New Left Review* (May/June), 112–29.

Romer, T. 1988. "On James Buchanan's Contributions to Public Economics." *Journal of Economic Perspectives* 2(1) (Fall): 165–79.

Rosenberg, Alexander. 1992. *Economics—Mathematical Politics or Science of Diminishing Returns?* Chicago: University of Chicago Press.

Rothbard, Murray N. 1957. "In Defense of Extreme Apriorism." *Southern Economic Journal* 23(3): 314–20.

———. 1962. *Man, Economy, and State*, 2 vols. Princeton, NJ: D. Van Nostrand.

———. 1963. *America's Great Depression*. Princeton, NJ: D. Van Nostrand.

———. 1972. "Praxeology: The Method of Austrian Economics." In *Foundations of*

Modern Economics, edited by E. Dolan. Repr., Kansas City, KS: Sheed & Ward, 1976.

———. 1974. *Egalitarianism as a Revolt against Nature*. Auburn, AL: Ludwig von Mises Institute, 2000.

———. 1992. "How and How Not to Desocialize." *Review of Austrian Economics* 6(1): 65–77.

———. 1995. *An Austrian Perspective on the History of Economic Thought: The Classical Economists*. Cheltenham, UK: Edward Elgar Publishing.

———. 2006. *For a New Liberty: The Libertarian Manifesto*. Auburn, AL: Ludwig von Mises Institute.

———. 2009. *Man, Economy, and State*. Auburn, AL: Ludwig Von Mises Institute.

Rothschild, Emma. 2001. *Economic Sentiments*. Cambridge, MA: Harvard University Press.

Sah, Raaj K., and Joseph Stiglitz. 1985. "Human Fallibility and Economic Organization." *American Economic Review* 75 (May), 292–97 .

———. 1986. "The Architecture of Economic Systems." *American Economic Review* 76 (September). , 716–27.

Salerno, Joseph. 1993. "Mises and Hayek Dehomogenized." *Review of Austrian Economics* 6(2): 113–46.

Samuels, Warren J. 1971. "Interrelations between Legal and Economic Processes." *Journal of Law & Economics*. In *Essays on the Economic Role of Government: Volume I—Fundamentals*, 139–55. Repr., New York: New York University Press, 1992.

———. 1972. "In Defense of a Positive Approach to Government as an Economic Variable." *Journal of Law & Economics* 15 (October): 453–59.

———. 1989. "Austrians and the Institutionalist Compared." *Research in the History of Economic Thought & Methodology* 6, 53–72.

———. 1989. "The Legal-Economic Nexus." *George Washington Law Review*. In *Essays on the Economic Role of Government: Volume I—Fundamentals*, 162–86. Repr., New York: New York University Press, 1992.

Samuels, Warren J., and James M. Buchanan. 1975. "On Some Fundamental Issues in Political Economy: An Exchange of Correspondence." *Journal of Economic Issues*. In *Essays on the Methodology and Discourse of Economics*, 201–30. Repr., New York: New York University Press, 1992.

Samuelson, Paul A. 1947. *Foundations of Economic Analysis*. Cambridge, MA: Harvard University Press.

———. 1948. *Economics,* 1st ed. New York: McGraw-Hill.

———. 1961. *Economics*, 5th edition. New York: McGraw-Hill.

Samuelson, Paul A., and William D. Nordhaus. 1989. *Economics*, 13th ed. New York: McGraw-Hill.

Sandmo, A. 1990. "Buchanan on Political Economy: A Review Article." *Journal of Economic Literature* 28(1) (March): 50–65.

Sautet, Frederic. 2000. *An Entrepreneurial Theory of the Firm*. New York: Routledge.

Say, Jean Baptiste. 1821. *Letters to Mr. Malthus*. Repr., New York: Augustus M. Kelley, 1967.

Schelling, Thomas. 1978. *Micromotives and Macrobehavior*. New York: Norton.

Schotter, A. 1981. *The Economic Theory of Social Institutions*. New York: Cambridge University Press.

Schumpeter, Joseph. 1954. *A History of Economic Analysis*. New York: Oxford University Press.

———. 2008. *Capitalism, Socialism, and Democracy*. New York: Harper Perennial.

Schutz, Alfred. 1967. *The Phenomenology of the Social World*. Evanston, IL: Northwestern University Press.

Selgin, George A. and Lawrence H. White. 1994. "How Would the Invisible Hand Handle Money?" *Journal of Economic Literature* 32(4): 1718–49.

Sen, Amartya. 1987. *On Ethics and Economics*. Oxford: Blackwell.

———. 1995. "Rationality and Social Choice." *American Economic Review* 85(1) (March): 1–24.

Sennholz, Hans F. 1955. *How Can Europe Survive?* Princeton, NJ: D. Van Nostrand.

———. 1979. *Age of Inflation*. Belmont, MA: Western Islands.

———. 1985. *Money and Freedom*. Spring Mills, PA: Libertarian Press.

———. 1987. *Debts and Deficits*. Spring Mills, PA: Libertarian Press.

———. 1987. *The Politics of Unemployment*. Spring Mills, PA: Libertarian Press.

Shackle, G.L.S. 1972. *Epistemics and Economics*. Cambridge: Cambridge University Press.

Shivakumar, S. 2005. *The Constitution of Development: Crafting Capabilities For Self-Governance*. New York: Palgrave.

Shleifer, Andrei, S. Djankov, E. Glaeser, R. La Porta, and F. Lopez-de-Silanes. 2003. "The New Comparative Economics." *Journal of Comparative Economics* 31 (December): 595–619.

Shleifer, Andrei, and Robert Vishny. 1998. *The Grabbing Hand*. Cambridge, MA: Harvard University Press.

Simmel, Georg. 1908. "How Is Society Possible?" In *On Individuality and Social Forms*, edited by Donald N. Levine. Repr., Chicago: University of Chicago Press, 1971.

Simons, Henry C. 1983. *Simons' Syllabus*, edited by Gordon Tullock. Fairfax, VA: Center for the Study of Public Choice.

Skidelsky, Robert. 1992. *John Maynard Keynes: The Economist as Savior, 1920–1937*. New York: Penguin.

Smith, Adam. 1759. *The Theory of Moral Sentiments*. Repr., Indianapolis, IN: Liberty Fund, 1982.

———. 1776. *An Inquiry into the Nature and Causes of the Wealth of Nations*, edited by Edwin Cannan. Repr., Chicago: University of Chicago Press, 1976.

Smith, B. 1990. "Aristotle, Menger, Mises: An Essay in the Metaphysics of Economics." *History of Political Economy*, Annual Supplement to vol. 22: 263–88.

———. 1994. "Aristotelianism, Apriorism, Essentialism." In Boettke, *The Elgar Companion to Austrian Economics*, 33–37.

———. 1996. "In Defense of Extreme (Fallibilistic) Apriorism." *Journal of Libertarian Studies* 12: 179–92.

Smith, Vernon. 1998. "The Two Faces of Adam Smith." *Southern Economic Journal*, 65(1): 2–19.

———. 2003. "Constructivist and Ecological Rationality in Economics." *American Economic Review* 93(3): 465–508.

Snowdon, Brian, Howard Vane, and Peter Wynarczyk. 1994. *A Modern Guide to Macroeconomics: An Introduction to Competing Schools of Thought*. Aldershot, UK: Edward Elgar Publishing.

Solow, Robert. 1997. "How Did Economics Get That Way and What Way Did It Get?" *Daedalus* (Winter), 39–58.

Stark, Rodney. 2005. *The Victory of Reason: How Christianity Led to Freedom, Capitalism, and Western Success*. New York: Random House.

Steele, David Ramsey. 1992. *From Marx to Mises*. La Salle, IL: Open Court.

Stewart, Dougald. 1793. "Account of the Life and Writings of Adam Smith, L.L.D." In *Essays on Philosophical Subjects*, edited by W.P.D. Wrightman, 269–351. Repr., Oxford: Oxford University Press, 1980.

Stigler, George. 1946. *Theory of Price*. Chicago: University of Chicago Press.

———. 1961. "The Economics of Information." *Journal of Political Economy* 16(3) (June), 213–25.

———. 1975. *The Citizen and the State*. Chicago: University of Chicago Press.

Stiglitz, Joseph. 1993. *Economics*. New York: Norton.

———. 1994. *Whither Socialism?* Cambridge, MA: MIT Press.

———. 2002. *Globalization and Its Discontents*. New York: Norton.

Stringham, Edward P. 2003. "The Extralegal Development of Securities Trading in Seventeenth Century Amsterdam." *Quarterly Review of Economics and Finance* 43(2): 321–44.

Summers, Lawrence. 1990. *Understanding Unemployment*. Cambridge, MA: MIT Press.

Swedberg, Richard. 1998. *Max Weber and the Idea of Economic Sociology*. Princeton, NJ: Princeton University Press.

_____. 2009. *Tocqueville's Political Economy*. Princeton, NJ: Princeton University Press.

Tabarrok, Alex. 2009. "Elinor Ostrom and the Well-Governed Commons." *Marginal Revolution*, October 12. Accessed 20 January 2010. http://www.marginal revolution.com/marginalrevolution/2009/10/elinor-ostrom-and-the-wellgoverned -commons.html.

Thomsen, Esteban. 1992. *Prices and Knowledge: A Market-Process Perspective*. New York: Routledge.

Tullock, Gordon. 1983. Preface to *Simons' Syllabus*, by Henry C. Simons. Fairfax, VA: Center for the Study of Public Choice.

_____. 1994. *The New Federalist*. Vancouver: Fraser Institute.

_____. 2004. "Entry Barriers in Politics." In *The Selected Works of Gordon Tullock: Virginia Political Economy*, edited by C.K. Rowley, vol. 1, 69–77. Indianapolis, IN: Liberty Fund.

_____. 2004. "The Welfare Costs of Monopolies, Tariffs, and Theft." In *The Selected Works of Gordon Tullock: Virginia Political Economy*, edited by C.K. Rowley, vol. 1, 169–79. Indianapolis, IN: Liberty Fund.

_____. 2006. "Adam Smith and the Prisoners' Dilemma." In *The Selected Works of Gordon Tullock: Economics without Frontiers*, edited by C.K. Rowley, vol. 10, 429–37. Indianapolis, IN: Liberty Fund.

Vaughn, Karen I. 1980. "Does It Matter That Costs Are Subjective?" *Southern Economic Journal* 46(1) (January): 702–15.

_____. 1980. "Economic Calculation under Socialism: The Austrian Contribution." *Economic Inquiry* XVIII: 535–54.

_____. 1994. *Austrian Economics in America*. New York: Cambridge University Press.

Veblen, Thorstein. 1899. "Why Is Economics Not an Evolutionary Science?" In *The Portable Veblen*, edited by M. Lerner, 215–40. Repr., New York: Viking Press, 1948.

Wagner, Richard E. 1989. *To Promote the General Welfare*. San Francisco: Pacific Research Institute.

———. 2004. "Public Choice as an Academic Enterprise." *American Journal of Economics & Sociology* 63 (January): 55–74.

———. 2007. "Value and Exchange." *Review of Austrian Economics* 20(2–3): 97–103.

———. 2009. *Fiscal Sociology and the Theory of Public Finance: An Exploratory Essay.* Northampton, UK: Edward Elgar Publishing.

Walicki, A. 1995. *Marxism and the Leap into the Kingdom of Freedom: The Rise and Fall of Communist Utopia.* Stanford, CA: Stanford University Press.

Weber, Max. 1904–1905. *The Protestant Ethic and the Spirit of Capitalism.* Repr., New York: Scribners, 1958.

———. 1927. *General Economic History.* Repr., New Brunswick, NJ: Transaction, 1995.

———. 1956. *Economy and Society: An Outline of Interpretive Sociology*, edited by Guenther Roth and Claus Wittich, vol. 1. Repr., Berkeley: University of California Press, 1978.

Weingast, Barry. 1995. "The Economic Role of Political Institutions." *Journal of Law, Economics and Organization* 11(1): 1–31.

Wicksteed, Philip H. 1910. *The Common Sense of Political Economy: Including a Study of the Human Basis of Economic Law.* London: Macmillan.

———. 1914. "The Scope and Method of Political Economy in Light of the 'Marginal' Theory of Value and Distribution." In *The Common Sense of Political Economy*, 2 vols. Repr., London: Routledge, 1938.

Wieser, F. von. 1927. *Social Economics.* New York: Adelphi.

Williamson, Claudia. 2009. "Informal Institutions Rule." *Public Choice* 139(3): 371–87.

Wright, Robert. 1988. "Kenneth E. Boulding," in *Three Scientists and Their Gods.* New York: Harper and Row.

Young, Jeffrey. 2005. "Unintended Order and Intervention: Adam Smith's Theory of the Role of the State," *The Role of Government in the History of Economic Thought, Annual Supplement to Volume 37, History of Political Economy,* edited by Steve Medema, 91–119.

Zaller, John. 1992. *The Nature and Origins of Mass Opinion.* Cambridge: Cambridge University Press.

Zingales, Luigi. 2009. "Keynesian Principles: The Opposition's Opening Remarks." *The Economist,* March 10. http://www.economist.com/debate/days/view/276.

Acknowledgements

Chapter 1, "Economics for Yesterday, Today, and Tomorrow," was prepared for the occasion of receiving the Adam Smith Award from the Association of Private Enterprise Education in April 2010. This article was originally printed in *The Journal of Private Enterprise* 26(2) (2011): 1–14. We gratefully acknowledge permission to reprint. I was (am) very grateful to have received this award from APEE, and my remarks from that evening can be found at: http://www.coordinationproblem.org/2010/04/2010-adam-smith-award-remarks-read-on-april-11th-in-las-vegas.html. I would like to thank Edward Stringham for editing the special issue of *The Journal of Private Enterprise* that consisted of essays of my former students in my honor that was organized to coincide with the Smith Award. I have learned more from these students than they can ever imagine, and I can only wish for them the wonderful experience in teaching economics throughout their careers that I have been able to have in mine because of them. Thank you.

Chapter 2, "On the Tasks of Economic Education," was originally published in *GMU Working Paper in Economics* No. 10–25. We gratefully acknowledge the permission to reprint. An earlier version was presented at the conference "Economic Freedom and the High School Curriculum" sponsored by the Freedom and Prosperity Academy in Tucson, AZ, November 5–8, 2010, and I thank Stephen Haessler for the invitation to present and to the participants for invaluable feedback.

Chapter 3, "Teaching Austrian Economics to Graduate Students," was originally published in the *Journal of Economics and Finance Education* 10(2) (2011): 19–30. We gratefully acknowledge permission to reprint.

Chapter 4, "Teaching Economics, Appreciating Spontaneous Order, and Economics as a Public Science," was originally published in the *Journal of Economic Behavior and Organization* 80(2) (2011): 265–74. We gratefully acknowledge permission to reprint. This paper was written for the FSSO conference honoring James Buchanan for lifetime contributions to spontaneous order studies. I have benefited greatly from the comments of Chris Coyne, Bill Dennis, Peter Leeson, Shruti Rajagopalan, and Virgil Storr. The usual caveat applies.

Chapter 5, "Relevance as a Virtue: Hans Sennholz," was originally published in *The Quarterly Journal of Austrian Economics* 5(4) (Winter 2002): 31–36, for a special issue on the occasion of Dr. Hans Sennholz's eightieth birthday. We gratefully acknowledge the permission to reprint.

Chapter 6, "The Forgotten Contribution: Murray Rothbard on Socialism in Theory and in Practice" was co-authored with Christopher Coyne and originally published in *The Quarterly Journal of Austrian Economics*, 2004 7(2): 71–89. We gratefully acknowledge the permission to reprint. An earlier version of this paper was presented at the 9th Austrian Scholars Conference at the Ludwig von Mises Institute in Auburn, Alabama, March 2003. Peter Boettke would like to thank Guido Hülsman and Joseph Salerno for encouraging him to present a paper on this topic at the conference. We would like to acknowledge the helpful comments of Andrew Farrant, Peter Leeson, Ben Powell, Edward Stringham, and John Robert Subrick, two anonymous referees, and the editor. We also appreciate the input from the students in Austrian Theory of the Market Process II course in the Spring 2003. Financial assistance from the program in Philosophy, Politics and Economics at the James M. Buchanan Center for Political Economy, and the Social Change Program at the Mercatus Center is gratefully acknowledged. The usual caveat applies.

Chapter 7, "Mr. Boulding and the Austrians," was co-authored with David L. Prychitko and originally printed in L. Moss ed., *Joseph A. Schumpeter, Historian of Economics* (New York: Routledge, 1996): 250–59. We gratefully acknowledge permission to reprint.

Chapter 8, "Putting the 'Political' Back into Political Economy: Warren Samuels," was originally published in Steve Medema and Jeff Biddle, eds., *Economics Broadly Conceived: Essays in Honor of Warren Samuels* (New York: Routledge, 2001): 203–16. We gratefully acknowledge permission to reprint.

Chapter 9, "Maximizing Behavior and Market Forces: Gordon Tullock," was originally published in *Public Choice* 135(1–2) (2008): 3–10. We gratefully acknowledge the permission to republish.

Chapter 10, "Methodological Individualism, Spontaneous Order, and the Research Program of the Workshop in Political Philosophy and Policy Analysis: Vincent and Elinor Ostrom," was co-authored with Christopher Coyne and was originally published in the *Journal of Economic Behavior and Organization* 57 (2005): 145–58. We gratefully acknowledge permission to reprint. Financial assistance from the Program in Philosophy, Politics and Economics at the Buchanan Center for Political Economy, the Social Change Program at the Mercatus Center, and the Earhart Foundation is acknowledged. We are grateful to many of the symposium participants for offering helpful comments on an earlier version of this paper, and particularly, to our two official discussants, Paul Dragos Aligica and Michael McGinnis. The usual caveat applies.

Chapter 11, "Is the Only Form of 'Reasonable Regulation' Self-Regulation? Elinor Ostrom," was originally published in *Public Choice* 143(3/4) (2010): 283–91. We gratefully acknowledge permission to republish. Paul Dragos Aligica, Chris Coyne, Daniel D'Amico, Peter Leeson, Steve Medema, Mario Rizzo and Daniel Smith provided helpful comments.

Chapter 12, "The Matter of Methodology: Don Lavoie" was adapted from an article originally published as "Obituary Don Lavoie (1950–2001)" in *Journal of Economic Methodology* 11(3) (2004): 377–79. We gratefully acknowledge the permission to reprint.

Chapter 13, "Invitation to Political Economy: Peter Berger and the Comedic Drama of Political, Economic, and Social Life," was originally published in *Society* 47(3) (2010): 178–85. We gratefully acknowledge permission to reprint.

Chapter 14, "Was Mises Right?" was co-authored with Peter Leeson and was originally published in *Review of Social Economy* 64(2) (2006): 247–65. We gratefully acknowledge permission to reprint. The authors thank the Editor of the *Review of Social* Economy and two anonymous referees for helpful comments and suggestions. The financial assistance of the Olofsson Weaver Fellowship, the Earhart Foundation, and the Mercatus Center are gratefully acknowledged. Leeson was the F.A. Hayek Fellow at the London School of Economics at the time of this research's acceptance. He wishes to thank the STICERD Center and the Hayek Fellowship for their support in this work.

Chapter 15, "The Genius of Mises and the Brilliance of Kirzner," was co-authored with Frederic Sautet and was originally published in *The Annual Preceedings of the Wealth and Well-Being of Nations* 3 (2011): 34–44. We gratefully acknowledge the permission to reprint.

Chapter 16, "Hayek and Market Socialism: Science, Ideology, and Public Policy," is an abridged version of the 2004 Hayek Memorial Lecture delivered at the London School of Economics on October 19, 2004, and was originally published in *Economic Affairs* 25(4) (2005): 54–60. We gratefully acknowledge the permission to reprint. I would like to thank Toby Baxendale for the opportunity to visit the London School of Economics as the Hayek Fellow in 2004 and Tim Besley for being such a gracious host during my stay. I want to thank the Ludwig von Mises Institute for their role in sponsoring the Hayek fellowship at the LSE. I also want to thank Jennifer Dirmeyer and Jennifer Smith for helping me to prepare this manuscript for publication. The usual caveat applies.

Chapter 17, "James M. Buchanan and the Rebirth of Political Economy," was originally published in Richard Holt and Steve Pressmen, eds., *Economics and Its Discontents: Twentieth Century Dissenting Economists* (Cheltenham, UK: Edward Elgar Publishing, 1998), 21–39. We gratefully acknowledge the permission to reprint. I would like to thank James Buchanan, Jack High, Israel Kirzner, Mario Rizzo, and Karen Vaughn for comments on an earlier draft of this chapter. In addition, I would especially like to thank Steven Pressman for his comments and suggestions for improvement. Financial assistance from the Austrian Economics Program at New York University is gratefully acknowledged. Responsibility for remaining errors is mine.

Chapter 18, "Where Did Economics Go Wrong? Modern Economics as a Flight from Reality" was originally published in *Critical Review* 11(1) (1997): 11–64. We gratefully acknowledge permission to reprint. I would like to thank Tyler Cowen, Jeffrey Friedman, Steven Horwitz, Israel Kirzner, Daniel Klein, David Prychitko, Mario Rizzo, and Edward Weick for their comments and suggestions, and gratefully acknowledge financial assistance from the National Fellows Program of the Hoover Institution on War, Revolution, and Peace, and from the Sarah Scaife Foundation in support of the Austrian Economics Program at NYU. Earlier versions of this paper were presented at the History of Economic Society meetings at the University of Notre Dame, June 1995; the Austrian Economics Colloquium at New York University, March 1993; and Central European University, Prague, January 1993.

Chapter 19, "Man as Machine," was co-authored with Christopher J. Coyne and Peter T. Leeson and was originally printed in *Annals of the Society for the History of Economic Thought* 43(1) (2003): 1–10. We gratefully acknowledge permission to reprint.

Chapter 20, "The Limits of Economic Expertise," was co-authored with Steve Horwitz and was originally published in *History of Political Economy*, Vol. 37, (2005): 10–39. We gratefully acknowledge the permission to reprint. We thank the conference participants and an anonymous referee for challenging and helpful comments on earlier drafts.

Chapter 21, "High Priests and Lowly Philosophers" was co-authored with Christopher Coyne and Peter Leeson and was originally published in *Case Western Reserve University Law Review* 56(3) (2006): 551–68. We gratefully acknowledge permission to reprint.

Index

417

About the Author

PETER J. BOETTKE is Research Fellow at The Independent Institute; University Professor of Economics and Philosophy at George Mason University; Director of the F.A. Hayek Program for Advanced Study in Philosophy, Politics, and Economics at the Mercatus Center; and Editor of the *Review of Austrian Economics*. He has been a National Fellow at the Hoover Institution, as well as Visiting Professor at the Russian Academy of Sciences in Moscow, Max Planck Institute for Research into Economic Systems, and London School of Economics. He is the recipient of the Golden Dozen Award for Excellence in Teaching from the College of Arts and Sciences at New York University, the 2009 Faculty Member of the Year Award from the George Mason University Alumni Association, and the 2010 Adam Smith Award from the Association of Private Enterprise Education.

Professor Boettke's books include *The Political Economy of Soviet Socialism: The Formative Years, 1918–1928; Why Perestroika Failed: The Economics and Politics of Socialism Transformation; Calculation and Coordination: Essays on Socialism and Transitional Political Economy; The Elgar Companion to Austrian Economics; Challenging Institutional Analysis and Development: The Bloomington School;* and *The Handbook on Contemporary Austrian Economics.*

He holds a B.A. in economics from Grove City College and a Ph.D. in economics from George Mason University, and has held faculty positions at Oakland University, Manhattan College, and New York University.

Independent Studies in Political Economy